MW00624831

Obama: The Dream And The Reality

Obama:
The Dream And
The Reality

National Review
Essays, 2008–2010

Victor Davis Hanson

Obama: The Dream And The Reailty

Copyright © 2012 by National Review

First Edition
Published and Printed in the U.S.A.

National Review
215 Lexington 10016
New York, NY 22480

Library of Congress Control Number: 2010903467

PREFACE

This is an anthology of weekly essays published by *National Review Online* between January 2008 and December 2010. I usually submitted one opinion editorial each Monday, between 800 and 2,000 words in length, about topics in the news—which means during these 36 months almost always some aspect of the strange ascendency of a heretofore mostly unknown Barack Obama.

Except for occasional reformatting and corrections of misprints in the original texts, the essays are reprinted unchanged from their original postings, both to reflect a sort of ongoing diary of the times and to offer some idea, with the benefit of hindsight, of how insightful or wrong about such contemporary events. The opinion pieces are now regrouped here into nine thematic chapters, in chronological sequence as they appeared over the three-year period.

As I look back over them, I am reminded of two general themes.

First, as I watched the rise of Barack Obama, I was struck by just how little we knew of his past or present life, his political agendas—and how even less we were going to know, given the media effort neither to report nor analyze fully any matters perceived to be injurious to the Obama cause. In response, I tried, as many did during the Obmaa ascendency, to point out how contradictory and orthodox was the reality of his hope and change agenda, an assessment more than born out by the record of his first-term in office.

Second, I confess to a certain naiveté. While I accurately predicted that the Rev. Wright matter, inconsistency in both Obama's campaign and governance, his often clumsy proclamations, and a certain petulance with critics and boredom with the mechanics of governance would all conspire to end the 2008 Obama hysteria and later send his presidential polls plummeting, I underestimated the resiliency of Obama, the candidate and the president—and in particular his iconic value.

Millions of Americans have invested in the abstract idea of Obama as a sort of talisman that might both heal their own perceived past transgressions and offer inoculation from any future charge of illiberal thoughts or deeds—a syndrome well known to, and amply capitalized on, by Obama himself.

As I write this introduction, the president's popularity hovers about 40%. In November 2010, he suffered the greatest midterm congressional setback since 1938 (a loss of 63 Democratic seats in the House). Gas prices are over $4 a gallon in many parts of the country. The 2011 budget deficit is slated to exceed $1.6 trillion, with $5 trillion added in aggregate debt since Obama's inauguration. Much of his foreign policy is characterized both by explicit rhetorical rejection of George W. Bush's agenda and implicit embrace or even expansion of it. Yet the idea of Obama is a very different thing from Obama, the concrete politician and president, now with a clear record of governance. For many, the latter fact hardly trumps the former mystique. So his political successes may well continue in a way other presidents have not been able to overcome similarly depressing news.

I would like to thank Jack Fowler at the *National Review* for inviting me to collect these essays for publication.

Victor Davis Hanson
Selma, California

CONTENTS

CHAPTER THREE: The "Good" War in Afghanistan, the "Bad" One in Iraq

CHAPTER FOUR: On Hating Israel

CHAPTER FIVE: The Sorta War on Terror

CHAPTER SIX: The World Can Be a Scary Place

CHAPTER SEVEN: The Bush and Palin Derangement Syndromes

CHAPTER EIGHT: Obama, Dream and Reality

CHAPTER NINE: We are Going to Make It

CHAPTER ONE

"HOPE AND CHANGE"

THE 2008 CAMPAIGN AND ITS AFTERMATH

JANUARY 3, 2008

Voting the War

Thoughts for early caucus and primary voters

T he question for Americans at the start of 2008 is not—after over four years and a great deal of American blood and treasure—whether we should leave Iraq (all agree that we should), but when and under what conditions. In this regard, consistency of belief reveals a lot, since it suggests that views are formed on principles rather than the prevailing, and constantly shifting, majority impression.

Senator Hillary Clinton voted for authorizing the war, then, as the costs mounted, became a critic—but not to such a degree that she could not still hedge should things still turn around. The result is that we now have a pro-war Clinton, a "suspension of disbelief" Clinton, and a quiet Clinton on the war, much in the way Bill Clinton initially supported the war, then proclaimed he had been against it from the beginning. But are there any core beliefs here about the wisdom or folly of removing Saddam and trying to foster consensual government in his place-other than 'if it is going well, I'm for it; if not, I'm against it-for now at least'? We should remember that one of the supposedly most astute politicians of our age, Hillary Clinton, gratuitously insulted with the "suspicion of disbelief" cast-off line, a commanding general who was on his way to becoming a genuine American hero.

Not smart at all.

Sen. Obama is believable when he states he was against Iraq from the beginning and still is, though we can't ascertain that fact, given he wasn't yet elected a senator at the critical moment of authorization. Sen. Edwards was for the war, and gave eloquent speeches why so, then moved hard left and damned the war and any who supported it—and now is relatively quiet on Iraq (other than wanting all U.S. troops out within 10 months) since his nearly acquired William Jennings Bryan populism seems for now to bring more dividends.

It is hard to determine much difference in the positions of the leading Republican candidates—the removal of Saddam was necessary, the three-week war was well run, the four-year occupation was marred by mistakes (made by someone else), and the surge has helped bring stability – one that requires a careful American drawdown, predicated by facts on the ground in Iraq. Much of this is gleaned through assertion since few of the candidates, excepting McCain, were in a position to go on record for or against the surge and staying the course. Thompson and Giuliani made the most effort to tie their support for the war to larger geostrategic anti-terrorism strategies.

There is a sort of Orwellian quality, however, in the Republican candidates' positions on the war: all seem to support the present Bush course but can't quite name the President, given his 36% favorable rating in the polls. The result is that we hear of little substantive difference from the present strategy, but frequent protestations about past mistakes—that seem intended as necessary cover for de facto associating oneself with George Bush's Iraq.

Where does all that leave us? Gen. Petraeus and the success in Anbar have radically changed the politics of the war in Iraq. Six months ago, we were supposed to have envisioned Iowa as an Iraqi battleground, where Middle American said 'no' to war, and those candidates with the most anti-war fides found traction.

But this past monthly period in Iraq was the least costly to America in terms of wounded and dead in Iraq, and the media is reduced to running back-page stories about poor graveyard workers with too little work, or supposedly lazy Iraqis who aren't cleaning up debris in prompt fashion. As the violent trends decrease, the positive ones—power, oil revenue, GDP, returning refugees, security forces—increase. The result is that we are in one-year, election-cycle holding period of "What's next?"

The voters have lately turned a deaf ear to anti-war activists; Michael Moore, Cindy Sheehan, and Code Pink are mostly receding as bad memories. Instead, the public is probably willing to continue to support a Petraeus-like counter-insurgency solution as long as the violence steadily abates and they can begin to see incremental withdrawals

4

of American troops, the fact of such, rather than the actual numbers, being initially what matters.

Bottom line: for now Iraq per se is not a major issue in the primaries, at least to the degree it is seen as something separate from Afghanistan and the general war against Islamic terrorism. Those on the anti-war side who harp that it is will sound strident, given public support for Gen. Petraeus and good news from the front. There are subtle differences among the Republican candidates, both in their past statements and positions and their recommendations; but for now they are not of much significance, at least for the immediate primaries.

What to look for? It depends on the pulse of the battlefield: Continued good news, makes the war less and less of an issue, especially if some troops are withdrawn either late summer or early next autumn.

The final irony? No candidate apparently argues that someone did something right to have prevented another 9/11-like attack for over six years, removed two dictatorships, fostered the continued, stubborn presence of democratic governments in Afghanistan and Iraq, helped change the Middle East dynamic from Lebanon to Libya, and at present won friendship and support from key countries as diverse as France, Germany, and India.

JANUARY 8, 2008

The Queen Is Dead . . .

. . . long live the king?

For the past year, I, like millions of others, have been bewildered by TV's talking heads, always assuring us that Hillary—before a single vote was cast, before a surge attack ad was made, before a single blunder or mini-crisis occurred—was to be coronated as the Democratic nominee and would inevitably go on to beat any Republican rival. (Many instead thought 'Never underestimate the ability of Bill Clinton to do damage to those around him').

Now after the first week of the primary season, these same genius-es are deifying Obama (formerly trashed as running a "surprisingly" dismal and uninspiring campaign) to the skies and writing Clinton's post mortem—even as her national polls are still even or ahead of Obama. Something similar is true of McCain as well—once worshiped, then pitied, and now admired.

What comes across to the viewer is the near complete absence of any independent judgment; instead, the 24-hour buzz makes someone hot or cold, and the pundits adjust accordingly with praise or blame. We've seen this before with the Gary Hart, Howard Dean, and Ross Perot pet-rock like craze—which are not that unusual in the popular landscape of radically democratic cultures such as our own.

The truth is that what a few thousand Americans think in Iowa and New Hampshire does not trump the tens of millions in states like Florida, New Jersey, New York, and California. The Clinton and Giuliani campaigns were based on this fact, and could still work—as long as the perceived momentum achieved by Obama or Huckabee among tiny populations in these two early states, amplified and exag-gerated by spin doctors on television, does not cause second and third thoughts in voters of these key mega-states, inasmuch as most have no firm or fixed views other than a desire to be associated with a winner.

Hillary is not comatose, but instead at a crossroads. If she distances herself from Bill, goes silent about her First Lady years, stops the play-safe, don't-blow-it-fourth-quarter strategy, and instead takes risks, talks about what she's going to do in simple, blunt terms, gives more inter-views, answers impromptu questions at her campaign stops, jettisons the canned laugh for real give and take, she could recover in two weeks.

Left unsaid is that America will soon—thanks to input from the shadows from various hit men from the Clinton 1992/1996 team—be hearing a lot more details about the relatively unknown life and views of one Barrack Obama and those around him. Right now voters know almost everything about Hillary and are troubled by that knowledge; they know almost nothing about Obama, and are happy for that igno-rance—but that too can change, since she has nothing left to disclose or lose, he everything.

JANUARY 9, 2008

The Crying Game

Hillary, Part Two

T he teary, compassionate Hillary and her "human moment" were just in time—and misinterpreted by the media:

(1) She didn't actually break down and "cry," but better yet, only teared up—a drop or two showing a human side, with glimpses of empathetic frailty, but not rivers of abject weakness and loss of composure.

(2) Contrary to popular wisdom, this was not an Ed Muskie New Hampshire moment. When a tall, lanky man breaks down in tears that's one thing; it's quite another to see a teary-eyed confessional woman. There is a double-standard, but it's not the one we're told: Men always seem to look weak when they tear up; women can look, well, empathetic and sensitive. In this regard, note when she "opened her heart" there was an enhancing soft light around her, and her make-up was understated and pastelish—an aura effect.

(3) The slur against her was that she was an iron-lady automaton, without emotion; so she needed that tearful introspection; it was not like a quirky, psycho-dramatic Pat Schroeder crying 20 years ago, and thereby confirming what we suspected—that as a fragile personality, she was subject to wild mood swings and undue passions. Hillary's quarter tear wasn't the weepy Cowardly Lion serially breaking down, but an appreciated sad drop or two coming from the heartless Tin Man.

(4) No comment on the authenticity of her "human moment," since the "I'm all choked up" is a one-time bromide. It did the trick—and can't be repeated.

Again, never underestimate the Clintonian team. (In this regard the astute Dick Morris's apparently obsessive worries are hardly obsessive, but very real.)

Hillary Clinton is in the midst of a complete focus-group/poll-driven/handler make-over. And to the degree she sticks to it (a big if), she will do fine. As we heard tonight, Hillary has now "found her voice"; she suddenly speaks more slowly, there are more bite-the-lip-like pauses, and she has been reminded not to go into frenetic panic mode or hit that screech-owl high note as much. She will seek out interviews, welcome questions, and be empathetic, accessible, and sensitive to the public.

Her New Hampshire victory speech was almost anti-Hillary (at least until the last two seconds of the old Hillary shrill-shouting): slow, deliberate, empathetic, a lot of personal voice—and Bill finally off the stage.

Note that she thanked her mother and almost everyone else imaginable (even Biden, Dodd, etc.), but not Bill!—who, of course, in albatross fashion, blew up again on his stump, and ranted on about himself and how he has suffered so for the rest of us.

A final note: The campaign talking heads and opinion makers this season have been lousy, about the worst in memory—especially the "she's won, she's lost, she's won ..." feeding frenzy, and then writing the silly "end of the Clinton era" essays—all based on a few thousand Iowans, some bad polls in New Hampshire, and catch-up to what some other wrong pundit wrote an hour earlier. And remember, these are "experts" who pontificated each week on the real Iraq war. They remind one of the ridiculous gnashing tropical carp, splashing about in Saddam's old Baghdad pond.

JANUARY 16, 2008

Absurd on the Left

Faux populism and pseudo-identity politics

In today's leisured, affluent, and globalized world, few elites are old-fashioned populists or on the perilous barricades of the civil-rights movement. Those who say they are—mostly the Democratic candidates—show us almost daily the contradictions and absurdity of it all.

John Edwards rails against the corporate elite and its strangulation of the little guy. But nothing in Edwards's own life (even aside from the haircuts, sub-prime mortgage investments, and "John's room") would lead one to think he could ever be serious. When he speaks to a University of California audience on poverty, he takes not $5,000 or even $10,000, but $55,000, from the public coffers.

When he won lawsuits as an attorney, whether against doctors or the American Red Cross, he often gobbled up not several hundred thousand dollars, but millions, in cuts. This money did not come from the hides of mustached bandits in mahogany boardrooms; the costs were eventually borne by taxpayers or passed on to consumers. Thank God for winner-take-all capitalism.

Hillary Clinton likewise preaches fairness and egalitarianism, but nothing in her and her husband's life suggests that they feel such a burden. Their appetites, expenditures, and tastes—in clothes, housing, transportation, and vacations—are no different from those of a John Kerry or an Al Gore. All behave like top-of-the-heap, carbon-spewing corporate CEOs.

The apologia for all this—that at least the liberal elite is pained enough to worry about others while indulging—rings hollow. Populism used to be the idea that someone from the lower and middling classes, or the laboring underbelly of America, would enlighten the public about the grimy ordeal of those not sharing in the fruits of our collective success. It was not selective noblesse oblige with a thin patina of Huey Long or William Jennings Bryan.

The same problems of consistency and authenticity arise these days with racial identity and all that comes with it. Bill Richardson—son of a banker, prep-school graduate, toiler in the vineyard of Kissinger Associates—assured us that he would be the first Hispanic president, due to his mother's lineage. But why was that information necessary, and to what purpose was that appeal?

His background seems a world away from the contemporary Mexican-American experience. And in our current fantasy world of racial identity politics, he was hoisted on his own petard by unfortunately having his father's English aristocratic name, William Blaine Richardson III. Had he taken on his mother's maiden name (with accent), and as others have done, Hispanicized his first name, he might have had more media resonance—as, say, one Guillermo Márquez.

Ditto Sen. Barack Obama. It is an inexplicably surviving legacy of the racist antebellum South that a drop of African blood apparently cements a black identity. Senator Obama is forced to be seen—or wishes to be seen—not as white or even half-white, but as a de facto African-American and thus emblematic of all the historical ordeal that such an identity might encompass.

But by the logic of his own memoirs, it was his upbringing by his Kansas-born white mother and his long residence with his maternal grandparents that shaped his values and aspirations. His Kenyan father was almost always absent.

Had he been named not after his father, but, say, in honor of both his often-present mother and his omnipresent grandfather, Stanley Dunham, we might well have had a superficially different conception of him. A Sen. Stan Dunham would require some of the footnotes that Gov. Bill Richardson had to provide.

The point is not hypocrisy really, but rather that there is little authentic populism, ethnic fides, or general misery to be found among anyone blessed enough to run for our presidency. To think otherwise is not just intellectually dishonest, but a mirror of the falsity of our media-driven age.

JANUARY 17, 2008

Living History

Hillary gone wild

The Clinton team was supposed to be known for sticking to the year-long make-over script, especially after the disastrous sound bite ("suspension of disbelief"), but lately the senator has gone wild. She egotistically claimed that ipso facto her election would bring down world oil prices. Then she claimed ownership of the surge she tried to stop, by boasting that those parochial Iraqis apparently listen to her every word, as Iraqis, the U.S. military, and the enemy all must adjust their strategy to her most current position on the war.

Then she offered a history lesson of the civil-rights movement as a way to explain the difference between her, the sophisticated and savvy parliamentarian, and Sen. Obama the inspirational naïf, who, apparently in the African-American rhetorical tradition, is a useful foot soldier to rile up the masses, before turning over the real legislative work to the pros.

Now she calls the president "pathetic" for his jawboning of the Saudis to lower oil prices. Far better I suppose just to wait for her election, when the price will tumble spontaneously as promised.

The egotism is only tag-teamed by narcissistic Bill's serial temper tantrums, finger-pointing, and revisionism. If the two keep it up, at some point I think we will see a steady surge for Obama, mostly as a cry of the collective heart to be free once and for all of these people.

I once thought it was suicidal of Obama to simply smile, talk inanely of "change," offer no concrete proposals, and play rope-a-dope deflection to nonstop Clinton innuendo and rumor-mongering. But he may have far more insight that most of us: The more Hillary talks, attacks, cries, pontificates, and rewrites history, the more he appears sympathetic and above her petty fray as she punches herself out.

JANUARY 22, 2008

Who Exactly Is Running for President?

The Bill Show

I wrote not long ago about Bill as the "Clinton Albatross," but now it is more apt to compare him to an attack dog unleashed. His (not her) victory speech in Nevada was quite extraordinary: He went on and on, while she stood next to him, mute. He gloated over her comeback, took digs at the other candidates, referenced himself of course, and was reluctant to give up his iron grip on the microphone.

Her expression was that of a classic "Don't dare ask me to muzzle that Doberman!" frozen bystander. If she can't control him, how could she control the country—or is that a fair comparison, given that his pathologies are far greater than those of our collective nation? It defies the laws of physics for such a narcissist to recede into the shadows, or yield to his wife, or play a private role, quietly calling in political debts.

In 2000, George Bush Sr. was careful not to be too partisan and mostly kept out of the campaign limelight. There was no sense that a vote for W. was simply an endorsement of a Bush I continuance. So Bill's ubiquity on the campaign—sharp partisan attacks and caricatures, misinformation about his own record, fiery outbursts to reporters—is quite unprecedented for an emeritus president, especially one who had so carefully cultivated his image as a global insider and international humanitarian.

If between 2001 and 2008 the Clinton legacy was something to be defended by all Democrats, Hillary's candidacy and Bill's unseemly behavior are calling it into question. Who knows—soon Democrats themselves, either Obama supporters or disillusioned Clintonites, may grudgingly concede to critics, "Yeah, you were right about that guy all along." If Bill keeps up the attack on Obama, he may become the first unblack president.

Of course, Bill sees his wife's election as a referendum on himself, a way to redeem himself for his impeachment and tawdry exit from the presidency, and a co-presidency—if the prefix "co-," in any sense, can ever be applicable to someone of such an extraordinary ego. Again, I pass on the Freudian aspect of him in part wanting her to lose. Handlers may think that Hillary's bounce came from Bill's suddenly frenetic pace, and indeed, he surely claims as much. But it is more like a shot of adrenalin to a floundering patient—necessary perhaps for one-time revival, but fatal if resorted to on a daily basis.

Again, the surprise is not that he has gnawed himself free, but rather how and why the old pros in the Clinton campaign did not have a steel chain rather than a mere leash. So far Obama has played off this gaffe in good fashion—when attacked, being both pained and confused in just the right mixture. But it would be wise for him to counter Bill a bit more, drawing on his much-more-even-tempered perplexity and sadness to challenge Bill's mendacity. If he does that and keeps his cool, it will remind voters that Hillary apparently has willingly chosen bystander status—and sooner or later, Bill will blow up big-time and irrevocably harm Hillary's candidacy. The Clintons know his snapping and biting must cease, but they also know he can't stop—sort of like the frustrated Queensland Heeler that has gone through extensive obedience training, only to snap at the first stranger he sees.

In the meantime, we witness the odd effect that the more Bill presses the attack, the more sympathetic and likable—and presidential—Obama becomes. How odd that, on the campaign trail, Obama appears more like a calm ex-president, while Bill comes off as the overeager, grasping wannabe we remember so well from the late 1980s.

OCTOBER 10, 2008

Not Over Yet

Reasons for hope on the first Tuesday in November

Of course, this is a Democratic year. The public is tired of George Bush and eight years of an incumbent administration. War, Wall Street, and the absence of a conservative Reagan-like charismatic figure should make it easy for a Democrat to win the presidency. After a nearly miraculous McCain surge in September, following the Republican Convention and Palin nomination, the Republicans are once again floundering—and a sense of utter despair has now set in among conservatives.

Wall Street melted down. The New York–Washington media elite went ballistic over vice presidential candidate Sarah Palin. The Alaskan mom of five in near suicidal fashion was ordered by the campaign to put her head in the Charlie Gibson-Katie Couric guillotine. A trailing McCain—while sober and workmanlike in the first two debates—failed to close the ring and hammer the agile Obama as a charismatic charlatan.

The result is that with not much more than three weeks left in the campaign, a number of conservatives have all but accepted (if a few not eager for) an Obama victory. Others are angry at the McCain campaign's supposed reluctance to go after Obama's hyper-liberal, hyper-partisan Senate record, his dubious Chicago coterie, his serial flip-flops, and his inexperience. And how, most wonder, can McCain regain the lead lost three weeks ago, when the media has given up any pretense of disinterested coverage, time is growing ever more short, prominent conservatives such as George Will, Charles Krauthammer, David Brooks, and Kathleen Parker have suggested Sarah Palin would be unfit to assume the presidency, and former Romney supporters are raising again their unease with the once again too moderate-sounding McCain?

Yet for all the gloom, there are several reasons why this race is by no means over.

First, it is not clear that panic, hysteria, and the "Great Depression" will continue to be the headlines and lead-ins each night for the next three weeks. We may be soon reaching a bottom in the stock market. Sometime in the next few days, wiser investors should see that trillions of global dollars are now piling up and could begin to prime the economy—and that still valuable stocks, for a brief period, are up for sale at once-in-a-lifetime bargains. With the sudden collapse of oil prices, the West has been given a staggering reprieve of hundreds of billions of dollars in savings on its imported fuel bills. That economy too will result in more liquidity at home. Given the shameless behavior of Wall Street, and Fannie Mae and Freddie Mac, it will be unlikely that we will revert soon to the Wild West speculation that had for the last six years transformed the once pedestrian notion of seeing a house as a home and refashioned it into either a politically correct entitlement or a Las Vegas poker chip to be thrown down on the roulette table.

It is still possible that, by the week before the election, there will be a sense of respite rather than continued anger and panic—and any day in which hysteria is not the topic of the day benefits McCain. In this regard, McCain must keep reminding in simple fashion that Freddie and Fannie were catalysts that drew in the Wall Street sharks: crooked officials cooked the books to get mega-bonuses; they got away with their crimes by lavishing money on mostly Democratic legislators (including Obama); and hand-in-glove they all covered—and still are covering—their tracks under a reprehensible politically correct cynicism.

Iraq is no longer the contentious issue of the primaries where Democratic candidates outdid each other in predicting failure, but mirabile dictu turning out to be a clear American victory. No one can now believe that withdrawal by March 2008, as Sen. Obama once advocated, would have been anything but an utter calamity. McCain needs to continue to emphasize the dire consequences of accepting such a defeat. The military is not broken, but now the most experienced, battle-hardened force in the world. Iraq is not, as Joe Biden once demanded, trisected into feuding fiefdoms, but an emerging consensual state. The more Iraq is out of the news, the more the growing public acceptance that it is becoming a success. McCain should continue to ask: Did Americans want victory in November 2008 or defeat in March 2008?

The Ayers controversy is cited by the in-the-tank media as signs of McCain's desperation. Perhaps. But amid the tsk-tsking, there are also certain deer-in-the-headlights moments among Obama's handlers. Why? There are simply too many ACORNs, Ayers, Khalidis, Pflegers, Wrights, et al. not to suggest a pattern unbecoming of a future President of the United States. Obama's past statements about his relationship with Ayers (and others) simply cannot be reconciled with the factual circumstances of their long association. McCain must focus on Ayers between 2001–2005. Then in the climate of national worry following 9/11, Ayers was on recent record as lamenting that he had not set off enough bombs, and yet until 2005 still in contact with Obama—about what and why, voters might wish to know.

When Iraq and Wall Street were off the front page, Obama went moribund in the last months of the Democratic primary. Why? Not because of racism, or even public weariness with Obama's hope and change fluff, or his flip-flops, or occasional striking ignorance about basic history and geography. He finally began to wear on the public—

as he continues to when events of the day do not smother the attention of the voter—for two reasons.

First, the public tires of all the media slant, the celebrity rants, and the shills in popular culture, that in concert hourly berate, beg, threaten, and ridicule voters on behalf of Obama. We are supposed to accept Obama's apotheosis, replete with Latinate seal, Greek columns, biblical injunctions about the seas and atmosphere, and prophesies that he is The One whom we have been waiting for. The creepy effect of ordering us to accept our own salvation becomes cumulative. So there is a quiet unease among the voters, as there always is in America, when someone finger-points and lectures them what they must do—or else!

Second, for all the two years of nonstop campaigning, Obama somehow still remains an unknown—and for apparently good reason. He has almost no record in the Senate to speak of—other than one as America's most predictably partisan and liberal Senator. What is known of his Chicago associates is not reassuring, and so the only defense can be silence rather than exegesis. No one knows anything of his record at Columbia University, how he got into Harvard Law School, or what he was doing until he reached Harvard, or exactly what he did as a community organizer in Chicago, or how a person with no record of legal scholarship was about to be offered tenure at the Chicago Law School. Each doubt in and of itself is of little import, but again in aggregate even the generalities make voters uneasy—especially when they hear of fraud among voter registration drives, swarming radio stations to stifle those critical of Obama, and threatened lawsuits to yank pro-McCain ads.

The odds always were against McCain. And the outcome in these last few days may be seem contingent in large part on breaking news beyond the candidates' control. Yet McCain still has it within his own power to win the election. Obama's view of America is mostly rosy emulation of the European Union; McCain's is to restore fiscal sanity, keep our defenses strong, and ensure that American exceptionalism remains a fact, rather than descends into an empty slogan. In that context, it makes no sense to sneer at McCain for being behind, but a great deal to hope that he isn't.

OCTOBER 31, 2008

The End of Journalism

Sometime in 2008, journalism as we knew it died, and advocacy media took its place

There have always been media biases and prejudices. Everyone knew that Walter Cronkite, from his gilded throne at CBS news, helped to alter the course of the Vietnam War, when, in the post-Tet depression, he prematurely declared the war unwinnable. Dan Rather's career imploded when he knowingly promulgated a forged document that impugned the service record of George W. Bush. We've known for a long time—from various polling, and records of political donations of journalists themselves, as well as surveys of public perceptions—that the vast majority of journalists identify themselves as Democratic, and liberal in particular.

Yet we have never quite seen anything like the current media infatuation with Barack Obama, and its collective desire not to raise key issues of concern to the American people. Here were four areas of national interest that were largely ignored.

CAMPAIGN FINANCING
For years an axiom of the liberal establishment was the need for public campaign financing—and the corrosive role of private money in poisoning the election process. The most prominent Republican who crossed party lines to ensure the passage of national public campaign financing was John McCain—a maverick stance that cost him dearly among conservatives who resented bitterly federal interference in political expression.

In contrast, Barack Obama, remember, promised that he would accept both public funding and the limitations that went along with it, and would "aggressively pursue an agreement with the Republican nominee to preserve a publicly financed general election." Then in June 2008, Obama abruptly reneged, bowing out entirely from government financing, the first presidential nominee in the general election to do that since the system was created in 1976.

Obama has now raised over $600 million, by far the largest campaign chest in American political history. In many states he enjoys a four-to-one advantage in campaign funding—most telling in his scheduled eleventh-hour, 30-minute specials that will not be answered by the publicly financed and poorer McCain campaign.

The story that the media chose to ignore was not merely the Obama about-face on public financing, or even the enormous amounts of money that he has raised—some of it under dubious circumstances involving foreign donors, prepaid credit cards, and false names. Instead, they were absolutely quiet about a historic end to liberal support for public financing.

For all practical purposes, public financing of the presidential general election is now dead. No Republican will ever agree to it again. No Democrat can ever again dare to defend a system destroyed by Obama. All future worries about the dangers of big money and big politics will fall on deaf ears.

Surely, there will come a time when the Democratic Party, whether for ethical or practical reasons, will sorely regret dismantling the very safeguards that for over three decades it had insisted were critical for the survival of the republic. Imagine the reaction of the *New York Times* or the *Washington Post* had John McCain renounced his promise to participate in public campaign financing, proceeded instead to amass $600 million and outraise the publicly financed Barack Obama four-to-one, and begun airing special 30-minute unanswered infomercials during the last week of the campaign.

THE VP CANDIDATES

We know now almost all the details of Sarah Palin's pregnancies, whether the trooper who tasered her nephew went to stun or half stun, the cost of her clothes, and her personal expenses—indeed, almost everything except how a mother of so many children gets elected councilwoman, mayor, and governor, routs an entrenched old-boy cadre, while maintaining near record levels of public support.

Yet the American public knows almost nothing of what it should about the extraordinary career of Joe Biden, the 36-year veteran of the Senate. In unprecedented fashion, Biden has simply avoided the press for most of the last two months, confident that the media instead would deconstruct almost every word of "good looking" Sarah Palin's numerous interviews with mostly hostile interrogators.

By accepted standards of behavior, Biden has sadly proven wanting. He has committed almost every classical sin of character—plagiarism, false biography, racial insensitivity, and serial fabrication. And because of media silence, we don't know whether he was kidding when he said America would not need to burn coal, or that Hezbollah was out of Lebanon, or that FDR addressed the nation on television as president in 1929 (surely a record for historical fictions in a single thought), or that the public would turn sour on Obama once he was challenged by our enemies abroad. In response, the media reported that the very public Sarah Palin was avoiding the press while the very private Joe Biden shunned interviews and was chained to the teleprompter.

For two months now, the media reaction to Biden's inanity has been simply "that's just ol' Joe, now let's turn to Palin," who, in the space of two months, has been reduced from a popular successful governor to a backwoods creationist, who will ban books and champion white secessionist causes. The respective coverage of the two candidates is ironic in a variety of ways, but in one especially—almost every charge against Palin (that she is under wraps, untruthful, and inept) was applicable only to Biden.

So we are about to elect a vice president about whom we know only that he has been around a long time, but little else—and nothing at all why exactly Joe Biden says the most astounding and often lunatic things. Imagine the reaction of Newsweek or Time had moose-hunting mom Sarah Palin claimed FDR went on television to address the nation as President in 1929, or warned America that our enemies abroad would test John McCain and that his response would result in a radical loss of his popularity at home.

THE PAST AS PRESENT
In 2004, few Americans knew Barack Obama. In 2008, they may elect him. Surely his past was of more interest than his present serial denials

of it. Whatever the media's feelings about the current Barack Obama, there should have been some story that the Obama of 2008 is radically different from the Obama who was largely consistent and predictable for the prior 30 years.

Each Obama metamorphosis in itself might be attributed to the normal evolution to the middle, as a candidate shifts from the primary to the general election. But in the case of Obama, we witnessed not a shift, but a complete transformation to an entirely new persona—in almost every imaginable sense of the word. Name an issue—FISA, NAFTA, guns, abortion, capital punishment, coal, nuclear power, drilling, Iran, Jerusalem, the surge—and Obama's position today is not that of just a year ago.

Until 2005, Obama was in communication with Bill Ayers by e-mail and phone, despite Ayers reprehensible braggadocio in 2001 that he remained an unrepentant terrorist. Rev. Wright was an invaluable spiritual advisor—until spring of 2008. Father Pfleger was praised as an intimate friend in 2004—and vanished off the radar in 2008. The media might have asked not just why these rather dubious figures were once so close to, and then so distant from, Obama; but why were there so many people like Rashid Khalidi and Tony Rezko in Obama's past in the first place?

Behind the Olympian calm of Obama, there was always a rather disturbing record of extra-electoral politics completely ignored by the media. If one were disturbed by the present shenanigans of ACORN or the bizarre national call for Americans simply to skip work on election day to help elect Obama (who would pay for that?), one would only have to remember that in 1996 Obama took the extraordinary step of suing to eliminate all his primary rivals by challenging their petition signatures of mostly African-American voters.

In 2004, there was an even more remarkable chain of events in which the sealed divorce records of both his principle primary rival Blair Hull and general election foe, Jack Ryan, were mysteriously leaked, effectively ensuring Obama a Senate seat without serious opposition. These were not artifacts of a typical political career, but extraordinary events in themselves that might well have shed light on present campaign tactics—and yet largely remain unknown to the American people. Imagine the reaction of CNN or NBC had John McCain's pastor and spiritual advisor of 20 years been revealed as a white supremacist who damned a multiracial United States, or had he been a close acquaintance until 2005 of an unrepentant terrorist bomber of abortion clinics, or had McCain himself sued to eliminate congressional opponents by challenging the validity of African-American voters who signed petitions, or had both his primary and general election senatorial rivals imploded once their sealed divorce records were mysteriously leaked.

SOCIALISM?

The eleventh-hour McCain allegations of Obama's advocacy for a share-the-wealth socialism were generally ignored by the media, or if covered, written off as neo-McCarthyism. But there were two legitimate, but again neglected, issues. The first was the nature of the Obama tax plan. The problem was not merely upping the income tax rates on those who made $250,000 (or was it $200,000, or was it $150,000, or both, or none?), but its aggregate effect in combination with lifting the FICA ceilings on high incomes on top of existing Medicare contributions and often high state income taxes.

In other words, Americans who live in high-tax, expensive states like a New York or California could in theory face collective confiscatory tax rates of 65 percent or so on much of their income. And, depending on the nature of Obama's proposed tax exemptions, on the other end of the spectrum we might well see almost half the nation's wage earners pay no federal income tax at all.

Questions arise, but were again not explored: How wise is it to exempt one out of every two income earners from any worry over how the nation gathers its federal income tax revenue? And when credits are added to the plan, are we now essentially not cutting or raising taxes, but simply diverting wealth from those who pay into the system to those who do not?

A practical effect of socialism is often defined as curbing productive incentives by ensuring the poorer need not endanger their exemptions and credits by seeking greater income; and discouraging the wealthy from seeking greater income, given that nearly two-thirds of additional wealth would be lost to taxes. Surely that discussion might have been of interest to the American people.

Second, the real story was not John McCain's characterization of such plans, but both inadvertent, and serial descriptions of them, past and present, by Barack Obama himself. "Spreading the wealth around" gains currency when collated to past interviews in which Obama talked at length about, and in regret at, judicial impracticalities in accomplishing his own desire to redistribute income. "Tragedy" is frequent in the Obama vocabulary, but largely confined to two contexts: the tragic history of the United States (e.g., deemed analogous to that of Nazi Germany during World War II), and the tragic unwillingness or inability to use judicial means to correct economic inequality in non-democratic fashion.

In this regard, remember Obama's revealing comment that he was interested only in "fairness" in increasing capital-gains taxes, despite the bothersome fact that past moderate reductions in rates had, in fact, brought in greater revenue to government. Again, fossilized ideology trumps empiricism. Imagine the reaction of NPR and PBS had John McCain advocated something like abolishing all capital gains taxes, or repealing incomes taxes in favor of a national retail sales tax.

The media has succeeded in shielding Barack Obama from journalistic scrutiny. It thereby irrevocably destroyed its own reputation and forfeited the trust that generations of others had so carefully acquired. And it will never again be trusted to offer candid and nonpartisan coverage of presidential candidates.

Worse still, the suicide of both print and electronic journalism has ensured that, should Barack Obama be elected president, the public will only then learn what they should have known far earlier about their commander-in-chief—but in circumstances and from sources they may well regret.

NOVEMBER 12, 2008

Win One for the Messiah!

Excuse me if I remain unmoved by the misguided religious fervor

J ust one punch of the ballot is all it took. Now suddenly almost every one, here and abroad, is supposed to appreciate the new-found morality of the American people, change their own prior wicked ways, and do what they must for newly elected Barack Obama.

Some columnists are now putting Europe, Russia, China—and the whole world—on moral notice: we Americans did the right thing in electing the first African-American president and a charismatic, hip, commander-in-chief. They must now, too—or else!

Our divine edict from on high is simple: O wide world of little faith: Don't blow it! So Europeans buck up for Barack, and get back in Afghanistan! Illiberal Russia, hands off those democracies on your borders and don't make Barack do something we will all regret later! China, keep Barack's air clean and don't dare burn any more dirty coal!

Excuse me?

The world may be temporarily awestruck with the wise and all-powerful Obama, but it's not quite ready to coalesce into a kinder, gentler global family—one people, under one Messiah, indivisible, with peace and justice for all.

In fact, Vladimir Putin doesn't care a whit that Barack Obama is a path-breaking African-American, much less the first person of color to be an American president. The Chinese can't quite appreciate in translation Obama's mellifluous cadences. France's cool Sarkozy isn't swayed much by the Obama sunglasses, snazzy polo shirt, or nifty outside jump shot.

All these states have interests—not deities. For the most part, either their enmity with or fondness for the United States antedated George

Bush. The world's mental map wasn't erased away when Bush took power. Being the planet's most powerful democracy, and a free and confident world peacekeeper, either excites admiration or earns envy—and even the most crude or the most elegant American president can't change much that simple fact of global human nature.

To the small degree Obama's superior charm and style will improve things, the Russians may toast, backslap, and bear hug Obama—before seeking to body slam him against the wall on Polish anti-missile sites. The smiling Europeans will scurry around mumbling "Yes, but of course!"—as they shirk even more. An unhinged President Ahmadinejad will endlessly write rambling letters to Barack Hussein Obama as the last centrifuges come on line. The jihadists will sigh rather than swear as they continue to try to blow us all up.

Next we are told by many in the media that African-American activists of the race industry will inevitably bow before the transcendent, postracial new President Obama—and recede into the background as they shut down the once-productive victimization assembly lines. After all, did not Americans just prove, through their magnanimous vote—again, it took just one punch of the ballot—that we are no longer racists and should be collectively, if not at least symbolically, relieved at last of an age-old charge of intolerance?

Excuse me, again.

An Al Sharpton, Jesse Jackson, or Charles Rangle is not about to close the plant, and issue lay-offs just because Americans elected an African-American president.

Why should they? Would a Rev. Sharpton really wish to confront his unresolved Tawana Brawley past? Would a Rev. Jackson welcome the public opprobrium accorded most pious white evangelicals, in leisure suits and pompadour hairstyles, who foster out of wedlock children? Or would Charles Rangel wish to pay all his taxes on time, without excuses, as do most other Americans who are not the Chairman of the House Ways and Means Committee?

Victimization for generations has proven lucrative, precisely by allowing self-appointed leaders to advance their careers through doctrinaire "they did it" complaints. The script is now old indeed: Blame the pathologies of the underclass that hamper economic progress—inordinate drug usage, illegitimacy, crime, or dismal graduation rates—on the racism of those with "power." "The Man" can find penitence only through perpetual apologies and the proper channeling of plentiful lucre. All that, too, antedated Obama and will transcend him—until either African-Americans en masse reject their leaders' racial scapegoating; or bored whites, Asians, and Hispanics simply cease listening to the shouting of "Racism! Racist!" and turn the channel.

Unfortunately, Barack Obama did not suggest to the nation that the forces behind John McCain were soon going to wage a racist campaign against him because he had any shred of evidence that they were. And he did not listen at the knee to Rev. Wright for 20 years because he found the venomous preacher to be a racial healer. Trinity Church was not renown for staunch opposition to anti-Semitism, its advocacy for Martin Luther King—style American integration, a self-help promotion of black middle-classness, or its stern criticism of ethnic stereotyping. After all, when Rev. Wright G-D-damned America, talked about those long Italian noses, and laughed about our 9/11 chickens finally coming home to roost, he was not met with jeers, but with wild, standing ovations.

President-Elect Obama once praised the Right Reverend as his spiritual mentor and a brilliant scholar because such an affinity was a wise investment. Not all that long ago, such pandering to, and subsidization of, Trinity ensured to his own budding political constituency that Obama was hardly an avatar of real change, but more safe business as usual. The "usual" was rightly understood as directing state monies into the coffers of various practitioners of victimization, and excusing all social pathologies under the banner of racism and "they raised the bar on you." Moral historians remind us that those who once sought power through disreputable means for supposedly lofty ends rarely change methodology when they finally achieve authority.

Then there are the intellectuals who are giddy that they finally got their Adlai Stevenson. Obama quotes big thinkers. Big thinkers like him. He reads big books. Like Bush, he went to Harvard—but in his case a real Harvard professional school, with an admission slot earned not by undue insider influence (unlike the case of the hated Bush), but on merit alone, and on the basis of an intellectual's sterling undergraduate record at Columbia. (So please, now, intellectuals of the world, unite—and ask that his undergraduate transcript be freed, so in comparison we can snicker one last time at the hated Bush's inferior Yale effort!).

Snide intellectuals are now told to cool it, and also win one for the Messiah as well. The usually hillbilly Palin-loving Americans—again with just one punch of the ballot—proved their intellectual seriousness and gave thinking men and women another rare Camelot gift comparable to the Pulitzer Prize—winning JFK.

Pointy-heads likewise better not blow it, with snarky rebuke and nasal whining, but thank their lucky stars that one of their own finally made it. No more nihilism from Nicholson Baker and his postmodern novel about killing a president. No more chic prizes at Toronto for Gabriel Range's "breathtakingly original" documentary about shooting a president. No more of Jon Stewart's neat little side-riffs about a moronic chief executive—perhaps (wink, wink, nod, nod) who thinks that we took our eye off the ball in Afghanistan by diverting all those much-needed Arab-speaking translators from Kabul to Baghdad.

Excuse me a third time.

Do intellectuals—real and imagined—believe, like Barack Obama, that those who were born in 1922 lived through the two world wars? Or that sometimes we have 57, sometimes 47 states? Or that brave Americans liberated Auschwitz? Or that old Kentucky borders on illiberal Arkansas, but not on progressive Illinois?

Were Barack Obama a mom of five from Alaska with a Fargo accent, long ago we would have learned the candidate was a weird sort of Chicago law professor who never wrote a scholarly essay, a strange sort of Harvard Law Review editor who never published a legal article, and not all that deep a thinker who thought inflating air tires negated the need to look for more oil.

And do intellectuals anyway necessarily make good Presidents? Maybe a John Adams or Teddy Roosevelt—maybe not a utopian megalomaniac like Woodrow Wilson. History is not encouraging when we ponder voracious book readers like Richard Nixon. Brilliant Antiphon tried to overthrow Athenian democracy. The friends of Socrates and Plato—mad writer Critias leading the pack—formed much of the bloodthirsty Thirty Tyrants. The poet Nero finally did away with his insider advisors, including the once sycophantic moralist Seneca and novelist Petronius. Reading a snippet of Thucydides in Greek about the helots at Pylos did not make Thomas Jefferson go out on the veranda and free all his slaves in the fields. Sorry, but quoting Niebuhr has zero relevance in suggesting Obama will out-think our enemies or—elbow on knee, chin on palm—figure out the enigmas of the economy, or offer moral guidance.

Unless Obama really is the Messiah, human nature won't change much just because we elected someone who we want to think might be divine. So give Obama, the man, not the god, a chance to earn, rather than merely assert, his respect. Quit the smug moralizing that we have somehow proved to the world and ourselves that we are now finally worthy and deserving of adulation—as if wisdom and morality were always only an easy punch of the ballot away.

NOVEMBER 21, 2008

What Went Wrong?

Well, it wasn't conservatism

C onservatives have already in the three weeks after the election come up with three competing explanations—and remedies— for their congressional defeats and the victory of the relatively unknown Barack Obama. Post-election voting patterns and statistical data can be interpreted in various ways to support any of the following three exegeses, which I understand as being roughly the following:

It was a sort of fluke. Party faithful will shrug that almost everything conspired this year against the conservative brand: two wars; the sinking economy; eight years of presidential incumbency; a biased, unethical media; Bush's low ratings; the absence of an incumbent president or VP candidate on the ticket; more exposed Republican congressional seats than Democratic ones; a charismatic path-breaking opposition candidate, etc. The stars were wrong, rather than the ideas.

So, the theory goes, just make McCain appear a little younger,

Obama sound a little bit more like John Kerry, and take away the mid-September financial meltdown, and—presto!—a Republican would now be in the White House.

Remedy? Not much other than fielding younger, more charismatic candidates. The failure was people, not ideas, and best symbolized by the damage done by the creepy Jack Abramoff, Larry Craig, Duke Cunningham, Mark Foley, or Ted Stevens whose ethical lapses became the Republican bumper-sticker.

Even had an ethical but colorless Bob Dole or Gerry Ford run in 1980 on Reagan's identical platform, he would have most likely lost to Carter. So it's the candidate, stupid. In this way of thinking, someone like Jindal, Palin, and other fresh new faces will save the party in 2012, especially as hope and change soon proves neither hopeful nor different. Democrats, after all, just replaced their 91-year-old Sen. Robert Byrd as Chairman of the Senate Appropriations Committee with equally entrenched 84-year-old Sen. Daniel Inouye; and are now talking about re-empowering the big unions that helped ruin Detroit, are hiring all the Clinton retreads for a second try in the Obama administration, and seem to want to use the ancient Freddie/Fannie/postal service model to expand the government.

It was too narrow a base, too exclusionary a message. This second theory—favored by New York and D.C. columnists, Schwarzenegger Republicans, and "helpful" Democrats of the "we miss the old good McCain of 2000" school—posits that all these new young, minority, and independent voters can't break through the anti–gay marriage, anti–illegal immigration, anti–affirmative action, anti-abortion firewall, and so are diverted from the low-taxes, small-government, and strong–national defense message that they otherwise might welcome.

Remedy? Junk the social agenda. Become more libertarian. Try to make existing Great Society programs run more efficiently, rather than shrilly barking at what you couldn't cut, even if you wanted to. Be a little more neo-isolationist abroad, a little more laid back at home. Turn off talk radio, and read more of the Wall Street Journal.

It was the namby-pamby, con-lite sell-out that did us in. In this view, conservatives and evangelicals didn't turn out as in the past, because the ticket and its short coat-tails abandoned a conservative message. Take away Bush's mega-deficits, and conservatives could have run on fiscal sanity. Why were right-wingers boasting about federal bailouts? Why print more money on top of the $10-trillion-and-rising national debt? No drilling in ANWR? Close down Gitmo? No talk about creepy Islamic terrorists? No more "personal responsibility" lectures about drugs, alcohol, illegitimacy, crime, and drop-out rates? Didn't the party see that gay marriage lost everywhere, and with help from minorities as well?

Remedy? Run as a true conservative, energize the base, and outdebate and outthink your liberal opponents.

* * *

I supposed one could cop out, and claim that there is truth in all three explanations. But my sense is that most people—who, after all, get a job, eventually buy a house and have to maintain it, have children, and respect the traditions of their families' past—end up by necessity more conservative than liberal. The challenge is not to water down the conservative message, but to beef it up, even while making it more persuasive to those who are skeptical.

Take so-called Hispanics. (I say "so-called" since the liberal notion of millions of progressive unassimilated brown block voters is mythical, given high rates of intermarriage, mutual suspicion between Cubans, Central Americans, and Mexicans, and right-wing tendencies among Spanish-speaking minorities.) Take race completely out of the equation and start with the notion that enforcing the border is the only way to restore the respect for immigration statutes whose non-enforcement is currently an embarrassment to every citizen who believes in the rule of law.

Automatic Mexican-American support for open borders is simply not a given. Why wouldn't Hispanic citizens bristle should a freighter beach on the coast of Northern California each day, to unload 1,000 illegal Chinese would-be immigrants? Given historical and present geographical realities, existing levels of legal immigration already privilege Hispanics over all other groups of immigrants. Conservative should emphasize and welcome that mostly neglected fact.

Legal immigration must be distinguished from illegal immigration at every juncture. It is no surprise that La Raza, the Democratic Left, and the cheap-labor, open-borders Right always make charges of "anti-immigrant" rather than anti–illegal immigration, since, if they cannot both personalize the issue and conflate it with legal immigration, they lose the debate. Conservatives' chief talking point should be the deleterious effect of unchecked illegal immigration on the wages of poor workers, coupled with the employers' discrimination against Mexican-American second-generation and African-American entry-level workers in preference for off-the-books and cheaper illegal laborers.

If one were to talk of party betrayal, it would involve supposedly conservative corporate elites who talk disingenuously of diversity and opportunity while they lobbied to ignore the law, and get their hands on as many illegal cheap laborers as they could to the callous detriment of the working citizen poor.

On social issues, there has to be some conservative touchstone, like reverence for uniqueness and beauty of individual life. What unites skepticism about euthanasia, abortion on demand, or embryonic stem-cell research is fear of a sort of soulless Brave New World notion that individuals don't matter, that ease of lifestyle trumps every other difficult moral consideration, and that such thinking is the beginning—not the end—of something frightening.

Rather than demonizing gay-marriage, conservatives should emphasize the availability of civil unions—and then ask: What exactly is not enough protection in such current contracts, and how can such legal statutes be improved to protect the legal rights of gay couples? Civil unions should be seen as an avant-garde institution for novel times, while traditional marriage is reserved as a retrograde stuffy institution for the hopelessly straight.

The problem with liberal notions of high taxes and big government (besides the obvious problem that they don't work) should be that they are elitist. Those born into particular social and economic castes are frozen: the government supplies just enough subsidized housing, food, and fuel for those in untaxed lower-income brackets to remind those citizens that it is not all that bad staying there. Meanwhile, those struggling to become prosperous and leave capital behind for their children are suddenly taxed to death just as they begin to succeed—as if, once the hyper-wealthy have gotten theirs, the rules change and no one else can follow.

The reason why Wall Street zillionaires like a Ted Turner, Warren Buffet, or George Soros endorse Obama's tax plan is that they make so much that increased taxes don't matter, or they can hire costly consultants to find exemptions not available to most plumbers or electrical contractors. Even when they choose to endow favorite causes they prefer tax exemptions—either now with write-offs, or postmortem without estate taxes—and de facto have the taxpayer subsidize their particular take on proper policy. Unfortunately, the Republicans failed to even develop such an argument that the very poor and the very wealthy in cynical fashion support liberal policies, while those in between who struggle in entrepreneurial fashion to do even better are caricatured as unpatriotic and selfish.

On foreign policy and national security, the battle of ideas is already won. A more articulate, persuasive defense of existing foreign policy, without gratuitous "they're wimps" lingo would help. But come January, the Left will in surprising fashion emulate most of what Bush did abroad, albeit under a fuzzy, kumbaya veneer. The removal of Saddam, the humiliating defeat of Al Qaeda in Iraq, and the creation of a constitutional government in Baghdad will seem better, not worse, as each month passes in which we see little American combat violence approaching a likely 2011 withdrawal date.

So for all the big talk of a cabal of Jewish neo-cons, I doubt Democrats want to promote Mubarak and the House of Saud as "at least they're our SOBs." They may dream grandly of flipping Syria and Iran, but shortly will remember how Carter, Reagan, Bush 41, and Clinton utterly failed on that score. They may close Gitmo (both trials and transference home of the detainees will prove a public-relations nightmare), but I doubt we will see precipitous pullouts from Iraq, repeal of the Patriot Act, or the end of the FISA accords. "Shredding the Constitution" is an opposition's cheap slur; in contrast, when responsible for governance or in fear of rumors of another attack, such former critics will worry more about suffering another 9/11 on their watch.

Should the Left dismantle homeland-security provisions taken since 2001, and embrace therapeutic approaches to radical Islam abroad—and as a result we then see a single repeat of September 11—the credibility of the Democratic Party will be lost for a decade. For all the campaign talk of a trumped-up, constructed war on terror, Obama's advisors—at least when they speak privately—know that keeping America safe since 9/11 was a Bush achievement rather than a natural occurrence. They also privately advise that Obama emulate Bush on key substantive foreign-policy issues (Iran really is a big threat, and can't have nuclear weapons; current strikes on terrorists in Pakistan are necessary, etc.), while grandstanding about "being liked" again.

The key is not to abandon conservative positions, but to explain them in novel ways to the majority who might find them more in tune with human nature—and consequently more humanitarian than their usual caricatures of being too selfish, tough, or insensitive. The conservative message the last eight years was to support freedom abroad as an absolute value that appealed to all, regardless of culture and background; the liberal multicultural message was not to rely on universal standards to judge the "other"—since supposed past oppression allows the "victim" to redefine morality on his own terms. The conservative message was that government without checks and balances, whether at the UN, the EU, or here in the massive bureaucracies of the federal government, naturally seeks to bully and stifle rather than empower the individual.

A final note. Conservatism also applies to bearing and comportment. There was something repugnant about greedy CEO and speculators on Wall Street wildly raking in hundreds of millions under the guise of "free-market conservatism"—as if Ace hardware store owners, truck drivers, and farmers would find them kindred spirits. Conservatism's social message used to be something like "Don't do all the things that you are otherwise free to do" or "Just because we don't make all your appetites illegal, does not mean that some are not immoral." Conservative populism is not anti-intellectualism at all, but rather a disdain for excess and arm-chair elitism.

In short, explain why conservatism appeals to the innate values of most ordinary Americans and the squabbling about the proper message disappears.

DECEMBER 5, 2008

Parallel Lives

In politics today, intention, symbolism, and rhetoric are everything; facts, nothing.

The Roman moralist Plutarch wrote a number of parallel lives of illustrious Greek and Roman notables to offer his Greek-reading audience ethical lessons about character, virtue, and culture. He was trying to teach his fellow Roman citizens the importance of ethics, and to remind them that their own ancestors were often as illustrious as the great Greeks of the past. Let us try to use his example to learn something about modern morality from the contrasts within a few matched pairs of contemporary notables, prominent in the recent news.

FINANCE

I know from media accounts that someone called Richard Fuld supposedly ran the once cash-laden and 158-year-old Lehman Brothers investment and banking house into the ground. Indeed, various newspapers and news shows convinced me I should dislike Fuld—given his apparent arrogance to his underlings, and insidious greed in harvesting an aggregate $300 million in salary and bonuses over eight years from his sick firm.

So I confess I was not particularly bothered to hear that someone in the company gym supposedly punched Fuld in the face after his brazen and shameless congressional testimony. But why have we not heard commensurate censure of former whiz kid Robert Rubin at Citigroup? The stock of that mega-lending institution has descended from blue-chip status to being now nearly worthless. I was recently talking to a teller in Fresno at a small branch office of Citibank, who sighed, "Who'd have thought I may lose my job because we knew more about running a tiny branch office than those guys in New York who ran us?"

While among the top echelon at Citigroup (as someone called "Citigroup Inc. director and senior counselor") Rubin took in an aggregate $115 million in pay and bonuses—even though his bank's stock crashed and lost 75 percent of its value, and now the conglomerate totters close to bankruptcy. On Wall Street it appears that the role of a "senior counselor" earning over $100 million is to use one's influence with people one has met in government to lobby them to do things for one's present employer that they would otherwise not necessarily think was ethical—such as trying to get the government to bail out a Citigroup concern like Ken Lay's bankrupt Enron.

I recall that Robert Rubin, as Bill Clinton's Treasury Secretary, oversaw the deregulation of Wall Street that certainly contributed to the present meltdown. But while we can associate the name Fuld with Lehman Brothers, and Ken Lay with Enron, and both with abject greed, probable malfeasance, and systematic incompetence, why are we unable to make the similar connection between Citigroup's near collapse, its reckless foray into the morass of subprime loans, and Robert Rubin's very lucrative, but ultimately disastrous leadership role within the banking conglomerate?

Such an examination might be useful inasmuch as Rubin's own protégés Lawrence Summers and Timothy Geithner will now oversee the nation's financial policy for the new Obama administration. On a final note, examine Rubin's Fuld-like response to such charges: Apparently he claims as a "senior advisor" and member of the board of directors of Citigroup, he had both no responsibility for lunatic decisions of his company, but yet enough responsibility to be worth $115 million.

POLITICS

I remember why most Republicans, other than Colin Powell, abandoned the soon-to-be convicted Ted Stevens. And the names of Mark Foley and Larry Craig are now understandably infamous. It is altogether fine and proper that Republicans turned on their own miscreants, who needed to be turned on for their various misdeeds. But why in the world is Rep. Charles Rangel still the Chairman of the House Ways and Means committee which oversees U.S. tax policy—especially at this critical juncture in our nation's financial history? I say "Why?" not out of sarcasm, but out of real bewilderment: Rangel's record of financial and ethical improprieties is no longer a matter of hypocrisy, but rather one of probable criminality.

Let us count the ways: (1) Rangel paid no federal income tax on some $75,000 in rental income from his Caribbean villa—that lapse would result in a felony tax-evasion charge for the rest of us who dared to try that year in and year out. (2) Something called Nabobs Industries gave $1 million to something called the Charles B. Rangel Center for Public Service at City College of New York—and, apparently in exchange, got tens of millions of dollars in tax waivers from Rangel's committee. Surely if Scooter Libby went to prison for faulty recall about not being the first one to "out" (non-covert) CIA operative Valerie Plame, a special prosecutor could also examine Rangel's role in what may have resulted in a nearly $1 billion shortfall to the federal treasury. (3) Rangel seems to be claiming his New York campaign office as his home in order to continue to garner rent-control exemptions, improperly saving him thousands of dollars through aggregate subsidies. That someone who oversees the drafting of American tax policies and regulation cannot follow them himself is now a statement of fact, not baseless slander.

LAW

Then we come to the office of the U.S. Attorney General. We all remember Alberto Gonzales's painful 2007 testimony before Congress, where he was publicly humiliated by outraged Congressional Democrats for his halting replies, failing memory, and apparent inability to advise administration kingpins that their anti-terrorism zeal was dangerously bordering on the unconstitutional and unlawful.

The subtext of liberal criticism was that Gonzales was both a moral weakling who could not speak Truth to Power, and a sort of affirmative-action mockery, an example of one of those cynical attempts by conservatives, in condescending fashion, to appoint less than qualified minorities to high posts, in the expectation that political correctness would offer cover to such compliant fellow-traveling right-wingers. Gonzalez resigned under Congressional and media pressure, his reputation so damaged he could not find work with any major Washington law firm.

Given such past sermonizing about the need for independence and ethical resolve at the attorney general's office, there should be little chance that someone who facilitated the pardon of Marc Rich, the odious fugitive tax and oil cheat, would ever be nominated—much less confirmed to the same post. Rich, remember, while on the lam and through surrogates, had donated monies to various Clinton and Democratic appendages. Then as a wanted fugitive in Europe (on the FBI's most wanted list, no less), expected and received a presidential pardon in return. It was about as quid pro quo as could be.

In turn, Eric Holder, as a compliant high official at the Justice Department, apparently was both afraid to cross the Clintons and, by his obsequious subservience to top Democratic insiders, perhaps conniving to ensure a top spot for himself in the then probable Gore administration to come. Thanks to Holder's deft efforts, Clinton pardoned Rich a few hours before he left office. Few mentioned that Rich had stealthily bought and sold Iranian oil while U.S. citizens were held hostage in Teheran.

If Gonzales could be faulted for unwise zealotry in pursuit of national security, then Holder could be damned for unwise zealotry in the pursuit of freeing a billionaire fugitive on the run to enhance his own career. I leave the reader to ascertain why the Hispanic Gonzalez was branded as inept and given no quarter despite his inspiring personal saga, while the suggestion that the African-American Holder has proven he could not be reliable as the highest law enforcement official of the land would be deemed insensitive. Who knows? Perhaps the distinction may have something to do with their respective politics.

SENIOR STATESMEN

Then there is the strange case of Sen. Chris Dodd. Future economic historians may trace the origins of the September financial collapse back to the deregulation of the federally affiliated Freddie Mac and Fannie Mae lending agencies, and the banking industry's shenanigans in allowing the unqualified to receive improper loans—all under political pressure from Congressional leaders.

Somehow Dodd seems to have had an uncanny ability to have been at Ground Zero of both implosions. Here are the facts: Chris Dodd is currently chairman of the Senate Banking Committee. As such, he refinanced his own mortgage property through (the now bankrupt) Countrywide's "V.I.P." program. That is, Dodd was given an unusually favorable loan discount that over the life of his mortgage in theory would have saved him several thousand dollars. Yet Senate rules make it illegal for members to knowingly receive gifts worth $100 or more a year from private businesses like Countrywide that makes use of lobbyists. What's more, Countrywide had also contributed $21,000 to Dodd's senate campaigns since 1997. Worse still, Dodd received about $70,000 in campaign gifts from Bank of America—which bought out the bankrupt Countrywide.

Remember, as well, that Sen. Dodd serially asserted that both Freddie Mac and Fannie Mae were fundamentally strong—even as both were on the verge of bankruptcy. Dodd was strangely confident in the insolvent entities perhaps because he had received more campaign contributions from the two failed agencies than did any other legislator in Congress.

think all our grandfathers at one time in this country might have thought it morally wrong for a congressional banking overseer to take money from banks—and in particular when they were in the process of being looted and run into the ground. If the Senate Banking Committee Chairman is improperly receiving mortgage preferences and outright cash from banking concerns, then who will police the police? Contrast Dodd's uninterrupted tenure with the case of the former Senate Majority Leader Trent Lott. Lott once foolishly shot off his mouth in odious fashion at the 100th birthday party of the late Dixiecrat, former segregationist and fellow Senate colleague Strom Thurmond.

Words matter. So although Lott quickly offered apologies for his endorsement of Thrumond's reprehensible candidacy over a half-century ago, at the moment he finished his salutation, he was through as a Senate leader. Under pressure from both Senate colleagues and the White House, he resigned his leadership position. The charge against Lott was a racially insensitive remark, not a systematic pattern of offering near bankrupt firms public approbation in exchange for cash contributions and preferential treatment.

Lott was understandably and with cause sacked by the powers that be in Washington; Dodd curiously now plays a crusading role in Congressional damnation of Wall Street greed, and the supposedly inept Bush administration's regulation of the banking industry.

COMPARITIVE MORALITIES

I could go on and on with these Plutarchean examples of Parallel Lives but you get the picture. Here, the contrast is not the respective virtues of Greece and Rome. Nor is there any regret whatsoever that liberals of good faith thankfully scrutinize the bad judgment and even criminal activity of wayward conservatives. The problem instead is why we continuously consider liberal transgressions as misdemeanors and their conservative counterparts as felonies.

If Plutarch once believed that action, not intention matters (otherwise, as Aristotle noted, we could all be moral in our sleep), we moderns believe the reverse—that proper thinking can often excuse improper acts. Why so? Perhaps we suspect that a Rubin or Dodd want to do more good things for the poor than do a Fuld or Lott, and so we should interpret their transgressions as atypical lapses rather than characteristic behavior.

Perhaps we think a Attorney-General designate Holder is properly cognizant of our long liberal efforts to force the system to change and therefore deserves some exemption for ethical blindness on the job. Again in contrast, Attorney-General emeritus Gonzales is unduly cynical in not appreciating that progressive thinking is responsible for his job, and therefore he must be held accountable immediately and for the rest of his professional life for supposed character flaws.

Perhaps we think a life-long crusading African-American like Rangel merely fudges a bit here and there in the twilight of a long exemplary career seeking to ensure racial harmony and parity for his nation, and therefore is absent-minded rather than felonious and hypocritical. Yet the sordid behavior of his white male conservative counterparts provides valuable elucidation about their depravity and bigotry—and is proper grounds for their eventual departures not merely from posts of influence, but from the Congress altogether.

Perhaps—as we saw from the asymmetrical media treatment of the two candidates during the recent campaign—in matters of power and politics today, intention, symbolism, and rhetoric are everything; facts essentially nothing.

Or maybe less cynically—in the minds of self-appointed liberal moralists concerned about the greater good—exalted ends at times necessarily entail regrettable means.

MAY 8, 2009

Why Did Republicans Lose Their Appeal?

And how can they get it back?

C olin Powell keeps insisting that the Republicans lost the presidency because of right-wing extremists like Rush Limbaugh and Ann Coulter, who, in his view, have become the public face of the Republican party, and thus will ensure its permanent marginalization. Others argue that the Bush administration had allowed Republicanism to become a cowboyish clique of the selfish who wanted a free hand to make money and let others less fortunate be damned. David Frum offered the novel notion that Rush Limbaugh's girth, past drug use, checkered marital career, and palatial digs were emblematic of the party's out-of-touch self-indulgence, especially when contrasted with the athletic, happily married, and transracial Barack Obama.

But none of these explanations rings true—especially since most of the current critics themselves were, in the heyday of 2002–03, either enthusiastically working for, or writing in praise of, the very administration whose policies they now claim caused the present mess.

LIMBAUGH & CO.?
First, the real public expressions of extremism in American politics recently have not been from the Right—not surprisingly, perhaps, given

that for much of this new century the Republicans smugly controlled most of the government. It was not Rush Limbaugh, for example, but Michael Moore who announced that the 9/11 killers wrongly selected a blue-state city, or that the al-Qaeda insurgents were Minutemen-like patriots. Moore, remember, was no marginal figure but the darling of the Democratic establishment, who flocked to the gala opening of his crude propaganda film Fahrenheit 9/11.

Indeed, if one were to follow the logic of this new Powell doctrine that public expression of extremism sinks a party, then the Democrats would never have won back the Senate and the House. Senators as diverse as Dick Durbin, John Kerry, and Ted Kennedy shrilly compared American soldiers to terrorists, Nazis, Pol Pot's thugs, and Saddam's Baathists.

The most inflammatory public figure of the last two years was, in fact, Barack Obama's own minister, Rev. Jeremiah Wright, who uttered vile racist characterizations of everyone from Italians to Jews, as part of his generic "G-d damning" of America. So far we have not seen a conservative version of Nicholson Baker's novel Checkpoint, or anything like Jonathan Chait's New Republic essay that began, "I hate President George W. Bush." Colin Powell himself has been demonized in scurrilous terms, but the epithets have come not from Rush Limbaugh, but rather from such observers as that old cultural icon of the Left, Harry Belafonte, who once quite unapologetically compared the secretary of state to a "house slave."

THE CYCLES OF AMERICAN POLITICS

There were historical reasons why it was unlikely that the Republicans were going to win the presidency last year. It has always been difficult to extend a party's control of the executive branch for 12 consecutive years; the Democrats themselves had not done it since the Roosevelt-Truman years. In 30 out of the last 50 years, Republicans have controlled the White House, hardly proof of a conservative implosion. Over the last half-century, the general rule was that a Democrat could not win the presidency unless he had the cover of a Southern accent. That both JFK and Obama defied that conventional wisdom suggests that only the rare appearance of a charismatic youthful Democratic candidate can balance the stigmatization of out-of-touch northern liberalism. The elections of 1964, 1976, and 1992 were all heralded as the beginnings of new permanent liberal majorities. In the first two cases, the inept governance of LBJ and Jimmy Carter ensured that Republicans were back in office in four years. Bill Clinton extended Democratic rule for eight years; but he did so without winning a majority of the votes in either election. Take Ross Perot out of the equation in 1992—and perhaps even in 1996—and Clinton might well not have won. Clinton survived Monica because no Americans were killed in his Balkans War, and because Dick Morris taught him the arts of triangulation, while the Republican Congress forced spending cuts that led finally to two years of budget surpluses. He left office popular, despite Monica, with balanced budgets and an assurance that the era of big government was over.

THE SEPTEMBER MELTDOWN

John McCain was ahead of Barack Obama when the September meltdown occurred. Had the financial panic not transpired until December, there was a 50-50 chance that McCain would have won—despite deep defections from the conservative base. In that case, we would be talking now about the continued Democratic propensity for self-destruction by nominating liberal northern presidential candidates like Obama, Kerry, Gore, Dukakis, and Mondale.

A STEALTH CANDIDATE

Obama was an especially charismatic candidate. His mixed racial heritage and exotic name were novelties that both intrigued and reassured elite white liberals, while galvanizing minorities in a way that Jesse Jackson and other traditional African-American candidates had previously not managed to do. Had the Democrats run Al Gore or John Kerry they might well have lost; or had Barack Obama, Kerry-like, paraded around in various costumes—duck-hunting camouflage, biker's spandex, a windsurfing wetsuit—or even kept up the arugula talk and the faux bowling appearances, he too would not have won.

On nearly every campaign issue—offshore drilling, nuclear power, NAFTA, guns, abortion, capital punishment, Iraq, the war on terror—

candidate Obama hedged or triangulated in favor of the more conservative view. Had he in late October outlined a $1.7-trillion deficit, the need for serial apologies abroad, and the nationalization of the banks and the auto industry, he would have lost.

RED INK

But the above are peripheral issues. The real cause of unhappiness with the Republicans was simply that they could not make a convincing case for conservatism to a changing electorate because so many of them were not acting as conservatives.

Take the seminal issue of spending and expanding government. The last Republican to balance a budget was Dwight Eisenhower. Had President Bush—despite 9/11, Katrina, and two wars—simply limited spending increases to the rate of inflation and natural growth, then he would have entered his last years of office with balanced budgets.

In contrast, once Republicans started talking about federal deficits only in terms of manageable percentages of GDP rather than as real money, they forfeited the entire issue of fiscal responsibility, and lost the moral high ground. Barack Obama can get away with unprecedented and astronomical of projected deficits, in part because the Republicans are not credible any more on spending.

COMPASSIONATE CONSERVATISM?

Compassionate conservatism was supposed to show the middle classes how, even with small government, lower taxes, and streamlining of existing programs, social protection was still ensured for those who did not do as well as the wealthy during the boom years. Instead, it ended up as a rather crude quid pro quo on things like No Child Left Behind and the Medicare prescription-drug benefit. Bush's embrace of big old-fashioned spending was supposed to be a demonstration of bipartisanship that might extend to united congressional support for the war. Instead, Democrats cherry-picked the Bush overtures, increased their anti-war rhetoric, and then, mirabile dictu, attributed the ensuing deficits not to the profligate spending but to "tax cuts for the rich"— despite the yearly increases in aggregate federal revenue.

THE WAR

Obama's continuance of the Iraq war, his escalation in Afghanistan, and his preservation of wiretaps, e-mail intercepts, renditions, Predator drone attacks, and, so far, the Guantanamo Bay detention center prove that Bush's war on terror per se, even the controversial Iraq war, did not lose Republicans the election. The problem was more complex than just the mayhem of the insurgency in Iraq, which was over by November 2008—as witnessed by Obama's constant campaign demagoguing against the very Bush anti-terrorism protocols and war policies in Iraq and Afghanistan that he was soon to embrace.

When conservatives advance tough foreign-policy initiatives, they naturally evoke hostility from the therapeutic media. Instead of tough "smoke-'em-out" talk that reinforces the cowboy caricature, they needed to explain exactly why the resort to force was needed, what the strategy was, and why such a bad choice was better than the existing worse alternatives.

Unfortunately, the Bush administration was not able to articulate exactly what Iraq was about, why the congressional Democrats had willingly joined them to authorize the war on 23 counts (nearly all of them not about WMD), and why it was both moral and in the United States' interest to remove Saddam and not abandon the nascent Iraqi democracy.

SPECTERIZATION

If the Republicans think they can outbid the Democrats for the support of feminists, gays, and growing numbers of minorities, then they will only add embarrassment and permanent failure to the present natural cycle of political correction. Instead, they must be ready to show that deficits of the present magnitude, when added to existing debt, are unsustainable and will sap the vitality of the entire American society.

Most people dread going to the DMV; that such a state-run blueprint will now be superimposed on manufacturing, energy, health care, and banking should scare the landscaper and the roofer alike. Precisely by showing to gays, women, minorities, and the young that none of us gets an exemption from the iron laws of nature—you cannot spend what you don't make; you can't apologize to unsavory characters and end up respected and safe; you can't expect government bureaucrats to make better decisions than private executives—conservatives can become inclusive.

Conservatives should remind the electorate that the very wealthy, the Wall Street big money, and the elite in the universities and foundations are now consistently voting Democratic. It was the nexus between Wall Street financiers and lax liberal Democratic congressional overseers—the former wanting profits, the latter able to cloak lavish campaign contributions with populist rhetoric about caring for the poor—that got us into the financial mess.

The reason Sarah Palin earned real hatred was the populist nature of her appeal. Her rallies did not draw many of the government-dependent poor, true; but they also did not draw the rich and liberal elite. If Palin had survived the press demonization, she might have been able to show the electorate why the current leadership of the Democratic Party is at odds with the middle classes, who do not require most of the government entitlements that liberals love to dispense, and yet don't share the aristocratic tastes that the elite in the media, foundations, universities, and Wall Street see as requisites for paternal governance.

If the Republicans can offer a sane alternative of balanced budgets to the current mega-deficits; if they demonstrate the nexus between those who don't pay taxes and those who have so much money that they don't worry about taxes; and if they can talk without braggadocio of the tough choices abroad that are not solved by apologies, then they will win again in 2012. Conservatism is the political belief that best mirrors human nature across time and space; but because its precepts are sometimes tragic and demand responsibility rather than ever-expanding rights, it requires adept communicators—not triangulators and appeasers whose pleasure is only for the moment.

OCTOBER 20, 2010

The Strange Summer of 2008

How our first postracial, postnational, bipartisan president has revealed himself to be a condescending doctrinaire ideologue.

Historians will look back at the 2008 campaign in the light of the 2010 midterm elections. Almost everything the president has done in the last two years is simply a continuance of that now strangely distant summer.

The only disconnects are (1) that the media are now embarrassed by Obama's rapid decline in the polls and so suddenly, in catch-up fashion, have chosen to highlight his inexperience and hypocrisy in a way they did not in 2008. And (2) that governance requires concrete action in a way campaign rhetoric does not, and thus the American public can evaluate the consequences of deeds rather than the implications of mellifluent hope-and-change rhetoric.

Remember the 2008 claims of bipartisanship and an end to the old style of politics? Yet there was nothing in Obama's prior career to substantiate those idealistic claims. In his first race, for the Illinois state senate in 1996, he sued to remove opponents from the ballot, and in his campaign for the U.S. Senate in 2004, the divorce records of both his primary- and general-election opponents were mysteriously leaked. Subsequently, Obama compiled the most partisan record in the entire Senate, proving that he was the least willing senator to veer from a doctrinaire ideology. So if we are surprised that Rush Limbaugh, Sean Hannity, Fox News, John Roberts, the tea parties, John Boehner, the Chamber of Commerce, Karl Rove, and Ed Gillespie have later become bogeymen of the week, we must remember that this is merely the logical continuance of Obama's earlier hardball modus operandi.

Remember Obama's praise for public campaign financing, with its attendant restrictions? Yet Obama was the first candidate in the history of publicly financed presidential campaigns to renounce such funding (after promising that he would accept it). His renunciation of the Carter-era program has probably wrecked the idea that presidential candidates will ever again be bound by public-financing protocols. In fact, Obama raised the largest pile of campaign cash in history, much of it from Wall Street, some of it from unnamed donors. So if we are surprised that he is now ritually attacking Wall Street financiers and alleging that his opponents are raising funds from unnamed sources, it is simply because he knows such landscapes firsthand only too well.

Remember the serial attacks on the Bush anti-terrorism protocols—questioning intercepts, wiretaps, and the Patriot Act, and decrying predator attacks in Afghanistan/Pakistan—and the promises to exit Iraq, close down Guantanamo, and end renditions and tribunals? Other than introducing some creative euphemisms (e.g., "man-made disasters," "overseas contingency operations"), Obama either kept or vastly expanded the Bush protocols, apparently on the assumptions that (a) they were always needed and his prior opposition was simply acceptable campaign demagoguery, and (b) the Left's opposition to the anti-terrorism efforts was always disingenuous and aimed only at sullying Bush, and therefore it would dissipate once Obama took them over intact.

Remember the condescending Pennsylvania clingers speech, and the psychoanalysis of his own grandmother's purported "typical white person" sort of racism? Such professorial tsk-tsking has simply now been channeled into deprecations of a new cast of yokels, whose denseness and emotionalism ensured that they also could not appreciate all that Obama had done for them.

Indeed, the supposedly limbic-brained voters of Pennsylvania would easily recognize some of Obama's later analyses: "So I've been a little amused over the last couple of days where people have been having these rallies about taxes. You would think they would be saying thank you." And, "At a time when the country is anxious generally and going through a tough time, then, you know, fears can surface—suspicions, divisions can surface in a society. And so I think that plays a role in it." And, "Part of the reason that our politics seems so tough right now and facts and science and argument does [sic] not seem to be winning the day all the time is because we're hardwired not to always think clearly when we're scared. And the country is scared." And (of his own disenchanted supporters), "If people now want to take their ball and go home that tells me folks weren't serious in the first place. If you're serious, now's exactly the time that people have to step up."

Remember all the right-wing furor over the Rev. Jeremiah Wright, Bill Ayers, Father Pfleger, Rashid Khalidi, and a host of other Obama associates that suggested in 2008 he was well out of the American mainstream? In that context, the appointment of a Van Jones or an Anita Dunn made perfect sense. Sonia Sotomayor's "wise Latina," Eric Holder's "cowards, " and Van Jones's white students engaging in mass murder and "white polluters . . . steering poison into the people of color's communities"; the president's own putdowns of the police, the Arizona law, and the opponents of the Ground Zero mosque; the apology tour, the bowing abroad, the snubbing of the British, and on and on were only elaborations of the same Chicago/Ivy League view of America as a largely racist, unfair, and deeply flawed society.

One could continue with numerous other examples from the summer of 2008 that have been reified during the first 21 months of Obama's governance, but the picture is clear enough. Almost all the current style and substance of President Obama were clear enough in the 2008 campaign. But in that long-ago, dreamy summer of mass hypnosis, the excitement about our first African-American president, a biased media, Bush/Iraq, the September 15 meltdown, the lackluster McCain candidacy, and an orphaned election with no incumbent running all conspired to convince voters that what they heard and saw was not so disturbing—or at least that it would end once Obama became president.

So the 2008 campaign, as brilliantly as it was waged in Machiavellian fashion by Obama, will be reinterpreted in the context of the 2010 setback.

The voters are rebelling because they believe they have been had. They now think that they were deceived in 2008 into voting for someone who never had any intention of governing in the bipartisan manner on which he had campaigned.

Conservative and moderate pundits and elite commentators who went for Obama then are rebelling now because they foolishly assured the country that the assumed intellectualism of the charismatic Obama—so in contrast to the twangy, evangelical Bush—far outweighed any Neanderthal right-wing worries that Obama had a long record of hard-Left associations and dubious proclamations.

The media are rebelling because they have wakened up to the current polls and concluded that Obama in 2008 had charmed them into sacrificing their reputations for disinterested reportage. Then once elected, he cynically counted on their continued subservience to destroy any shred of credibility that they had left.

The Democratic establishment is rebelling because it fell for the hard-left agenda of a charming pied piper who promised them that he could disguise and package extremism to ensure years of Democratic majorities and an FDR-like omnipresence—only to destroy thousands of their careers at the local, state, and national levels.

The left wing is rebelling because a postracial, postnational Obama deceived them into thinking that his non-traditional heritage, his glibness, and his own godhead would carry through their ultra-liberal agenda that historically the American people did not want—only to discover that it was impossible, and that he would now sermonize to them that it was in fact impossible.

Yet they were all warned—in that strange summer of 2008.

CHAPTER TWO

WHEN THINGS DON'T MAKE SENSE

FEBRUARY 12, 2009

Hardly the Best and Brightest

The institutions run by our elites aren't trustworthy,
so why should we put any faith in them?

Most historians agree that earthquakes, droughts, or barbarians did not unravel classical Athens or imperial Rome. More likely the social contract between the elite and the more ordinary citizens finally began breaking apart—and with it the trust necessary for a society's collective investment and the payment of taxes. Then civilization itself begins to unwind.

Something like that has been occurring lately because of the actions on Wall Street and in Washington, D.C. The former "masters of the universe" who ran Wall Street took enormous risks to get multimillion-dollar bonuses, even as they piled up billions in debt for their soon-to-be-bankrupt companies. Financial wizards like Robert Rubin at Citicorp, Richard Fuld at Lehman Brothers and Franklin Raines at Fannie Mae—all of whom made millions as they left behind imploding corporations—had degrees from America's top universities. They had sophisticated understanding of hedge funds, derivatives, and sub-prime mortgages—everything, it seems, but moral responsibility for the investments of millions of their ordinary clients.

The result of such speculation by thousands of Wall Street gamblers was that millions of Americans who played by the rules, and put money each month in their 401(k) plans and elsewhere, lost much of their retirement savings. Many likely will have to keep working well into their 60s or 70s, and delay passing on their jobs to a new generation awaiting employment.

Yet most disgraced Wall Street elites will retain their mega-bonuses and will not go to jail. Their legacy is having destroyed the financial confidence of a society that depends on putting capital safely away to be directed for investment by responsible overseers. A sort of unraveling of the entire system of credit and debt may follow from the loss of confidence in Wall Street. Ads on radio now blare out to the rest of us how to renegotiate our mortgages, how to avoid paying the IRS, and how to walk away from freely incurred credit-card debt. We hear not to trust in mutual funds or even banks—but instead, like medieval hoarders, to revert to the age-old safety of gold.

Apparently, the institutions run by our elites aren't trustworthy, so why should we put any faith in them? Meanwhile, we are learning that the brightest and best-educated Americans at the highest levels of government simply refuse to pay their required taxes. Yet because the IRS audits a tiny percentage of taxpayers, voluntarily compliance with our tax code is the glue that holds together a sophisticated society and separates it from a failed state. Rep. Charles Rangel (D., N.Y.) is the chairman of the Ways and Means Committee that oversees our tax laws. But his lawyer recently admitted that Rangel didn't report some $75,000 in income. Timothy Geithner is the new Treasury secretary and oversees the IRS. Yet Geithner improperly wrote off his son's summer camp fees as a dependent-care expense, and failed to pay thousands of dollars in Social Security and Medicare taxes. Then there is former senator Tom Daschle, who was nominated to be secretary of health and human services. It was revealed that he owed the IRS over $140,000 in taxes on unreported free limo services; as a result, he had to ask President Obama to withdraw his nomination.

Nancy Killefer, who just withdrew her name from consideration as "performance czar," did not pay required taxes for domestic help. The husband of labor secretary nominee, Hilda Solis, had over a dozen liens for back taxes on his property and just now paid up amid public outcry. (The issue is relevant, since the couple filed a joint income-tax return.) Daschle, Geithner, Killefer, and Solis did not disclose their tax liabilities until they were nominated to high office and scrutinized by the press. And they apparently did not pay their back taxes until their appointments were in jeopardy from public disclosures. That raises disturbing questions: Would we have known about such tax dodging had our best and brightest not wished career advancement in government? And would they have ever paid up if they had not been caught?

Take your pick—on the one side, we have free-market capitalists who took huge amounts of money as their companies eroded the savings of tens of millions; on the other, we have supposedly egalitarian liberals who skipped paying taxes.

The result is the same. Our best educated, wealthiest, and most-connected in matters of finance proved our dumbest—and our political leaders were less than ethical in meeting their moral responsibilities as citizens. If ordinary Americans were to follow the examples of Wall Street and Washington elites, the nation would neither collect needed revenue nor invest its capital. All that is a recipe for national decline and fall.

OCTOBER 2, 2009

The Obsolescence of a Slur

Criticisms of Obama are increasingly met by cries of "Racist!" Are his critics racists?

The charge of racism has been leveled against critics of President Obama's health-care reform by everyone from *New York Times* columnists, racial activists, and Democratic legislators to senior statesmen like Jimmy Carter ("It's a racist attitude"), Bill Clinton ("some . . . are racially prejudiced"), and Walter Mondale ("I don't want to pick a person [and] say, 'He's a racist,' but I do think the way they're piling on Obama . . . I think I see an edge in them that's a little bit different").

But are Obama's critics really racists?

It is a serious charge. If true, it means the hope of a color-blind society is essentially over after a half-century of civil-rights progress. If false, it means that we have institutionalized vicious smears as legitimate political tactics—and, in the process, discredited the entire dialogue that surrounds racial prejudice.

How do we determine the accuracy of the "racism" charges?

1) Is the criticism of Barack Obama unusual by recent presidential standards?

No. Bush hatred was even more intense. Furthermore, it very soon went from fierce partisanship into a deviant desire for the president's injury or death. Such derangement was tolerated or indeed enhanced by mainstream liberal establishment figures. Alfred A. Knopf published a novel speculating about killing the president. The Toronto Film Festival gave a prize to a docudrama about an envisioned assassination of George W. Bush. His death became the stuff of a New York play, the dream of a Guardian columnist, and a common theme in the left-wing blogosphere.

A certain amount of this kind of venom was evident in the opposition to Bill Clinton, who was accused of everything from covering up murders to being a serial rapist. By any fair standard, nothing so far in the health-care pushback has approached the smears and dirt directed at Presidents Bush and Clinton.

2) Is there a systematic racialist attack on other black politicians and leaders?

No. Gov. David Paterson of New York, for example, alleges a new racism as the chief cause of his own decline. But it is President Obama himself, not white racists, who is pressuring Paterson not to run for reelection. Charles Rangel cited racism for much of the public outrage over his behavior. But clearly his problems were caused by his own tax fraud, inability to tell the truth, and violations of ethical standards— which would have destroyed most other politicians long ago. There may well be some racially motivated criticism of prominent at-risk black politicians, but so far there is no evidence that anything other than their own actions accounts for their political troubles.

3) Is President Obama's agenda, or Obama himself, the problem?

Barack Obama could not have been elected without millions of white voters, coupled with a near-monolithic black base. To believe that innate racism has caused many of the millions who voted for him spontaneously to withdraw their support makes no sense. Take moderates and independents who were once strong Obama supporters. Why would someone vote for a black man, then eight months later decide that he could not support a black man? Clearly, Obama's problems derive not from his race, but from his radical agenda for out-of-sight government spending, high taxes, mega-deficits, nationalized health care, cap-and-trade, and an apologetic foreign policy.

In this regard, imagine two counterfactuals:

a) Had Obama delayed his liberal initiatives and first devoted his attention to controlling federal spending, winning in Afghanistan, and balancing the budget, would his polls have dropped to near 50 percent? (President Clinton's own up-and-down experience between 1993 and 1996 is instructive here.)

b) Should Obama now escalate in Afghanistan, delay his liberal agenda, and balance the federal budget, would not more of his criticism come from the Left—and if so, would it then be considered racist? If a protester at an anti-war march carried a sign that read, "I love Afghanistan—Bomb Chicago!" would that be racist? Indeed, Obama's adherence to the Patriot Act, renditions, wiretaps, intercepts, tribunals, Predator attacks, and the Petraeus plan in Iraq—and his inability to close Guantanamo on his promised one-year date—have already incurred furor from the hard Left. But again, will that growing anger be termed racially motivated?

4) Has the Right recently been more racially conscious in its attacks than has the Left?

Not really. We forget that the left-wing blogosphere savaged Michael Steele in racialist terms when he was running for the Senate from Maryland. Harry Belafonte—to the silence of the Left—called Secretary of State Colin Powell a house slave. No one on the Left objected to the racist cartoons, both here in the United States and abroad in the Arab world, caricaturing Secretary of State Condoleezza Rice. Much of the liberal hostility against Clarence Thomas suggested in thinly disguised terms that he was an unqualified beneficiary of affirmative action. The assumption is that the heartless Right is guilty of racism unless proven innocent, while the utopian, humanitarian Left could not possibly resort to racist attacks for partisan advantage. So far Barack Obama has seen less virulent opposition than what Alberto Gonzales, Condoleezza Rice, or Michael Steele faced.

5) Is racial polarization more pronounced among whites or among blacks?

Here there seems no general trend of racial animosity by any particular group. The occasional over-the-top sign at a tea party, or right-wing minor official who crosses the line, seems balanced by prominent blacks who talk in racially oriented terms. Obama himself has stereotyped whites in Pennsylvania in quasi-racist terms, and has employed banalities like "typical white person." The most prominent racist in the United States currently may well be the Rev. Jeremiah Wright, the president's own former pastor, who has insulted in racist fashion whites in general, Jews, Italians, and just about everyone other than African-Americans.

When Eric Holder called his fellow citizens "cowards," his comments were understood to have been directed at white America's unwillingness to discuss race on his terms. Green-jobs czar Van Jones promiscuously threw around the terms "whites" and "white people," associating them with polluters and high-school mass murderers. Again, there seems no greater white propensity for using stereotypes. Bill Clinton, husband of the current Secretary of State, now points to a white propensity to play a racial card against President Obama; last year, Bill Clinton, husband of Obama rival Hillary Clinton, charged that candidate Obama himself had "played the race card" on him.

6) Are there trends in the general society that suggest a new racial polarization?

Again, not really. Recently a number of high-profile controversies may have had racial overtones, but they did not suggest a pre-existing climate of white racism. Had a white counterpart of Professor Gates insulted a black arresting police officer, made a pejorative reference to "your mama," and then counted on his friendship with a white president for support, there might have followed charges of racism. Had a white country-and-western singer grabbed the microphone from a diminutive

18-old-year black gospel singer to announce to a national television audience that another white country-and-western singer was more deserving of the award, there could well have been charges of racism leveled. And had a marquee white tennis player lost her cool, charged a small Asian line judge, and threatened her person, there might well have been charges of racism. In all these and other lurid news stories splashed about on YouTube (cf. the bus attack by several black youths against a white passenger), there has not been much of a larger reaction along racial lines that suggests either that whites or blacks in general are racist, or that either group thinks the other is.

In short, there is little, if any, evidence that the millions of voters who are losing confidence in the president are doing so for racist reasons. But there is a great deal of evidence that his own extremist positions on spending, government, taxes, foreign policy, and health care, along with a few high-profile, out-of-the-mainstream appointments, have convinced many Americans that Obama, like the Bill Clinton of 1993, is not the moderate voice he appeared to be during the campaign, but a partisan ideologue racing to expand the government before his popular support collapses.

So why is the faux charge of "racist" so freely bandied about—given that polls suggest it is a losing tactic for liberals?

The most obvious reason is that a popular president believed he could enact an unpopular agenda on the basis of his own magnetic personality. When he discovered that he could not—and in the process revealed a pattern of partisanship and intolerance—some of his diehard supporters were flabbergasted by the turn of events and resorted in desperation to the "racist" charge to regain sympathy for both their cause and their president.

Second, liberals never envisioned that they would so quickly regain the House and Senate, as well as the presidency—partly through tough invective and a demonization of both George W. Bush and a Republican "culture of corruption." Their noble ends were felt to justify their often over-the-top rhetoric. Now they most surely do not wish the same level of street invective legitimized and used against themselves. "Racist!" then serves as a preemptive firewall against possible conflagrations to come.

Third, there is an almost hysterical fear that "Racist!" has lost all currency as an effective political tool. Indeed, the charge has been rendered almost meaningless by the frequency of its use and the rarity of its accuracy. Counterintuitively, some believe the more the discredited charge is repeated, the more likely it might be to regain its prior effectiveness.

Thousands on the left, both black and white, have for decades invested in the notion of ubiquitous racism that must be addressed by either material or psychic reparations. At risk now with the discrediting of the charge are government-mandated quotas and affirmative action, and indeed the postmodern gospel that oppressed people of color could not, de facto, ever be racist themselves. If charges of racism no longer end the discussion, by sidetracking the accused into first proving his long record of racial tolerance, then the political atmospherics may well be altered.

Polls show that the public does not believe criticism of Obama to be racially motivated, and further that the majority has become exasperated at the tired charge. What we are seeing, then, in the latest hysterical resort to "Racist!" is a growing realization not only that this once-effective scapegoating has become obsolete, but that it has become a boomeranging liability for all who employ it.

MARCH 17, 2010

Sun and Socialism

Plant a welfare state in a warm climate, and it will grow like Jack's beanstalk

Sun and socialism are seemingly a bad mix. Socialism—or at least communitarian practices that in their ultimate manifestations would result in socialism—doesn't go well with 300 days of sun, long summers and short winters, sandy beaches and seaside cafés, and shorts and swimsuits. Each tends to bring out the worst in the other.

Take weather, climate, and geography. Few places in the world are as beautiful as California. Its autumns are like summers elsewhere; its winters, others' normal springs—but without the humidity and clouds. You are no more than about five hours from the sea anywhere in California; in fact, most of the state's 36 million residents are within three hours of the beach.

One does not have to be a geographical determinist to see that good weather, a predictably warm climate, and natural beauty promote the pursuit of leisure. On a February Friday afternoon, it is harder to stay in an office in Santa Monica, in the low 70s, than it is in a blizzard in St. Paul. Those who can swim or skateboard all year long in their Speedos at Venice Beach—well, they seem to think they can approach life with that same carefree attitude, as if things in general sort of sprout up spontaneously, just as the sun, blue water, and warm breezes naturally appear each morning, with little worry over a Kansas-style twister or an Albany-style deep freeze.

I would not wish to enter into a chicken-or-egg controversy over whether California's natural enticements drew in a certain laid-back sort of person, or whether once tight-fisted, no-nonsense citizens crossed the border, they were altered into bohemian types by places like Carmel and Tahoe. And I grant that there are plenty of communitarians in harsh climates like Manhattan's, and conservative, small-government types in Mobile. I also realize that warm Texas is the antithesis to warm California—though I would suggest there is nothing quite like California beaches or Yosemite in the rather scenic Lone Star State.

My point again is one of force multiplication rather than cause and effect. A high-tax, big-government, expansive-entitlement, plentiful-public-worker landscape naturally becomes higher, bigger, more expansive, and ever more plentiful when located in paradise—perhaps explaining why California is in even worse shape than, say, New Jersey. It is as if nature offers no reality check to human naïveté, no reminder to the would-be utopian that, yes, there are rigorous impediments like snow and constant storms that transcend man's ability to ensure the good life with tenured, high-paying government jobs, lavish payouts for housing, food, education, and legal help, and all sort of rules and regulations to make us into perfect egalitarians.

In other words, a communitarian statist morphs out of control in a place like Mill Valley in a way he would not in equally liberal Minneapolis. The sun multiplies the therapeutic efforts of the state; in addition, the natural bounty that good weather and geography bring can, for a while at least, cover the results of human foolishness.

Consider Europe as well. A great many scholarly studies (less so in the politically correct age of the last three decades) have suggested that the more Protestant northwestern European countries, with Atlantic ports open to the New World, had leapfrogged the old classical centers of wealth in warmer Greece and Rome even before the coal-driven Industrial Revolution. A certain religious sanction for hard work in the here and now, trade with North and South America, and greater distance from the Ottomans fostered economic vibrancy, despite the traditionally poorer northern climate—which from classical times had been cited as a natural obstacle to open-air democratic assemblies and outdoor civic intercourse.

But with the rise of the modern European socialist state, and the decline of religion of any sort, it seems that a Mediterranean climate and weather pattern now ipso facto have institutionalized traditional patterns of behavior—siestas, long lunches and dinners, more holidays, open-air labor strikes and demonstrations—marrying the naturally pleasant skies and seductive good life to the notion that someone else should pay one to enjoy it all. Socialism may have trouble up in Sweden and Germany, but in warm, seaside areas like Greece, Italy, Portugal, southern France, and Spain it can become a veritable lotus land of 14 monthly pay periods, two-hour lunches, three-day weekends, and dinners at nine. That's why wealthier northerners love to vacation there—while they invest, hire, fire, and make money back home in the cold.

So far, the sunny socialist state has gotten by on two general truths: Most people won't leave the beautiful coastlines, sunny weather, and scenic landscapes no matter how high the taxes go to subsidize less productive or more needy others; and, second, lots of tourists will visit to bask in the beauty and warmth—and pay quite a lot for even that brief taste of natural paradise.

Yet those smug assurances of the Lala Land redistributive state may be ending. An estimated 3,500 upper-income Californians are leaving their beautiful state each week. They seem to think that crumbling highways, schools rated at near to last in the nation, 5 to 7 million illegal aliens, and overfilling prisons aren't worth the 10 percent sales tax, 10 percent income tax, and 63-cent-a-gallon combined state and federal gasoline taxes. And they don't think that Barbara Boxer, Nancy Pelosi, or the California legislature can or wants to fix things.

If things don't change for the better, tourists might soon come to find that flying into LAX, driving up a crumbling 101 to Carmel, risking getting off the wrong freeway ramp into Oakland or East LA, and walking through a grimy San Francisco are all beginning to cancel out the wine country, Yosemite, Fisherman's Wharf, and Disneyland.

Socialist Greece is becoming likewise problematic for the tourists whose euros are so necessary to subsidize the failing Greek welfare state. I try to go there every other summer, and I once lived there off and on for over two years. But I now brace for each visit, expecting to find Syntagma Square entertaining a loud protest by a particular unionized public-worker clique that is angry that another one has gotten a bigger piece of the shrinking pie. Surely the itinerary will need to be reshuffled because of a two-day strike by airline baggage handlers or ferryboat captains, or the highway will be blocked by the tractors of farmers whose subsidies are supposedly too small, or the banks will suddenly close in the afternoon because of an obscure regional holiday, or the car mechanic will be willing to fix the brakes only for off-the-books cash in hand. Then there is the near-death experience if one were to break an ankle on the Acropolis or eat a bad strawberry and end up in the state-run Greek health-care system—whose Inferno I once barely survived through 30 days of 19th-century hospitalization.

What an odd paradox!

Clear skies and warmth have made socialism even worse through encouraging leisure and an escape from reality, and yet with their siren calls have drawn onto their shoals enough new paying sun-worshipers to offer temperate statism a reprieve from its own chronic mismanagement. California and its legions of dependents wager that most of the state's citizens, no matter how high the taxes and severe the government misery, just won't leave—and that if they do, there will always be enough newcomer naïfs and tourists to keep subsidizing the state's failure.

MARCH 26, 2010

Chicago Does Socialism

Connect the dots of Obama's first year in office, and an ugly picture emerges.

We can have a rational debate on any one item on President Obama's vast progressive agenda, arguing whether adjectives like "statist" or "socialist" fairly describe his legislative intent. But connect all the dots and lines of the past year, and an unambiguous image starts to materialize.

NEW PROGRAMS

The problem is not individual legislation, whether passed or proposed, involving the gamut of issues: health care, bailouts, stimuli, education loans, amnesty, cap and trade. Rather, the rub is these acts in the aggregate. The president promises a state fix for health care; then student loans; and next energy. There are to be subsidies, credits, and always new entitlements for every problem, all requiring hordes of fresh technocrats and Civil Service employees. Like a perpetual teenager, who wants and buys but never produces, the president is focused on the acquisitive and consumptive urges, never on the productive—as in how all his magnanimous largesse is to be paid for by someone else.

That Medicare and Social Security are near insolvency, or soon will be; that the Postal Service and Amtrak are running in the red; that a day at the DMV, county-hospital emergency room, or zoning department doesn't inspire confidence in the matrix of unionized government workers and large unaccountable bureaucracies—all this is lost on the Obama administration. Utility means nothing. So long as the next proposed program enlarges a dependent constituency and is financed by the "rich" through higher taxes and more debt, it is, de facto, necessary and good. Equality of result is to be achieved both by giving more to some and by taking even more from others.

TAXES

The same pattern emerges when it comes to taxes. Most Americans could live with Obama's plan to return to the Clinton tax rates of about 40 percent on the top brackets. But that promise is never made in a vacuum. Instead, there is an additional, almost breezy pledge to lift caps on income subject to Social Security and Medicare payroll taxes—15.3 percent in some cases—on top of the income-tax increase.

At other times, an idea like a new health-care surcharge is tossed about—on top of the previous proposals for payroll- and income-tax increases. That new bite likewise, in isolation, perhaps is not too scary. But Obama is planning these 1-2-3 increases at a time when most of the states are already upping their own income-tax rates—in some cases to over 10 percent.

Once again, Obama never honestly connects the dots and comes clean with the American people about the net effect: On vast swaths of upper income, new state and federal taxes—aside from any rises in sales, property, capital-gains, or inheritance taxes—could confiscate an aggregate of 65 to 70 percent.

These proposals thus raise the question: Exactly what sort of total tax bite does the president think is fair for those making more than $200,000 or $250,000? Can the citizen be allowed to retain 45, 40, 35, or 30 percent of his income? And if, with combined governments starting to take 60 to 70 percent of income through the various tax increases, we still have record annual budget deficits, how much higher should these high taxes go to prevent national insolvency? Eighty percent? Ninety? One hundred?

Perhaps we could have a rate of 110 percent: Those who make $250,000 might pay a redemptive $275,000 to the government on the theory that in the Bush era they "made out like bandits."

"LET ME BE PERFECTLY CLEAR . . ."

Then there is Obama's chronic dissimulation. Most Americans were indifferent rather than outraged when Obama became the first presidential candidate to renounce public campaign financing in the general election—despite both earlier promises that he would not, and later crocodile tears over the Supreme Court's rollback of some public-financing rules.

Perhaps most Americans also were only mildly irked that Obama demagogued the Bush anti-terror protocols during the campaign, only to continue unchanged precisely those practices that he had most fiercely railed against—tribunals, renditions, Predators, the continuing presence in Iraq. And perhaps most Americans did not believe Obama when he promised to close Guantanamo within a year and to try Khalid Sheikh Mohammed in a civilian court in New York—and they were right. These too were isolated Obama untruths.

Then some of us were troubled that Obama had once decried passage of health-care reform by mere 51 percent majorities—only to do precisely that last weekend. Candidate Obama likewise damned the use of executive orders to countermand legislative action—and then did just that on matters of abortion and Obamacare. Chalk it up to the Chicago style of the ends justifying any means necessary. So was anyone surprised that the health-care bill did not sit on the president's desk for five days before the signing, as he once bragged would be the new administration's policy, for reasons of transparency? And wasn't that reminiscent of his continued, but reneged on, pledges to air all the health-care debates on C-SPAN?

I could go on and on, but again the pattern is clear. Each time Obama prevaricates, we grant him an exemption because of his lofty rhetoric about bipartisanship and his soothing words about unity. Only later do we notice that in retrospect each untruth is part of a pattern of dissimulation within just a single year of governance. Obama has proven so far that in fact one can fool a lot of the people a lot of the time.

ABROAD

In foreign policy, Americans were okay with one bow to the Saudi king

— until they saw a deeper bow to the Japanese emperor. One so-so apology was then followed by many more embarrassing meae culpae. His reaching out to Chávez was only one link in a chain that included Cuba, Libya, Syria, and Iran. We thought his serial gratuitous rudeness to Britain in matters of protocol was an aberration—until it proved to be the norm with the Czech Republic, Israel, Honduras, Poland, and the Dalai Lama. Smackdowns by Russia might have seemed singular, until China followed in suit.

One perhaps can forgive erstwhile Obama adviser Zbigniew Brzezinski's stupid hypothetical speculation about shooting down Israeli planes over Iraq. And maybe the nominations of Charles Freeman and Samantha Power—not known as friends to Israel—were of no importance. Some raised an eyebrow, too, over Obama's past close affinities with the anti-Semitic Reverend Jeremiah Wright and anti-Israelis like Bill Ayers and Rashid Khalidi. But finally, the most recent outreach to the terrorist regimes in Damascus and Tehran, when juxtaposed with the hysterics over a few apartment buildings in Jerusalem, has cemented the notion that Obama really has radical ideas about altering the traditional American support for the Jewish state.

In other words, again, connect these seemingly isolated dots and a picture emerges of a new radical foreign policy of "neutralism." Traditional allies are ignored, and old enemies are courted—until both are on the same moral and political plane. The one constant is that a socialist anti-Western philosophy abroad (which blames the West for a nation's own self-inflicted misery) wins sympathy with the Obama administration, while capitalist Western culture is seen as mostly passé.

In any isolated circumstance, we are willing to give the president of the United States a pass on a particular disturbing decision. But after 14 months of them, the Obama particulars add up to a remaking of America that is now clear and consistent: Grow government; redistribute income; establish permanent political constituencies of dependents; increase entitlements; hike taxes; demonize "them" while deifying their supposed victims; seek global neutrality abroad; and always play fast and loose with the truth.

What do we end up with?

You might call it: Chicago does socialism.

MARCH 31, 2010

Next Battle: Immigration

What we will—and will not—hear in the upcoming debate over illegal immigration.

After the health-care fight, we can expect the Obama administration to use the same template to pass "comprehensive immigration reform." That is a euphemism for permanently ceasing construction of the still-incomplete border fence; institutionalizing a large guest-worker program; treating illegal residents as de facto citizens in terms of receiving earned-income credits, health care, and general entitlements; and providing virtual amnesty for 11 million illegal aliens.

And what exactly is that model for passage of something that promises to be so unpopular? We know the boilerplate well after a year of health-care acrimony. First, immigration policy—like health care, and cap-and-trade to come—will be cast as a civil-rights issue. That is, free access to the United States and, for some, its entitlement industry for millions of impoverished Mexicans will be redefined as comparable to ending discrimination in the South in the 1960s.

Next, skeptics will be branded "racists" and "nativists," as is being done now to the tea partiers. A few House members will wade through anti-illegal-immigration rallies, and within minutes the media will announce "racial slurs" and "a scary atmosphere" suggesting "violence" and "hatred." This polarization is critical for the bill's passage, since it does not have 50 percent public support—and won't unless a series of constituencies can be united to see the issue in polarities such as us vs. them, whites vs. people of color, rich vs. poor. Blacks will be told it is Birmingham all over again. The Mexican-American middle class, highly skeptical of open borders, will be told that opposition to amnesty is "anti-Hispanic."

So the debate will be personalized—and, above all, blurred. Opponents, we will also be told, are not bothered by illegal immigration per se. Rather they are "anti-immigrant"—as the issue is transmuted into one of hating real people rather than opposing an illegal activity. Fence-sitting House members will be promised all sorts of special multi-million-dollar earmarks to allay "voter concern." Executive orders will be pledged to override the more disturbing elements of congressional legislation. Anecdotes about starving children, and accusations of responsibility for the deaths of hundreds trying to cross the border in the desert, will pepper the rhetoric of open-border advocates.

The key will be to redefine as liberal something as inherently illiberal as illegal immigration. Thus there will be no discussion of what the surge over the last two decades of more than 11 million illegal aliens has done to poorer American workers.

We won't hear from the Democrats that upper-middle-class suburbanites—many quite liberal —apparently see themselves as aristocratic, at least in the sense of being entitled to cheap labor for their lawn care, domestic cleaning, and child care.

They will not talk about the crisis that will occur in entitlement funding for the American poor, once additional millions of Mexican nationals overburden a finite system of health, housing, and food subsidies. There will absolutely no discussion of the $40 to $50 billion that is sent annually back to Latin America in remittances, a great part of it by illegal aliens, who, in turn, rely on American federal, state, and local governments to make up the shortfall in their weekly paychecks. In effect, the off-the-hook Mexican government is the beneficiary of American tax dollars.

Expect silence about the current status of legal immigration from Mexico—specifically, that we accept more legal immigrants from Mexico than from any other nation in the world, hardly the behavior of a racist or nativist society.

Also, don't mention the deleterious effects that sudden influxes of millions of illegal immigrants have on the processes of assimilation, intermarriage, and integration—the traditional mechanisms by which legal arrivals successfully melt into the American mainstream. To suggest that one's tribe, race, or ethnicity should be incidental to being an American, or to point out that vast enclaves of unassimilated aliens live in virtual segregation, is now a heresy of the first order.

We can be sure that no one on the left side of the aisle will cite the utter cynicism of the Mexican government, which exports poor brown people from its interior, whom it does not wish to help, even as it welcomes largely rich white people to its picturesque coast. What else but cynical is it to provide little housing support for millions of your own in Oaxaca while encouraging second-home construction by foreigners in Baja?

So Obama and his congressional allies will make every effort to prevent discussion of the issues, because they revolve around a simple matter of following the law and ensuring that those who emigrate from Mexico do so in the same manner as thousands do from Kenya, South Korea, or Russia—legally and in reasonable numbers.

There would be no debate if each day freighters were arriving to unload on the coast of Texas or California 3,000 illegal aliens from Nigeria or China, most of whom did not speak English or have a high-school diploma.

So-called immigration reform, in other words, is not about the concept of illegal immigration from poor countries in general; rather, it is about massive illegal immigration from Latin America and in particular Mexico—and it hinges entirely on political considerations. Millions of illegal aliens have become citizens through past blanket amnesties, and they are likely, at least for a while, to vote in bloc for liberal and/or Hispanic candidates. The idea of enlarging that pool of loyal constituents by another 5 to 6 million people of voting age is too great a temptation to refuse, especially given the decisive effects to be expected on close elections in the American southwest. The more entitlements are extended to illegal aliens, the more liberal politicians can remind continued generations that they alone were responsible for such institutionalized federal subsidies.

For a smaller fringe of Hispanic activists—found largely in academia, the foundations, journalism, and politics—illegal immigration is a matter of ethnic pride, some racial chauvinism (cf. the old MEChA slogan, "For the race everything; outside the race, nothing"), and a welcomed sense of irony that demography is now redefining the old Spanish northern provinces once lost through war. After all, in 2010 there is still a national lobbying organization with the fossilized name

La Raza (The Race), a racially chauvinistic term that would be considered uncouth if employed by whites—but one that enhances a small group of Spanish-surnamed elites through their self-appointed representation of millions of illegal aliens.

Unfortunately, though, this is not only a left-wing issue. The corporate Right in many industries—tourism, hotels, restaurants, meat-packing, landscaping, agriculture—also welcomes illegal immigrants. These employers are as happy to have hard-working first-generation poor immigrants on their payroll as they are willing to outsource the subsequent problems of acculturation to society at large.

Will the bill pass?

We can be assured only that the debate will be as nasty as the one over health care. Yet recent developments may suggest greater difficulty than the administration imagines. We are in a deep recession. Unemployment is still over 9 percent in some of the southwestern states, and nearly 20 percent in the inland counties of California. The old myth that native-born Americans will not clean hotel rooms or weed gardens is fading, as the unemployed now seem willing to work at jobs once considered taboo. That trend will only increase if the recession endures and unemployment benefits finally wind down.

State budgets are in a mess, and even liberals grant, for example, that some part of the California meltdown is due to the presence of some 5 to 7 million resident illegal aliens, which drives up the cost of everything from education to incarceration. Liberal teachers—California has the highest-paid teachers in the nation while its student scores rank nearly dead last—don't like to acknowledge that the abject failure of their public schools is due to poor teaching and administration rather than in part the presence of millions who do not speak English.

The public is sensitive to the overused charge of racism. When everything from health care to immigration law is to be defined in terms of racial prejudice, it has a dulling effect. This round of the immigration debate comes after the acrimony over Eric Holder's "cowards," the president's "acting stupidly" reference in the Professor Gates affair, Sonia Sotomayor's "wise Latina," Van Jones's "white polluters"—all on top of the president's earlier quips about a "typical white person" and rural whites' "clinging" to guns and religion. By now millions see the evocation of race as more reflective of the biases of the accuser than his target.

In 2010 we are also subjected to almost nightly news stories of horrific violence in Mexico, much of it along the border. Fairly or not, many Americans associate Mexico with lawlessness, corruption, and mayhem—the death tolls there have been far higher recently than in either Afghanistan or Iraq—and want its problems to stay on the southern side of the border.

A wiser administration would call in opponents and, in bipartisan fashion, agree to finish the border fence, toughen up employer sanctions, issue a tamper-proof ID, deport alien felons and recent arrivals, and then work out a process through which illegal aliens who are longstanding residents of the United States could reapply for residency and embark on a pathway to eventual citizenship, contingent upon payment of fines, lack of criminality, compliance with current law, and mastery of English. Then legitimate debate could take place over the thorny issue of whether aliens would first need to return home in order to begin going through these legal channels and processes.

Instead, we will see a replay of the health-care controversy. The administration has decided that winning another legislative victory in an agenda aimed at remaking America is worth the cost of dividing the country and whipping up heroes and demons. Momentum, not compromise, is the order of the day.

MAY 19, 2010

The Technocrats' New Clothes

Climategate, the Icelandic volcano, the Greek melt-down—suddenly the bureaucratic Masters of the Universe don't look so omnipotent.

I n the last year, many of the dreams of an emerging international elite have imploded—and this, in a new century that was to usher in a regime of global liberal ecumenism. The lies and academic fraud of Climategate reminded us that it is almost impossible for even disinterested scientists to fathom the complex history of global climate change. But it also—and more importantly—reminded us how Western universities have turned into rigid medieval centers of intolerant orthodoxy. Our new academic monks, in their isolated sanctuaries—cut off by grants, subsidies, tenure, and cadres of obsequious graduate students from the grubby efforts of others to stay alive—have for years breezily issued all sorts of near-religious exegeses and edicts about the public's ruination of the planet. We lesser folk were supposed to find salvation through installing windmills and junking our incandescent light bulbs under the tutelage of wiser overseers.

Meanwhile, in the last few weeks, nature did what no human industry had ever quite done—shut down much of European airspace with a huge toxic cloud. But the mess was not a DuPont emission, or soot from Eastern Europe's network of coal plants, or any such man-caused disaster, but the work of a prosaic volcano. The ensuing economic chaos and toxic air pollution were accepted with a shrug in that they were natural and had nothing to do with Halliburton.

Another dream—the European Union—is also imploding. Beneath the hysteria over Greece is a simple truth: All the capital that Germany piled up over the last 20 years through its export-driven economy was never really there; it must now be forfeited to those who borrowed from Germany in order to buy from Germany. In some sense, if a taxi driver in the Peloponnese drove a Mercedes beyond the reach of most Americans, it was not because of his capital-creating productivity, but rather because of his country's ability to lure the Germans into lending Greece euros at nearly nonexistent interest.

For decades we were lectured about the EU's nuanced practice of "soft power," and we were told how life was at last good when one garnered cradle-to-grave government entitlements, retired early, and expected American arms to protect and German money to subsidize the collective borrowing binge. Apparently because Europeans did not drawl and go to church, we were supposed to believe that they had reinvented finance, and loans could be floated rather than paid back.

In 2009, the vision of the new Obama administration was European: foreign-policy triangulation, government takeovers of private enterprises, higher taxes, more entitlements and public workers, and always more "them/us" class-warfare rhetoric from members of a technocratic guardian class who had played the very system they were now to oversee. Apparently Obama's high-level appointees—from Timothy Geithner to Van Jones—thought they were our versions of Brussels bureaucrats, who could say and do anything with no need to worry about popular reaction.

Then came the Greek meltdown. The music of this parlor game stopped, and all the poor players standing—German banks, anonymous bondholders, EU technocrats, Greek politicians and public unions—lunged for the far too few seats. What are we left with? At best, a slow devolution to something like the original Common Market of northwestern European nations, a strengthening of NATO (to keep America in, Germany down, and Russia out), and loud diplomacy to stop the rising European tensions—all too reminiscent of 1939—that seem to hinge on unresolved historical grievances, cultural stereotypes, and the old north/south, cold/hot divide.

Here in the United States, we will have a last chance in November to brake before following the European bus into the abyss. Who would have thought, a mere year ago, that the theme of 2010 would be: How lucky is Turkey that it has not been accepted into the European Union! Aside from the passing of messianic environmentalism and European utopianism, we are also seeing the unraveling of Obama's reset-button foreign policy, announced to such fanfare in January 2009. It was apparently predicated on the assumption that much of the tension in the world was caused by George W. Bush's United States, and therefore could be ameliorated through apology, retrenchment, dialogue, public self-critique, and criticism of prior presidents.

So add it all up: the Al-Arabiya interview, the Cairo speech, the distancing from Israel, the euphemisms like "overseas contingency operations" and "man-caused disasters," the politically correct banishment of any anti-terrorism phraseology associated with Islam, the repeated announcements of the closing of Guantanamo and the trying of KSM in New York, the strange case of Attorney General Eric Holder, who can call his own fellow citizens "cowards" but not associate radical Islam with recent attempts by Muslims to kill those fellow citizens en masse—and we get Syria supplying terrorists with missiles, Iran ever closer to a bomb, and the largest number of terrorist attempts inside the U.S. over the past year than during any other twelve-month period since September 11, 2001.

Indeed, a trait of this administration is to speak far more harshly of fellow Americans than it does of our enemies: Arizonans vote to enforce federal immigration laws, so the administration offers them up to the Chinese as an example of American civil-liberties violations. In our morally equivalent world, a government that would enforce laws against those who entered the country illegally is not all that different from a government that not long ago killed more than 40 million of its own.

If Europe is our model of soft power; if Syria, Jordan, Saudi Arabia, and other autocracies are the moral equivalents of democratic Israel; if it is not radical Islam that empowered a Hasan, an Abdulmutallab, or a Shahzad; if Iran can be reasoned with to abandon its nuclear agenda; and if Russia can be flattered into acting responsibly—then the world suddenly does not work in the way it has in the past 2,500 years of civilization.

What is common to all these disillusionments—the intolerance and dishonesty of environmental extremism, the European Union crackup, and Barack Obama's renewal of Jimmy Carter's failed foreign policy? They all can be traced to a global Western elite that in its intellectual arrogance confused late-20th-century technological progress with a supposed evolution in human nature itself. Heaven on earth was to be ushered in by those who deemed themselves so wise and so moral that they could remake civilization in their own image—even if that sometimes meant the end of disinterested research, basic arithmetic, and simple common sense.

MAY 19, 2010

Death of the Postmodernist Drama

As crises mount abroad and voters' anger grows at home, Obama's dream of a new world order has died a quiet death.

I n just a few months the brave new dream world as we knew it has died—but with a whimper, not a bang. There will be no more lectures on soft power and a Baltic-to-Mediterranean postmodern culture. Suddenly European Union expansion is dead in its tracks. The question of Turkish membership, after a decade-long controversy, has been settled without so much as a demonstration. The Europeans don't want another Greece in their midst; the Turks don't want German bankers running their sagging finances. A soaring Euro was supposed to reflect the sobriety of socialism; instead, it hid its profligacy, but only for a while.

So the welfare state is discredited. In the past, we used to be warned that static population growth, vast public-sector employment, early and generous retirement benefits, and high taxes were not sustainable. In recent years, those lectures were caricatured as partisan or hypothetical. No longer. The Greek meltdown—with Ireland, Italy, Portugal, and Spain on the brink—has shown that European socialism does not work. Bankruptcy, not politics, is the final arbiter: Individuals, firms, and nations either buy particular bonds or they don't. And a nation like

Greece, in turn, either pays what it has borrowed or it doesn't. All the op-eds in the *New York Times* cannot change that fact.

Al Gore will continue to channel from his Montecito hilltop the latest green consensus of the international academic community. But fairly or not, neither he nor it will be listened to all that much: He has made one too many millions off his hysteria, and professors have fudged one too many publicly funded studies. The result is that almost at once both have lost the people's trust. A volcano, not hot weather, shut down European air travel. The Sierra Nevada is still buried under snow in late May. At least this year, a wet, cold state of California is not going to blow away, as Energy Secretary Chu warned not long ago.

It is fine and good to invest in wind and solar power, and other alternative energy sources—if for no other reason than to drain the swamp of the oil-rich Middle East—but soon Americans will be paying a fortune for gasoline and electrical power. As gas hits $4 a gallon, they will want more oil drilling, more coal mining, and more nuclear, hydro, and natural-gas energy, not less. Green mongering is not what it was just a few months ago.

Then there is Arizona. Over 70 percent of the American people support the state's efforts to stop illegal immigration, which amount to nothing more than enforcing currently unenforced federal laws. The hackneyed charges of racism and nativism are ignored. The Left can cite California's Proposition 187 and warn the Republicans that they will lose the Hispanic vote, but 70 percent margins reflect angry citizens of all races and ethnicities, who are tired of seeing laws ignored, their state governments bankrupted, and Mexican presidents shaking fingers at them. That Mexico treats illegal aliens far less humanely than does the United States, and that it deliberately encourages its own citizens to break U.S. immigration law (to the extent of publishing a comic book advising on how to illegally cross the border) reminds us that Barack Obama knows as little about Mexico as he does about Arizona's law when he talks of an age to come without borders.

I do not think the word "reset" will be used much longer to characterize American foreign policy. Reset from what to what? After all, is Iran closer to getting a bomb or further away than it was a year and a half ago? Are terrorists more or less likely to attack and kill inside the

United States? Is Syria now a more or a less helpful player in the Middle East? Is Israel safer or less safe, more or less a U.S. ally? Are Putin and Chávez now more helpful players on the world scene, in appreciation of Obama's olive branches? Does a North Korea or an Iran feel more or less emboldened to run risks in testing the status quo? Is China more or less provocative in the Pacific?

The more provocation is ignored in one region, the more it is pursued in the other. The new audacity is predicated on the universal notion that the new United States either cannot or will not fulfill its retrograde function of deterrence—or might even privately sympathize with the assorted grievances that serve as pretexts for ignoring the sanctity of the border, selling missiles to terrorists, pursuing the bomb, or aiding in uranium enrichment.

The new world order as envisioned by Obama in January 2009 was, I think, supposed to look something like the following: A social-democratic America would come to emulate the successful welfare states in the European Union. These twin Western communitarian powers would together usher in a new world order in which no one nation was to be seen as preeminent. All the old nasty ideas of the 20th century—military alliances, sovereign borders, independent international finance, nuclear arms, religious and cultural chauvinism—would fall by the wayside, as the West was reinvented as part of the solution rather the problem it had been in its days of colonialism, imperialism, and exploitation. A new green transnationalism would assume the place of that bad old order, a transnationalism run by elite, highly educated, and socially conscious technocrats—albeit themselves Western—supported by a progressive press more interested in effecting social change than in merely reporting the tawdry news.

Obama can still push that story, but more and more Americans disagree with his 21st-century vision. Stuck in the past, they instead believe that capitalism, not socialism, brings prosperity; that to reach a green future we need to survive for now in a carbon and nuclear present; that all, not some, laws must be enforced; that our country is different from others and needs to maintain the integrity of its borders; and that there are always going to be a few bad actors abroad who must be deterred rather than appeased.

We will hear all sorts of angry charges as these dreams die, but that will not mean they are not dead—even if we are lucky and they go out with a whimper rather than a bang.

JUNE 25, 2010

The Law? How Quaint!

'Change you can believe in' is working out in practice to mean: If you don't like the Constitution's separation of powers—ignore it.

W e are well into revolutionary times, but perhaps not in the way we traditionally think of political upheaval. Instead, insidiously, the law itself is becoming negotiable—or rather, it is becoming subservient to what elite overseers at any given time determine is a higher calling of social change. Of course, progressive federal judges have been creating, rather than interpreting, law for decades. Yet seldom in memory have we seen such a systematic attack on our framework of laws as the present assault from the executive branch.

Federal immigration statutes mandate a clearly defined American border, which aliens may not cross without authorization. Yet the Obama administration not only does not fully enforce those statutes (in this regard, it is not behaving much differently from the prior administration), but also is preparing to sue the state of Arizona for implementing enforcement that follows the intent of neglected federal laws on the books. Apparently, the president believes that enforcement of existing law is a bargaining chip that can be used to obtain "comprehensive immigration reform"—a euphemism for blanket amnesty.

Other states and even cities are now marching in lockstep to boycott Arizona. Meanwhile, the president of Mexico recently blasted Arizonans from the White House Rose Garden, no less, apparently counting on the president of the United States to go along with this demonization of one of his own states. All this is eerie; it has a whiff of the climate of the late 1850s, when the federal government was in perpetual conflict with the states, which in turn were in conflict with one another, and which often appealed to foreign nations for support.

Recently, as if on cue, the secretary of labor, Hilda Solis, produced a video advising workers to contact her office should they feel that they have been shorted wages by their employers. Fair enough. But then she goes on to explicitly include workers who are not documented and to promise them confidentiality, i.e., de facto federal protection for their illegality: "Every worker has a right to be paid fairly, whether documented or not."

"Undocumented" is part of the current circumlocution for breaking federal law and residing here illegally. In short, although Solis is a federal executive sworn to uphold existing federal law, she has decided which laws suit her and which do not. She rightly promises to pursue law-breaking employers, but quite wrongly not to pursue law-breaking employees.

Yet when we become unequal before the law, the entire notion of a lawful society starts to erode. If Secretary Solis has decided that law-breaking aliens can in confidence count on her protection, then can those who don't pay their taxes (perhaps citing some sort of prejudice) likewise find exemption from Treasury Secretary Geithner? Can citizens pick and chose their particular compliances—run red lights, but still want shoplifters arrested? Break the speed limit, but insist that cars stop at crosswalks? Do questions of race, class, and gender determine the degree to which the federal government considers enforcing existing law?

Recently in Port Chester, N.Y., a federal judge made a mockery of the concept of one man, one vote. Apparently the magistrate felt that Hispanics in Port Chester needed help to elect someone with whom they can identify along racial lines. So, to ensure the election of an Hispanic to the village Board of Trustees, the judge created a system of cumulative voting. Each voter was given six votes, and the explicit hope was that Hispanics would give all their votes to Hispanic candidates, voting on the basis of race rather than policy. Now we hear this may well become a precedent that the federal government will use to ensure diversity elsewhere.

When an "Hispanic" was duly elected as one of the six trustees, the judge and other observers were pleased that Hispanic voters had achieved the intended result. There was no thought, of course, about what constituted "Hispanic." Does it require three-quarters Hispanic blood? One-half? One-quarter? One-eighth? Does Puerto Rican count, but not Spanish? Mexican, but not Portuguese or Basque? There was also no thought about whether such racial pigeonholing was good for the country. After all, focusing on race, while violating the cherished notion of each citizen enjoying one—and only one—vote, might also conjure up some disturbing memories from our not-too-distant past.

BP has acted in derelict fashion in the Gulf. But that does not justify the Obama administration's decision—without a court order and without legislation passed by Congress—to ignore past legal precedent capping oil-company liability. Instead, this administration promises to "kick ass" and put a "boot on their necks" until BP coughs up, say, $20 billion in reparations. If a president by fiat can demand $20 billion from a corporation to create a payout fund, why not $30 or perhaps $100 billion? Or better yet, in South American style, why not simply nationalize BP altogether?

We saw something like this before from the Obama administration, when it bailed out the bankrupt Chrysler Corporation and by executive order overturned the legally determined order of creditors. "Senior" creditors were to have been, by contract, the first paid, while junior creditors waited in line. But the latter group included union workers. So Obama derided the senior lenders as "speculators" and simply put his own constituents and campaign donors in front of them. The first sign of a debauched society is that it does not honor contracts, but reinterprets them according to perceived political advantage.

Now there is talk of an executive decree from the Environmental Protection Agency to implement provisions of cap-and-trade legislation that Congress will not pass. Republican senators are already worried that the administration will likewise simply begin to grant amnesty to illegal aliens en masse, without introducing such a proposal to Congress, which alone has the right and responsibility to make our laws. And the recent executive order to ban all offshore drilling in the Gulf clearly circumvented the legal process. (Does the government have the right to shut down every flight if one airplane crashes, or to mothball all nuclear plants should one leak?) Instead of putting a moratorium on the sort of deep-drilling procedure and pipe fittings that BP used, the Obama administration simply issued a blanket ban on all offshore drilling—as if the real intent was not to allow the crisis of an oil spill to go to waste in the larger environmental effort to reduce carbon emissions.

What do all these ends-justify-the-means examples portend? Mostly, they reflect an effort by a technocratic class to implement social change through extralegal means if it finds that its agenda does not meet with public approval. In some sense, the Obamians have lost all faith that our democracy shares their vision, and so they seek to impose their exalted will by proclamation—as if they are the new Jacobins and America is revolutionary France throwing off the old order.

In late 2008, the liberal hope was that an elected President Obama, with large Democratic majorities in both the Senate and the House, could do just about whatever he wanted. But then a number of obstacles arose, from occasionally recalcitrant Democratic legislators to bothersome things like filibusters. In response, Obama was not content with achieving his liberal ends, but sought to change the very means of obtaining them; even *New York Times* columnists suddenly resented the calcification of American politics, and pointed to the ease with which dictatorial China can simply impose green change.

Note the logic of all this. Federal officials determine a supposed good and then find the necessary way to achieve it. The law be damned. "Diversity," unions, environmentalism—any of these anointed causes trumps the staid idea of simply following the letter of the law.

The final irony? It was law professor Obama who campaigned on respect for the rule of law as he serially trashed elements of the Bush administration's war on terror—almost all of which he subsequently kept or expanded. Note how what was deemed illegal before 2009 has suddenly become quite legal and worthy of emulation and indeed expansion.

As Obama's polls continue to erode and congressional support for his agenda further dwindles, expect his cabinet to continue to seek ways around the enforcement of existing law. You see, in the current climate, the law is seen as retrograde, an obstacle to the advancement of long-overdue social change—which is to be implemented by a law professor and a past fierce critic of George Bush's supposed constitutional transgressions.

While the media still rail about fanciful threats to constitutional stability from right-wing Tea Party types, we are getting real usurpation—but with a hope-and-change smile.

JULY 21, 2010

Not Obama Is Not Enough

There are risks involved, but if Republicans are to be taken seriously, they must be willing to detail specific alternatives to the Obama agenda.

Republicans will shortly need to stand for something more than just being against much of the Obama agenda. Only a superior and detailed alternative can win more lasting support than just a midterm correction. Obama, after all—with nationalized health care, amnesty, cap-and-trade, financial overhaul, government absorption of private enterprise, takeover of the student-loan industry, and gorge-the-beast deficits that will ensure a generation of higher taxes—at least seems to have some sort of plan to change America.

The absurdity of $1.5 trillion annual deficits is easy to run on; but where in the budget should we freeze or cut spending? To restore fiscal sanity, we need details rather than vague promises to reduce red ink to a particular percentage of GDP. Is there to be an across-the-board spending freeze or targeted cuts? How much, if at all, does defense get cut? If it does, where and how?

Fairly or not, we are at the stage where, at least in the short term, each proposed dollar of tax cuts needs to be matched by a proposed dollar of spending reduction. The supply-side notion of expanding federal revenue through tax cuts and business stimulation remains of course valid. But in the here and now, the public needs concrete reality, not assurances about more money to come in within a year or two.

Amnesty—under the euphemism of "comprehensive immigration reform"—would be a disaster. But in critiquing Obama's policies, Republicans need to explain precisely how employer sanctions, increased patrols, and the completion of the fence will result in near-zero illegal entry. Then they must detail what exactly to do with the existing population of illegal aliens, which may well exceed 12 million—of whom most are neither felons nor unemployed.

What exactly is earned citizenship, and how does it differ from amnesty? Does one have to go back to Mexico to apply for readmission for American residency or to obtain citizenship? How would fines be levied and collected? Are we to close the border first, and let various agencies incrementally deport illegal aliens over several years as they come across them?

If the Republicans are not prepared to answer these questions and more, then they will get hit with the charge of advocating "mass deportations"—and with 60 Minutes—style stories of a valedictorian Victoria Lopez or a football star Jorge Garcia detained during a traffic stop and cruelly put on a bus to Oaxaca.

Obama seems lost on Afghanistan. He avoided General McChrystal for months. He foolishly, as with his promises on Guantanamo, set an arbitrary date for phased troop withdrawals. And he is imprisoned now within his own self-created paradox of the supposed good war in Afghanistan turned bad, and the bad war in Iraq turned good.

But what is the alternative? Can Republicans articulate a simple three-step policy that will set out: (1) our objectives and aims in Afghanistan, (2) how we are going to achieve them, and (3) a rough estimate of the costs and sacrifices necessary? Can they explain why continuing the war is preferable to leaving? Without some specificity about what would constitute victory and how we can secure it, we are back to Nixon's campaign promise of a "secret plan" to abruptly end the Vietnam War, which turned out to be Vietnamization stretched out over four years.

Obama's reset foreign policy is heading for a Carter-like collision with reality. But so far has anyone in the opposition explicitly explained why the new alignment policy is wrong, and how it can be changed? Should we reemphasize our ties with Britain, Colombia, Israel, and India, while ceasing to talk to Iran and Syria? What would the conservative reset-button diplomacy with Russia and China look like?

It is easy to denounce the pathetic apology tours, but what exactly is the Republican vision of how to explain an exceptional America without being haughty? Instead of U.N. guidance, is there to be a determined effort to encourage democratic and free-market nations to join America in resisting autocracy? Can we hear that Guantanamo both is a humane detention center and fulfills a need in a war in which terrorist killers do not fit the traditional criteria of the Geneva Conventions, as Eric Holder himself once explained? Could a Republican explain how these new $1.5 trillion deficits cripple U.S. foreign-policy options?

Cap-and-trade looms as a calamity. The billions Obama has spent on wind and solar subsidies seem to be yet another boondoggle. Fine—but exactly how are we going to transition to new fuels without going broke? Will the Republicans explain why oil, natural gas, clean coal, and nuclear, hydroelectric, wind, and solar power are all necessary, and state the rough percentage of our energy profile that each should make up? Can they retool "Drill, baby, drill" for the post-BP age?

The more we learn about Obama's health-care solution, the more we see that it will be the source of vast new problems. Okay. But do the Republicans have a way to manage costs for the aged and ill, who in their last year often exceed the aggregate health-care expenditure of their entire life up until then? Can the opposition address that issue in ways other than dismissing "death panels"? Do kids between age 23 and their first job need health insurance? And if so, how are they going to get it? How does the middle-class family with a house, two cars, and a 401(k) not lose everything if the suddenly out-of-work father develops lymphoma? Or does it lose everything?

Entitlement costs are slowly strangling the American economy. Medicare and Social Security are unsustainable. We can all agree on that, and on the fact that the Democrats' usual response is to demagogue anyone who points it out. But what exactly would Republicans do? Raise the age for Social Security eligibility? Raise Medicare premiums? The days of simply adding on prescription-drug benefits without the means to pay for them are long over. And yet the last time Republicans offered the solution of quasi-private retirement and health-care accounts, in 2005, they were massacred politically. Have they got better ideas now—or a better notion of how to present these largely good ideas?

Cannot Republicans insist on an ethics pledge, so that the careers of a Charles Rangel and a Chris Dodd are not followed by another Jack Abramoff and Duke Cunningham?

Republican politicos will quite accurately lecture that presenting such detailed alternative plans would be foolhardy: The key now is simply to be against what an unpopular Obama is for. I accept that offering detailed solutions might well turn the public as much against the proposed medicine as against the original malignant disease.

Yet at some point, blanket Obama-bashing without a comprehensive alternative will turn stale. Critics of Obama—if they are to be taken seriously—will have to be about more than not being Obama. Instead, conservatives must identify exactly how to undo the Obama agenda—and do so in a way that does not earn them the disdain that the Republican Congress earned between 2001 and 2006, and the Republican administration between 2005 and 2009.

We need some notion of a contracted agenda, so that conservative voters can hold conservative politicians to account in this age of anti-incumbency. Voters wanted closed borders, balanced budgets, ethical members of Congress, and less government between 2001 and 2006. They believed that all of that had been promised—and then were sorely disappointed.

In short, conservative voters want to see something specific—as much to keep their own honest as to defeat the other.

AUGUST 18, 2010

The Cynical Brilliance of Imam Rauf

There are thousands of sites where the imam could locate his monument to interfaith tolerance. But away from Ground Zero, the irony would be lost.

Start with the notion of a "Cordoba Initiative." In the elite modern Western mind, Cordoba has been transmogrified into a mythical Lala Land of interfaith tolerance. To invoke the city is to prove one's ecumenical credentials. Just ask our president, who, in his June 2009 Cairo speech, fantastically claimed that the Muslim city taught us tolerance while Christians were launching the Inquisition (1478)—quite a feat two and a half centuries after most of the Muslims of Cordoba had fled, converted, or been cleansed during the city's fall (1236) to the Christian forces of the Reconquista. But no matter, we got the president's drift about who was supposedly tolerant and who was not.

In truth, apart from a brief cultural renaissance, Cordoba, during its five centuries of Islamic rule, was not especially tolerant of nonbelievers. And, like most medieval cities, it was plagued by coups, assassinations, and right-wing clerical intolerance; it was a place where books were both burned and written. But that is not the point of citing Cordoba. Surely Feisal Abdul Rauf knows all that and more: Cordoba is as much a mythical construct of a long-ago multicultural paradise so dear to elite liberals as it is a fantasy rallying cry to Islamists to reclaim the lost Al-Andalus. So Cordoba is a two-birds-with-one-stone evocation: in the liberal West proof of one's ecumenical bona fides; in the Middle East proof of one's Islamist bona fides. It would be easy to find a city emblematic of interfaith outreach other than the Andalusian Cordoba—from Jerusalem to Ann Arbor—but then the irony would be lost.

Then we come to Imam Rauf himself. To his liberal defenders, he is a sort of respectable Deepak Chopra who at respectable places like Aspen mouths pop platitudes of interfaith tolerance—so much so that our own State Department has employed him, apparently for quite some time, for goodwill gallivanting abroad.

But to those in the Middle East, he is known equally well for doing what he can, as a Western liberal, to contextualize terrorism, bin Laden, and Islamic extremism within the tired Western postmodern tropes of cultural relativism: "The United States' policies were an accessory to the crime that happened" on 9/11; "In fact, in the most direct sense, Osama bin Laden is made in the U.S.A."; "The U.S. and the West must acknowledge the harm they have done to Muslims before terrorism can end"; "The issue of terrorism is a very complex question"; "The Islamic method of waging war is not to kill innocent civilians. But it was Christians in World War II who bombed civilians in Dresden and Hiroshima, neither of which were military targets"—blah, blah, blah, like all the thinkery that one hears in the faculty lounge.

If the now mysteriously absent Mr. Rauf were not cynical, he simply could do the Oprah/Katie Couric circuit and convince the public that all of the above is taken out of context and that the implications are belied by his longstanding efforts at interfaith outreach. But then he tried that once, on 60 Minutes, with disastrous consequences; and, anyway, the irony of speaking obliquely to two audiences would surely be imperiled.

Now we are fighting over how far the perimeter of Ground Zero extends, and where "hallowed" or "sacred" ground begins and ends. But again, the entire notion of a "Ground Zero mosque" was the brainchild of Imam Rauf himself. He grasped at once the brilliant cynicism involved: Here at home well-meaning liberals would applaud the audacity of hope in positioning a mosque near the 9/11 site in order to "commemorate" the "tragedy," as a token of tolerance where all could come together and thus avoid another misunderstanding of the sort that sent two airliners crashing into two skyscrapers.

Abroad, the message would, of course, be interpreted quite differently: To the radical Islamists, a mosque rising near Ground Zero well before a new World Trade Center is constructed is a message of Islamic triumphalism—in the long tradition of minarets on the conquered Santa Sophia in Istanbul, the eighth-century Al-Aqsa mosque in Jerusalem rising on the site of the destroyed Jewish Second Temple, and the great mosque at Cordoba retrofitted from the gutted Christian Church of St. Vincent. Again, there are thousands of sites in New York where another mosque could be built; but without the Ground Zero resonance, the irony would be lost.

Then we come to the funding of the supposed $100 million, 13-story Islamic center ("mosque" has become a right-wing defamation for a complex devoted to contemplation and meditation). Mr. Rauf is not engaged in a nationwide fundraising drive of the sort Americans are used to for preserving iconic ships or refurbishing the Statue of Liberty. Instead, he is apparently counting on petrodollars from the Middle East. Given the authoritarian, and religiously intolerant, regimes in most of the Gulf sheikdoms, one can assume that donations will not be predicated on Imam Rauf's supposed efforts at an Islamic Reformation. Otherwise, what better place to start than Saudi Arabia?

But all that might be unfair second-guessing and right-wing demagoguing. After all, Mr. Rauf can simply embrace transparency, and galvanize Americans to donate to his interfaith center. (Governor Paterson has already offered the help of the New York taxpayer.) Do that, and Gulf money becomes redundant.

Then there is the image of America. Note that the world is not talking about banning the burqa in France, or shutting down a mosque in Germany. Much less are we familiar with the Russians leveling Muslim Grozny or the Chinese rounding up and jailing or shooting Muslims. And, of course, few care that the Saudis, whether the public or the government, would jail a Christian who built a church in Riyadh, or kill a nonbeliever who tried to enter Mecca.

No, Imam Rauf wanted to show the world that the most religiously tolerant country in the world was, in fact, hypocritically intolerant. It is hard to do that in an anything-goes America, where Piss Christ art and shoot-Bush Knopf novels are considered hip creative expressions. But build a mosque a stone's throw away from Ground Zero? Now that was a brilliant move, one that would draw a reaction from everyone from Glenn Beck to the New York labor unions. All Imam Rauf had to do was propose the mosque site, scram out of the country for a month, and let the liberal elite and the media lecture the world on how nativist, xenophobic, and intolerant the most tolerant nation in the world really was—sort of like lighting a firecracker, tossing it into a crowd from a moving car, speeding away, and watching the ensuing human fireworks in the rear-view mirror.

Finally, we come to the greatest irony of all, the politically suicidal entry of President Obama into the fray. After himself invoking Cordoba for just the sort of therapeutic mythmaking that Imam Rauf is far better at, how could the president now stay out? Rauf knew that he had a legal right to build the mosque, that the cultural elite would rally to his defense, that the right wing would go ballistic, and that his "outreach" would be deeply offensive to the vast majority of Americans of all faiths.

In other words, Rauf is just the sort of Venus's flytrap that would lure in the unthinking multicultural, multi-everything president, eager to score political points with his omnipresent tolerance, and apparently having learned nothing from his disastrous beer summit and his declaration that clinging Arizonans would arrest Mom and Pop and the kids as they went out for ice cream. Obama could not resist weighing in, and once more he ended up looking the law-professor fool, who in sonorous tones reminds Americans, on the one hand, of the banal (it is perfectly legal to build a mosque near Ground Zero), while, on the other, he plays the Chicago legislator who voted present whenever he could (to a Muslim audience, he kinda, sorta wanted it built; to an American audience the next day, he kinda, sorta really didn't).

Imam Rauf is a rascal, but he is at least a brilliantly cynical one.

OCTOBER 26, 2010

Wikileaks' Selective Morality

Despite its claims of uncovering bad behavior by governments around the world, WikiLeaks chiefly targets the U.S. military.

There has never been anything quite like WikiLeaks in American military history. We are engaged in a great experiment to see whether the U.S. military can still persist in a conflict when it knows that any and all of its private communications can become public—and will be selectively aired and hyped by people with a preconceived bias against it. Had the public known in real time from periodic media leaks about operational disasters surrounding the planning for the D-Day landings, intelligence failures at the Bulge or Okinawa, or G.I. treatment of some German and Japanese prisoners, the story of World War II might have been somewhat different. But then, in those Paleolithic days FDR and Winston Churchill did not have to be flawless to be perceived as being far better than Adolf Hitler.

So we now have a war within a war—one to defeat the enemy, and quite another, to preemptively backtrack, footnote, and explain the context of one's actions for future armchair judges and jurors who will adjudicate battle behavior from the library carrel. Note here that no other government bureau or private entity functions under quite such rules of engagement—the communications of Mr. Obama's staff are not public; we don't read the internal memos of Warren Buffett or Bill Gates; the minutes of *New York Times* editorial meetings remain private; we don't even get to read the private communications and discussions that the often petulant Julian Assange conducts with his own WikiLeaks team and learn whether there is dissent among his staff over his own ethics and methods. Surely a leaker of any and all things should not demand privacy for himself?

Note also that there is no attempt at systematic or coherent leaking.

WikiLeaks mostly targets the West. It may now and then leak to us something about dastardly behavior by an African or Chinese bureau or religious sect, but it really does not tend to uncover things about the Russian, Iranian, Cuban, or Chinese armed forces in any way commensurate with its fixation on the U.S. military. It either has no wish to, has no means to, or is very afraid of the consequences—in the fashion of the reaction to the Danish cartoons—should it choose to do so. I suppose that WikiLeaks believes that the Western military can "handle" a climate of zero confidentiality and still protect the likes of Mr. Assange and his team. After all, as a high-profile, elite Westerner, he assumes a level of comfort, security, civil rights, freedom, and affluence in his many international travels and operations not accorded to most who live under other systems, and impossible without the protective umbrella of the military he seems so bent on destroying.

Nor do we know why some documents are leaked and published and others are not. In one sense, Mr. Assange is a rogue version of Bob Woodward: The would-be archival leaker knows that if he gets his particular documents to WikiLeaks promptly, his own preferred narrative will emerge; if he does not, perhaps someone else will preempt him by leaking different archives, which may include evidence of his own culpability, or at least a version of events not to his liking.

So WikiLeaks' morality is quite selective. Mr. Assange takes a divine view that as judge and juror—and executioner—it is up to him to decide the ethics of what to, and what not to, release—though the public has no idea of his nontransparent modus operandi. But while we may be shocked for a while at the Machiavellian nature of our own military, that morning outrage soon passes amid the sheer clutter of the daily news. What persists, however, is the danger to thousands in the field who helped the U.S. military—not on the WikiLeaks supposition that we must be perfect to be good, but in the more mundane belief that we were far better than the wretched alternative on the battlefield. So, yes, we ponder the morality of WikiLeaks in the newsroom; thousands of others less fortunate do so far, far away, anticipating a bullet to the head.

Finally, I expect Mr. Assange's organization soon to implode. You see, despite all its utopian chest-thumping about seeking out secretive evil the world over, it is really designed, in Daniel Ellsberg fashion, to expose bad faith and cruelty on the part of the evil capitalist military-industrial Western state. But right now, that apparatus here in the Great Satan is being run by the likes of the hyper-liberal Barack Obama, Nancy Pelosi, and Harry Reid, with the enthusiastic sanction of the *New York Times*, NPR, the *Washington Post*, *Newsweek*, and CBS News. Bush's Iraq War was and is still fair game, and we can all indulge in groupthink outrage about his minions. But WikiLeaks is now flitting around within the red zone, and any leaks about Afghanistan or Iraq post January 2009 reflect upon a left-wing Obama government. A public perception of inappropriate military policy would endanger an entire far-left social experiment at home. The result will be that either Mr. Assange and his team pull back, or, more likely, the outraged media will abruptly decide that his leaking grows stale and he has already had more than his 15 minutes of fame.

Who knows, maybe the head of NPR will soon scoff that Mr. Assange should first check in with his psychiatrist or his publicist—take your pick.

NOVEMBER 12, 2010

The Obama Fabulists

It's as if Bush had explained his nosedive in the polls by his failure to invade Syria and Iran or expand Freddie Mac and Fannie Mae.

During the 2008 campaign, Barack Obama was billed as a cool rationalist—a sober and judicious intellectual so unlike the inattentive and twangy "smoke 'em out" George W. Bush, so rational in contrast to the herky-jerky and frenetic John McCain. Like Senator Kerry, our professor president now laments Americans' descent into emotion. "Facts and science and argument does [sic] not," our president moans, "seem to be winning the day."

The largely academic intellectuals whom Obama brought into his administration promised to bring their erudition and logic both to reading public opinion and to providing commensurate winning solutions. Sympathetic liberal pundits also cited their own empirical thinking as proof of a scientific method that they find sorely lacking in the gush and rancor of talk radio, the Tea Party, and Fox News. But in its first 21 months, this administration has serially proved inept at analyzing public opinion, and seems instead governed by predetermined ideology that trumps basic empiricism.

It all started in January 2009, when a giddy Barack Obama failed to appreciate how he got elected. He concluded that his victory was proof of a radical shift to the left on the part of the American electorate. In fact, it was a combination of the novelty of the first serious African-American presidential candidate, a so-so McCain effort, the traumatic financial meltdown of Sept. 15, 2008, unhappiness with the Bush administration's Iraq war, fawning media, an orphaned presidential election with no incumbent running, and Obama's centrist campaigning that explained the near impossible election of a northern liberal, when kindred sorts such as Dukakis, Kerry, McGovern, and Mondale had all failed. The country clearly wanted a corrective to the big spending and borrowing of the Bush administration—and soon discovered that, instead, it was going to get a far larger second serving of it.

From the outset, European expansive government was the model for this administration. But a statist antidote to the financial crisis was a complete misreading of ongoing events at home and abroad. The Wall Street meltdown was a result of a two-decade-long state intervention in the mortgage industry. Big government had guaranteed lower-income Americans that they could buy homes they could not afford, while those who built, sold, or financed subsidized houses were aided and abetted by the con—assured of exorbitant government-backed profits with the ethical cover of helping the poor achieve home ownership.

In reaction, quite fabulously the Obama administration explained this government-backed Ponzi scheme in terms of popular distrust of private enterprise and a need for a radical expansion of government as a share of GDP—or, in the now-infamous quip of Rahm Emanuel, "Never let a serious crisis go to waste." More ironic still, the implosion of much of southern Europe and the belt-tightening and cost-cutting of the European Union's strongest economies offered ongoing proof that the redistributive state was unsustainable, at the precise moment we Johnny-come-lately Americans were rushing to embrace just that failed paradigm. The almost stealthy departure from the Obama administration of academics who so prominently guided our economic policy until recently—Peter Orszag, Christina Romer, Larry Summers—suggests that they wished to get out of fantasy town ahead of the reasoning posse that was bound to follow.

The same flight of logic explains the Obamians' weird post-election political triumphalism about the first two years of unpopular legislation promoted or passed by the administration. The takeover of health care, passage in the House of cap-and-trade, bailouts, expansions of entitlements, and huge deficits should—given their low poll ratings—have been something to hide rather than parade. Yet Obama and his loyalists point to these very accomplishments as proof that a now unpopular administration should be proud of its unpopular record.

Of course, the American people did not see it that way, in the greatest outpouring of anger in any midterm election of the last 72 years. Apparently the voters liked very little of what Obama had envisioned for them—and felt that it didn't take a political genius to increase government spending with borrowed money. Only a fabulist would keep bragging of a political legacy that led to political catastrophe. Two years of stasis and gridlock would have done better for the Democrats at the polls.

There also emerged an equally unhinged postmortem analysis that cited almost every cause of Democratic defeat—except the unpopular record of 2009—10 and the weak economy: The most visible and exposed president in American history had not "gotten the message out." The inordinate loss of blue-dog Democrats in key swing congressional districts that are barometers of national opinion "proves" that the defeated Democratic incumbents there were not liberal enough. The referendum was supposedly a warning to both parties in general and Washington in particular—and therefore the loss of 60 or more Democratic seats in the House is analogous to the wave of public frustration that Obama rode into office in 2008. Again, the reasoning class clings to fantasy instead of the "facts and science and argument" that explain why all the House gains of 2006 and 2008 were wiped out at one stroke. Twenty-one months of Barack Obama's vision proved more deleterious to Democrats than what six years of Iraq and the mortgage meltdown did to Republicans.

The list of mythologies could be expanded: A public furious over open borders and looming amnesty was supposedly frustrated about the lack of "comprehensive immigration reform," the new euphemism for amnesty. The failure to act on unpopular promises like closing Guantanamo, trying KSM in a civilian court, and ending "Don't ask, don't tell," apparently disappointed voters. Calling fellow Americans "enemies" and telling Republicans to sit in the back seat were symptomatic of Obama's inability to rev up the base in partisan style.

What's going on with this folklore? In a word, the Left appreciates that Barack Obama in 2008 was, for a variety of reasons, their best hope in a half-century to force a center-right country to embrace a liberal agenda. Everything now follows deductively from that premise. To the extent that the agenda fails and the Democratic Congress gets shellacked, exegeses must arise explaining that things could have been worse, that such a singular midterm rebuke is fairly normal, that the bipartisan statesman Obama might have erred by being too centrist, that the great communicator, in his zeal for quickly serving the electorate, ignored the more mundane arts of public relations and communication. It would be as if Bush supporters explained the president's nosedive in the polls by his unwillingness to invade Syria and Iran or expand Freddie Mac and Fannie Mae. Perhaps Bill Clinton's agenda got trounced in the 1994 midterm elections because voters were disappointed that Hillary had failed to deliver a promised single-payer federal takeover of the health-care system.

So the most logical explanation of the problem is the most shunned, given its ramifications for liberalism: Even with a young, charismatic African-American president who rode to victory on the unpopularity of Bush and of the war, on the upheaval on Wall Street, and with the aid of the media—with all that, in just 21 months Obama finds himself well below 50 percent in approval and his agenda incurring the largest midterm legislative losses since 1938.

In short, the truth is unbearable, reason fails, and the self-described rationalists have become fabulists.

NOVEMBER 17, 2010

Voting Present Beats Losing

With enemies like Michael Moore and Bill Maher, Obama needs fewer friends.

O bamism was repudiated in the midterm election. Not since 1938 has the Democratic party lost so many House seats. The losses of state legislatures and governorships were as bleak for liberals. Obama's frantic campaigning in the last two weeks before the election did little to stop the tide, but did much to remind the country how easily the president reverts to a natural partisanship and divisiveness. Nancy Pelosi's promise to "drain the swamp" of congressional corruption ended four years later with a disgraced Charles Rangel offering up the Magna Carta as a defense of his ethics violations. The congressional elections of 2012 could be just as depressing for liberals, given the greater exposure of Democratic incumbents. George W. Bush now polls roughly even in approval ratings with Barack Obama, who has neither the political experience nor the ideological deftness of a Bill Clinton to triangulate and reinvent himself as a moderate.

For Obama to continue pressing his agenda would further the ongoing destruction of the Democratic party in 2012. However, there are some reasons to believe that he may well instead prefer to vote present, as in his Illinois past, and thereby stave off catastrophe. Why?

The anger of the unhinged Left—the high-profile but ultimately irrelevant rantings of a Michael Moore or a Bill Maher—has the effect of making Obama seem more centrist than he is: With enemies like these, he needs fewer friends. Obama had offered such hope-and-change promises to a progressive America that many naïfs assumed he could turn a country that polls 60 percent conservative into another Sweden—and then onward to even more still. Now that Obama has been rendered politically impotent, he can stop with Obamacare, relieved of the burden of a liberal congressional majority. The extreme Left will become shriller the less the president does. And both their furor at presidential inaction and Obama's own inability to press on with his leftist projects will help him politically.

We can already sense how the president is not going to take the bipartisan lead in cutting out-of-control expenses. Key Democrats have already turned on the centrist recommendations of the president's deficit-reduction commission. Republicans will ultimately have to look at everything from Social Security and Medicare to defense. Obama can benefit from their fiscal responsibility while deploring their heartlessness.

The economy is bound to recover, especially when Americans with capital are assured that Obamism has stalled and it is time to reenter the market—to resume investing, hiring, and buying equipment. Consumers have reduced debt. The world economy is healing. Obama can do very little and take credit for very much. Things should be better by November 2012 than they are now—as long as the private sector is assured that Obama will do no more harm.

Obama's class warfare will not end, but it may be refocused and refined. The problem for many Americans was not that he attacked the wealthy per se, but that he gored those who were not really wealthy—at least as defined by a ridiculous $250,000-annual-income rubric that demonized any above and patronized those below. Expect the president to up his them/us Mason-Dixon line to, say, a million dollars in annual income. Such a hike will reassure his upscale liberal supporters in the media, the universities, and the law that they are not exploiters and need not pay higher taxes, while also exempting most small businesses from increased income, capital-gains, and payroll taxes. Everyone knows of someone noble who makes somewhat over $250,000 a year; most people don't worry much about a mostly unknown "they" who, as class enemies, pile up $1 million or more in annual income.

Abroad, the president is quietly starting to curb the bowing and apologizing. His team is learning that cynical foreign leaders appreciated Obama's fawning only to the degree that they could take advantage of it at the expense of America—and of Obama's reputation.

For all the past talk of hitting the reset button, Obama has quietly accepted the entire Bush anti-terrorism policy. There is no more bragging about closing Guantanamo, ending renditions and tribunals, or trying KSM in a civilian court; idiotic parlance like "overseas contingency operations" and "man-caused disasters" hasn't been heard for months. We are now witnessing the surreal world of Hillary Clinton ("suspension of disbelief") defending America's use of force in Afghanistan against international criticism and explaining why a Petraean surge is working this time, when she is in charge of U.S. foreign policy.

When Obama urges the American people to have patience with his war plans, as he ups the number of Predator drone attacks and special-forces hit missions, then we are living in quite an alternative universe to wanting all troops out of Iraq by March 2009 and declaring the Bush surge a failure.

By 2011, American foreign policy in practice will resemble nothing of what presidential candidate Obama outlined in 2008 and thought he could deliver in winter 2009. Instead, the damage that Obama has wrought in 2009—10 will be passed off as inevitable American "decline" that he was trying to "manage." In his first two years in office, Obama said and did some ridiculous things abroad, and assorted monsters in Iran, Lebanon, North Korea, Syria, and Venezuela are still calibrating to what degree they can (literally) get away with murder. Opportunists in China and Russia are still trying to decide whether it is time to humiliate Obama, cashing in their chips and taking their winnings home, or whether they can get more still from our gullible president.

Obama's reelection chances could hinge on international crises to come. His fate may rest not on whether at home he triangulates like Bill Clinton or continues to sermonize like Jimmy Carter, but on whether abroad he is up to something like Clinton's confrontation with Milosevic, or whether he prefers instead an appeasement akin to Carter's enlistment of Ramsey Clark to help out with the hostage release.

How odd that, 22 months into his presidency, the best reelection chances for the president of the United States are suddenly found in keeping quiet, abandoning his agenda, adopting the security protocols of his hated predecessor, and sounding more like a Reagan or a Bush than a Carter when he reaps abroad in 2011—12 what he has sown in 2009—2010.

Weirder still? The more Obama's polls improve from his not being Obama, the more moderate Democrats will probably praise him for his virtual progressivism.

DECEMBER 15, 2010

Two Californias

Abandoned farms, Third World living conditions, pervasive public assistance—welcome to the once-thriving Central Valley

The last three weeks I have traveled about, taking the pulse of the more forgotten areas of central California. I wanted to witness, even if superficially, what is happening to a state that has the highest sales and income taxes, the most lavish entitlements, the near-worst public schools (based on federal test scores), and the largest number of illegal aliens in the nation, along with an overregulated private sector, a stagnant and shrinking manufacturing base, and an elite environmental ethos that restricts commerce and productivity without curbing consumption.

During this unscientific experiment, three times a week I rode a bike on a 20-mile trip over various rural roads in southwestern Fresno County. I also drove my car over to the coast to work, on various routes through towns like San Joaquin, Mendota, and Firebaugh. And near my home I have been driving, shopping, and touring by intent the rather segregated and impoverished areas of Caruthers, Fowler, Laton, Orange Cove, Parlier, and Selma. My own farmhouse is now in an area of abject poverty and almost no ethnic diversity; the closest elementary school (my alma mater, two miles away) is 94 percent Hispanic and 1 percent white, and well below federal testing norms in math and English.

Here are some general observations about what I saw (other than that the rural roads of California are fast turning into rubble, poorly maintained and reverting to what I remember seeing long ago in the rural South). First, remember that these areas are the ground zero, so to speak, of 20 years of illegal immigration. There has been a general depression in farming—to such an extent that the 20- to-100-acre tree and vine farmer, the erstwhile backbone of the old rural California, for all practical purposes has ceased to exist.

On the western side of the Central Valley, the effects of arbitrary cutoffs in federal irrigation water have idled tens of thousands of acres of prime agricultural land, leaving thousands unemployed. Manufacturing plants in the towns in these areas—which used to make harvesters, hydraulic lifts, trailers, food-processing equipment—have largely shut down; their production has been shipped off overseas or south of the border. Agriculture itself—from almonds to raisins—has increasingly become corporatized and mechanized, cutting by half the number of farm workers needed. So unemployment runs somewhere between 15 and 20 percent.

Many of the rural trailer-house compounds I saw appear to the naked eye no different from what I have seen in the Third World. There is a Caribbean look to the junked cars, electric wires crisscrossing between various outbuildings, plastic tarps substituting for replacement shingles, lean-tos cobbled together as auxiliary housing, pit bulls unleashed, and geese, goats, and chickens roaming around the yards. The public hears about all sorts of tough California regulations that stymie business—rigid zoning laws, strict building codes, constant inspections—but apparently none of that applies out here.

It is almost as if the more California regulates, the more it does not regulate. Its public employees prefer to go after misdemeanors in the upscale areas to justify our expensive oversight industry, while ignoring the felonies in the downtrodden areas, which are becoming feral and beyond the ability of any inspector to do anything but feel irrelevant. But in the regulators' defense, where would one get the money to redo an ad hoc trailer park with a spider web of illegal bare wires?

Many of the rented-out rural shacks and stationary Winnebagos are on former small farms—the vineyards overgrown with weeds, or torn out with the ground lying fallow. I pass on the cultural consequences to communities from the loss of thousands of small farming families. I don't think I can remember another time when so many acres in the eastern part of the valley have gone out of production, even though farm prices have recently rebounded. Apparently it is simply not worth the gamble of investing $7,000 to $10,000 an acre in a new orchard or vineyard. What an anomaly—with suddenly soaring farm prices, still we have thousands of acres in the world's richest agricultural belt, with available water on the east side of the valley and plentiful labor, gone idle or in disuse. Is credit frozen? Are there simply no more farmers? Are the schools so bad as to scare away potential agricultural entrepreneurs? Or are we all terrified by the national debt and uncertain future?

California coastal elites may worry about the oxygen content of water available to a three-inch smelt in the Sacramento—San Joaquin River Delta, but they seem to have no interest in the epidemic dumping of trash, furniture, and often toxic substances throughout California's rural hinterland. Yesterday, for example, I rode my bike by a stopped van just as the occupants tossed seven plastic bags of raw refuse onto the side of the road. I rode up near their bumper and said in my broken Spanish not to throw garbage onto the public road. But there were three of them, and one of me. So I was lucky to be sworn at only. I note in passing that I would not drive into Mexico and, as a guest, dare to pull over and throw seven bags of trash into the environment of my host.

In fact, trash piles are commonplace out here—composed of everything from half-empty paint cans and children's plastic toys to diapers and moldy food. I have never seen a rural sheriff cite a litterer, or witnessed state EPA workers cleaning up these unauthorized wastelands. So I would suggest to Bay Area scientists that the environment is taking a much harder beating down here in central California than it is in the Delta. Perhaps before we cut off more irrigation water to the west side of the valley, we might invest some green dollars into cleaning up the unsightly and sometimes dangerous garbage that now litters the outskirts of our rural communities.

We hear about the tough small-business regulations that have driven residents out of the state, at the rate of 2,000 to 3,000 a week. But from my unscientific observations these past weeks, it seems rather easy to open a small business in California without any oversight at all, or at least what I might call a "counter business." I counted eleven mobile hot-kitchen trucks that simply park by the side of the road, spread about some plastic chairs, pull down a tarp canopy, and, presto, become mini-restaurants. There are no "facilities" such as toilets or washrooms. But I do frequently see lard trails on the isolated roads I bike on, where trucks apparently have simply opened their draining tanks and sped on, leaving a slick of cooking fats and oils. Crows and ground squirrels love them; they can be seen from a distance mysteriously occupied in the middle of the road.

At crossroads, peddlers in a counter-California economy sell almost anything. Here is what I noticed at an intersection on the west side last week: shovels, rakes, hoes, gas pumps, lawnmowers, edgers, blowers, jackets, gloves, and caps. The merchandise was all new. I doubt whether in high-tax California sales taxes or income taxes were paid on any of these stop-and-go transactions.

In two supermarkets 50 miles apart, I was the only one in line who did not pay with a social-service plastic card (gone are the days when "food stamps" were embarrassing bulky coupons). But I did not see any relationship between the use of the card and poverty as we once knew it: The electrical appurtenances owned by the user and the car into which the groceries were loaded were indistinguishable from those of the upper middle class.

By that I mean that most consumers drove late-model Camrys, Accords, or Tauruses, had iPhones, Bluetooths, or BlackBerries, and bought everything in the store with public-assistance credit. This seemed a world apart from the trailers I had just ridden by the day before. I don't editorialize here on the logic or morality of any of this, but I note only that there are vast numbers of people who apparently are not working, are on public food assistance, and enjoy the technological veneer of the middle class. California has a consumer market surely, but often no apparent source of income. Does the $40 million a day supplement to unemployment benefits from Washington explain some of this?

Do diversity concerns, as in lack of diversity, work both ways? Over a hundred-mile stretch, when I stopped in San Joaquin for a bottled water, or drove through Orange Cove, or got gas in Parlier, or went to a corner market in southwestern Selma, my home town, I was the only non-Hispanic—there were no Asians, no blacks, no other whites. We may speak of the richness of "diversity," but those who cherish that ideal simply have no idea that there are now countless inland communities that have become near-apartheid societies, where Spanish is the first language, the schools are not at all diverse, and the federal and state governments are either the main employers or at least the chief sources of income—whether through emergency rooms, rural health clinics, public schools, or social-service offices. An observer from Mars might conclude that our elites and masses have given up on the ideal of integration and assimilation, perhaps in the wake of the arrival of 11 to 15 million illegal aliens.

Again, I do not editorialize, but I note these vast transformations over the last 20 years that are the paradoxical wages of unchecked illegal immigration from Mexico, a vast expansion of California's entitlements and taxes, the flight of the upper middle class out of state, the deliberate effort not to tap natural resources, the downsizing in manufacturing and agriculture, and the departure of whites, blacks, and Asians from many of these small towns to more racially diverse and upscale areas of California.

Fresno's California State University campus is embroiled in controversy over the student body president's announcing that he is an illegal alien, with all the requisite protests in favor of the DREAM Act. I won't comment on the legislation per se, but again only note the anomaly. I taught at CSUF for 21 years. I think it fair to say that the predominant theme of the Chicano and Latin American Studies program's sizable curriculum was a fuzzy American culpability. By that I mean that students in those classes heard of the sins of America more often than its attractions. In my home town, Mexican flag decals on car windows are far more common than their American counterparts.

I note this because hundreds of students here illegally are now terrified of being deported to Mexico. I can understand that, given the chaos in Mexico and their own long residency in the United States. But here is what still confuses me: If one were to consider the classes that deal with Mexico at the university, or the visible displays of national chauvinism, then one might conclude that Mexico is a far more attractive and moral place than the United States.

So there is a surreal nature to these protests: something like, "Please do not send me back to the culture I nostalgically praise; please let me stay in the culture that I ignore or deprecate." I think the DREAM Act protestors might have been far more successful in winning public opinion had they stopped blaming the U.S. for suggesting that they might have to leave at some point, and instead explained why, in fact, they want to stay. What it is about America that makes a youth of 21 go on a hunger strike or demonstrate to be allowed to remain in this country rather than return to the place of his birth?

I think I know the answer to this paradox. Missing entirely in the above description is the attitude of the host, which by any historical standard can only be termed "indifferent." California does not care whether one broke the law to arrive here or continues to break it by staying. It asks nothing of the illegal immigrant—no proficiency in English, no acquaintance with American history and values, no proof of income, no record of education or skills. It does provide all the public assistance that it can afford (and more that it borrows for), and apparently waives enforcement of most of California's burdensome regulations and civic statutes that increasingly have plagued productive citizens to the point of driving them out. How odd that we overregulate those who are citizens and have capital to the point of banishing them from the state, but do not regulate those who are aliens and without capital to the point of encouraging millions more to follow in their footsteps. How odd—to paraphrase what Critias once said of ancient Sparta—that California is at once both the nation's most unfree and most free state, the most repressed and the wildest.

Hundreds of thousands sense all that and vote accordingly with their feet, both into and out of California—and the result is a sort of social, cultural, economic, and political time-bomb, whose ticks are getting louder.

DECEMBER 22, 2010

The Obamaites About-Face

Like Orwell's farm animals, we have awakened to
see the new commandments on the barnyard wall.

Californians have been experiencing ten days of the wettest, snowiest weather in recent memory. In the usually arid San Joaquin Valley, flooding is ubiquitous. The high Sierra passes are locked in snow well before the first of the year. If the United Kingdom is dealing with the irony of its elites' recently warning of an end to snow on a now snowy island, out here our version of that embarrassment is water everywhere after Energy Secretary Chu warned us that our farms would blow away and that he could envision an end altogether of California agriculture—logically, he asserted, given that 90 percent of the annual Sierra snowpack would soon disappear.

While the state struggles with flooding and blizzards, Governor Schwarzenegger is advertising himself to the Obama administration as a possible post—Van Jones green czar, to regulate energy for the country as he has done for a now insolvent California. But then, once global warming morphed into climate change, too much rain, snow, and cold could become as symptomatic of too much man-made carbon being released as too little rain, snow, and cold once were. Start that engine, and thou shalt both burn and freeze in hell.

This week Attorney General Holder was warning about the threat of terrorism—but not terrorism in the usual liberal Timothy McVeigh, "even Christians can be terrorists" sort of gobbledly-gook. Rather, Eric Holder, as this Christmas's new Dick Cheney, is warning about U.S. citizens who are stealthy radical Islamists. Holder fears that they wish to succeed where the would-be Times Square, subway, Portland, and Christmas airliner bombers all failed. He assumes that the terrorists among us for some reason did not read the Al-Arabiya interview, fully appreciate the Cairo speech, see the famous bow to the Saudi king, or

hear of administration pressure on Israel. In short, "All religions produce terrorists," is now followed by "But some religions produce more
terrorists than others."

So, gone for the moment at least are we "cowards" who racially
stereotype, oppose the Ground Zero mosque in Neanderthal fashion,
and fail to appreciate Holder's own commitment to shutting down
Guantanamo and trying KSM in a New York federal court. Much like
his colleague Harold Koh (who, as an Obama State Department justice
official rather than a Yale law dean, is no longer suing to put an end to
waterboarding at Guantanamo, but is instead opposing those who are
suing to stop Predator assassination missions), Holder in a blink of an
eye went from trashing the Bush-Cheney anti-terrorism protocols to
sighing that it is almost a matter of when, not if, home-grown Islamic
radicals will kill lots of us. Holder's road to Damascus is eerily reminiscent of the sudden conversion in 1938 of British intellectuals, who,
as Czechoslovakia was swallowed, abruptly went from 15 years of
trumpeting League of Nations pacifism to calling for British military
deterrence against fascism. Unlike Holder, however, they at least
explained why they had made their about-faces.

To be fair, the Obamaites are simply channeling their commander-
in-chief, who spent a near decade, from 2001 to 2009, pontificating on
the illegality or superfluousness of the Patriot Act, renditions, tribunals,
Predators, Guantanamo, and overseas wars, and then as president
embraced or even expanded all of them—with not a word of remorse
that his earlier demagoguing might have done great harm both to the
efficacy of the programs and to the reputations of those involved in
them, as well as to his country's image abroad. I suppose we are all
Orwell's farm animals now, mystified but quiet as we wake to see the
commandments on the barnyard wall crossed out and written over.

On the matter of taxes, two years after borrowing $2 trillion to
expand, stimulate, change, and reset the economy, and after talking of
limb-lopping doctors, fat-cat bankers, junketeering CEOs on their way
to Vegas and the Super Bowl, and how "at a certain point you've made
enough money," Obama has now embraced the abhorrent Bush-era tax
rates, and he is courting CEOs. The latter are apparently sitting cata-
tonic on the sidelines, with hundreds of billions in cash but unwilling to

expand operations for fear that Obama will adopt EU-like socialism. At exactly what point did the caterpillar of massive borrowing and government spending emerge from his chrysalis as the butterfly of not raising taxes on anyone in a recession and of balancing budgets? At 8, 9, or 10 percent unemployment? At 50, 48, or 43 percent approval? Or at the idea of 30, 40, 50, or 63 lost House seats?

Obama reset-button diplomacy rested on two assumptions: (1) all problems abroad either started with or failed to transcend George W. Bush; and (2) multicultural non-judgmentalism must replace neo-conservative promotion of human rights across cultures and nations. Now? I don't think anyone argues that China, Russia, or Venezuela has become a little softer on dissidents, or that North Korea is a little more quiet, or that Iran is a little less likely to press ahead with its nuclear proliferation, or that Japan, Britain, or Eastern Europe is a little more confident in American leadership, or that Iraq is lost or Afghanistan saved because we put "our eye back on the ball." As a result, in six months, U.S foreign policy will probably be indistinguishable from that of the second George W. Bush term—even as we continue to hear sermons about bold new multicultural initiatives delivered in Nobel-laureate rhetoric. When did "Bush did it" become "And we did too!"?

When one loses one's faith, the aftermath can be startling. As gas hits $3 a gallon at Christmas, with fears of $4 by summer-vacation time, expect suddenly to hear of plans to tap more natural gas, build more nuclear reactors, and lift the suppression of offshore drilling—all beneath a loudly trumpeted but very thin wind and solar veneer. What are we to expect next—a few windmills fastened atop a drilling rig in the Arctic National Wildlife Refuge, some solar panels on the domes of new nuclear-power plants, a supercharger as an upgrade on the Chevy Volt?

An unrepresentative but quite influential intellectual elite—in the media, the universities, the arts, and government—is vested in Barack Obama, in his unpopular doctrinaire agenda, but even more so in the symbolism of his person. The result is paradoxical. For his political survival, Obama now accepts that his faith-based ideas about the environment, radical Islam, taxes, stimulus, the economy, national security, and foreign policy are not supported by any evidence in the real world. Yet he knows as well that the more he must become empirical, the more he must assure his flock of believers outside the farmhouse window that he still walks on four rather than two legs.

The wonder is not that politicians change as politics dictate, but that the most vehement leftism now accepts nonchalantly what it not long ago so ardently demonized. The oddity is not that Obama must back up after driving his country into a brick wall at the end of a dead-end street, but that as he backs up, turns around, and heads in the other direction, he can still be praised as if he had dematerialized and gone ahead right on through the wall.

CHAPTER THREE

THE "GOOD" WAR IN AFGHANISTAN, THE "BAD" ONE IN IRAQ

FEBRUARY 12, 2008

Iraq Is Not the Worry

It is surrender and self-destruction at home.

General David Petraeus—a sort of combination of Fabius Maximus ("unus homo…") and Matthew Ridgway—has changed the entire Iraqi war, and thereby given us a breathing spell to reflect on our longer-term strategies of victory. Most of the conventional pessimism about Iraq is being proven wrong. For example, the recently translated captured diary of the dead al-Qaeda terrorist—Abu Maysara, a senior adviser to Abu Ayyoub al-Masri—reveals a sort of hopelessness. The dead Maysara laments that al-Qaeda has lost the hearts and minds of the people to the U.S. and its Iraqi allies, while suffering terrible battlefield losses. Abu Maysara did not write as some civilian defeatist, the equivalent of our own Moveon.org antiwar protesters. He was instead a frontline fighter, once confident of victory in the field, but realistically broken by defeat—before he was killed.

For all the Western gloom, the forces trying to break up Iraq are not as strong as the fears of seeing it so trisected. Federal Iraq has survived Iranian subterfuge, the House of Saud terrorist subsidies, Turkish invasion, and Kurdish nationalism—and is still there. It won't be quite Kansas, but the Iraqi state has a good chance to evolve into something no more violent than the usual Middle Eastern state, but without either murderous dictators or theocrats—or, of course, the genocidal murderer Saddam Hussein.

The combination of new American tactics, the surge, shared fear of Iran, vast oil revenues, sheer attrition of jihadists over the last five years, and growing Iraqi hatred of Wahhabi terrorists over the same period, have all led to a perfect storm for al-Qaeda. It now suffers the almost unbelievable humiliation of having Arab Muslims willingly join Americans to expel it from the ancient caliphate.

John McCain was pilloried for his "100 years" in Iraq quip. But the logic of some sort of longer-term presence still stands: Should we continue to bring brigades home slowly as the situation warrants, then the stationing of smaller contingents of Americans abroad in Iraq could become analogous to our presence in South Korea, Japan, the Balkans, or Europe, where deployments are no more dangerous, nor that much more costly than having them here in the United States. Far from being worn out, the U.S. military has evolved into the world's only capable anti-insurgency military force—as we sadly see through contrast with the dismal performance of our NATO allies in Afghanistan.

On the other fronts, the outlook is not so encouraging. Iran was given a great gift with the National Intelligence Estimate's de facto clean bill on nuclear proliferation, a finding that undermined almost all current multilateral efforts to embargo or boycott the theocracy until it is transparent about enrichment. Somehow our politically tainted intelligence agencies argued the near laughable: claiming that Iran stopped making the bomb in 2003 (so that we need not worry now), and yet insisting that such abrupt cessation had nothing to do, as was true in the case of Libya, with our removal of Saddam Hussein (so that no one gets any credit). Far from drawing us back from the brink, the naïve and politicized findings—meant to restrain the much caricatured Bush—have instead only eroded much of the peaceful avenues to prevent Iran's acquisition of a nuclear weapon.

Stabilization in Iraq helps. So does regional Arab worries about Iran. But we are in a holding pattern with three or four unknowns that will ultimately determine whether Iran gets the bomb: What will Israel do? Will Russia, given its past Islamic problems, really want a nuclear theocracy on its border? Is Iran for a few months laying low and quiet, waiting for a change in administration, and with it the assurance that it can sneak through and offer the West its nuclear capacity as a fait accompli, as Pakistan did in 1998?

Oil remains our greatest wartime liability. Since the spikes started in 2003, trillions in wealth have been transferred from the producing nations of America, Europe, China, and India to the otherwise failed societies of the Arab Middle East, Russia, Iran, and Venezuela. It is naïve to think that beneficiaries like Iran or Saudi Arabia will opt for the Dubai route of self-indulgent, but peaceable and largely humane development. For us, the transfer of such massive amounts of capital is both a cause and symptom of our financial vulnerability in a war in which global perceptions are everything—and the United States increasingly seen as an insolvent debtor, its enemies, like vultures on the ever lower branches, awaiting the massive stag below to finally stumble under its wounds.

Ironically our greatest asset is Middle Eastern greed, or the notion that pumping oil at $3 to $4 a barrel and selling it at, say, $50 is not enough for the House of Saud, when it can squeeze out $90. Only that permanent price gauging ensures that we won't see a drop back to $20 a barrel, and with it a relaxation of our efforts to find new energies. Thus eventually both liberals with their Volvo SUVs and conservatives in their 4×4s will agree to develop nuclear power, flex and alternative fuels, gasification of coal, mandatory conservation, and increased oil exploration—and thereby free us from the current extortion, and at last dry up the petrodollars that feed the terrorists.

In terms of Western morale, the picture is likewise not so encouraging. Although the worst days of Cindy Sheehan and Michael Moore have faded, American public opinion is inconsistent. It is angry over the cost of Iraq, but supports the Petraeus plan and rejects the Democratic alternative of mandatory withdrawal and subsequent defeat. It bridles at Guantanamo and wiretaps, but wants the protections of such surveillance and the Patriot Act in continuance. It complains about lost liberties, but neither explains in any detail how exactly we are no longer free nor appreciates that the nation has not experienced another 9/11, despite repeated terrorist attempts.

Immigrants from the Middle East, as least as we determine their sentiments in the media and the universities, complain about current U.S. policy, but rarely voice sustained appreciation of our system they fled to in rejection of their own. Opposition leaders bash Bush as preemptive, unilateral, and incompetent, but do not adduce any alternative peace plan for the Middle East, a new innovative strategy for Iran, a better way of handling Pakistan, new directions in Afghanistan, or something other than quick withdrawal from Iraq. What little we've seen and heard—Obama's worldwide Muslim peace conference and call for an armed incursion into nuclear Pakistan, Pelosi's visits to dictatorial Syria, Joe Biden's trisection of sovereign Iraq—are more frightening than novel.

Abroad, the European public is more schizophrenic. It wants to make no sacrifices to stop the jihadists, but fears them terribly. It damns the U.S. as responsible for the tense, unpleasant global environment, but then—apparently in private—votes to ensure it has leaders favorable to us. Europeans offer moral lectures to Americans who are paying a great price in blood and treasure for constitutional alternatives in Iraq, even as their own elites in shameful timidity mortgage the Western Enlightenment to two-bit thuggish Islamists.

Afghanistan is not seen as a line in the sand to stop the spread of jihadism, but an embarrassing entanglement that can be blamed on George Bush's inordinate anger following 9/11. The European attitude toward America seems to be "you must intervene in the Balkans to lead us in the fight against the twilight, but we won't follow you into Afghanistan to battle against abject darkness."

For those who thought that the level of European appeasement could not be surpassed following the Dutch murderers, the opera and cartoon fiascos, the pope's remarks, or the Iranian kidnapping of British sailors, we now are to listen to the Archbishop of Canterbury's admission that the implementation of sharia law in Britain is "unavoidable" and probably useful as well. Never was so much surrendered by so few to so many.

The new multicultural and relativist British elite in just a decade or so has managed to make in comparison the 12th-century England of Thomas Becket seem humane. In the last analysis, the real worries about the survival of the West in this war are not with America and its courageous twenty-something suburban kids in Anbar trying to offer something better than the sharia morality of the seventh century, but with the likes of sanctimonious and cowardly churchmen in England trying to spread it.

MARCH 14, 2008

Mirror, Mirror . . .

Looking at Iraq

By now everyone sees what he wishes in Iraq—a disaster of many proportions, a necessary war that will still be won. Liberals who used to demand that we promote democracy abroad are fierce critics of Iraqi democracy; conservatives, who want an iron hand dealing with a hostile Middle East, support spending hundreds of billions of dollars in rebuilding Iraqi society.

So it will be left to historians, as has been true in the case of the far-more-costly Korean and Vietnam wars, to adjudicate the final verdict. Meanwhile, the war in Iraq has entered yet another manifestation. The fickle American public and its media have switched and flipped on the war as much as they have on Hillary Clinton's chances—in the last two months she's been a shoo-in, a has-been, a comeback kid, a loser, and now a contender.

In late 2003, Iraq transmogrified suddenly, from an overwhelmingly popular and brilliant three-week war to remove a genocidal Saddam Hussein, into a bitterly divisive effort of four years to defeat an insurgency that threatened to topple the postwar elected government.

Now, despite the obligatory throat-clearing epithets used by journalists and politicians—"the worst," "nightmare," "disaster," "fiasco," "catastrophe," "quagmire"—Iraq is beginning to be seen as something that just might work after all, as the violence subsides and a stable constitutional government hangs on. Once promised to be the singular issue of the current presidential campaign, the war has receded to background noise of the primaries. An ascendant Barack Obama pounded home the fact that, unlike Senator Clinton, he never supported the removal of Saddam Hussein and always wanted to get Americans out of there as fast as he could; it may well prove that a more circumspect Obama soon won't want to mention the war and, as hinted by aides, wouldn't jerk the troops out should he be the next president.

Rarely in American history has a war been so often spun, praised, renounced, disowned, and finally neglected. And the result is that a number of questions remain not just unanswered, but unasked. We have not been hit since 9/11, despite the dire predictions from almost everyone of serial attacks to come. Today if a Marine recruitment center is bombed, we automatically assume the terrorist to represent a domestic anti-war group, not al-Qaeda—a perverse conjecture impossible to have imagined in autumn 2001.

In response to that calm, the communis opinio is that we hyped the threat, needlessly went to war, mortgaged the Constitution—just collate the rhetoric from the Obama and Clinton campaigns—when there was never much of a post-9/11 threat from a rag-tag bunch of jihadists in the first place.

What is never discussed is how many Islamists flocked to Iraq, determined to defeat the U.S. military—and never got out alive. Or, more bluntly, how many jihadists did the U.S. Army and Marines kill in Iraq rather than in Manhattan? And what was the effect of that defeat not only on the jihadists, but also on those who were watching carefully to see whether the terrorists should be joined in victory or abandoned in defeat? Who really took his eye off the ball—the United States by going into Iraq, as alleged, or Osama bin Laden and his jihadist lieutenants by diverting thousands there to their deaths, as is never mentioned?

When the war started, contrary to the current rhetoric, Osama bin Laden was popular in the Middle East, and the tactic of suicide bombing had won a sizable following. But after the war was fought, and despite years of anti-American rhetoric, bin Laden has never polled lower while support for suicide murdering in the Muslim Middle East continues to decline.

In 2001, the Arab street apparently thought, for all the macabre nature of suicide bombing, that it at least had brought the United States to its knees and such a takedown was considered a good thing; in the latter reflection of 2007 and 2008, it worried that such a tactic brought the United States military to its region, and guaranteed the defeat of jihadists along with any who joined them.

Iraq, as no one ever imagined, ended up as a landscape in which the

United States and al-Qaeda would battle for the hearts and minds of the Arab world on the world stage. And in Anbar Province, the jihadists are losing—losing militarily and losing the support of the local Sunni population. Again, whereas the conventional wisdom holds that we have radicalized an entire generation of young Muslims, it may turn out instead that we have convinced a generation that it is not wise after 9/11 to wage war against the United States. In any case, there is no other constitutional Arab government in the Middle East that actively hunts down and kills al-Qaeda terrorists.

When the insurgency took off in late 2003, Europe immediately triangulated against the United States, courted the Arab world, and hoped to deflect jihadists by loudly proclaiming they were vehemently against the war in Iraq. This is in itself was quite remarkable, since the entire recent expansion of the European Union to the south and east had been predicated only on a partnership agreement with the United States to extend NATO membership—alone ensuring these weak new European affiliates American military protection.

Irony abounds: Since 2003, Europe—not the United States—has experienced a series of attacks, and near-constant threats, ranging from bombed subways and rail stations to Islamic demands to censor cartoons, operas, films, and papal exegeses.

It is in Europe, not in post-Iraq Kansas, where a Turkish prime minister announces to Muslim expatriate residents that they must remain forever Turks and assimilation is a crime; it is in post-Iraq Europe, not Los Angeles, where politicians and churchmen talk of the inevitability of Sharia law; and it is in post-Iraq Europe, not the United States, where honor killings and Islamic rioting are common occurrences.

Why? A number of reasons, but despite all the misrepresentation and propaganda, the message has filtered through the Middle East that the United States will go after and punish jihadists—but also, alone of the Western nations, it will risk its own blood and treasure to work with Arab nations to find some alternative to the extremes of dictatorship and theocracy. Europe, in contrast to its utopian rhetoric, will trade with and profit from, but most surely never challenge, a Middle Eastern thug.

Iraq is purportedly a mess left to the next president. In fact, by January 2009 it may well be far less a strategic problem than was

Saddam Hussein's regime, the no-fly zones, Oil for Food, and the punishing UN embargoes. And the next president may well see a stabilized country in which periodic steady American withdrawals, not an insurgency, are the norm—and far fewer jihadists with far fewer supporters worldwide.

George Bush will be blamed for getting us into Iraq and staying there—he's already seen some of the lowest poll ratings since Harry Truman or Richard Nixon. The next president will be praised for beginning to withdraw troops in 2009 on a schedule established in late 2008. After all, if a pundit's column these days has a headline blaring "A Plan for a Way Out" or "Quagmire," we automatically assume a way to unlock the Democratic primary mess, not leave Iraq. In the first ten days of March, before the most recent losses, there was one American combat fatality among 160,000 troops at war.

Iraqi was always an optional war, one that could either do great harm to our national interest and security or offer great advantage to the United States and the region, depending on its costs and the ultimate outcome. Between 2005 and 2006, public support for the war was mostly lost—trisection of the country and American withdrawal were considered our options. In 2008 there is instead a real chance that the original aims of the war—establishing a constitutional government, defeating terrorism militarily, and convincing the Arab population to reject terrorism—are at last possible.

It is the nature of this strange war that we know far more about who failed and what went wrong, far less about who succeeded and what went right. We believe that the dividends of the war—a constitutional government in Iraq and a stunning defeat of radical Islamic jihadists—happened by accident, while the 4,000 dead are the responsibility of our leaders, not the tenacity of the enemy or the costs of waging war in general. The more that the violence subsides and the costs wind down, the more Americans in a near recession will complain of the expense. The more the Iraqis finally begin to exercise responsible political power, the more Americans will lament there is no way to translate tactical victory into long-term strategic advantage.

Iraq, you see, long ago has become a mirror in which we all see only what we want.

JUNE 13, 2008

Iraq in Review

Is there anything left of the antiwar Left's criticism of the Iraq war?

Many commentators on Iraq had no strong ideas about the wisdom of removing Saddam Hussein, but often predicated their evolving views on the basis of whether we were perceived as winning or losing—and later made the necessary and often fluid adjustments. So in light of the changing pulse of the battlefield, it is time once again to examine carefully a few of the now commonplace critiques of the Iraq war.

1. *We took our eye off the ball in Afghanistan by going into Iraq, thereby allowing the Taliban to regain the advantage.*

Any two-theater war can result in less resources allotted to one of the two fronts. But such multiple-front wars, whether in World War II or the Cold War, have never stymied the United States military. More importantly, if we are truly in a global war against Islamic extremists— as al-Qaeda itself reminded us when it announced that Iraq was the key front in their jihad against infidel crusaders—then the problem is not necessarily fighting the insurgents in Iraq, but whether it is a theater conducive to our aims and resources—and can be won. In other words, Iraq simply upped the ante of a larger war, promising disaster if we lost, and enormous advantages if we won. Progress in Iraq is already having positive effects in Afghanistan, where an experienced American counterinsurgency force is fighting extremists who know that their kindred are on the verge of losing militarily and politically in Iraq, and are afraid that the same bitter calculus now applies to them.

In the first years, the odds were with the terrorists—given indigenous Muslim local populations, the hostile neighborhood of a Syria, Iran, and Saudi Arabia, and anti-war fervor at home and abroad. But once the U.S. military defeated al-Qaeda in Anbar, the population turned on Islamic terrorists, and the elected Iraqi government gained stature, then Islamists in and out of Iraq suffered a terrible defeat. We learned to fight a war of counterinsurgency and win hearts and minds far from home; they lost an insurgency—and with it the support of the local and once naturally sympathetic Muslim population. Note that suddenly journalists, intelligence analysts, and politicians are struck by al-Qaeda's implosion, as the Muslim street turns on radical Islamists, who themselves are torn apart by internal ideological schisms.

While many critics remain too heavily invested in antiwar positions staked out between 2003–7 to cite the war as a contributory cause, the obvious catalyst for al-Qaeda's fiasco is its terrible performance in Iraq. Remember, if Americans adjusted their own support for the war on their perceptions of the success or failure of the U.S. military, why wouldn't millions in the Middle East do the same with radical Islamists like al-Qaeda, whose fortunes on the battlefield have only gone from bad to worse?

2. Bush lied about the war and entered it under the false circumstances of fears of WMD and Iraqi ties to al-Qaeda.

Bush erred in focusing on WMDs when the Senate and House approved over 20 writs for war, all of them as valid now as they were in October 2002. That said, it is hard to find a single prominent congressional critic of the war who has made the case that the administration itself altered intelligence information, doctored reports, or had substantially different assessments than those provided to Congress or offered up by foreign governments. The reason recent critics of the war such as Sen. Rockefeller are utterly unconvincing in their allegations of administration malfeasance is that the record shows that they themselves had access to the same information, and often outdid the President in their prewar rhetoric and saber-rattling about Saddam.

But again, the battlefield, rightly or wrongly, colors these controversies. In a world in which there is no longer a Saddam Hussein (who would now have had his hands on trillions of dollars in oil revenue), a Libyan WMD program, and Dr. Khan's nuclear export business, the proliferation issue is becoming less contentious. (If one were to believe the National Intelligence Estimate, Iran ceased its weapons-grade nuclear track opportunely right after Saddam's capture). Since 2003, thousands of Islamic extremists and al-Qaeda's notables have been killed, and the organization routed and discredited; it is hard to see how Iraq has not had positive effects in curbing proliferation and damaging the organization that was responsible for 9/11. Moreover, disputes about Abu Musab al-Zarqawi's post-Afghanistan odyssey, assorted terrorists in Saddam's Baghdad in 2003, or al-Qaeda in Kurdistan during Saddam's rule become less contentious with the knowledge that al-Qaeda, between 2003–7, tried to win, and then lost, Iraq.

3. Mistakes in Iraq were legion and irreversible.

It is better to see such controversies in terms of long- and short-term consequences. Examine the two most discussed—the Iraqi army and troop levels. Disbanding the Iraqi army without providing temporary financial support for young males with military skills was disastrous. Yet in the long-term, building a new army without tens of thousands of hard-core Baathists—as was true of the de-Nazification program with German army in 1946–7—offered a greater chance for eventual success.

Did we send too few troops? Apparently we had enough manpower to take out Saddam, which we did brilliantly in three weeks—a force determined partly in reaction to the first Gulf War, when current critics then alleged that we had needlessly sent over far too many troops, both our own and those of the unwieldy coalition.

Evaluating the surge is more complex, since in a vast theater the size of Iraq, an increase of a little more than 20 percent in troop strength probably does not per se win wars. We forget now that many supporters of the surge were calling for 80,000-100,000 more troops in 2004–7. The 30,000 troops was a compromise figure, given our commitments elsewhere.

As important as the 30,000 reinforcements were, just as critical were three other factors associated with it: a signal to both Iraqi friends and enemies that we were staying on and fighting to win; a radical change in tactics from counterterrorism based in compounds to counterinsurgency intended to protect the local populations from terrorist reprisals; and the appointment of Gen. Petraeus as senior commander in Iraq who won the confidence of the Iraqis; silenced critics at home; and energized his officers on the ground with a new commitment to victory.

Again, there were tragic mistakes—focusing on WMDs as a sole casus belli, the pullback from the first siege of Fallujah, and bellicose Presidential rhetoric coupled with operational tentativeness—all of them regrettable, none of them fatal or comparable to the disastrous foul-ups of World War II, Korea, or Vietnam.

4. Democratization was naïve and bound to fail, given the realities of the tribal Middle East.

In fact, the promotion of constitutional government, however clumsy our efforts in 2003–4, was the only chance the U.S. had after the fall of Saddam Hussein to stabilize the country and hurt our terrorist enemies. No development infuriated al-Qaeda more than U.S. support for elections and a constitutional Iraq that undercut the slander of a 21st-century crusade to annex the ancient caliphate, and invested the Iraqi people themselves in the fight against terrorism for their own future. Iraq is not comparable to the Hamas plebiscite, in that its elections were in concert with a ratified constitution and a result of an American-led effort to depose Saddam Hussein.

One of the most surreal developments of the war has been the Left's caricature of American idealism and our support for a democratic Iraqi government—a brave group of reformers who have been more tarred and demonized by American politicians than have been their al-Qaeda enemies. Should we see a President Obama, and he realizes that Iraq is working, expect the Left to cease its criticisms of neocon democracy fantasies, and instead adopt Iraq's democracy as yet more proof of Obama's hope-and-change idealism in foreign policy.

5. The real winner of the war was Iran.

In the short-term, yes—Iran benefited from the removal of its traditional enemy, Baathist Iraq, and from the initial pan-Islamist rallying against the U.S. presence in Iraq. But in the long-term, should Iraq succeed, nothing will be more destabilizing to Iran than to have a free society next door, where Shiites say, write, and read what they wish, and do so in pluralistic fashion. Again, the ante has been raised. Should Iranian-backed militias lose in Iraq, the theocracy will have suffered a terrible defeat, at a time it diverts precious oil dollars to failed military adventures while its silenced population rations gas. Iran's theocratic government must either incite a U.S. preemptive strike, or destroy Iraqi democracy—or it is doomed.

6. President Bush's presidency was ruined in Iraq.

If we were to lose the war, then yes. But should we win, should a constitutional government stabilize, should al-Qaeda keep unraveling, and should the hiatus of terrorist attacks against Americans at home and abroad continue, then historians will rank Bush in Trumanesque terms: a similarly orphaned presidency that ended disliked—even as it crafted a strategy to defeat global Islamic terror by taking the fight to the heart of the Middle East, while establishing proof of America's good intentions by fostering constitutional government that offered Iraqis an alternative other than the usual Middle East non-choice of theocracy or autocracy.

Bush was terribly damaged by a series of poor spokesmen, his own bellicose sound bites of 2002–3, a series of tell-all defections of former intimates and officials, and an inability to cut U.S. consumption of imported petroleum. But that said, years from now, historians will look at the record and the results, not the present rhetoric, and his legacy could well be—"He kept us safe."

7. Our military is nearly ruined and the war was never worth the cost.

We have paid a high price for our efforts with thousands of dead and wounded, and billions spent. But if the deterioration of a-Qaeda continues, America is kept safe, and the Middle East at last has some alternative to the dismal autocratic norm—one that curbs future oil-fed extremism—then Iraq will be the most important American achievement since the end of the Cold War. If we lose or quit, and Iraq devolves along the lines of the badlands of Pakistan, then, yes, the losses were not worth it.

For all the wear and tear on our military, recruitments are up, we have developed the most sophisticated and experienced anti-insurgent force in the world, and we are just beginning to shake-up the entire military by promoting a new generation of brilliant officers who came of age in the cauldron of Iraq.

In the end, the U.S. military has achieved the near impossible by removing the worst government in the Middle East and fostering what has a real chance to become by far the best. In some sense, whether Iraq was worth the high cost depends on whether one thinks the present-day liberal and humane democracies in Europe, Japan, and Korea were likewise worth the past, and far more terrible, price that America paid in blood and treasure to secure their enduring freedom.

JULY 18, 2008

More Iraq Ironies

Our short memories.

T here is by now only one constant in the entire sad Iraqi saga since the brilliant three-week victory of 2003, and the subsequent violent reconstruction that followed. In our collective exasperation almost all the bad news from the front is due to someone else's stupidity; any good reports are always the result of one's own insight and sobriety. The result is irony, but also amnesia about what was written and said in the recent past. Consider the paradoxes we've witnessed.

We were paralyzed for a year over Ambassador Joe Wilson's carnival-like mission, in part due to the prompt of his wife at the CIA Valerie Plame, to find out whether Niger sold, or tried to sell, yellowcake to Saddam. Meanwhile unmentioned is the fact that all the time 1.2 million pounds of yellowcake continued to sit in a warehouse in pre- and postwar Iraq. We chose a special prosecutor to find the culprit who, in some sort of supposed conspiratorial retaliation to Wilson's flamboyant but erroneous claims, divulged the employment status of his wife. The result is that the special prosecutor found the culpable party, but ensured that he is free from indictment, and indicted and convicted the person who, we know, did not first divulge Ms. Plame's identity—the object of the original inquiry.

The war was initially damned as a naked effort to grab cheap, accessible Middle Eastern oil. The war is now damned as naïve and foolish in empowering our enemies to manipulate and sell high-priced Middle Eastern oil.

Iraq is considered a puppet state when its officials express a desire for a continued U.S. presence to transition it to full security; it is considered fully autonomous when one of its politicians talks of a desire for us to leave promptly.

Iraq was supposedly failing because it lacked the proper model of the truly multilateral, U.N.-fully- sanctioned, NATO-led effort in Afghanistan, where we fought al-Qaeda on the proper ground on which they had planned 9/11. And now? The failed war in Iraq has succeeded and the good war may have turned bad?

In 2003 al-Qaeda sent thousands of jihadists to Iraq in a supposedly brilliant effort to widen the war. We, in contrast, "took our eye off the ball" by fighting, defeating, humiliating, and routing them there. The defeated are seen as insightful; the victorious foolhardy, the only constant being what the United States does is always misdirected, what our enemies do consistently inspired.

In 2004 critics asked "Where is the Iraqi Karzai?"; in 2008 they will no doubt ask "Where is the Afghan Maliki?"

Afghanistan is still proof of the success of multilateralism? North Korea was once not, but now is? And Iran deserves direct unilateral U.S. diplomacy, and no longer multilateral European negotiation? Somehow the use of American "soft power" and "diplomacy" is never derided as unilateral; military action, even in concert with others, always so.

In 2005-6 the critique was (a) that our military didn't understand counterinsurgency, had too few troops, sidetracked maverick leaders like David Petraeus, and sought only a military solution, while (b) the Shiite-led Iraqi democracy had no oil-revenue-sharing plan, alienated and ostracized the Sunni tribes, and was a civilian front for Iranian-backed militias. In 2008 all those concerns either being now irrelevant or met, critics shifted to argue that the war was not worth the human and material cost, was responsible for the oil-price hike (although daily world oil production is greater than in 2003), and all the gains temporary.

In 2003, as a state legislator, Barack Obama opposed the war. In 2004, as a state legislator, Obama said, "There's not much of a difference between my position on Iraq and George Bush's position at this stage." In 2007, Sen. Obama said his desired pullback would lead to all U.S. troops gone from Iraq by March 2008. In spring 2008, he said his timetable of withdrawal would lead to all U.S. troops home within 16 months. In July 2008, he said his desired withdrawal would now be predicated on events on the ground and the recommendations of ground commanders in Iraq. In fall 2008, I suggest, candidate Obama will add that due to his consistent criticism we properly changed our policy in Iraq and found success, and so he would now be as careful in withdrawing troops according to military advice, as others who put them there were reckless in ignoring it.

In worry over Bush's alleged desire to invade or bomb a hostile and meddling Iran over its nuclear program and infiltration into Iraq, Barack Obama called instead for more diplomacy with Tehran at the highest levels. In worry over a friendly but meddling Pakistan, Obama called for unilaterally invading it.

I think a conventional narrative is slowly forming about Iraq something like the following:

I supported the successful three-week war. I opposed the flawed occupation. My principled criticism, however, led to the salvation of Iraq, which is important and necessary. Yet I did not support the idea of being in Iraq, but now don't oppose it either. My model of intervention in Afghanistan was the proper one; difficulties there are due either to others' improper implementation or an unwise diversion of resources to Iraq.

If the president employs unilateral action, he should be more multilateral; if multilateral, he is an outsourcer and should by more directly involved and unilateral.

Just remember the details of this narrative, monitor how it is modified to fit the daily pulse of the battlefield, and then almost everything we hear makes sense.

AUGUST 29, 2008

What Happened to Iraq?

So many opinions on the war, so few of them constant.

S uddenly there are no longer any more litmus tests—remember the Democratic primary bickering in autumn 2007?—over who was, and was not, always against the war in Iraq. There are no more hearings in which a Sen. Obama or Clinton seek to outdo each other in grandstanding condemnations of the war effort. We see no more discounted "General Betray-Us" ads in the *New York Times*. The protestors on our street corners have taken down the "No blood for oil!" signs and replaced them with "Hands off Iran!" placards. A Sen. Durbin or Rep. Murtha is quiet about supposed American war crimes and cruelty. That Barack Obama said he wanted all U.S. troops out by March 2008 is quietly forgotten.

In other words, it is now a good time to reflect back on the last five years of conventional wisdom about the war. When the histories of the Iraq War are written—in contrast to the dispatches published in mediis rebus by critical journalists and born-again antiwar critics—expect to see a much different narrative from the conventional ignorance that became the gospel these last five years.

THE GOOD VERSUS BAD WAR?

For years now, we have been lectured that Iraq was the hopeless unilateral preemptive war—one that diverted attention from Afghanistan, the proper multilateral retaliation. But the truth is that both were singular wars with their own particular challenges. Afghanistan remains uniquely difficult because, unlike Iraq, it is a landlocked, hard-to-supply tribal land with a nuclear Islamic neighbor, Pakistan, that provides almost perpetual sanctuary for cross-border terrorists.

That NATO and later the UN were involved in Afghanistan only meant that a Germany or France would make an appearance there in a way they did not in Iraq—not that they would fight shoulder-to-shoulder with America in real numbers and without restrictions. That several countries were deployed to Afghanistan under the aegis of NATO was of not much more significance than that others went to Iraq as a coalition of the willing. Note that as Iraq quiets, Afghanistan, with its particular challenges, does not necessarily thereby get any easier. Expect new sloganeering to replace "took our eye off the ball." In that regard, the expertise acquired in Iraq more likely will help—than the wear and tear on the military hindered—the efforts in Afghanistan. Without defeating al Qaeda in Iraq, the only other option to have met and engaged such Islamic terrorists in real numbers the last five years would have been to invade Pakistan.

THE RECORD OF THE U.S. MILITARY

The performance of our military in Iraq was never suspect, and our soldiers were hardly the terrorists, criminals, and storm troopers as implied at various times in slanders voiced by Sens. Durbin, Kennedy, and Kerry or Rep. Murtha—and in a series of failed and reprehensible Hollywood movies. Instead, the U.S. military removed the genocidal Saddam Hussein, stayed on to fight a second war and defeat and humiliate Al Qaeda, and fostered democracy in the heart of the ancient caliphate. Both the quality of our troops and the generalship of Gen. Petraeus matched anything in American military history, and will be recognized as such once the significance of their achievement is recognized.

The story of the National Guard was not one of exhausted and demoralized reservists, but of skilled, often more senior soldiers whose civilian expertise enhanced reconstruction at every turn, as anyone can attest who has seem them at work in Iraq.

HONORABLE (AND DISINGENUOUS) ANTIWAR OPPOSITION

There were two honorable positions in opposing the war. One was the hard left and paleoconservative opposition to an optional war for a variety of moral and practical considerations. When over 70 percent of the public favored the invasion, and such support even widened with the fall of Saddam's statue, most such critics nevertheless maintained their then unpopular opposition.

The second group of principled critics were those that confessed that the unforeseen opposition to reconstruction, evident by late 2003, convinced them, albeit belatedly, that the cost in blood and treasure would not be worth the goal of a democratic Iraq. During the optimism of the subsequent Iraqi elections, and the recent spectacular success of the surge, such critics still insisted the war was misguided and their newfound opposition irrevocable. Note here that revisionists did not blame others, or claim they were brainwashed, but simply acknowledged that their initial expectations were wrong and the war thus in retrospect unwise.

That said, there was certain reprehensibility to the positions of most other opportunistic critics, whose Protean fluidity was not even empirical, but rather, predicated on the 24-hour news cycle and the perceived pulse of the battlefield. Some were former neoconservative zealots, whose saber-rattling about Iraq dated back to the Clinton administration; but when the occupation became difficult, they not only withdrew their support as our troops came under fire, but claimed either that they were misled or, worse still, someone else was to blame.

An equally unfortunate but convenient claim for erstwhile pro-war pundits and politicians was that they were duped by hyped-up threats of WMD, and thus otherwise would have never supported the war. Remember, however, that the Congress authorized 23 reasons to remove Saddam, the majority or writs well beyond worries over WMD—a prewar consideration voiced by intelligence agencies as diverse as the French and Egyptians.

Rather than blaming Donald Rumsfeld or George Tenet, the principled position of the "my three-week perfect war was loused-up by your five-year occupation" critic would have been an honest admission that they underestimated the potential of Iraqi insurgency, and that even its defeat was simply not worth the commensurate American costs.

Instead, what we have now are dozens of loud, pick-and-choose opportunists who were for the war, then soured on it, then came back some during the purple-finger elections, then got angrier during the February 2006 insurgency, then damned the surge, then grew quiet during the Petraeus success—always, in retrospect, citing a particular past phase of their ongoing metamorphoses when it now seems to best amen the current status in Iraq.

Few recalled that the errors and miscalculations in Iraq paled in comparison to the tragic lapses in the Civil War, World War I, or World War II that cost the lives of tens of thousands, but nevertheless did not imperil eventual American victory. But in the utopian landscape of the contemporary West, Iraq—as is the case of almost every other contentious issue—followed the logic of what did not prove perfect could therefore not be good.

THE NO-MILITARY-SOLUTION CANARD

Any reasonable observer could make the banal observation that Iraq required a combination of political savvy to reunite various factions, and military force to kill or quiet the terrorists. In fact, only the U.S. military—and, in particular, its evolving tactics in 2007—provided the window of security necessary for Iraqi civilians to step up and participate in politics and economic reconstruction.

Yet, given the echo chamber in Washington, one could predict that almost anytime a DC politician pontificated that "there is no military solution in Iraq" at that exact moment there was a dire need for armed action to put down insurgents and terrorists to restart the political process.

In truth, the cumulative toll on al Qaeda over five years, the Anbar military awakening, David Petraeus's change of tactics and aggressive military innovations, and the surge of 30,000 additional fighters were as important to restoring stability to Iraq as earlier political lapses were to prompting the initial unrest.

THE WORST WHATEVER . . .

We have heard ad nauseam that Iraq was the worst—fill in any synonym for fiasco one wishes for Iraq. Given the long history of the United States—the terrible summer of 1864, the ill-preparedness before World War II, the naiveté about the postwar Soviet Union and Mao's China, the surprise and early flawed conduct of the Korean War, or the tragedy of Vietnam in 1973-5—such an appraisal was simply political hyperbole. In truth, in the present post-September 11 climate, Iraq always had the potential of making the war against Islamic extremism and terrorism much worse or much improved, depending on our ability to take out Saddam, and foster a constitutional replacement.

Note well that, as we look back to the landscape of 2001-3, we can now appreciate the present progress that we then did not anticipate. America has not been hit again—but not for want of trying on the part of dozens of terrorist plots. The two worst regimes in the Middle East are gone; constitutional states are in their place. Al Qaeda is discredited and in disarray, its leadership in large part dead, in hiding, or in captivity. Bin Laden's popularity and Middle Eastern support for suicide bombing—sky-high before Iraq, peaking during the Abu Ghraib hysteria—are now at all-time lows. European anti-American politicians are largely gone; governments in Germany and France are unusually pro-American. Boutique table-talk about distant American preemption has been replaced by elemental fears of Russian aggression and energy leverage on the frontiers of Europe. The European worry is not any more that the American Sheriff is popping off his six-shooter, but that he may have ridden out of town and left the timid townspeople to their own devices.

While it is popular to say that we are hated abroad, two billion in India and China are not particularly anti-American, and Eastern Europeans respect Americans more than their shaky Western European brethren. In short, if Iraq remains stable, support for the American effort to promote Iraqi freedom will grow in direct proportion to when it waned when many saw our setbacks as precursors for defeat.

Sadly, most have no ethical bearings, and wrongly judged our presence in Iraq in terms of wishing to identify with a winner and to distance themselves from a perceived loser. The irony, of course, is that in the months to come many abroad will begin to respect our support for Iraqi democracy only for the self-interested reasons that it proved successful rather than principled.

A final word about George W. Bush. It was not his rhetorical skills, political agility, or shared prewar intelligence that convinced old Democratic political pros, Washington analysts, and savvy pundits to support the attack on Saddam Hussein and to stay on and allow Iraq the chance at constitutional government. Instead, many, by their own logic and political calculations, came to the same conclusion as the president to remove Saddam. But whereas the president stayed the course, and suffered the dire consequences during dark times, not all of the latter did. And there will come a time, when Iraq is stable and successful, that this constancy of President Bush when most around him lost their heads also will be acknowledged—as it always has been in America's past wars, when history alone has the last word.

JULY 2, 2010

Afghanistan Agonistes

Obama needs to shake free of his past rhetoric, commit to our mission in Afghanistan, and give Petraeus a chance to do the job he has taken on.

T he growing consensus is that the United States and its NATO allies cannot prevail in their aim of creating a stable constitutional government in Afghanistan, free of radical Taliban insurrectionists who will facilitate terrorism beyond their borders and seek to reinstitute their medieval theocracy. We need to calm down and take a deep breath. Here are ten considerations that suggest that Afghanistan is hardly lost.

1. General Petraeus.
By all accounts he is an historic figure. Take his willingness to step down from Centcom, after achieving global fame, only to enter into the Inferno of Afghanistan, at a time when he has seen nonstop service and dealt with health issues—and when there is not much that can be added to his reputation but a great deal that might diminish it in Afghanistan.

All that is in marked contrast, for example, to the 2003 behavior of Gen. Tommy Franks, who did the opposite: He retired abruptly after basking in the glow of a three-week victory—even as he saw the insurgency brewing—seemingly in order to capitalize on his newfound and transitory fame. Petraeus's moral capital and past successes are worth a great deal, here and abroad, and bring a new dimension to the struggle—even though he will be apparently working with diplomatic personnel quite unlike the gifted and selfless Ryan Crocker.

Remember, he surged in Iraq without the sort of wide-scale criticism over his rules of engagement that has been directed at current counterinsurgency methods in Afghanistan. Again, for a national icon to willingly step down into the fray, when conventional wisdom is writing Afghanistan off, and under the aegis of former senators—Biden, Clinton, Obama—who deprecated his efforts when he most needed public support is nothing short of heroic. And that too will help for a while in rallying military and civilian opinion behind the effort.

2.   The mission.
President Obama needs to remind America of the mission. We seek to foster a stable constitutional system in Afghanistan that will keep radical Islamists from offering sanctuary to international terrorists. That is our main objective. Shutting down the opium industry, fostering a civil society that does not butcher its own, and enlisting the support of Pakistan to stop terrorism—all these are important corollaries and aid our objective, but are ipsis factis not the main reason why we are fighting in Afghanistan. For nearly a decade, those on the left have simply defined Afghanistan as not Iraq and left it at that—without telling us why in fact they would fight the "good war." Now they must do so without invoking Bush or Iraq: We need to hear from the president what Afghanistan is, rather than what it is not.

3.   Losses.
We have suffered tragic deaths, but they must be seen through the prism of other, far more lethal and difficult conflicts. Through 2007, America had lost cumulatively about the same number of troops in Afghanistan that we lost in just that one year in Iraq. Indeed, in the single year 2004—three years after the war began in Afghanistan—America had lost a total of 52 soldiers; in contrast, in 2006, similarly three years after the commencement of the Iraq war, 822 were killed in Iraq—a figure

15 times higher. The total American fatalities in nearly nine years are 1,130—less than 2 percent of those lost in Vietnam. Afghanistan is no Iraq, much less a Vietnam. In a war nearly a decade long, the United States has been remarkably adept in not losing its soldiers.

4. *Karzai in perspective.*

Yes, the Karzai government is probably corrupt. But not long ago, during the relative quiet of the mid-2000s, we openly wondered of Iraq, "Where is the Iraqi Karzai?"—as if Iraq might yet be salvaged if only we had an ally of the sort we counted on in Kabul. Apparently that is why, in 2004, the Liberty Medal—past recipients include the likes of Mikhail Gorbachev, Colin Powell, and Kofi Annan—was bestowed upon Hamid Karzai. He cannot have been so good in 2004 only to suddenly have become so bad in 2010. In fact, he is mostly what he always was, an Afghan pragmatist who follows his own perceptions of relative American strength, especially the degree to which we seem to be winning or losing. Meanwhile, the Taliban has been out of power for nearly nine years, and most Afghans have gotten used to its not being around.

5. *Afghanistan was not always so.*

We hear that the country has always been ungovernable. But the British achieved their aims between 1878 and 1919 in preventing chaos. Russia's disaster is often evoked, but its decade-long misadventure brought on an odd alliance among China, Pakistan, most of the Arab world, and the United States, which all poured in supplies and in some cases manpower to aid the Taliban. Nothing analogous to all that is now happening. The present planned surge of 30,000 alone is probably three times larger than the Taliban's insurgent forces, which have little international support. Afghanistan for the half-century between 1919 and 1973 was sustainable, when a decentralized constitutional monarchy made it as stable as any society in that rather rough region. Just as Iraq is a more sane place than soon-to-be-nuclear Iran, so too Afghanistan can be stable in comparison to nuclear Pakistan—explaining why both those neighbors are to varying degrees invested in seeing us not succeed in either country.

6. *Eye off the ball?*

Nor does the conventional charge that we "took our eye off the ball" quite explain the upsurge in violence. Afghanistan was relatively quiet when Iraq was most violent and was drawing in enormous amounts of our money and manpower; it oddly started to heat up when Iraq slowly began to quiet down. We forget that radical Islamists have mostly lost in Iraq. Apparently, however, that setback has rallied the Taliban and discouraged us, the winners—when the opposite should have been more likely. At some point, historians will remark that the United States succeeded in preventing another 9/11-like attack for nearly a decade when that was once thought impossible (e.g., "Not if, but when"), deposed a murderous regime in Iraq and offered its people a real chance of consensual government, and rid Afghanistan of a barbaric regime that fostered deadly international terrorism. We are doing well, then, on two fronts, and it would be a mistake to give up on the third.

7. *Executive inconsistency.*

President Obama campaigned on the good-war/bad-war false dichotomy, and so in 2009 got caught off guard. Indeed, by late 2007, candidate Obama was promising that he would end Bush's unnecessary war and reenergize the necessary effort in Afghanistan—approved by the UN and NATO and directed against many of the architects of 9/11. Apparently, Obama assumed as president that Afghanistan would stay quiet and that Iraq was lost. Suddenly, reality turned his campaign rhetoric upside down, as Obama could no longer be a peace icon by ending the supposedly bad Iraq war, but instead had to step up and assume a Churchillian persona to keep his promises to focus on Afghanistan and defeat the Taliban. As a senator seeking to realize his presidential hopes, Obama used fierce antiwar rhetoric about the doomed nature of the surge and about General Petraeus as a naïve proponent of the impossible. Obama must now, as president, bring in that same Petraeus to surge in Afghanistan. All these paradoxes, along with artificial deadlines for withdrawal, convey the sense that the commander-in-chief is not fully committed to a successful Afghan strategy. The window for blaming Bush for Afghanistan has long been closed, and we will do far better when the administration accepts this.

8. *Diplomatic mess.*

The result of all this confusion has been 18 months of loud rhetoric about "fixing" Afghanistan, as a disengaged president has outsourced the war to a number of different interests and dithered both on adopting a strategy and on consulting with General McChrystal, his own appointee as ground-forces commander in Afghanistan. During the Bush administration, Ryan Crocker and Zalmay Khalilzad worked well with both our senior military command and the Afghan government; they brought confidence to our diplomatic mission in Kabul and the region at large. In contrast, our current ambassador, General Eikenberry, and Obama's "special representative," Richard Holbrooke, have alienated both. Should we find one—and only one—diplomat who can partner with both General Petraeus and President Karzai, things will improve.

9. *Obama's advantages.*

The fact is that Obama enjoys several advantages that George W. Bush did not have. The Left, for all its sniping, will not so easily sacrifice its agenda on the altar of antiwar rhetoric. So we will see no "General Betray Us" ads or acrimonious confirmation hearings on Afghan appointments. IEDs in Afghanistan will no longer be on the front pages of our newspapers. It is also a truism that Democratic commanders-in-chief are more immune from wartime criticism of the sort that can become hysterical against Republican presidents. Wilson, FDR, Truman, Kennedy, LBJ (for a time), and Clinton were all seen as reluctant warriors in a way Nixon and the Bushes were not.

In short, the *New York Times*, the *Washington Post*, NPR, *Time* and *Newsweek*, the major networks, and PBS will not cover Afghanistan in the manner they did Iraq. Why endanger cap-and-trade or amnesty for illegal aliens by emphasizing the weekly body count, when the media know well that such attention is an effective mechanism for destroying a presidency? All of that translates into a greater unity and empathy for the problems we face in Afghanistan.

10. *We have no choice but victory.*

A failure in Afghanistan will reenergize radical Islam, as did the Soviet defeat, with implications that will affect everything from the current quiet in Iraq and the nuclearization of Iran to the behavior of Turkey, and the chances of more terrorist attacks within the United States. Failed invasions are more grievous even than lost battles. Those who think we can just leave Afghanistan and call it quits are sorely mistaken. Fairly or not, we are well beyond that: Either we stabilize the country, with all the accruing advantages from that achievement, or we withdraw in defeat and expect to reap a bitter harvest from that defeat.

SEPTEMBER 9, 2010

October Surprises

Will the Obama administration tackle Iran's nuclear ambitions?

In less than 60 days, the Democrats will probably suffer historic losses in both the House and the Senate. The eleventh-hour campaigning of the now-unpopular Barack Obama on behalf of endangered congressional candidates will not change much. In fact, most embattled Democratic candidates don't want the president to even set foot in their districts.

The public knows that the stimulus packages are played out. Unemployment rose, instead of falling as promised. All that is left are the higher taxes due next year to pay back the borrowed money that was squandered. Those in Congress who went along with the Obama borrowing agenda now find themselves on the wrong side of the American people on almost every issue—from federalized health care, higher taxes, and bailouts to proposed cap-and-trade and amnesty.

Could things still turn around before November? The Democrats' best hope is a major crisis overseas that would rally the American public around their commander-in-chief. Usually, cynical journalists refer to an unexpected autumn bombing run, missile launch, or presidential announcement of a cease-fire or needed escalation as an "October surprise."

These are the "wag the dog" moments that might turn angry Americans' thoughts elsewhere. And they have a checkered history that began long before August 1998, when critics alleged that Bill Clinton, before the midterm elections, had ordered bombing missions in Afghanistan and Sudan to distract public attention from his embarrassing dalliance with Monica Lewinsky in the Oval Office. He looked decisive and presidential; his Republican opponents looked nitpicking and petty. Abraham Lincoln could have lost the 1864 election to peace candidate Gen. George McClellan, given that over the summer Gen. Ulysses S. Grant had almost ruined the Army of the Potomac without taking the Confederate capital of Richmond. Then, suddenly, Gen. William Tecumseh Sherman captured Atlanta on Sept. 2. Overnight, Lincoln went from an inept bumbler to a winning commander-in-chief. An exasperated McClellan never recovered.

Less than two weeks before the 1972 election, national security advisor Henry Kissinger, without warning, announced that "peace is at hand" in Vietnam (it was not). Democratic nominee George McGovern would have lost anyway to Richard Nixon, but his peace candidacy abruptly appeared redundant.

Suspicious liberals were convinced that in 2004 George W. Bush would pull off some sort of surprise to distract voters from the bad news in Iraq. A year before the election, a paranoid Madeleine Albright, the former secretary of state, floated a crazy suggestion: "Do you suppose that the Bush administration has Osama bin Laden hidden away somewhere and will bring him out before the election?"

In panic over the depressing polls, Obama is now scrambling to find any good news overseas that he can, to turn voter attention away from near-10 percent unemployment and record debt. He has just addressed the nation about the long-scheduled troop reductions in Iraq. And suddenly, all Mideast leaders are now equally welcome at the White House in hopes of reaching a dramatic Israeli-Palestinian breakthrough that would showcase his presidential leadership before the midterm elections.

Neither of these events is likely to change things in November.

Only a headline crisis could rally Americans around their now-unpopular commander-in-chief and his beleaguered supporters in Congress. What would that entail? Most probably something like a showdown with soon-to-be-nuclear and widely despised Iran.

As a candidate, Obama criticized the Bush administration for not reaching out and talking with Iran's theocratic leadership. As president, Obama has done that. He even muted his criticism of the brutal Iranian crackdown on pro-democracy demonstrations after the 2009 election. But Obama soon found that the Iranians saw his outreach as appeasement, and so only increased their breakneck efforts to get a bomb.

Now everyone from the Israelis to the Sunni Arab nations is pressuring the United States to do something before a radical and nuclear Iran changes the complexion of the entire Middle East. If the erstwhile peace candidate Barack Obama were to confront Iran, conservatives might well support his resolve. Then Democratic candidates would find a more united nation that was suddenly far more worried about Mideast Armageddon than unemployment and record deficits. Unlike past October surprises, in this one the pro-Obama media would probably be far less cynical in its coverage of presidential motives.

But Iran won't go nuclear in the next two months. So let us hope that the current unpopular administration waits for a while before deciding between the rotten choice of using military force against Tehran and the even worse alternative of a nuclear Iran.

CHAPTER FOUR

ON HATING ISRAEL

JANUARY 14, 2008

Nonviolence Nonsense

Gandhi, again.

T hose who do not necessarily associate the name Gandhi with either humanitarian brotherhood or wisdom, and those who remember Mahatma's idiotic thoughts about those facing the Holocaust ought to examine the latest Gandhi take on "the Jews" in the online edition of the *Washington Post*, this time from one Arun Gandhi.

He is self-identified as the "President and co-founder of the M.K. Gandhi Institute for Nonviolence" and "the fifth grandson of India's legendary leader, Mohandas K. "Mahatma" Gandhi. He is president and co-founder of the M. K. Gandhi Institute for Nonviolence, now at the University of Rochester in New York." In the Post, he writes:

The holocaust was the result of the warped mind of an individual who was able to influence his followers into doing something dreadful. But, it seems to me the Jews today not only want the Germans to feel guilty but the whole world must regret what happened to the Jews. The world did feel sorry for the episode but when an individual or a nation refuses to forgive and move on the regret turns into anger... We have created a culture of violence (Israel and the Jews are the biggest players) and that Culture of Violence is eventually going to destroy humanity...

Everything in that brief excerpt is untrue for the following reasons:

1. The Holocaust was not just Hitler and a few SS "followers"; rather, it involved millions of followers (some of whom were active, some of whom were passive) in a systematic and near successful genocide of an entire people.

Neither Hitler, nor Himmler, nor Goebbels, nor any of the Nazi hierarchy could have wrought what they did without millions of

German non-party guards, railroad employees, informants, and clerks and bureaucrats in the industry of death. Tragically this complaisance did not happen over night, but was prepped by years of National Socialist indoctrination that systematically and incrementally whipped up centuries old anti-Semitism by blaming—take note here, Mr. Gandhi—"the Jews" as being the "biggest players" in the world's violence and problems.

2. Gandhi makes an incredibly asinine suggestion when he says, "But, it seems to me the Jews today not only want the Germans to feel guilty but the whole world must regret what happened to the Jews." Should the whole world not "regret" what happened to the Jews? Maybe sorta, kinda regret it? Are the Germans not supposed to feel guilty about the loss of six million under their auspices? And if all this should not be, as Gandhi implies, then is his assumed antithesis then correct? To illustrate, try this counterfactual: "But it seems to me the Jews today should not only not want the Germans to feel guilty, but the whole world must not regret what happened to the Jews."

3. "The world did feel sorry for the episode but when an individual or a nation refuses to forgive and move on the regret turns into anger." Creating an autonomous, self-sufficient nation, as well as the only liberal democracy in the Middle East, seems to qualify as both forgiving and moving on. Yet after five major wars against Israel since 1947, it is apparent that its neighbors can neither forgive its creation nor move on to accept its existence. And what exactly does "regret turns into anger" mean? Is it anger such as blowing up civilians through suicide attacks, rocketing day-care centers from 'liberated' Gaza—or writing puerile, half-educated homilies, like Gandhi's, from a "nonviolence" center on an American college campus?

4. "We have created a culture of violence (Israel and the Jews are the biggest players) and that Culture of Violence is eventually going to destroy humanity."

Despite the scare capitals, I doubt whether Israel and "the Jews" are "the biggest players." All one has to do is tally up the numbers murdered in the last decade in India, Pakistan, Rwanda, Darfur, Somalia, Nigeria, Congo, Chechnya, the Balkans, (and the list goes on), and discover that "the Jews" are pretty much bit players. If Mr. Gandhi disputes that, then let him produce evidence that shadowy "Jews" or "Israel" were, in fact, involved in the above various slaughters. If the "Culture of Violence is eventually going to destroy humanity," then I suggest such an assumed Armageddon most likely will begin either along the India/Pakistan border where two nuclear-armed countries share an existential hatred of each other—or it will emanate from Iran, which has promised to wipe out Israel. Clearly, Mr. Gandhi could do far more for world peace by leaving the University of Rochester and proselytizing against violence in the field, perhaps either in Waziristan or Teheran.

Moreover, it is worth noting, had anyone on a university campus written anything comparable about "the Arabs" and Islam, there would very likely be outrage rather than the present silence.

In this regard, one should remember that Gandhi primus offered to almost everyone from the British to the "Jews" his wisdom of nonviolent resistance to Hitler, suggesting that the slaughter might be a valuable lesson in humanitarian martyrdom. But then his own modalities were put into practice against a post-Victorian liberal Britain, not the Third Reich or Stalin's collectivization project.

To put Arun Gandhi's present musings in proper context, I leave you with an excerpt, somewhat similar in spirit, from his grandfather's famous 1938 essay, "The Jews," offering advice to the Jews of Germany about how to achieve "joy" (note the key counter-factual "If I were…") through mass annihilation.

"If I were a Jew and were born in Germany and earned my livelihood there, I would claim Germany as my home even as the tallest gentile German may, and challenge him to shoot me or cast me in the dungeon; I would refuse to be expelled or to submit to discriminating treatment. And for doing this, I should not wait for the fellow Jews to join me in civil resistance but would have confidence that in the end the rest are bound to follow my example. If one Jew or all the Jews were to accept the prescription here offered, he or they cannot be worse off than now. And suffering voluntarily undergone will bring them an inner strength and joy which no number of resolutions of sympathy passed in the world outside Germany can. Indeed, even if Britain, France and America were to declare hostilities against Germany, they can bring no inner joy, no inner strength. The calculated violence of Hitler may even result in a general massacre of the Jews by way of his first answer to the declaration of such hostilities. But if the Jewish mind could be prepared for voluntary suffering, even the massacre I have imagined could be turned into a day of thanksgiving and joy that Jehovah had wrought deliverance of the race even at the hands of the tyrant. For to the god-fearing, death has no terror. It is a joyful sleep to be followed by a waking that would be all the more refreshing for the long sleep. It is hardly necessary for me to point out that it is easier for the Jews than for the Czechs to follow my prescription."

It is commonplace to compare our present complaisance about the dangers of radical Islam to the liberal democracies' past failure to galvanize against the creed of fascist Europe. Much of what has been written since 9/11 (one can also compare the naiveté of Mr. Arun Gandhi on that as well) is both dangerous and silly—but no more so than what was offered up in the late 1930s.

The more things change, the more they stay the same.

JANUARY 29, 2008

A Modest Proposal for Middle East Peace

The U.N. need only take five simple steps.

There seems to be a growing renewed animus against Israel lately. Arun Gandhi, grandson of the purported humanist Mahatma Gandhi, thinks Israel and Jews in general are prone to, and singularly responsible for, most of the world's violence. The Oxford Union is taking up the question of whether Israel even has a right to continue to exist. Our generation no longer speaks of a "Palestinian problem," but rather of an "Israeli problem." So perhaps it is time for a new global approach to deal with Israel and its occupation.

Perhaps we ought to broaden our multinational and multicultural horizons by transcending the old comprehensive settlements, roadmaps, and Quartet when dealing with the Israeli-Palestinian dispute, a dispute which originated with the creation of Israel. Why not simply hold an international conference on all of these issues—albeit in a far more global context, outside the Middle East?

The ensuing general accords and principles could be applied to Israel and the West Bank, where the number of people involved, the casualties incurred, and the number of refugees affected are far smaller and far more manageable.

Perhaps there could be five U.N. sessions: disputed capitals; the right of return for refugees; land under occupation; the creation of artificial post-World War II states; and the use of inordinate force against suspected Islamic terrorists.

In the first session, we should try to solve the status of Nicosia, which is currently divided into Greek and Turkish sectors by a U.N. Greek Line. Perhaps European Union investigators could adjudicate Turkish claims that the division originated from unwarranted threats to the Turkish Muslim population on Cyprus. Some sort of big power or U.N. roadmap then might be imposed on the two parties, in hopes that the Nicosia solution would work for Jerusalem as well.

In the second discussion, diplomats might find common ground about displaced populations, many from the post-war, late 1940s. Perhaps it would be best to start with the millions of Germans who were expelled from East Prussia in 1945, or Indians who were uprooted from ancestral homes in what is now Pakistan, or over half-a-million Jews that were ethnically cleansed from Egypt, Jordan, Iraq, and Syria following the 1967 war. Where are these refugees now? Were they ever adequately compensated for lost property and damages? Can they be given promises of the right to return to their ancestral homes under protection of their host countries? The ensuing solutions might shed light on the Palestinian aspirations to return to land lost sixty years ago to Israel.

A third panel would take up the delicate issue of returning territory lost by defeat in war. Ten percent of historic Germany is now part of Poland. The Russians still occupy many of the Kurile Islands, and Greek Cyprus lost sizable territory in 1974 after the invasion by Turkey. The Western Sahara is still annexed by Morocco, while over 15 percent of disputed Azerbaijan has been controlled by Armenia since 1994. Additionally, all of independent Tibet has been under Chinese occupation since 1950-1. Surely if some general framework concerning these occupations could first be worked out comprehensively, the results might then be applied to the much smaller West Bank and Golan Heights.

In a fourth panel, the international conference should take up the thorny issue of recently artificially created states. Given the tension over Kashmir, was Pakistan a mistake—particularly the notion of a homeland for Indian Muslims? North Korea was only created after the stalemate of 1950-3; so should we debate whether this rogue nation still needs to exist, given its violent history and threats to world peace?

Fifth, and finally, is there a global propensity to use inordinate force against Muslim terrorists that results in indiscriminate collateral damage? The Russians during the second Chechnyan War of 1999-2000 reportedly sent tactical missiles into the very core of Grozny, and may have killed tens of thousands of civilians in their hunt for Chechnyan terrorists—explaining why the United Nations later called that city the most destroyed city on earth. Syria has never admitted to the complete destruction of Hama, once home to Muslim Brotherhood terrorists. The city suffered the fate of Carthage and was completely obliterated in 1982 by the al-Assad government, with over 30,000 missing or killed. Did the Indian government look the other way in 2002 when hundreds of Muslim civilians in Gujarat were killed in reprisal for Islamic violence against Hindus? The lessons learned in this final session might reassure a world still furious over the 52 Palestinians lost in Jenin.

In other words, after a half-century of failed attempts to solve the Middle East crisis in isolation, isn't it time we look for guidance in a far more global fashion, and in contexts where more lives have been lost, more territory annexed, and more people made refugees in places as diverse as China, Russia, and the broader Middle East?

The solutions that these countries have worked out to deal with similar problems apparently have proven successful—at least if the inattention of the world, the apparent inaction of the United Nations, and the relative silence of European governments are any indication.

So let the international community begin its humanitarian work! Greek Cypriots can advise Israel about concessions necessary to Muslims involving a divided Jerusalem. Russians and Syrians can advise the IDF on how to deal properly and humanely with Islamic terrorists. Poland, Russia, China, and Armenia might offer the proper blueprint for giving back land to the defeated that they once gained by force. A North Korea or Pakistan can offer Israel humanitarian lessons that might blunt criticisms that such a recently created country has no right to exist. Iraq and Egypt would lend insight about proper reparation and the rights of return, given its own successful solutions to the problems of their own fleeing Jewish communities.

But why limit the agenda to such a small array of issues? The world has much to teach Israel about humility and concessions, on issues ranging from how other countries in the past have dealt with missiles sent into their homeland, to cross-border incursions by bellicose neighbors.

No doubt, Middle East humanitarians such as Jimmy Carter, Arun Gandhi, and Tariq Ramadan could preside, drawing on and offering their collective past wisdom in solving such global problems to those of a lesser magnitude along the West Bank.

JANUARY 3, 2009

The Gaza Rules

Completely at odds with the past protocols of war.

The Israelis just struck back hard at Hamas in Gaza. In response, the United Nations, the European Union and the Arab world (at least publicly) expressed their anger at the killing of over 300 Palestinians, most of whom were terrorists and Hamas officials.

For several prior weeks, Hamas terrorists had been daily launching rockets into Israeli towns that border Gaza. The recent volleys of missiles had insidiously become more frequent—up to 80 a day—and the payloads larger. Iranian-backed Hezbollah terrorists were reportedly supplying their own training and expertise.

These terrorists point to the Lebanon war of 2006 as the proper template for provoking an Israeli counter-response that will bog down the Israeli Defense Forces in the streets of urban Gaza and ensure that Palestinian civilians are harmed on global television.

Watching both this week's war and the world's predictable reaction to it, we can recall the Gaza rules. Most are reflections of our post-modern age, and completely at odds with the past protocols of war. First is the now-familiar Middle East doctrine of proportionality. Legitimate military action is strangely defined by the relative strength of the combatants. World opinion more vehemently condemns Israel's counter-measures, apparently because its rockets are far more accurate and deadly than previous Hamas barrages that are poorly targeted and thus not so lethal.

If America had accepted such rules in, say, World War II, then by late 1944 we, not the Axis, would have been the culpable party, since by then once-aggressive German, Italian, and Japanese forces were increasingly on the defensive and far less lethal than the Allies.

Second, intent in this war no longer matters. Every Hamas unguided rocket is launched in hopes of hitting an Israeli home and killing men, women, and children. Every guided Israeli air-launched missile is targeted at Hamas operatives, who deliberately work in the closest vicinity to women and children. Killing Palestinian civilians is incidental to Israeli military operations and proves counterproductive to its objectives. Blowing up Israeli non-combatants is the aim of Hamas' barrages: the more children, aged, and women who die, the more it expects political concessions from Tel Aviv.

By this logic, the 1999 American bombing of Belgrade—aimed at stopping the genocide of Slobodan Milosevic—was, because of collateral damage, the moral equivalent of the carefully planned Serbian massacres of Muslim civilians at Srebrenica in 1995. Third, culpability is irrelevant. The "truce" between Israel and Hamas was broken once

Hamas got its hands on new stockpiles of longer-range mobile rockets—weapons that are intended to go over Israel's border walls.

Yet, according to the Gaza rules, both sides always deserve equal blame. Indeed, this weird war mimics the politically correct, zero-tolerance policies of our public schools, where both the bully and his victim are suspended once physical violence occurs. According to such morally equivalent reasoning, World War II was only a tragedy, not a result of German aggression. Once the dead mounted up, it mattered little what were the catalysts of the outbreak of fighting.

Fourth, with instantaneous streaming video from the impact sites in Gaza, context becomes meaningless. Our attention is glued to the violence of the last hour, not that of the last month that incited the war. Israel withdrew from Gaza in 2005 to great expectations that the Palestinians there would combine their new autonomy, some existing infrastructure left behind by the Israelis, Middle East oil money and American pressure for free and open elections to craft a peaceful, prosperous democracy.

The world hoped that Gaza might thrive first, and then later adjudicate its ongoing disputes with Israel through diplomacy. Instead, the withdrawal was seen not as a welcome Israeli concession, but as a sign of newfound Jewish weakness—and that the intifada tactics that had liberated Gaza could be amplified into a new war to end the Zionist entity itself.

Fifth and finally, victimization is crucial. Hamas daily sends barrages into Israel, as its hooded thugs thump their chests and brag of their radical Islamic militancy. But when the payback comes, suddenly warriors are transmogrified into weeping victims, posing teary-eyed for the news camera as they deplore "genocide" and "the Palestinian Holocaust." At least the Japanese militarists did not cry out to the League of Nations for help once mean Marines landed on Iwo Jima.

By now, these Gaza asymmetrical rules are old hat. We know why they persist—worldwide fear of Islamic terrorism, easy anti-Westernism, the old anti-Semitism, and global strategic calculations about Middle East oil—but it still doesn't make them right.

JUNE 4, 2009

The Age of Middle East Atonement

Therapeutic efforts to disguise the truth never really work.

P resident Obama made an earnest effort—as is his way in matters of discord—to split the difference with the Islamic world. His speech essentially amounted to: "We did that, you did this, tit-for-tat, now we're even, and can't we all just get along?" He should be congratulated for expressing a desire for peace and for gently reminding the Muslim world of the way to reform, even if he did so while inflating Western sins.

But the problem with such moral equivalence is that it equates things that are, well, not equal—and therefore ends up not being moral at all. To pull it off, one must distort both the past and the present for the presumed higher good of getting along. In the 1930s, British intellectuals performed feats of intellectual gymnastics in trying to contextualize Hitler's complaints against the Versailles Treaty, assignment of guilt for the First World War, and French bellicosity—straining to overlook the intrinsic dangers of National Socialism for the higher good of avoiding another Somme. Over the short term, such revisionism worked; over the longer term, it ensured a highly destructive war.

Whatever a well-meaning President Obama thinks, occasional American outbursts against Muslims are not analogous with the terrorism directed at Westerners or the hostility toward Christianity shown in most of the Muslim world. Try flying into Saudi Arabia with a Bible, as compared to traveling to San Francisco with a Koran. One can easily forsake Christianity; one can never safely leave Islam. European worries about headscarves are not the equivalent of the Gulf states' harassment of practicing Christians. Sorry, they're just not.

Pace Obama, Arab learning in the Middle Ages, while impressive, did not really fuel either the Renaissance or the Enlightenment. If anything, the arrival in Europe of the learned of Byzantium fleeing Islam over two centuries was a far stronger catalyst for rediscovery of classical values, while enlightened European sympathy for Balkan peoples enslaved by the Ottomans rekindled romantic interest in Hellenism in the 18th and 19th centuries. Colonialism and the Cold War—both of which have now been over for decades—do not account for present Arab pathologies. The far more pernicious Baathism, Nasserism, Pan-Arabism, and Islamism were all efforts, in varying degrees, to graft ideas of European socialism and Communism onto indigenous Arab and Muslim roots.

Today, Russia and China are much harder on Muslims than is the West. (Consider Russia's actions in Chechnya and China's treatment of the Uighurs.) Neither country pays any attention to Muslims' grievances, and therefore Muslims respect and fear Russia and China far more than they do the United States. There are no Arab coffeehouse discussions today about the nearly 1 million Muslims killed over two decades by the Soviets in Afghanistan and the Russian government in Chechnya, yet there is constant haranguing over Abu Ghraib, where not a single inmate was killed by rogue American guards. In short, neither logic nor morality is in abundance on the Arab Street, and conjuring up American felonies will not change that.

"On the one hand, on the other hand"—what Greek rhetoricians knew as men/de—when delivered in mellifluous tones, can suggest a path to reconciliation. But denial of fundamental differences leads nowhere. Our problems with the Middle East will dissipate, as have to varying degrees our problems with Japan, Southeast Asia, South Korea, and South America, when the region adopts, in part or in toto, open markets, consensual government, and human rights. Until then, we are in an uneasy and dangerous waiting period.

Conflating Western misdemeanors with Middle Eastern felonies is classical conflict-resolution theory, and laudably magnanimous. But privately the world knows that Muslims are treated better in the West than Christians are in Muslim countries. That Muslims migrate to the lands of Westerners, and not vice versa. That disputes over a border between Palestinians and Israelis do not explain the unhappiness of the Arab masses, suffering from state-caused poverty and wretchedness. That American military assistance to Afghanistan, Bosnia, Kosovo,

Kuwait, and Somalia, direct aid to Egypt, Jordan, and the Palestinians, and moral condemnation of Chinese, Russian, and Balkan treatment of Muslims, coupled with a generous U.S. immigration policy, are not really cause for apology or atonement. In short, few Arab leaders wish to give a "speech to the West." They would have to take responsibility, directly or indirectly, for either fostering or appeasing radical Islam, while denying their culpability for its decades of mass murdering. They would also have to lament the global economic havoc caused in part by oil cartels and energy price-fixing.

President Obama's intent is noble, but therapeutic efforts to disguise the truth never really work. We will see how the short-term good created by his therapeutic speechmaking compares to the long-term harm caused by telling the Muslim world, once again, that its problems were largely created by us—and, therefore, that we are largely responsible for providing the remedies.

Neither is true.

JUNE 4, 2009

Helen Thomas, Turkey, and the Liberation of Israel

The world cares deeply about refugees, disputed territory, and divided cities—when Israel is involved. Otherwise, otherwise.

I t is hard to become much more influential than the doyen of the White House press corps, who is given a ceremonial front-rows seat at press briefings and press conferences. So when Helen Thomas suggested that the Israelis should leave their country and "go home" to Poland and Germany, this was not some obscure, eccentric anti-Semite, but a liberal insider who has come to enjoy iconic status and a sense of exemption from criticism. Note that Ms. Thomas did not call for just a West Bank free of Jews. And she did not just wish for the elimination of the nation of Israel itself. Rather, Thomas envisions the departure of Israelis to the sites of the major death camps seven decades ago where six million Jews were gassed.

Turkey's role in aiding and abetting the flotilla, and its subsequent anti-Israeli outbursts, were excessive even by the often sick standards of the Middle East—but not exactly new. State-run Turkish television has aired virulent anti-Semitic dramas like the 2006 Valley of the Wolves, in which a Jewish doctor harvests organs from captured Iraqi civilians. Former Turkish prime minister Necmettin Erbakan once claimed that the Jews had instigated World War I in order to create Israel. Israel, Erbakan further asserted, in full-blown Hitlerian prose, was a "disease" and a "bacteria" that needed to be eradicated. The current prime minister, Recep Tayyip Erdogan, talks of sending in the Turkish fleet to confront the Israeli blockade, says he is sick of Israeli lies, and warns that his new Turkey is not "a young and rootless nation," as Israel presumably is (note the code word "rootless"). So speaks our NATO partner and EU wannabe. This week, in reaction to criticism from the West, Erdogan labeled such concerns "dirty propaganda"—note well, not just propaganda but a "dirty" sort.

In an odd way, Thomas's sick suggestions and Turkey's new Islamist and vehemently anti-Israel foreign policy will have a liberating effect on Israel. After all, if the ceremonial head of the White House press corps wants Israel's citizens either gone or dead, there is a legitimate suspicion that things are not quite right in the capital of Israel's staunchest ally. And if the most secular, democratic, and pro-Western Muslim country in the Middle East wishes to pick a fight to prove its Muslim fides, then there is not much hope that Israel is going to win over anyone else in that region.

Anti-Semitism as displayed by both Thomas and Turkey's leaders is not predicated on criticizing Israel, much less disagreeing with its foreign policy. Instead, it hinges upon focusing singularly on Israeli behavior, and applying a standard to it that is never extended to any other nation. There are plenty of disputes over borders and land in the world. But to Helen Thomas or the Turkish government, Kashmir or the

Russian-Chinese border matters little—although the chances of escalation to nuclear confrontation are far greater there than on the West Bank. Has Thomas ever popped off, "Why don't those Chinese just get the hell out of Tibet?" or "Why don't those Indians just get out of Kashmir?" The Palestinian "refugees"—a majority of whom are the children, grandchildren, or great-grandchildren of people actually displaced in 1948—compose a small part of the world's refugee population. There are millions of refugees in Rwanda, the Congo, and Darfur. Well over a half-million Jews were ethnically cleansed from the major Arab capitals between 1947 and 1973, each wave of expulsion cresting after a particular Mideast war. Again, few care to demonstrate for the plight of any of these people. Prime Minister Erdogan has not led any global effort to relocate the starving millions in Darfur, despite his loud concern for "refugees" in Gaza. The United States gives far more millions of dollars in aid to the Palestinians than does their Muslim protector in Turkey, who saves cash in winning Palestinian support by practicing anti-Semitism on the cheap. Nor have I heard of any German suicide bomber blowing himself up over lost ancestral land in Danzig or East Prussia, although that land was lost about the same time as some Palestinians left Israel. Few worry that in 1949 tens of thousands of Japanese were forcibly expelled by the Soviet Union from Sakhalin Island.

The world likewise cares little for the concept of "occupation" in the abstract; it is only the concrete example of Palestine that earns its opprobrium. We can be assured that President Obama will not bring up Ossetia with President Putin. He will not raise the question of Tibet with the Chinese or occupied Cyprus with Prime Minister Erdogan. Will Helen Thomas ever ask, "How can Turkey be allowed to keep Nicosia a divided city?" Will she worry whether Greeks are allowed to buy property in the Turkish sector of that capital?

There is no European outcry over the slaughter of South Koreans in a torpedo attack by a North Korean vessel. I don't recall President Sarkozy weighing in on that particular moral issue. The United Nations is angrier at Israel for enforcing a blockade against its terrorist neighbor than it is at Somalia for allowing pirates to kill and rob right off its coast. There was not much of a global outcry when Iran hijacked a

British naval vessel; few in Turkey demonstrated when the French blew up a Greenpeace protest vessel.

"Disproportionate" is a term used to condemn Israeli retaliation. It does not apply to other, far more violent reprisals, such as the Russian leveling of Grozny, or the Turkish killing of Kurds, or occasional Hindu mass rioting and murdering of Muslims in India. Does Prime Minister Erdogan wish to allow "peace activists" to interview Kurds detained in his prisons, or to adjudicate the status of Kurds, Armenians, or Christian religious figures who live in Turkey? Can we imagine a peace flotilla of Swedish and British leftists sailing to Cyprus to "liberate" Greek land or investigate the "disappearance" of thousands of Greeks in 1974? And if they did, what would happen to them? About the same as would happen if they blocked a road to interdict a Turkish armored column rolling into Kurdistan.

Nor do human-rights violations mean much any more. Iran executes more of its own citizens each year than Israel has killed Palestinians in the course of war in any given year. Syria murders whomever it pleases in Lebanon without worry that any international body will ever condemn its action. I have heard a great deal about the "massacre" or "slaughter" at Jenin, where 52 Palestinians and 23 Israelis died. Indeed, the 2002 propaganda film Jenin, Jenin was a big hit on college campuses. But I have never seen a documentary Hama, Hama commemorating the real 1982 slaughter of somewhere between 10,000 and 40,000 civilians by the criminal Assad regime in Syria, with which we now so eagerly wish to restore ties. I find a 1,000-to-1 fatality rule generally applies: Each person killed by the Israel Defense Forces warrants about as much international attention as 1,000 people killed by Africans, Russians, Indians, Chinese, or Arabs.

I used to think that oil, Arab demography, fear of Islamic terrorism, and blowback from its close association with the United States explained the global double standard that is applied to Israel. But after the hysteria over the Gaza flotilla, the outbursts of various members of the Turkish government, and Ms. Thomas's candid revelations, I think the mad-dog hatred of Israel is more or less because it is a Jewish state. Period.

Let me explain. Intellectuals used to loudly condemn anti-Semitism because it was largely associated with those deemed to be less sophisticated people, often right-wing, who on either racial, nationalistic, or religious grounds regarded Jews as undesirable. Hating Jews was a sign of boorish chauvinism, or of the conspiratorial mind that exuded envy and jealousy of the more successful. But in the last two decades especially, the Left has made anti-Semitism respectable in intellectual circles. The fascistic nature of various Palestinian liberation groups was forgotten, as the "occupied" Palestinians grafted their cause onto that of American blacks, Mexican-Americans, and Asian-Americans. Slurring post-Holocaust Jews was still taboo, but damning the nation-state of Israel as imperialistic and oppressive was considered principled. No one ever cared to ask: Why Israel and not other, far more egregious examples? In other words, one could now focus inordinately on the Jews by emphasizing that one's criticism was predicated on cosmic issues of human rights and justice. And by defaming Israel the nation, one could vent one's dislike of Jews without being stuck with the traditional boorish label of anti-Semite.

So an anti-Semitic bigot like Helen Thomas could navigate perfectly well among the top echelons of Washington society spouting off her hatred of Israel, since her animus was supposedly against Israeli policies rather than those who made them. Only an inadvertent remark finally caught up with her to reveal that what she felt was not anger growing out of a territorial dispute, but furor about the nature of an entire people who should be deported to the sites of the Holocaust.

Finally, as I say, all this may have a strangely liberating effect on Israel. We know now that whatever it does, the world, or at least its prominent political and media figures, is going to damn it. Its longtime patron, the United States, now sees not much difference between Israel's democratic achievement and the autocracies around it, which we are now either subsidizing or courting. As a result, the global censors have lost leverage with Israel, since they have proven to be such laughable adjudicators of right and wrong when Israel is involved.

Israelis should assume by now that whether they act tentatively or strongly, the negative reaction will be the same. Therefore why not project the image of a strong, unapologetic country to a world that has completely lost its moral bearings, and is more likely to respect Israel's strength than its past concern for meeting an impossible global standard?

How odd that the more the activists, political leaders, and media figures issue moral strictures against Israel, the more they prove abjectly amoral. And the more they seek to pressure Israel, the more they are liberating it to do what it feels it must.

CHAPTER FIVE

THE SORTA WAR ON TERROR

JANUARY 8, 2010

Beating the Dead Terrorist Horse

September 11 taught us many lessons.
To our peril, we have forgotten them.

Most of the current acrimony over counterterrorism is stale. The debate is simply a rehash of issues that were discussed and, in fact, resolved early last decade.
Let us review them one more time.

MOST TERRORISTS ARE NOT POOR AND DOWNTRODDEN
September 11 taught us that a Mohammed Atta or a Khalid Sheikh Mohammed does not commit mass murder out of hunger, want, illiteracy, or Western oppression. No doubt Middle Eastern poverty contributes to religious violence. But the poor in Palestine, Saudi Arabia, Egypt, and Yemen are no more impoverished than those in the slums of São Paulo, Mexico City, Ho Chi Minh City, or Johannesburg. And the latter, despite their frequent claims against the West, do not feel a need to murder in mass in the name of their particular religion.

A Major Nidal Hasan or an Umar Farouk Abdulmutallab wishes to kill Westerners not because he is poor or even on behalf of the poor, but rather out of a warped sense of pride, hurt, and anger. Such passions derive from a radical religious creed that insists that comparative failure in the modern Middle East is not self-induced—much less a product of fundamentalism, anti-Enlightenment thinking, autocracy, gender apartheid, tribalism, corruption, and statism. Instead the fact that there is no longer an intercontinental caliphate of rich and powerful believers is due to some sort of contemporary Jewish or Western oppression.

The wealthier, better educated, and more Westernized the radical Muslim, often the greater the sense of shame, alienation, and anger that he and his religion are not shown proper deference. We knew all that in 2001, but have apparently forgotten it during eight years of relative calm. Hasan hated American soldiers not because our system had discriminated against him, much less because of "secondary post-traumatic-stress syndrome," or any of the other wacky excuses that followed his crime. Instead, in part he sensed that the American military had bent over backwards for him and accommodated his extremism—and was therefore, in his own distorted worldview, weak, decadent, and deserving of what he would dish out.

THERAPY IS NO ANSWER

Radical Islam's anger is irrational. It is not predicated on the degree of outreach shown by the United States. A contrite and compliant Jimmy Carter, after all, prompted the creation of the slur "The Great Satan." The year 2009 saw the greatest number of foiled terrorist plots against America since 9/11. Indeed, one-third of all such attempts in the last eight years happened last year—the time of the Obama Al Arabiya interview, the Cairo speech, the bowing to Saudi royals, the promises to close Guantanamo Bay, and the ritual trashing of the Bush anti-terrorism policies.

We need not be gratuitously rude. There surely is a role for sober diplomacy and soft speech. But the degree to which radical Islam will be aggressive toward the West hinges a lot on what it imagines will be our reaction—in terms both of military responses, and of the sense of confidence we project about our own civilization.

Islamists, after all, ignore past American help to, and support for, Islamic peoples in Afghanistan, Bosnia, Chechnya, Indonesia, Iraq, Kosovo, Kuwait, and Somalia—only to pay far more deference to the Chinese and Russians, who have systematically oppressed and often butchered fellow Muslims. Apparently, Dr. Zawahiri and Osama bin Laden would rather recommend reading by Noam Chomsky and Jimmy Carter than offend Vladimir Putin and earn another Grozny. The popularity of bin Laden and the tactic of suicide bombing itself plummeted throughout the Middle East between 2001 and 2009. And that was not because of the mellifluousness of George Bush's Texas twang or a sudden love for our policy in Iraq.

Rather, the change of heart developed because bin Laden and his epigones were considered to be losing in Afghanistan and Iraq. They were endangering those who supported them, and murderously turning on their own—even as the United States was projecting both an image of confidence and readiness to extend support for consensual government and personal freedom.

In contrast, the current policy of apology and kowtow—coupled with a cynical realism (albeit cloaked in nonjudgmental, multicultural relativism) and presented abroad with a sense of hesitation and self-doubt—is, in fact, a prescription for reviving radical Islam.

That lesson likewise was apparent after 9/11.

A PROJECTION OF WEAKNESS IS DANGEROUS

Much of radical Islam's posture is predicated on our expected response. When we did nothing during the Iranian hostage crisis, more or less whined after the Marine-barracks bombing, sent a few cruise missiles after the East African embassy attacks, litigated the 1993 World Trade Center bombing, and forgot the *USS Cole*, bin Laden concluded that the West was the "weak horse" and pressed on.

To some degree, Afghanistan and Iraq changed that impression, especially the devastating defeat of al-Qaeda in al-Anbar province in 2006–2008. But that costly progress was accompanied by more recrimination against the Bush administration than anger directed at radical Islam. Equally important, the Western world said very little about the Danish-cartoon threats, the killing of Theo Van Gogh, and various premodern Muslim actions like rioting after the Pope's Byzantine exegesis and the false stories of Koran burning in Guantanamo. Had Europe and the United States shown a united front on behalf of freedom of expression, rather than a fear of Islamic reaction, such incidents would have been written off as the lunacy they were.

Instead of reacting to perceived Muslim grievances, we should be continually directing questions to Islam: Why are there numerous mosques in the West, but few churches in Islamic countries? Why are Korans freely disseminated in the West, but Bibles not so under Islamic rule? Why do Muslims enjoy more freedom and rights under Western secular law than in their own countries? The aim of such interrogatories is not to score points, but to suggest to radical Muslims that we hold them to the same standards as we hold ourselves.

ISRAEL IS NOT THE PROBLEM

Just because radical Muslims and the Arab Street claim that a Jewish presence on the West Bank is the catalyst for terrorist outrage does not make it so—any more than Hitler's insistence that Versailles drove him to the invasion of Poland in 1939, or Argentinians' claims that their problems in the early 1980s originated with the British "occupation" of the Malvinas. No Germans today are blowing up Poles for the loss of Danzig and East Prussia. Greek Cypriots are not planting IEDs at Turkish embassies to force the return of ancestral homelands. And the world is not concerned about the divided city of Nicosia or Russian occupation of the Kuriles.

No, what privileges the Palestinian question is largely three factors that have nothing to do with disputed ground: the presence of huge amounts of oil on Arab lands, endemic anti-Semitism in the West and at the U.N., and fear of radical Islamic terrorism.

Take those considerations out of the equation, and the West Bank is about as important to the world as a disputed South Ossetia. We forget that there were three Middle Eastern wars well before the so-called occupation of Palestine. Gaza did not become a calm place once the Israelis left. Should Palestinians cease the violence, welcome investment from elsewhere in the Arab world, and establish a consensual government, one transparent and free of corruption, the West Bank could become like Dubai—and deal with Israel as a responsible neighbor adjudicating a common border. And yet radical Islamic terrorism in general would nevertheless continue with fresh and always mutating grievances.

All that was clear around 2001—but apparently now ignored.

THE SO-CALLED WAR ON TERROR WAS WORKING

We constantly argue and bicker about what we should be doing rather than showing some appreciation for our past successes. Our country has not experienced another terrorist attack on the scale of 9/11. For all the tragedy of Iraq, what was unthinkable in 2006 has now become accepted—a continuing constitutional government and a month of "war" without a single American fatality. The U.S. military is not broken; in fact it has fought brilliantly in both Iraq and Afghanistan. General Petraeus's surge, unfairly caricatured at the time and now largely forgotten, was a remarkable military and political victory.

There are now proven protocols for dealing with terrorism that work and are not at odds with the Constitution. For all the talk of al-Qaeda's resilience, it has lost thousands of its top echelon. The regime in Iran is shaky—and shakier still for the continuance of a constitutional system in neighboring Iraq. Europe is shedding its politically correct appeasement of Islam, and several countries have already enacted statutes about Islamic dress and mosques unthinkable in the United States.

"Bush did it" is becoming ironic, and having the unintended consequence of reminding us how well we once defended ourselves—and how risky it is not to appreciate why and how.

WILL WE NEVER LEARN?

In short, soon after September 11 the United States correctly sized up radical Islam, its nature, its aims, and its pseudo-grievances. We may have made mistakes in implementation, and at times in tactics and strategy, but in large part we had contained the threat, and radical Islam was losing its currency.

Apparently we've forgotten why that was so, and thus continue to beat the old dead horse in our own self-recrimination.

JANUARY 15, 2010

Our Sorta, Kinda War on Terror

*President Obama has not signed up for
a serious effort against radical Islam.*

After Germany invaded Poland on Sept. 1, 1939, Great Britain and France sorta, kinda declared war on Germany. The formal declaration of war was real enough, but the allies' initial responses were laughable.

Two days after Germany started to slaughter the Poles, Britain began conducting "truth raids," which were to drop 6 million leaflets over Germany. These milk runs were supposedly aimed at "showing" the Germans that Britain someday might be able to bomb them, "enlightening" them about the sins of the then widely popular and victorious Adolf Hitler, and demonstrating the Brits' desire for peace and quiet rather than another Somme or Verdun.

For much of that autumn of 1939 and the winter of 1940, the enormous French army stayed put—except occasionally to "push" a mile or two into German territory, and then retreat back, all to prove the country's supposed fighting ability. Somehow during the nine-month-long "phony war," the pre-Churchillian allies managed to convey a sense of weakness and timidity, while being bellicose sounding enough to offend their enemies. Hitler, in contrast, smiled and pressed on, invading Denmark and Norway, launching unrestricted submarine attacks, rounding up Jews in the east, bombing Britain, and preparing for a massive invasion of the Netherlands, Belgium, Luxembourg, and France.

We are back in a such a sorta, kinda war against radical Islam—whose name we almost never reference. We send more troops into Afghanistan, but only on the condition that we announce deadlines when they will start leaving. We damn the now-successful Iraq War as ill-conceived and not worth the effort, even as we stay in Iraq and consider the present calm and enduring democracy a (quiet) success.

The president has libeled tribunals, renditions, the Patriot Act,

Predator attacks, wiretaps, and intercepts as either shredding the Constitution or unfairly persecuting Muslims—only to keep all these protocols intact. Obama loudly promised the whiny Europeans and the angry Islamic world that he would close the supposed gulag at Guantanamo within a year—and then found he could not do without its apparent utility.

Deadlines are a favorite of our president. But does anyone believe that Guantanamo will be closed on January 21? Iran was to desist from its efforts to obtain the bomb before the U.N. summit in New York, and then before the G-20 summit, and then before the face-to-face negotiations in October, and then by the first of the year.

Sometimes we "reach out" to the unhinged Ahmadinejad and ignore his brave opponents who are risking their lives in the streets; at other times, we lecture the theocracy about its bad behavior in sponsoring terror and violating nuclear non-proliferation agreements. We both damn and praise Israel for its "settlements"—appointing its enemies to the Obama administration, while assuring its friends that U.S. policy remains unchanged.

When Mr. Abdulmutallab tried to blow himself up, along with 300 other passengers, Obama's initial, though belated, reactions were that the terrorist had "allegedly" tried to commit mass murder, and that he was an "isolated extremist," despite clear ties to Yemeni terrorists. Our Homeland Security head proclaimed that the system had "worked"—for about 24 hours, until she was politely disabused of that lunatic notion. Abdulmutallab was promised a civilian trial, apparently on the grounds that this non-uniformed enemy combatant was caught on American soil—although his intent was instead to float down upon it as human ash.

CIA agents are to be tried for supposedly being too rough on the architect of 9/11, who in turn, despite past bragging about his role in killing 3,000 Americans, will now as another non-uniformed terrorist be given a public trial in New York.

The 19th-century discipline of philology argued that words were the key to understanding the past—if something in the past had existed, there surely was a proper recoverable word for it. And in turn, how a culture used vocabulary was a window into its very values. So when

Barack Obama had his administration scrap the Manichean "war on terror" for "overseas contingency operations" aimed against "man-made disasters," we understood that he had not signed up for a serious effort against radical Islam.

Instead, Obama apparently felt the war was due mostly to misunderstanding and was only exacerbated by President Bush's crude Texanisms, rather than being due to the multifaceted pathologies of the radical Muslim world.

Obama by his nomenclature, race, and self-referenced unique life experiences would co-opt and confuse the terrorists and their sponsors rather than have to confront them with force in Neanderthal fashion. Indeed, if one were to go back and count the times Obama has trashed his predecessor, and then collate that list with a list of his comparable slurs and slights against radical Islam, one would conclude that our present federal animus is directed against George Bush rather than Dr. Zawahiri and his cohort.

All this is not lost on the enemy.

The problem is that despite all the appeasement rhetoric and the finger-pointing at prior federal officials, we are still sorta, kinda at war. The Nobel peace laureate Obama has ordered far more judge/jury/executioner Predator raids than did "smoke 'em out" Bush. That is, we regret waterboarding self-confessed mass murderers, but not executing suspected terrorists by remote control in Waziristan—along with anyone unfortunate enough to be sitting in the suspected terrorist's living room. Americans are bravely fighting radical Muslims in Afghanistan, and are on guard in Iraq—while their commander-in-chief promises to leave the former theater, and shows regret for even being in the latter.

Rendition is said to be the product of Dick Cheney's dark mind, but Barack Obama is now employing that tactic to its fullest extent. And while Obama continued to blow up Muslims in Afghanistan and simultaneously claimed that Bush had gone overboard in his war against terrorists, there were more foiled terrorist plots in his inaugural year of 2009 than during any other year since 2001.

In other words, we are in very dangerous territory. Barack Obama is doing just enough to infuriate our enemies, while at the same time trying to deny that we are in an existential war against them. He has caricatured the notion of victory as archaic and perhaps surreal in our complex postmodern world, as if the enemy agrees. Obama does not seem to understand that while we conduct a seminar on the meaning of victory, the Islamists believe that its antithesis, our defeat, is both very real and achievable.

While Obama offers false historical analogies, apologies for his country, and exaggerated accounts of Muslim achievement, he nevertheless tries to now follow/now deny the hated Bush anti-terrorism protocols and the Bush/Petraeus plans for Afghanistan and Iraq. Nothing is more dangerous in war than fighting an enemy while trying to beg peace from him at the same time. Ask Neville Chamberlain, Edouard Daladier, Lyndon Johnson, or Jimmy Carter.

So, like the British and French in 1939, LBJ in the 1960s, and Jimmy Carter, the Great Satan of 1979, we are sleepwalking through a real war, mixing therapy and tragedy, peace and war, appeasement and violence, outreach and Predators.

Soon the enemy will take our sad measure, reenergize and escalate, and make us choose either to fight or to desist—as we pray that another Churchill or Reagan rides in over the horizon.

FEBRUARY 10, 2010

Victory—How Quaint an Idea!

Defeating Islamic terrorism is not only definable and possible, but closer than ever before

There is a common—and understandable—perception in the postmodern age of nuclear proliferation that victory is an obsolete concept.

Is it that too many nuclear players have provided too many eleventh-hour reprieves to the losing sides in conventional wars?

Or is it the non-uniformed status of our increasingly common terrorist enemies?

Or perhaps the "ends" of wars seem inconsequential because of the ubiquity of terrorism and unconventional tactics, the mess of post-battle reconstruction and nation-building, and the power of instant global communications that bring us unedited and unrepresentative sound bites from the front.

In reality, such pessimism discourages Western military action, and cynical postmodern societies seem to be stymied by their zealous premodern opponents.

"I'm always worried about using the word 'victory,' because, you know, it invokes this notion of Emperor Hirohito coming down and signing a surrender to MacArthur."

So asserted our president in a July 2009 interview with ABC News. Aside from the fact that Emperor Hirohito never himself went "down" anywhere to surrender to General MacArthur, the president reflected the prevailing sense that wars are now amorphous, never-ending, and without clear benchmarks of success or failure.

But is all this quite accurate?

If it is true that human nature is unchanging, then the very human enterprise of war—with understandable allowances for changing technologies and ideologies—should itself, at least in its essence, have remained unchanged since antiquity.

In other words, while particular wars in any age may not end in victory or defeat for either side, the concept of such finality is very much possible for either, given their shared human nature. In short, if a war is stalemated, it is usually because both sides, wisely or stupidly, come to believe victory is not worth the commensurate costs in blood and treasure—not because victory itself is an anachronism.

In fact, for all the laments about American impotence in a nuclear age, we have won most of our wars since World War II. Despite the stalemate at the 38th parallel in Korea, the U.S. military achieved the stated goal of the Truman administration: keeping North Korea from destroying the South, and ensuring a viable autonomous state there. That was victory as defined before the war broke out.

The first Vietnam War ended in an American victory: the 1973 Paris Peace Accords that accepted an independent South—the original reason to intervene. We most certainly lost the second Vietnam War when our congressional leaders deemed that the postbellum vigilance of keeping the North from overwhelming the South was not worth the additional costs. A Watergate-damaged Nixon administration was unable to honor its commitment to use U.S. airpower to stop renewed Communist aggression.

The British clearly won the Falklands War. The United States won the small wars in the Balkans, Grenada, and Panama. It was victorious in both Afghanistan and Iraq, having removed the Taliban and Saddam Hussein. In the latter two instances, we are fighting second wars in which victory is defined as ensuring the survival of successive consensual systems under the countries' elected governments.

So far, we are winning both. Victory is definable: when these states are able to stay autonomous largely through their own efforts—with the understanding that Europe, for 65 years, and South Korea, for 60, have both required American military support to ensure their independence.

Iran could not possibly resist the economic and military power of Europe and the United States, should we decide that the mullahs will not have the Bomb. If they get the Bomb anyway, it will not be because stopping the theocracy is impossible, or because such a victory is too abstract a notion. It will be the result of American and European political leaders concluding that the costs would not be worth the benefits.

But what would victory in the now-derided War on Terror look like?

It would require three conditions, all of them closer to fruition than we think. The first condition of victory: Due to offensive operations in the Middle East and defensive measures at home, it would become almost impossible for an individual or small cadre to pull off another 9/11. We have done great damage to al-Qaeda in both Afghanistan and Iraq, in addition to less publicized attacks on the organization from Pakistan to Yemen. If we continue such offensive operations, at some point the enemy will equate anti-Western terrorism with a death sentence. At home, we have yet to create a zero-tolerance climate for radical Islamic propagandizing. That toughness would mean, among other things, that anyone on a watch list simply would not be allowed to fly. A Major Hasan should have long ago been disciplined and investigated for his Islamist proselytizing—and shamed by his local Muslim community. His past mosques must realize that publicly condemning radicals in their midst is a far wiser course of action than continuing to protest government vigilance against suspected terrorists on U.S. soil. In short, a Major Hasan should have been treated the same way a lone-wolf Nazi would have been treated in 1943—once it was revealed that he was mouthing Hitlerian doctrine on a U.S. military base and communicating with Nazi-sympathizers in Argentina.

Second condition: Middle East governments would no longer wish to aid and abet Islamic terrorists. They would fear both international ostracism in matters of trade and global intercourse and the unpredictability of the United States, which sometimes might conclude that a Damascus or a Tehran was as responsible as the terrorists who magically camped on their soil. Here we had made some progress—the Cedar Revolution in Lebanon, Qaddafi's surrender of his WMD projects, the long incarceration of Dr. Khan, and Pakistan's occasional attacks on terrorists in Waziristan. Do Middle Eastern countries openly praise the objectives of radical Islam more now or in the past? Despite this country's change in administration and the '03–'06 ordeal in Iraq, Arab governments, in fact, seem less likely to harbor terrorists than before.

Third: Radical Islam would become less successful at channeling Middle Eastern discontents into anti-Western terrorism. For years, al-Qaeda's popularity and its favored tactic of suicide bombing have been declining precipitously in international polls. Democracy promotion erodes the old nexus between the dictator and the terrorist—as we can see from unrest in Lebanon and Iran and the positive efforts of the Afghan and Iraq governments. There are more democracies today than at any time in history.

Critical here is the message and attitude of the United States. If "smoke 'em out" and "bring 'em on" sometimes sent the wrong message, so too did the Cairo fantasy speech of 2009 about a Muslim-fueled Renaissance and Enlightenment, not to mention the nonsense about a tolerant Islamic Cordoba during the Inquisition.

Neither gratuitous boasting nor therapeutic myth-making will convince Middle Easterners to pull away from radical Islamic terrorism. Instead, the message has to be uncompromising, yet understated, something like the quiet motto of Sulla's: "No better friend, no worse enemy." That there was no visible German opposition to Hitler in 1939 and no visible support for him in April 1945 was due both to overwhelming Allied power and to the knowledge that a magnanimous reconstruction was possible.

That we will be unmerciful to radical Islam and quite benevolent to those who reject it—that is the proper message. And, to some degree, that duality has been followed since 9/11. That a Middle Eastern Muslim can hope for a freer, more prosperous life without bin Ladenism; and that if he chooses to join bin Laden, he will die and cause havoc to his community, is more true since 9/11, not less.

The Obama administration entered office determined to repudiate the Bush war protocols and show the Muslim world that America had been at fault in its previous war against radical Islam. But in the end, all that it has done so far, ironically, is strengthen U.S. resolve and show the radical Muslim world that America's therapeutic alternative was a brief and failed deviation—given the continuance of Predator drone attacks, tribunals, renditions, intercepts, and wiretaps, as well as the difficulty in closing Guantanamo, the public outrage over the Christmas Day bomber and the proposed KSM trial, and the realization that appeasement of radical Iran was idiotic. I still cannot see how offering KSM his Miranda rights is any more humane than the on-site killing of suspected terrorists—and any living thing in their general vicinities—in Pakistan.

In short, "victory" in the War on Terror can be defined. We are slowly achieving it; the enemy is not. That's why the culture of the larger Middle East is becoming much more sympathetic to us than we are to radical Islam, and why the architects of al-Qaeda live incognito and seem more shrill than ever.

It may be unwise in such a delicate effort to win hearts and minds to trumpet notions of victory, but it is equally silly to deny the likelihood of our ultimate aims. Victory is an ancient and enduring concept, despite the multifarious and confusing faces of war over the ages. Defeating Islamic terrorism is not only definable and possible, but closer than ever before.

FEBRUARY 17, 2010

The Tragic Truth of War

What we dare not say: Killing the enemy brings victory.

Victory has usually been defined throughout the ages as forcing the enemy to accept certain political objectives. "Forcing" usually meant killing, capturing, or wounding men at arms. In today's polite and politically correct society we seem to have forgotten that nasty but eternal truth in the confusing struggle to defeat radical Islamic terrorism.

What stopped the imperial German army from absorbing France in World War I and eventually made the Kaiser abdicate was the destruction of a once magnificent army on the Western front—superb soldiers and expertise that could not easily be replaced. Saddam Hussein left Kuwait in 1991 when he realized that the U.S. military was destroying his very army. Even the North Vietnamese agreed to a peace settlement in 1973, given their past horrific losses on the ground and the promise that American air power could continue indefinitely inflicting its damage on the North.

When an enemy finally gives up, it is for a combination of reasons—material losses, economic hardship, loss of territory, erosion of civilian morale, fright, mental exhaustion, internal strife. But we forget that central to a concession of defeat is often the loss of the nation's soldiers—or even the threat of such deaths.

A central theme in most of the memoirs of high-ranking officers of the Third Reich is the attrition of their best warriors. In other words, among all the multifarious reasons why Nazi Germany was defeated, perhaps the key was that hundreds of thousands of its best aviators, U-boaters, panzers, infantrymen, and officers, who swept to victory throughout 1939–41, simply perished in the fighting and were no longer around to stop the allies from doing pretty much what they wanted by 1944–45.

After Stalingrad and Kursk, there were not enough good German soldiers to stop the Red Army. Even the introduction of jets could not save Hitler in 1945—given that British and American airmen had killed thousands of Luftwaffe pilots between 1939 and 1943. After the near destruction of the Grand Army in Russia in 1812, even Napoleon's genius could not restore his European empire. Serial and massive Communist offensives between November 1950 and April 1951 in Korea cost Red China hundreds of thousands of its crack infantry—and ensured that, for all its aggressive talk, it would never retake Seoul in 1952–53.

But aren't these cherry-picked examples from conventional wars of the past that have no relevance to the present age of limited conflict, terrorism, and insurgency where ideology reigns? Not really. We don't quite know all the factors that contributed to the amazing success of the American "surge" in Iraq in 2007–08. Surely a number of considerations played a part: Iraqi anger at the brutish nature of al-Qaeda terrorists in their midst; increased oil prices that brought massive new revenues into the country; General Petraeus's inspired counterinsurgency tactics that helped win over Iraqis to our side by providing them with jobs and security; much-improved American equipment; and the addition of 30,000 more American troops.

But what is unspoken is also the sheer cumulative number of al-Qaeda and other Islamic terrorists that the U.S. military killed or wounded between 2003 and 2008 in firefights from Fallujah to Basra. There has never been reported an approximate figure of such enemy dead—perhaps wisely, in the post-Vietnam age of repugnance at "body counts" and the need to create a positive media image.

Nevertheless, in those combat operations, the marines and army not only proved that to meet them in battle was a near death sentence, but also killed thousands of low-level terrorists and hundreds of top-ranking operatives who otherwise would have continued to harm Iraqi civilians and American soldiers. Is Iraq relatively quiet today because many who made it so violent are no longer around?

Contemporary conventional wisdom tries to persuade us that there is no such thing as a finite number of the enemy. Instead, killing them supposedly only incites others to step up from the shadows to take their places. Violence begets violence. It is counterproductive, and creates an endless succession of the enemy. Or so we are told.

We may wish that were true. But military history suggests it is not quite accurate. In fact, there was a finite number of SS diehards and kamikaze suicide bombers even in fanatical Nazi Germany and imperial Japan. When they were attrited, not only were their acts of terror curtailed, but it turned out that far fewer than expected wanted to follow the dead to martyrdom.

The Israeli war in Gaza is considered by the global community to be a terrible failure—even though the number of rocket attacks against Israeli border towns is way down. That reduction may be due to international pressure, diplomacy, and Israeli goodwill shipments of food and fuel to Gaza—or it may be due to the hundreds of Hamas killers and rocketeers who died, and the thousands who do not wish to follow them, despite their frequently loud rhetoric about a desire for martyrdom.

Insurgencies, of course, are complex operations, but in general even they are not immune from eternal rules of war. Winning hearts and minds is essential; providing security for the populace is crucial; improving the economy is critical to securing the peace. But all that said, we cannot avoid the pesky truth that in war—any sort of war—killing enemy soldiers stops the violence.

For all the much-celebrated counterinsurgency tactics in Afghanistan, note that we are currently in an offensive in Helmand province to "secure the area." That means killing the Taliban and their supporters, and convincing others that they will meet a violent fate if they continue their opposition. Perhaps the most politically incorrect and Neanderthal of all thoughts would be that the American military's long efforts in both Afghanistan and Iraq to kill or capture radical Islamists has contributed to the general safety inside the United States. Modern dogma insists that our presence in those two Muslim countries incited otherwise non-bellicose young Muslims to suddenly prefer violence and leave Saudi Arabia, Yemen, or Egypt to flock to kill the infidel invader.

A more tragic view would counter that there was always a large (though largely finite) number of radical jihadists who, even before 9/11, wished to kill Americans. They went to those two theaters, fought, died, and were therefore not able to conduct as many terrorist operations as they otherwise would have, and also provided a clear example to would-be followers not to emulate their various short careers. That may explain why in global polls the popularity both of bin Laden and of the tactic of suicide bombing plummeted in the Middle Eastern street—at precisely the time America was being battered in the elite international press for the Iraq War.

Even the most utopian and idealistic do not escape these tragic eternal laws of war. Barack Obama may think he can win over the radical Islamic world—or at least convince the more moderate Muslim community to reject jihadism—by means such as his Cairo speech, closing Guantanamo, trying Khalid Sheikh Mohammed in New York, or having General McChrystal emphatically assure the world that killing Taliban and al-Qaeda terrorists will not secure Afghanistan.

Of course, such soft- and smart-power approaches have utility in a war so laden with symbolism in an age of globalized communications. But note that Obama has upped the number of combat troops in Afghanistan, and he vastly increased the frequency of Predator-drone assassination missions on the Pakistani border.

Indeed, even as Obama damns Guantanamo and tribunals, he has massively increased the number of targeted assassinations of suspected terrorists—the rationale presumably being either that we are safer with fewer jihadists alive, or that we are warning would-be jihadists that they will end up buried amid the debris of a mud-brick compound, or that it is much easier to kill a suspected terrorist abroad than detain, question, and try a known one in the United States.

In any case, the president—immune from criticism from the hard Left, which is angrier about conservative presidents waterboarding known terrorists than liberal ones executing suspected ones—has concluded that one way to win in Afghanistan is to kill as many terrorists and insurgents as possible. And while the global public will praise his kinder, gentler outreach, privately he evidently thinks that we will be safer the more the U.S. marines shoot Taliban terrorists and the more Hellfire missiles blow up al-Qaeda planners.

Why otherwise would a Nobel Peace Prize laureate order such continued offensive missions?

Victory is most easily obtained by ending the enemy's ability to resist—and by offering him an alternative future that might appear better than the past. We may not like to think all of that entails killing those who wish to kill us, but it does, always has, and tragically always will—until the nature of man himself changes.

MARCH 3, 2010

Politically Correct Killing?

The increase in targeted killings makes urgent the need for Obama to clarify hiw whole anti-terrorism policy.

B y all accounts, President Obama has vastly increased the number of Predator drone strikes during his 13 months in office and expanded the theater of missile operations by thousands of square miles. Indeed, since inauguration day, 2009, Predator and Reaper drone attacks may have killed over 500 suspected terrorists in Waziristan and Pakistan.

In January of this year alone, the United States conducted ten strikes, and may have killed some 70 suspected al-Qaeda or Taliban terrorists—along with additional unknown others in their vicinity. When we killed Baitullah Mehsud, the leader of the Taliban in Pakistan, last summer, eleven others were blown up with him, among them his wife and father-in-law—and, earlier, dozens of others were killed in strikes that failed to target him. In the first two months of 2010, the Obama administration conducted almost half the number of strikes that were conducted in all of 2008, the last full year of the Bush administration.

Why has Obama expanded a killing program that seemingly is at odds with his own past statements ("We've got to get the job done there, and that requires us to have enough troops so that we're not just air-raiding villages and killing civilians, which is causing enormous pressure over there")—as well as with his general efforts to envision the war on terror as more a criminal-justice operation where terrorists are tried in civilian courts and given their Miranda rights?

First, drone aircraft reflect our technological superiority and sensitivity about suffering casualties—and give the U.S. enormous advantages in an asymmetrical war that often favors the enemy. Drones are far cheaper than conventional attack planes, and if they are downed, they cost no American lives.

Second, because of improved technology in the Predator program, a substantial increase in the number of our drones, and increased cooperation from the Pakistani government, the United States is now able to target far more suspected terrorists—and kill them—than ever before.

Third, killing suspected terrorists is far easier than capturing and detaining them. Apparently the Obama administration has concluded that dead men need no cells in Guantanamo, no interrogations, no Miranda rights, no sympathetic ACLU lawyers, and no trials in New York.

Fourth, the Obama administration apparently has been won over to the Bush notion that the number of terrorists is finite. Just as the Bush administration believed that the killing of top al-Qaeda operatives in Iraq—Abu Musab al-Zarqawi for one—weakened the insurgency, so too the Obama administration now believes that key individuals are unique, and that their lost terrorist expertise is not automatically replaced.

Fifth, the Obama administration apparently understands that there will be few political attacks from the Left on the Predator targeted-killing policy of the sort once voiced by candidate Obama. Obama understands that most of the loud leftwing criticism of the Bush anti-terrorism policy was less principled than political in nature, part of a larger effort to discredit the administration in general. Thus, the Constitution-shredding Bush-Cheney protocols of yesteryear—renditions, military tribunals, intercepts, wiretaps, troops in Iraq, Guantanamo—are apparently no longer subversive, but instead are considered useful tools in maintaining U.S. security.

Note that the characterization of the attacks as "assassinations" is not hyperbole; it is a more descriptive term than "bombings." We are not always focusing on generic terrorist training camps and compounds to eliminate anonymous killers, but often targeting specific individuals whose names and profiles we know—just as, say, the 1943 American P-38 fighter-squadron assassination of Admiral Yamamoto in the Pacific ("Operation Vengeance") was different in character from the usual fighter and bomber missions against unknown Japanese.

So plenty of issues are raised by the Obama administration's escalation of targeted assassinations that heretofore have not been fully voiced.

(1) The most obvious is the contradiction not just between the rhetoric of candidate Obama and President Obama (that is now old hat, as we have seen with renditions, tribunals, Guantanamo, etc.), but between Obama's refashioning of the war on terror itself and the new greater reliance on targeted airborne assassinations. Investigations of Bush-administration officials who approved the waterboarding of three known terrorist masterminds responsible for thousands of American deaths seem incompatible with the more lethal tactics of executing suspected terrorists (and their families) in Pakistan and Waziristan. One difference, of course, as noted above, is that terrorists we execute are not technically in our custody. True, but in today's sophisticated technological world, once the televised image of someone in Waziristan is beamed into Nevada, the soldier with his hand on the firing button seems to have more jurisdiction over a suspected terrorist than a jailer does over a known one in Guantanamo.

(2) I think the Obama administration will have to cease the commonplace U.S. criticism of targeted assassinations abroad, such as the objections we used to make to the Israelis' missile attacks on Hamas officials. When one removes the word "war" from "war on terror," and begins Mirandizing would-be mass murderers such as the Christmas Day bomber, then conflict devolves into the realm of espionage and criminal justice. Thus the line between a team of Israeli agents executing a known Hamas kingpin in Dubai and a squadron of Predators taking out dozens of suspected terrorists in Pakistan seems somewhat blurred. Was the conflict in Gaza and its aftermath any less a "war" than our own efforts in Afghanistan? More to the point, in the context of Obama's voicing sharp criticism of the previous administration, promising Mr. Abdulmutallab his Miranda rights, and planning to try

Khalid Sheikh Mohammed in New York, his administration's assassination plans strike a false note. One expects Texans in loudly announced "wars on terror," not Nobel peace laureates in "overseas contingency operations," to order the summary execution of suspects—and anyone unlucky enough to be nearby when the Hellfire missile hits.

(3) Once the Obama administration played to the media by announcing preliminary investigations of Bush-era CIA personnel and lawyers for the waterboarding of three terrorists, a dangerous precedent was established. One of the reasons the administration has not clarified its expanded Predator policy may well be that no liberal jurist now serving in the Justice Department wants his own imprint on a policy that, according to Obama's past accusations, would be considered suspect in nature and its advocates perhaps criminally culpable at some future date. (Indeed, according to the current protocols of liberal jurisprudence, some current Department of Justice grandee might in a few years find a summons delivered to his Ivy League dean's office, charging him with authorship of an "illegal" policy of targeted killing.)

I wholeheartedly support the president's expanded use of Predators against suspected terrorists in Pakistan and its environs—if we agree that we are in a global war on radical Islamic terrorism, and are also consistent in seeing our adversaries as non-uniformed enemy combatants not subject to the normal rules of war. But the expansion of targeted assassinations does not square with the administration's past rhetoric and its present interest in seeing anti-terrorism as more akin to criminal justice than war.

In short, we need an examination of our entire policy from an administration that has expanded a controversial wartime tactic without the sort of legal clarifications it once insisted were essential in operations professed not to be exactly war.

Chapter Six

The World Can Be
A Scary Place

FEBRUARY 22, 2008

Yippi Ti Yi Yo, Europe!

Neuroticism abroad

In the last few days, we've been reminded yet again that Europe's radical secularism, atheism, socialism, multiculturalism, childlessness, and aging population make a fascinating but unstable mix—a lovely, fragile orchid in a thinly protected greenhouse.

Kosovo has just declared its independence from Serbia, and what follows could be nightmarish. An oil-rich, bellicose, and rearming Russia doesn't much like the new breakaway state. But France, Germany, and most of the European Union—other than its Orthodox members and those in close proximity to Vladimir Putin—encouraged it. To paraphrase Joseph Stalin, "How many divisions does the EU have?"

Recently Turkey's prime minister, Recep Tayyip Erdogan, speaking on German soil, told cheering Turkish workers and Germans of Turkish ancestry that assimilation is "a crime against humanity"—in between demands that the European Union admit his increasingly Islamicized Turkey to full membership. The American press passed over Erdogan's broadside, but it was a revolutionary, nationalist appeal to German residents of Turkish backgrounds, over the head of, and contrary to, the German government itself–eerily like, mutatis mutandis, Hitler's appeal in the late 1930s to the supposedly oppressed Germans of Czechoslovakia. Meanwhile Norway is about to request 100,000 Turkish guest workers for its cash-rich but labor-poor economy. The French, however, are sighing 'been there, done that,' as police sweep public housing projects in the Paris suburbs looking for Muslim immigrants implicated in past riots.

The British press claims that Muslim immigrants committed over 17,000 acts of "honor" violence in Britain last year. Perhaps in response, the Archbishop of Canterbury conceded that imposition of a parallel system of sharia law in the United Kingdom might be "unavoidable." Iran just warned Denmark to silence its newspapers, which once again are republishing caricatures of the Prophet Mohammed.

Meanwhile, many European NATO troops in Afghanistan rarely venture into combat zones, even as U.S. Secretary of Defense Robert Gates pleads in vain for Europe to send over a few more thousand from its nearly two-million-man standing army. A recent Pew poll revealed that in many European countries only about 30-40 percent of those surveyed have a positive opinion of the United States.

How do all these diverse narratives and agendas add up? The vaunted European multicultural, multilateral, utopian and pacifist worldview is now on its own and thus will get hammered as never before in the unrelenting forge of history. Very soon there will be no more George W. Bush to dump on, hide behind, and blame for the widening cracks in the Atlantic alliance. Instead Europeans may well have to call on the old pro, Commander-in-Chief Barack Obama, to lead them in negotiating sessions with jihadists, Iran, and Russia.

Consider Kosovo again. Europe is invested, quite rightly I think, in promoting its independence. But it is a Muslim country in a post-9/11 landscape, with a history of drawing not only Albanian but also Middle Eastern jihadists to its defense. Russia and Serbia together have the military wherewithal to invade it tomorrow—Serbia by land, Russia by air—and end its breakaway experiment—to the relief of some Eastern European and Orthodox European states, and to the humiliation of the EU. What stops them is not a few NATO peacekeepers but the commitment of the United States to use its vast resources to further the European agenda of stopping Serbian ethnic cleansing and aggression.

Yet consider our dilemma. Why would we intervene abroad in a third war when our allies have lectured us ad nauseam about the amorality of military intercession, have shown little interest in fighting jihadism in Afghanistan or Iraq, and have made clear that they want very little to do with the United States? And after 9/11, why would the United States rush to the aid of a Muslim country in a war whose earlier incarnation, under Bill Clinton, was never authorized by the U.S.

Congress or the U.N.? In short, I doubt the United States will "surge" anything in the Balkans. We will be quite happy to see a postmodern European solution to an essentially European problem. No doubt Sen. Harry Reid or Speaker Nancy Pelosi will remind the public that President Bill Clinton never got a formal congressional treaty authorization to deploy and station American troops in the former Yugoslavia.

The more labor that a secular, increasingly sterile European populace imports, the more social problems will accrue from unassimilated Muslim immigrants who like the economy and freedom of the West but are reluctant to relax any of their own religious and cultural views to participate fully in the postmodern society of their hosts. The resulting "can't live with them, can't live without them" is not a static situation, but one that will be resolved either in multicultural/appeasement fashion (grant de facto sharia law at home and seek friendly realignment with Middle Eastern dictatorships abroad) or with tough assimilationist and immigration policies, coupled with increasingly explicit distrust of expansionary Islam.

Europe is short on energy and depends on illiberal Russia and the Middle East for its fuel. Both these regions are sick and tired of Europe's empty lectures about human rights and feel only disdain for its absence of military might to back up its sermonizing. But Europe is also anti-American, and now in a world of Ahmadinejihads, Putins, Chinese communist apparatchiks, and thuggish Latin American strongmen, it has more or less alienated the only reliable and capable resource it might have drawn on—the goodwill of the United States.

So Europe is in a classic paradox. Emotionally and culturally, Europeans are invested in a leftist such as Obama who reflects their soft socialist values and fuzzy multilateralism. But given their inherent military weakness and rough neighborhood, they have grown to count on an antithetical America—religious, conservative, militarily strong— that is not afraid to use force to fulfill its obligations to preserve the shared Western globalized system from its constant multifarious challenges. I'm not sure they privately want a President Obama calling Sarkozy or Merkel and announcing, "I think we should co-chair a worldwide Islamic conference to hear out Iran's grievances." Much better it would be for the U.S. to ensure that Iran doesn't get the bomb—at which point the French elite would trash America in Le Monde for being unilateral, cowboyish, and preemptive.

Our response to this Euro-neuroticism?

We are weary and tired of it. As our ancestors out West used to sing, "Yippy ti yi yo, get along little dogies, It's all your misfortune and none of my own…"

MAY 28, 2008

When Success Is the Orphan

Some insist on turning a blind eye to the benefits of our efforts in the Mid-East

Recent studies showing a decline in global incidents of Islamic terror have been interpreted as solely a Middle-East intramural affair. Sometimes the good news is said to be a naturally occurring phenomenon. We are supposed to believe that American policies of counter-terrorism at home have been of little value, if not McCarthyesque. Beefed-up security, the fight against the terrorists in Afghanistan and Iraq, and the cultural creation of a repugnance—and penalty—for jihadism (as in contrast to the 1990s), have likewise supposedly played no role.

But surely the catalyst for the decline in terrorist incidents worldwide was the radically different response of the U.S. to terrorism and 9/11 that finally brought jihadism into an open-shooting war against the West (e.g., cf. the Left's "creating terrorists"), in which the terrorists are losing the battle-space, along with the hearts and minds of those in the Middle East—as their own websites and cries of anguish attest.

The successful toppling of Saddam was followed in short order by the shutdown of Dr. Khan's atomic shop, the surrender of WMDs by the Libyans, and the supposed sidetracking of the Iranian nuclear bomb program (at least according to the National Intelligence Estimate)—and yet no one thought the timing of all these events was odd (even when Ghaddafi himself reportedly connected his decision to abandon a weapons of mass destruction program to Saddam's fate).

By the same token, the rise of governments that are sympathetic to the U.S. in France, Germany, and elsewhere in Europe is never associated with a shared and growing worry over Islamic radicalism—or a grudging, often private acknowledgment of the U.S. role abroad in beating back jihadism. How surreal to see a constitutional government in Iraq, with broad popular support, fighting and defeating terrorists and insurgents of both the Wahhabi and Iranian brand—at a time when the consensus is that Iraq only made terrorism much worse. As we've seen from recent events, there are many governments abroad that deserve criticism, whether in China, the Sudan, or Burma, but Iraq is not one of them.

So these are upside-down times when facts and events on the ground simply do not support the general pessimism of the Western media, the serial publication of gloomy he-did-it,-not-me memoirs about the post-9/11 supposed failures, and the shrill rhetoric of the Democratic primaries.

In general, the hard efforts of the last six years against radical Islam—that bore fruit by the radically changed atmosphere in Iraq, the decline in terrorism worldwide, the lack of a follow-up to 9/11, and polls that showed a marked fall in approval for al-Qaeda, Bin Laden, and the tactic of suicide bombing—are explained away in various ways. The common theme, however, is that one never mentions the efforts of the bogeyman George Bush.

The orphaned presidency of Harry Truman during the 1952 election year was likewise damned for stirring up Soviet and Chinese communism—tarred by the isolationist Right for getting us bogged down in hopeless quagmires, and by the Left for creating a climate of paranoia at home and abroad—until decades later appreciated for establishing the general framework and mind-set of an eventually successful containment.

We have not won the war on terror, but we are starting to see how the combination of domestic security, international cooperation, military action, cultural ostracism of those who condone terrorism, and promotion of constitutional government in the Middle East can, and will, marginalize and eventually defeat the jihadists. We know this not just by the anguished complaints of the Islamists themselves, and real progress on the ground—but also by the mantra of increasingly ossified critics who still insist that things are either worse, or were never that bad, or abruptly got better on their own.

JULY 24, 2008

'This Is the Moment'

And now we are loved again?

G iven the size of the audience in Berlin Thursday, the enthusiastic response, and the standard lines about how we-were-, -are-, and -will-be-friends boilerplate, one wonders whether all it took to win the Euro-hearts and minds was to have a charismatic, multiracial American spice up a standard George W. Bush speech about helping the world, addressing AIDs, more troops in Afghanistan, etc.?

So supposedly sophisticated Europeans, who constantly dissect American politics and culture, seem suddenly to like us now, because a younger, more mellifluous figure repackaged the standard American trans-Atlantic rah-rah speech, dressed up with a little Obama messianic sermonizing: "People of Berlin—people of the world—this is our moment. This is our time!" along with some throwaway lines about global warming and Darfur?

That's all it took?

A few minutes of Obama's Elvis-like hope and change? And now the Europeans will pour troops into Afghanistan, match our AIDs-relief dollars, stand up to Iran, be balanced in the Middle East, get off our backs about Iraq, and stiffen their spines with the Russians, because the days of Bushitler are by fiat over with?

Besides the usual rock-star stuff that he excels at, Obama still does not do history well. He started, as in now usual, almost immediately by mentioning his race ("I know that I don't look like the Americans who've previously spoken in this great city.") But that simply was not true, given the fact that for the last seven years both American Secretaries of State – who have been the faces of American foreign policy in Europe—were African-American.

His reference to why Berlin did not starve in 1948 ("But in the darkest hours, the people of Berlin kept the flame of hope burning. The people of Berlin refused to give up. And on one fall day, hundreds of thousands of Berliners came here, to the Tiergarten, and heard the city's mayor implore the world not to give up on freedom.") seems somewhat misleading: the city was kept alive not by "the world" or even the courage of the hungry Berliners, but by skill and courage of the U.S. Air Force.

Three conclusions: One, the public spectacle was of enormous political value to Obama, given the vast press coverage and the enthusiastic crowds. Two, pundits will probably praise—and then forget—the speech in the same manner they did his embarrassing "I can no more disown Rev. Wright . . . " race sermon which they once compared to the Gettsyburg Address—before quietly deleting it. Three, I doubt aping the European line about U.S. torture, global warming, Darfur, etc. will result in any more NATO troops to Afghanistan, or anything else forthcoming from Europe. As it is, they want less, not more, military spending; their extra-constitutional anti-terror laws, spy-cameras, and preventive detentions make the Patriot Act look like Cub Scout bylaws; and their new anti-immigration protocols would earn calls of "fascism" if enacted here at home.

JULY 25, 2008

It's America, Obama

A modest dissent to the citizens of the world

What disturbed me about Barack Obama's Berlin speech were some reoccurring utopian assumptions about cause and effect—namely, that bad things happen almost as if by accident, and are to be addressed by faceless, universal forces of good will. □□Unlike Obama, I would not speak to anyone as "a fellow citizen of the world," but only as an ordinary American who wishes to do his best for the world, but with a much-appreciated American identity, and rather less with a commonality indistinguishable from those poor souls trapped in the Sudan, North Korea, Cuba, or Iran. Take away all particular national identity and we are empty shells mouthing mere platitudes, who believe in little and commit to even less. In this regard, postmodern, post-national Europe is not quite the ideal, but a warning of how good intentions can run amuck. Ask the dead of Srebrenica, or the ostracized Danish cartoonists, or the archbishop of Canterbury with his supposed concern for transcendent universal human rights.

With all due respect, I also don't believe the world did anything to save Berlin, just as it did nothing to save the Rwandans or the Iraqis under Saddam—or will do anything for those of Darfur; it was only the U.S. Air Force that risked war to feed the helpless of Berlin as it saved the Muslims of the Balkans. And I don't think we have much to do in America with creating a world in which "famine spreads and terrible storms devastate our lands." Bad, often evil, autocratic governments abroad cause hunger, often despite rich natural landscapes; and nature, in tragic fashion, not "the carbon we send into atmosphere," causes "terrible storms," just as it has and will for millennia.

Perhaps conflict-resolution theory posits there are no villains, only misunderstandings; but I think military history suggests that culpability exists—and is not merely hopelessly relative or just in the eye of the beholder. So despite Obama's soaring moral rhetoric, I am troubled by his historical revisionism that, "The two superpowers that faced each other across the wall of this city came too close too often to destroying all we have built and all that we love." I would beg to differ again, and suggest instead that a mass-murdering Soviet tyranny came close to destroying the European continent (as it had, in fact, wiped out millions of its own people) and much beyond as well—and was checked only by an often lone and caricatured US superpower and its nuclear deterrence. When the Soviet Union collapsed, there was no danger to the world from American nuclear weapons "destroying all we have built"—while the inverse would not have been true, had nuclear and totalitarian communism prevailed. We sleep too lightly tonight not because democratic Israel has obtained nuclear weapons, but because a frightening Iran just might.

When Obama shouts, "Will we reject torture and stand for the rule of law? Will we welcome immigrants from different lands, and shun discrimination against those who don't look like us or worship like we do, and keep the promise of equality and opportunity for all of our people?" it is the world, not the U.S., that needs to listen most. In this regard I would have preferred Sen. Obama of mixed ancestry to have begun with "In the recent tradition of African-American Secretaries of State Colin Powell and Condoleezza Rice," rather than the less factual, "I don't look like the Americans who've previously spoken in this great city."

I want also to shout back that the United States does stand for the rule of law, as even the killers of Guantanamo realize with their present redress of grievances, access to complex jurisprudence, and humane treatment—all in a measure beyond what such terrorists would receive anywhere else. It is the United States that takes in more immigrants than does any country in the world, and thus is the prime destination of those who flee the miseries of this often wretched globe.

American immigration policies are humane, not only in easy comparison to the savagery shown the "other" in Africa or the Middle East, but fair and compassionate in comparison to what we see presently accorded aliens in Mexico, France, and, yes, Germany. Again, in all this fuzziness—this sermonizing in condescending fashion reminiscent at times of the Pennsylvania remonstration—there is the whiff of American culpability, but certainly not much of a nod to American exceptionalism. Politicians characteristically say to applauding audiences abroad what they wish to hear. True statesmen often do not.

In terms of foreign affairs, I think Americans will finally come to vote for a candidate, who with goodwill, a lot of humility, and a little grace, can persuade the world that universal moral progress, freedom, and material prosperity best advance under the aegis of free markets, constitutional government, and individual freedom, rather than for someone who seems to think, in naïve fashion, that these are necessarily shared and natural human practices, or are presently in force outside the West—or will arise due to dialogue or international good intentions.

AUGUST 12, 2008

Moscow's Sinister Brilliance

Who wants to die for Tbilisi?

L ost amid all the controversies surrounding the Georgian tragedy is the sheer diabolic brilliance of the long-planned Russia invasion. Let us count the ways in which it is a win/win situation for Russia.

THE HOME FRONT
The long-suffering Russian people resent the loss of global influence and empire, but not necessarily the Soviet Union and its gulags that once ensured such stature. The invasion restores a sense of Russian nationalism and power to its populace without the stink of Stalinism, and is indeed cloaked as a sort of humanitarian intervention on behalf of beleaguered Ossetians.

There will be no Russian demonstrations about an "illegal war," much less nonsense about "blood for oil," but instead rejoicing at the payback of an uppity former province that felt its Western credentials somehow trumped Russian tanks. How ironic that the Western heart-throb, the old Marxist Mikhail Gorbachev, is now both lamenting

Western encouragement of Georgian "aggression," while simultaneously gloating over the return of Russian military daring.

SINISTER TIMING

Russia's only worry is the United States, which currently has a lame-
duck president with low approval ratings, and is exhausted after
Afghanistan and Iraq. But more importantly, America's attention is pre-
occupied with a presidential race, in which "world citizen" Barack
Obama has mesmerized Europe as the presumptive new president and
soon-to-be disciple of European soft power.

Better yet for Russia, instead of speaking with one voice, America
is all over the map with three reactions from Bush, McCain, and
Obama—all of them mutually contradictory, at least initially.
Meanwhile, the world's televisions are turned toward the Olympics in
Beijing. The autocratic Chinese, busy jailing reporters and dissidents,
are not about to say an unkind word about Russian intervention. If anything, the pageantry at their grandiose stadiums provides welcome dis-
tractions for those embarrassed over the ease with which Russia smoth-
ered Georgia.

COMEUPPANCE

Most importantly, Putin and Medvedev have called the West's bluff. We
are sort of stuck in a time-warp of the 1990s, seemingly eons ago in
which a once-earnest weak post-Soviet Russia sought Western economic help and political mentoring. But those days are long gone, and
diplomacy hasn't caught up with the new realities. Russia is flush with
billions. It serves as a rallying point and arms supplier to thugs the
world over that want leverage in their anti-Western agendas. For the last
five years, its foreign policy can be reduced to "Whatever the United
States is for, we are against." The geopolitical message is clear to both
the West and the former Soviet Republics: don't consider NATO membership (i.e., do the Georgians really think that, should they have been
NATO members, any succor would have been forthcoming?).

Together with the dismal NATO performance in Afghanistan, the
Georgian incursion reveals the weakness of the Atlantic Alliance. The
tragic irony is unmistakable. NATO was given a gift in not having made

Georgia a member, since otherwise an empty ritual of evoking Article V's promise of mutual assistance in time of war would have effectively destroyed the Potemkin alliance. The new reality is that a nuclear, cash-rich, and energy-blessed Russia doesn't really worry too much whether its long-term future is bleak, given problems with Muslim minorities, poor life-expectancy rates, and a declining population. Instead, in the here and now, it has a window of opportunity to reclaim prestige and weaken its adversaries. So why hesitate?

Indeed, tired of European lectures, the Russians are now telling the world that soft power is, well, soft. Moscow doesn't give a damn about the United Nations, the European Union, the World Court at the Hague, or any finger-pointing moralist from Geneva or London. Did anyone in Paris miss any sleep over the rubble of Grozny? More likely, Putin & Co. figure that any popular rhetoric about justice will be trumped by European governments' concern for energy. With just a few tanks and bombs, in one fell swoop, Russia has cowed its former republics, made them think twice about joining the West, and stopped NATO and maybe EU expansion in their tracks. After all, who wants to die for Tbilisi? Russia does not need a global force-projection capacity; it has sufficient power to muscle its neighbors and thereby humiliate not merely its enemies, but their entire moral pretensions as well. □ □

APOLOGISTS IN THE WEST

The Russians have sized up the moral bankruptcy of the Western Left. They know that half-a-million Europeans would turn out to damn their patron the United States for removing a dictator and fostering democracy, but not more than a half-dozen would do the same to criticize their long-time enemy from bombing a constitutional state.

The Russians rightly expect Westerners to turn on themselves, rather than Moscow—and they won't be disappointed. Imagine the morally equivalent fodder for liberal lament: We were unilateral in Iraq, so we can't say Russia can't do the same to Georgia. (As if removing a genocidal dictator is the same as attacking a democracy). We accepted Kosovo's independence, so why not Ossetia's? (As if the recent history of Serbia is analogous to Georgia's.) We are still captive to neo-con fantasies about democracy, and so encouraged Georgia's efforts that provoked the otherwise reasonable Russians (As if the problem in Ossetia is our principled support for democracy rather than appeasement of Russian dictatorship).

From what the Russians learned of the Western reaction to Iraq, they expect their best apologists will be American politicians, pundits, professors, and essayists—and once more they will not be disappointed. We are a culture, after all, that after damning Iraqi democracy as too violent, broke, and disorganized, is now damning Iraqi democracy as too conniving, rich, and self-interested—the only common denominator being whatever we do, and whomever we help, cannot be good.

POWER-POWER

We talk endlessly about "soft" and "hard" power as if humanitarian jawboning, energized by economic incentives or sanctions, is the antithesis to mindless military power. In truth, there is soft power, hard power, and power-power—the latter being the enormous advantages held by energy rich, oil-exporting states. Take away oil and Saudi Arabia would be the world's rogue state, with its medieval practice of gender apartheid. Take away oil and Ahmadinejad is analogous to a run-of-the-mill central African thug. Take away oil, and Chavez is one of Ronald Reagan's proverbial tinhorn dictators.

Russia understands that Europe needs its natural gas, that the U.S. not only must be aware of its own oil dependency, but, more importantly, the ripples of its military on the fragility of world oil supplies, especially the effects upon China, Europe, India, and Japan. When one factors in Russian oil and gas reserves, a pipeline through Georgia, the oil dependency of potential critics of Putin, and the cash garnered by oil exports, then we understand once again that power-power is beginning to trump both its hard and soft alternatives.

PARALYSIS

Military intervention is out of the question. Economic sanctions, given Russia's oil and Europe's need for it, are a pipe dream. Diplomatic ostracism and moral stricture won't even save face. Instead, Europe— both western and eastern—along with the United States and the concerned former Soviet Republics need to sit down, conference, and plot exactly how these new democracies are to maintain their independence and autonomy in the next decade. Hopefully, they will reach the Franklinesque conclusion that "We must, indeed, all hang together, or most assuredly we shall all hang separately."

SEPTEMBER 11, 2008

The Other 9/11 Story

What has and hasn't happened in the seven years since September 11, 2001

Seven years ago today we suffered the worst attack on the American homeland in our history. The material damage proved far greater than the 1814 British burning of Washington, the human losses more grievous than the almost 2,400 Americans lost at Pearl Harbor. Years later, we tend to forget all the dimensions of that sinister homicidal bombing of our institutions. Radical Islam brazenly signaled that it need not have missiles or sophisticated bombers to burn 16 acres in the heart of Manhattan and set the Pentagon afire. Instead, it could turn from the inside out our own technology against us, in a manner that we were scarcely aware of—and in an iconic fashion at the heart of our greatest cities, ensuring collective psychological trauma that trumped even the terrible loss in blood and treasure.

Some bewildered Americans offered apologies that either the attacks were tit-for-tat payback for America's overreaching global presence, or—more preposterously still—that our record against Muslims incited such hatred. And so yet another cultural war broke out over the "causes" of 9/11. Only with difficulty were the American people reminded that we had, in fact, helped Muslims in Bosnia, and in Kosovo against European Christian Serbia, and in Somalia against gangs and thugs, and in Afghanistan against the Russians, and in Kuwait against Saddam, and that the record of the Chinese, or Indians, or Russians using force against Muslims was far more frequent and cruel than our own.

Only with difficulty was the case made that the jihadists had no legitimate cause, but rather hated modernism, globalization, and Westernization—and were either abetted in their fury by illegitimate Middle East dictatorships to deflect public unrest, or even bought off by such dictators to turn their furor westward. We forget now, seven years later, just how many scolded us, alleging (from the Right) that our liberalism and decadence, and our falling away from God, or (from the Left) our help to Israel, our overseas bases, and our need for oil caused 9/11, rather than the devilish hatred of bin Laden and the sick mind of Mohammed Atta and his ilk—emboldened by the hunch that America, as in the past, either could not or would not retaliate in serious fashion to serial terrorists attacks against its people and property.

The cruel irony of the terrorists' methods was not limited to inversion of our modern technology: in reaction to Mohamed Atta's breezy walk through our American airport security, tens of millions of Americans, billions of times over, were stalled in security lines, taking off their shoes, and, in humiliating fashion, undoing their belts and emptying their purses. Yet given the nature of the postmodern liberal West, the more we checked immigrants from the Middle East to ensure that there were no more wolves in sheep's clothing, and the more we monitored charities and mosques that had at times sponsored fringe Islamic hate groups, all the more we were pilloried as illiberal, as extremist on the defensive as the terrorists had been on the offensive. Thousands of hours were wasted refuting empty charges that a Timothy McVeigh's isolated terrorist attack in Oklahoma City was the moral or factual equivalent of years of constant Islamic terrorism, worldwide, that had killed thousands of innocents.

The more we sought to prevent "another 9/11" through increased security, and the more therein we found success in preventing another attack, so too the more we faced yet another paradox: renewed security prompted a sense of complacence which in turn questioned the need for increased security in the first place. In short order, civil libertarians—enjoying the unforeseen hiatus from the promised repeated attacks—accused the administration of unduly terrifying the nation.

And if they could not precisely explain to the American people how their daily lives were now stripped of constitutional protection, they nevertheless were able to charge, as the peace here at home continued, that our government police needed more policing than did Bin Laden and al-Qaeda.

Critics demanded an end to wiretaps, FISA protocols, Guantánamo, and the Patriot Act. Yet when a Democratic majority took over the Congress, there was a strange unwillingness to repeal such measures— almost as if the louder they charged homeland security agencies with unconstitutional transgressions, all the more they paused, sought no legislative repeal, and suspected that the American people at least felt that through such despised protocols they had thereby in part been kept safe.

The question arose: Against whom, and when, and where, and how to hit back? Voices of doom answered that the Taliban's Afghanistan was not the al-Qaeda perpetrator, but rather the graveyard of both British and Russian imperial troops, given its peaks, snow, warlords, and tribal badlands. Yet within five months following 9/11, the Taliban and al-Qaeda alike were routed to Pakistan and a constitutional government was in place. And while the effort to pacify Afghanistan still continues, so does the constitutional government in Kabul, which is rebuilding the country rather than hiding out in the caves of Waziristan.

It would be cruel to relate by name all those prominent Americans—including politicians, think-tankers, pundits, and military analysts—who felt once, and vehemently so, that the rogue and genocidal regime of Saddam Hussein—in violation of UN accords and 1991 armistice agreements, and the object of 12 years of no-fly zones—was an impediment to the need to change the conditions that had fostered 9/11. Yet suffice it to say that, when Iraq went from a brilliant three-week victory to someone else's flawed and bloody five-year occupation, almost no prior supporter of the need to remove Saddam could be found. It was not just that most changed their minds as the pulse of the battlefield changed; but rather that many prior supporters insidiously convinced themselves that in the now distant past they had never advocated such a supposedly preposterous war in the first place.

Seven years later, hundreds of billions of dollars have been expended; over 4,000 Americans have been lost in Iraq and Afghanistan; and

America's preexisting cultural wounds have had their thin scabs torn off by acrimony over warring abroad and security at home. And yet herein lies the greatest paradox of all that followed from September 11. If no one on September 12, 2001 thought it possible that the United States would not be hit again by a terrorist attack of similar magnitude, here we are still free from a major terrorist assault over 2,500 days later.

Bin Laden and Dr. Zawahiri are still hiding out in the caves of tribal Pakistan, in fear of daylight sorties by deadly American drones, but counting on safety from coalition ground attack through the auspices of their wink-and-nod—and nuclear—Islamic Pakistani hosts. The top cadres of al-Qaeda, nonetheless, are now either mostly dead, captured, or in hiding. When al-Qaeda now whines in its infomercials, the complaint is about Shiite Iran who supposedly helped the infidel Americans, not the Americans themselves who alone sent them to the caves of Pakistan and defeated them in, and routed them from, Iraq.

In response, polls reveal that Middle Eastern support for bin Laden, al-Qaeda, and the tactic of suicide bombing are at an all-time low. Constitutional governments remain in power in both Afghanistan and Iraq. Al-Qaeda has suffered a terrible material and public-relations defeat in the heart of the ancient caliphate.

While many rightly point to lapses in the conduct of the Iraq war, faulty intelligence, and wrongheaded emphasis on supposed arsenals of WMDs rather than the casus belli outlined in the 23 writs authorized by the Congress, few can answer a more existential question: Had we not met, defeated, and humiliated tens of thousands of jihadists on the battlefields of Iraq, where else might we have inflicted such a terrible defeat on our enemies—given the nuclear sanctuary of Pakistan, the bellicose governments of Iran and Syria, and the duplicity of the Gulf monarchies? And if we had not killed, captured, scattered, and turned our enemies abroad, how then might we have prevented them from coming back here to attack us at home? And are the governments of Afghanistan and Iraq, as in the past, aiding anti-American terrorists, or helping to hunt them down?

The truth is, we chased al-Qaeda from Iraq and Afghanistan and it is now in lunatic fashion chasing Danish cartoonists, European novelists, and opera producers as it cuts the fingers off smokers, tries to cover up the genitalia of animals, and looks for the mentally ill to strap on suicide belts. Long after Jacques Chirac, Michael Moore, Gerhard Schroeder, and Cindy Sheehan have come, gone, and nearly disappeared, a General David Petraeus and thousands of American soldiers and diplomats like him remain. George W. Bush is reviled, in part because of an inability to articulate what the war against terror was, and what it was for. But Bush hatred has been reduced to a sort of politically correct trinket, worn around the neck of the clannish critics as a reminder of the President's ineptness in expression or supposedly dangerous views—without examining what others might have done to achieve the same results of achieving freedom from further attack.

But in years to come it may well be said that the president kept us safe for years when none thought he could, and removed the two most odious regimes in the Middle East and replaced them with the two best—and confronted a confident and ascendant radical Islam and left it demoralized and discredited among its own host Arab and Muslim constituents. In the present toxic environment, all of that is not to be spoken—but all that has nevertheless happened since September 11.

SEPTEMBER 23, 2008

Fossilized Foreign Policy

On the international scene, Barack Obama is five years out of date

Much of what Barack Obama has said about the world beyond our shores is about five years out of date. Its pedigree is the stale campaign rhetoric of years past. But the world of 2009 will be far different from 2003. And if elected, a President Obama would probably not do much differently abroad than what we are doing right now.

Take Afghanistan. It is not the proverbial "good" war—as if the Taliban thinks they are more likely to lose than was al-Qaeda in Iraq, because the United Nations and NATO were always more supportive of American operations in Afghanistan than in Iraq. Even the tired cliché "Taking our eye off the ball" rings hollow, given that radical Islam suffered a terrible defeat in Iraq in a way it did not in the Hindu Kush. Seasoned American troops also gained critical anti-insurgency skills in Iraq in a way short-leashed NATO soldiers in Afghanistan did not.

Instead, the dilemma of the last seven years remains the de facto sanctuary offered to the Taliban and Islamic terrorists by nuclear Islamic Pakistan. Yet our options do not include overt invasions into Pakistan as once suggested by Obama. Most likely, after the election we will continue to do what are doing—killing terrorists on Pakistani soil through airborne drone attacks and occasional stealthy incursions—most denied by both us and the Pakistani government; promoting democratic reform; using American aid and the threat of its suspension to force government action against the tribal badlands; and strengthening ties with democratic India.

The Afghan government, while constitutional, remains far more ossified than is the much maligned Maliki administration in Iraq. It cannot win the hearts and minds of Afghans unless it proves to tribes that it is less corrupt and more competent than the seventh-century Taliban thugs who once ran the country. Rhetoric about Iraq timetables, surges, and who voted for this and should apologize for that are talking points of the 2007 primary that were already fossilized when they were made. Like it or not, much of Iraq is quiet. Fewer Americans are being killed in Baghdad each month than are in Detroit, Chicago, or Los Angeles.

The argument is now only over when and how—rather than if—Americans withdraw. Two paradoxes predominate: We have to leave carefully as conditions on the ground allow and the autonomous Iraqis advise. And once we start leaving, it is highly unlikely that we will return in force. The general public consensus has been that the American occupation was aimed at achieving post-Saddam calm, not an endless guarantee of a perpetual quiet that does not currently pertain in Pakistan, Yemen, Turkey, or any other Islamic country. The objectives of the removal of Saddam and the creation of a calm landscape for constitutional government have been achieved. What follows in the next decade will be the choice and responsibility of the Iraqi people as our own dwindling presence reverts to something analogous—albeit to a much smaller degree—to the insurance forces now in Korea and Europe. Obama advocated all forces out by March 2008; he would be lucky to accomplish half that by 2010.

Obama also has suggested that both sides were at fault in Georgia, that the U.N. might solve the crisis, and that Iraqi preemption was the green light for Russian invasion. All that was mostly incorrect, and again part of the old 2003 blame-America-first, rely-on-the-U.N. harping. The fact is that a past bipartisan American effort to offer former Soviet republics constitutional government and integration with Western economies—while often clumsily enacted and poorly thought out—was, in principle, well worth the risk. The gambit worked. The result is that, despite hotheaded Georgian leaders, today we are dealing with a shrinking, isolated Russian oligarchy of 140 million people, not an imperial colossus of 300 million with compliant puppet states.

Wounded Russian pride and the soaring price of oil have honed Russian foreign policy into whatever the U.S. is for, they are against. We should understand that to expect any Russian help in Iran or the Middle East, or full integration with European countries, we would probably either have to see true democracy emerge in Russia—or, barring that, our own acquiescence to Russian attempts to subvert the proud democratic republics on its borders. Neither is likely. Obama's past sermonizing about dismantling nuclear weapons, stopping weapons development, high-level talks with Russia to reduce strategic arms, ending anti-ballistic missile development, and cutting the Pentagon sounded like glitzy "hope and change" on the eve of the Iowa caucus, but is embarrassing to listen to a near year later.

The old mantra is still to talk with Iran. But we have done that frequently in past administrations, and the present Bush rhetoric is hardly bellicose. Our present uninterest in provoking Iran may explain why Teheran keeps screaming to nonexistent audiences about destroying Israel. Meanwhile, the mullahs look at Pakistan and North Korea and see that prestige, influence, money, and latitude are given to nuclear powers, even as the world claims proliferation brings ostracism and global disdain. All choices with Iran are bad. Obama may grandly talk with Ahmadinejad, but will end up doing about what he is criticizing

Bush for doing now—hoping that Iraq stabilizes and thus destabilizes Iran, rather than vice versa; hoping that sanctions weaken the Iranian economy to the point of prompting democratic reform; hoping that Europe, China, or Russia might help in stopping nuclear proliferation— all the while insisting that the military option is still open while privately expecting that Israel may act at the eleventh hour, bringing as much Western relief as it does condemnation of Israeli preemption and unilateralism.

Obama for years has been talking grandly of curbing anti-Americanism. But reciting myths to screaming Berliners—that the world, rather than the U.S. Air Force, once saved Berlin from the Russians—or citing our own misdemeanors to applause, is not a remedy. Mobs in Turkey, Pakistan, and Egypt may scream, "Death to America!" But each of those countries—all recipients of billions of American aid—is undergoing Islamic fundamentalist challenges that transcend what we say or do. Their former furor was spurred on by the idea we had invaded Iraq and failed, and is subsiding as we are restoring calm and sponsoring reform.

The truth is that much of Africa, India, and Japan are pro-American. So are the governments of Britain, France, Germany, and Italy. It is easy to cite the old acrimony of 2003 over Iraq. But privately, disarmed Europeans these days are terrified of an energy-rich bullying Russia, Islamic terrorism and their own demographic nightmares, a nuclear Iran, and a carbon-spewing, commercial China—and look for "unilateral" U.S. leadership.

In the war against terror, Obama may dismantle Guantánamo in deference to global furor. But he will then be presented with a dilemma of what to do with captured insurgents. He will earn new problems of his own, either having to let jihadists go, set up Guantánamo-like prisons out of sight in Afghanistan, or to conduct costly trials—as if a killer without a uniform caught in combat on the Pakistani border shares the same Miranda rights as a teenager pulled over for an open beer container.

For all the rhetoric about a shredded Constitution, Obama will do nothing about the FISA laws. He won't repeal the Patriot Act. Homeland Security will stay as it is. A President Obama won't overhaul domestic security because we all privately assume that we have stopped hundreds of planned terrorist operations through vigilance here and fighting abroad over the last seven years. Even as a President Obama does nothing differently, watch the talk of America as a police state among his loud supporters suddenly cease.

When Obama talks of change abroad, he really means nothing much of substance, however effective his own personal story and multilateral rhetoric might be to win friends. But to achieve real enhancements in our global stature and influence, we need a financially stronger and less dependent United States. For that to transpire, we would have to curb the near trillion dollars we send abroad for energy imports; develop more oil, coal, natural gas, and nuclear power at home; curb government spending; pay down debt; and forgo further government expansion and new programs.

The worst thing a new administration could do to weaken American influence abroad would be to repeal free trade agreements and rail at foreign producers, while ignoring fossil fuel production and nuclear power at home; to create a trillion-dollar new network of government entitlements; and to raise taxes in times of American uncertainty.

So far the Obama foreign policy has been whatever George W. Bush does, it must be inherently wrong—without realizing that the current administration is simply doing abroad what any sane president, liberal or conservative, would do in similar circumstances. Obama won't change much overseas, but his policies at home of trade renegotiation, higher taxes, more government spending, strategic-arms cuts, billions invested in subsidies to unproven energy sources, and less fossil fuel production are reminiscent of the Carter administration. They would make us weaker, and thus ultimately even less liked abroad—disdain being the stronger emotion than envy.

MARCH 13, 2009

Europeanizing Europe

Europeans wanted Barack Obama. They may have got more than they bargained for.

L ast summer, with several other Americans, I went to a garden reception attended by some French barristers, generals, and assorted professionals in Versailles. Most of them, conservatives and liberals alike, were quite ecstatic about the prospect of Barack Obama as the next American president—except one. He glanced around and then quietly whispered to me, "There is only room for one Obama—and, you remember, we already are the Obama."

I think we are beginning to understand something of what he meant.

Europe went gaga over the campaign of Barack Obama—especially his serial references to multilateralism, vows to leave Iraq, eco-utopianism, and the soothing way in which he trumped Europe's own disgust with the Bush administration. Promises of nationalized health care, higher taxes, Kyoto redux, and more government cheered Europeans, leading them to believe that Obama would steer America on a path closer to their own. (That the French, German, and Italian governments may be slightly to the right of Obama was never mentioned—nor was the fact that in their lethargy Europeans occasionally like to come over here for a swig of old-fashioned rip-roaring America.)

Yet after the first seven weeks of the Obama administration some in Europe may be reminded of the old adage, "Be careful what you wish for." Take unilateralism. After the invasion of Iraq, Europe mostly lambasted Bush as a go-it-alone cowboy who ridiculed "Old Europe." They forgot about American attempts to lead a joint effort to stop nuclear proliferation in North Korea and Iran, fight the Taliban in Afghanistan, beat back al-Qaeda, and ensure European autonomy in the face of an ascendant Russia. Tell a European that the U.S. military killed some pretty awful Islamic terrorists in Afghanistan, Waziristan, and Iraq—

terrorists who liked Europeans no better than us—and he was likely to play-act that we had created such creepy killers.

But now President Obama seems to be taking Europe at its multi-culturalist, multilateralist word. He asks for more European troops in Afghanistan, and yet before they even arrive he wants to open dialogue with the "moderate" elements of the Taliban—sort of like searching out reasonable Nazis around 1942, or looking for circumspect Japanese after Iwo Jima. (Apparently, he thinks the Taliban haven't heard of his $1.7-trillion deficit and his trashing of the cowboy Bush, or read his sympathetic press rebranding the once "good" Afghan war as the "quagmire.") Meanwhile Obama is playing Jacques Chirac in the Middle East, seeking talks with both Bashar al-Assad and Mahmoud Ahmadinejad without preconditions. His Al Arabiya interview put him squarely to the left of the old European colonialists. (It was not for nothing that he sent back the bust of Winston Churchill and offered the visiting British pith helmets some fire-sale DVDs as presidential presents.)

Recently, in a letter to Russian leaders, Obama tried his hand at Kissingerian quid pro quo, apparently offering to give up Eastern European missile defense (had the Poles and Czechs heard about that?) if Russia would help stop the nuclear program it had helped jumpstart in Iran. That would be like asking Dr. A. Q. Khan, strangely released last month from house arrest, if he might talk sense to North Korea's rogue nuclear scientists. In any case, those missiles were expensive in times of dearth, and how can you press the reset button with Putin if those pesky Eastern Europeans insist on chest-thumping to their former overlords?

Unlike the strutting but committed free-trader Bush, Obama is far more likely to arrange some quiet protection for American industries from subsidized foreign competition. So he may well back off from open markets and free-trade leagues, just as he promised in the campaign—and just as jittery EU functionaries worry in their pro forma praises of America's commitment to globalization. And if European technocrats come over here to bitch about new trade realities, they will surely get a dose of mellifluous "Hope and Change" and elegant denials that will shame them into never suggesting that we had become Buchanan-like protectionists.

Europeans once loved to ridicule Bush as a laissez-faire capitalist as they racked up trade surpluses with the United States. Now a far more sympathetic Obama may well make it harder for Europeans to send in goods without encountering some sort of tariff. And if Europeans and everyone else once looked to a wide-open, low-tax, risk-it-all United States to jumpstart the world economy and help spread globalization, well, from now on, we will be consulting with Europe for joint government initiatives on convincing the Indians and Chinese to shut down their coal plants—as we ask the lattermost to lend us more cash.

It was easy to ridicule straw-in-the-mouth Bush for cracking down on Islamic terrorists. Now Obama may well send some of them back from Guantanamo to face European postmodern justice. It was also easy for Euros to slur the Patriot Act and "extraordinary rendition" as signs of the new American fascism, even as their own judiciaries, immigration services, and investigative units quietly did things that we haven't dreamed of since the Civil War. But now the Europeans are confused—is Obama to the left of them in the war on terror (does the war on terror even exist any more?) or is he Bush without the twang? Can we Americans at last lecture our allies about the absence of habeas corpus in some European countries, or their illiberal practice of preventive detention?

What is going on here? Europeans got what their hearts wanted, but forgot what their heads told them. For 50 years, they have caricatured America as it served as the dumping ground for the export economies of the world. It (often clumsily) defended Europe at no cost, and got snickers and triangulation as its thanks. America's belching cars and smokestack industries were the object of disdain by the supposedly green Euros, who in fact never met any of the Kyoto guidelines that they preached to everyone else.

Europe talked a great multicultural game, as the antithesis to America's dirty role as the world's cop that had to do nasty things like get Saddam out of Kuwait and then Iraq itself, rid the world of Milosevic, and chase the Taliban from Afghanistan.

Europeans gave Nobel Prizes to Jimmy Carter and Al Gore with the idea of poking in the eye the conservative American establishment—not as proof that in their wildest dreams they would wish to see once again Carter's 1977–80 governance or enact Al Gore's ideas for shutting down the West's industrial infrastructure within a decade. (French nuclear plants and Eastern European coal-based production have no place in the Goreist wind-and-solar global paradise.) Suddenly America has flipped, and Europe is bewildered and afraid that we may be the new, but more powerful and influential, Europe—and thus Europe will be left alone, with no foil. Its intellectuals talk of post-colonialism and post-imperialism, as they brag of their new multicultural fides. Quietly they worry about unassimilated minorities in their cities with names like Hussein. And while they accept that a Barack Obama would never make it to a major European ministry, they cannot accept that he knows that all too well himself—and should have little problem from time to time reminding the world of it as well.

What will soon scare London and Paris and Berlin is that when the Russians "haggle," or squeeze Ukraine, or play games with gas exports, Americans will be right behind them in referring all such crises to the United Nations for multipolar talks. We may slice our deficit by cutting a carrier group or three, content to suggest that the Charles de Gaulle dock off Darfur to do a little air recon, or visit Georgia to reassure the people of Western support.

In the Middle East, we will worry about the sorry legacy of colonialism, as our multicultural president opens new initiatives with some pretty rough customers. (Europe, not the U.S., will be in range of the new Iranian missiles.) Europe can't even get its old rise out of us by bashing Israel, not when we are giving Hamas-controlled Gaza $1 billion in aid, and when the administration wanted Samantha Power and Charles Freeman as our regional experts. Re-empowered unions, Democratic protectionism, high taxes, big government, astronomical deficits, idealistic 1930s isolationism—not the globalization and free-market trade once demanded by the now moribund masters of the universe on Wall Street—are America's new creed. Who knows? Soon our elite may be thinking of emigrating to the Netherlands or Denmark to avoid America's high taxes and its new redistributive government regulations. Who knows? Soon a European eccentric may have to come over here, Churchill-like, to warn us about the storm clouds on the global horizons.

In short, we are going to Europeanize Europe in a manner far beyond what they ever dreamed of doing to us.

APRIL 15, 2009

President of the World

The globe is hearing a deeply pessimistic view of what America was and is

G iven Obama's performance on his recent trip, three developments were quite astounding. First, despite this fresh climate of atonement, there was a complete absence of a single apology from any other foreign leader—odd for the new shared spirit of multi-polarity and reciprocity. Not a word came from Britain about colonialism. Nothing from Germany on the Holocaust, or its trade with Iran. Not a peep from France about Algeria or Vietnam. Turkey was mum on the Armenian killings and its own tough anti-Kurdish policies. Russia said nothing about the 30 million murdered by Stalin—or its present assassinations abroad, much less its leveling of Grozny or its destruction of Afghanistan. Nothing came from China about the 70 million who perished under Mao or its present role in subsidizing North Korean nukes—or its violation of global copyright laws. We won't hear anything in the "New Asian Hemisphere" about Muslim Uighurs or Tibet.

Second, there was no other example of "He did it!" about supposedly inept predecessors. Mr. Medvedev said nothing about Putin's brutish rule. Sarkozy and Merkel did not trash the shady Chirac or Gazprom's bought lobbyist Schroeder, and their role in harming the Atlantic alliance. Gordon Brown was quiet about Tony Blair and Iraq. China did not mention a reset button. The new Berlusconi did not trash the old Berlusconi.

Third, we saw no concrete evidence of any help—or hope and change—from any foreign leader. Zilch. There were expectations of American concessions, but nothing new or helpful from anyone else. Instead I think a number of astute foreign leaders—rivals, enemies, and friends alike—have already drawn the following conclusions.

I. An Obama visit.

A vast entourage will descend on your capital in campaign mode.
Most of your functionaries will wish to get a photo-op with the rock-star president. The American president at some point will request a "town-hall meeting," press conference, or open-air handshake session with the crowd. All this is largely for domestic consumption back home, and is designed to offer an antidote for the concessions or apologies that follow. It is quite successful in generating temporary goodwill toward the new Obama administration.

II. "I'm sorry."

Obama will apologize for almost anything one can imagine. First comes the generic lamentation about Bush, the need for a reset button, and America's characteristic "arrogance." Then there are the "we are at fault" lines on spec, tailor-made mea culpas for the country in question. If you are Turkish and Islamic, you get a threefer: the morally equivalent reference to the American treatment of the Indians, the pledge that we are not at war with Islam (forget that no president ever said we were), and the reminder that we are not a Christian nation. In Europe, you receive apologies for Bush, Iraq, and the financial meltdown. Each leader gets a unique version of Obama's somewhat narcissistic "Them, not me"—either a strain of something like "Bush did it" or "Every American except me is arrogant." We can console ourselves only that Obama has not contextualized or apologized to the Somali pirates—yet.

III. "You're Right!"

Differences that your country has with the United States will be resolved in your favor. Foreign leaders already sense that Obama's success hinges on his "hope and change" ecstasy back home—which cannot for long sustain stories of difficult diplomacy and public manifestations of international trouble and acrimony, of anything really that suggests he is not mesmerizing the world in the manner he did the American electorate. Europe? Take your pick. No more combat troops to Afghanistan; an international financial "czar"; no additional financial deficit stimuli; no Guantanamo prisoners on European shores; American acknowledgment of culpability for the financial crisis; no mention of Europe's own reckless lending, protectionism, or pre-September 2008 declining GDP. But goodwill aplenty. China? It gets praise when it ridicules the dollar, but offers no help on North Korea. Nothing new about trade violations. Hope is expressed that they will still buy our growing debt. Russia? Let us count the ways. No more missile defense for Eastern Europe; no mention of Russia's human-rights violations or its policy of serial assassination abroad; de facto abandonment of advocacy for former Soviet republics' autonomy; Russia's energy blackmail is Russia's business; no help with de-nuclearizing Iran. Turkey? Yes, Europe must let you in the EU. The new Danish NATO supreme commander must apologize for defending free speech—and, as relish, hire some of your generals; continued American assurance that we are not a Christian nation.

The Islamic World is not to be inconvenienced by any mention of radical Islam, or 9/11, or of the endemic pathologies that nourished al-Qaedism in the first place—such as gender apartheid, religious intoler-ance, autocracy, statism, and tribalism. Instead there is plenty of Bush-bashing, courting of Iran and Syria, caricatures of the "war on terror," and talk of Iraq as a "mistake."

IV. "Them"

Then comes the "separation." Obama makes it clear to any host or for-eign leader that both he and his vision of America are strangely exempt from America's past, from Bush, and from our innately arrogant nature. That is accomplished in a number of adroit ways. There is evocation of his once-taboo middle name "Hussein" to win affection in the Middle East, but also to suggest a more Third Worldish resonance such as "I am one of you too who has grievances against 'them.' " He is beginning to mention the novelty of his racial heritage a lot, usually in the context that we are now in a new world of Obama, and that his very presence is a rejection of the old and illiberal America.

That the veteran Colin Powell and Russian-speaking Condoleezza Rice ran American foreign policy the last eight years, in a way unthink-able in Europe, is never voiced. Suggesting that China would have an Uighur foreign minister, that Saudi Arabia would have a Christian for-eign minister, that France would have an Algerian foreign minister, that

Germany would have a Turkish foreign minister, or that Russia would have a Chechen foreign minister is as absurd as suggesting that a Powell or Rice was never a big deal.

So what Obama leaves out about America is telling. He touches on slavery, lack of voting rights for blacks in the South (although he conflates this issue and implies to foreigners that African Americans could not vote in the North as well), our past treatment of Native Americans, and the dropping of the bomb against Japan. These transgressions are rarely put in any historical context, much less referenced as sins of mankind shared by all of his hosts (the pedigree of murder, exploitation, and rapine of his foreign interlocutors is quite stunning). We don't hear many references to the American Revolution, or the great tradition of American ingenuity embodied by Bell, Edison, or the Wright brothers.

We hear nothing about our Gettysburg, or our entry into World War I. Iwo Jima and the Bulge are never alluded to. Drawing the line in Korea and forcing the end of the Soviet monstrosity are taboo subjects. That we pledged the life of New York for Berlin in the Cold War is unknown. Liberating Afghanistan and Iraq from the diabolical Taliban and Saddam Hussein is left unsaid. The Civil Rights movement, the Great Society, affirmative action, and present billion-dollar foreign-aid programs apparently never existed. Millions of Africans have been saved by George Bush's efforts at extending life-saving medicines to AIDS patients—but again, this is never referenced. □ □

V. What's Next?

At present the world is watching, probing, and digesting the Obama presidency. But it has already concluded that Obama is nourished by applause and will work to maintain it—not merely for personal gratification, but because he realizes that loud public endorsement is essential to his perpetual candidacy, given its absence of experience and sagacity. Those abroad are also reassured that the American media, so heavily invested in hope and change, will do almost anything to transmogrify American embarrassments into Obama successes. Meanwhile, the contours of the new world order are clear. Iraq's democrats are snubbed; Iran's cutthroats are courted. A Saudi royal receives a bow;

the British queen, a presumptuous squeeze—while her prime minister receives unplayable DVDs.

Pakistan released Dr. Khan and wants us to idle our Predators. Iran is adding to its centrifuges. North Korea will ready ever-more missiles. Syria lectures on the putative peace it is begged to participate in. The former Soviet republics will fall back into line, closing American supply bases or bracing for the next Putin push. Israel gets a Charles Freeman nomination; Gaza a billion U.S. dollars in aid.

The odious governments of Cuba, Libya, and Syria quite logically have now expressed warmth of some sort for Obama and expect similar treatment in return. Russia fears little challenge to the reestablishment of its 19th-century influence. Pirates in Somalia, though slightly fewer in number today, likely have little to fear going forward. Europe had better prepare for its own defense. So should Japan. They may get more expressions of outrage when crises loom, more calls for U.N. action, but not much more than that. Expect a world of more nukes, not fewer—in direct proportion to Obama's calls for their entire elimination.

In short, we have a return of Jimmy Carter's postnational idealism, but this time with the charismatic face of a Ronald Reagan. For 40 years we have had well-meaning moral equivalence, utopian pacifism, and multiculturalism taught in our schools, and we are now learning that all that was not just therapy, but has insidiously become our national gospel. The world is hearing a deeply pessimistic view of what America was and is—now offered in mellifluous cadences by a messianic president who not so long ago in more unguarded moments called for more oppression studies and reparations.

President Obama will get his much-needed praise and adulation abroad, and Americans will finally be somewhat admired for a while. And thereafter, there will be real hell to pay—either abject U.S. appeasement as the world heats up, or some sort of frantic eleventh-hour hyper-response to restore stability and lost deterrence.

Just watch.

APRIL 15, 2009

A Thug's Primer

How to win liberal friends and oppress your people.

How strange that our rather nondescript, sober friends abroad do not garner attention from the current administration, yet overt enemies in Cuba, Nicaragua, Iran, Venezuela, and the West Bank most certainly do. Is there some covert code of conduct known to these dictators that allows them to win a pass from supposedly liberal Americans, who profess to value human rights, religious tolerance, and consensual government? Here's a tutorial for up-and-coming thugs abroad, who wish to ingratiate themselves with Western elites, not worry about "legitimacy," and not have someone meddle in their affairs.

DRESS MATTERS

Remember: Wear anything but a suit and tie. (Look at the drab Western wannabes Maliki and Netanyahu, and see what their suits got them.) The Iranian no-tie look impresses a lot of Americans, as it "makes a statement" that you are not part of a global conformist class, but instead deliberately challenge the norms of bourgeois dress. The full-length robe works too, given the Western image of the Gandhian Holy Man (the one-bare-shoulder look is preferable to the Saudi trailing style). Better still is the Mao-style wardrobe that allows you to appear as if you just left an organizing rally on the shop floor.

If you must go the touchy military route, please avoid the four-star-general look, with gold braid, sunglasses, and high-crested, bronze-starred hat. Remember, you are still a private in spirit. If you insist on braid and medals, then no higher than a colonel's: a man of the barracks who leads the rank-and-file in a global war against capitalism.

Best of all are camouflage, boots, and a baseball-type cap, in the manner of Castro and Chávez. The olive-drab jump suit of Kim Jong Il doesn't cut it. If one insists on the caudillo persona, then do it with wacky flair, as did Qaddafi—that is, be more a goofy, braided Michael Jackson moonwalker than a grim-peacock shah or Pinochet.

DON'T FORGET GROOMING

Try the perpetual three-day beard, Arafat-style, as if you're always shaving in the field with your comrades. Next best is mangy facial hair, à la Ahmadinejad, which suggests you once were an artist, novelist, or dissident of some sort. Castro's bushy beard and curls also convey an admirable defiance of the man in the gray flannel suit. In South America and the Middle East, the black moustache alone will do. Che-style hair and beard do well for the revolutionary phase, but they should be tamed to the Daniel Ortega half-bad look once you've taken over the government. Again, watch the sunglasses: They evoke a Greek colonel or South American strongman. Go instead with the nerd look of a 1950s intellectual: plastic rims on top, bare glass on the bottom. The more studious, the more bookish—the more you can jail. Think Allende or Trotsky, not Somoza.

SPEECH CODES

Don't use the hobgoblin word Communism: It's always socialism when you nationalize, steal property, take over businesses, shoot protestors, and shut down newspapers. Stay on message: The enemy is "globalization," capitalism, imperialism, racism, sexism, and always the United States. Be sure to use the buzz words "democracy" or "republic" in all your briefings, as in "The People's Republic of . . . " or "The Democratic Federation of . . . " Throw in "rule of law" and "constitution" anytime you shoot more than 100; evoke an Egyptian novelist, Martin Luther King, or Nelson Mandela when you send out the tanks. Abu Ghraib cannot be overused.

If in doubt about what resonates in the West, pick up a course catalogue online from UC Santa Cruz or Vassar, and just cut and paste some course descriptions into your next communiqué. Always play offense: It is Mossadeq, Bay of Pigs, United Fruit, Exxon, Vietnam, and Guantanamo all the time. Don't be afraid to dig up any fossil you can.

One stale My Lai reference still gets you a pass for 1,000 jailed; an Abu Ghraib is worth 5,000 in your gulag. Play full-court press until the U.S. cracks and turns it over with, "I'm sorry for slavery, the Native American genocide, the A-bomb, Dresden, ethnically profiled airport security, the Klan, the Greek coup . . . " Once the Americans start blabbering, they won't stop—and you can step up the killing, jailing, and torturing without much worry.

MILK THE U.N.

Get on as many U.N. committees as possible. The more slots you have on the Human Rights Commission and its appendages, the more you can imprison. Send a few goons to serve on a U.N. peacekeeping force. They'll like the money and sex, and it wins you cover later on. (Who knows: When the shooting starts at home, they may send some of your own blue-hats to patrol your streets.)

Anything with the word "High," as in High Commission, or a phrase containing the word "Refugees," earns exemption. Israel is always a winning slur (but watch Holocaust denial; it works three or four times, but gets old quickly). In general, avoid the overt "Jews" and just keep it to "Zionists." Most people will know what you mean.

Jew-hating is always a win-win situation: The Euros love the rarified anti-Israel shtick (Israel has no oil, no terrorists, no mobs, and few people), and you can sprinkle in "apartheid," "racist," and "colonialist" as cover to liven it up if anyone objects. Don't laugh: "The Jews did it" still works. Ask Ahmadinejad about last week.

DON'T FORGET RACE

Race is a good grenade. If you're going to kill people here and there, at least start with any white males you can dredge up—a colonial remnant, a poor attaché, a wandering journalist. Follow the Mugabe mode. You can destroy an entire country, loot it, send it back to the stone age, ruin a generation of Africans—but only if you start and finish with a few white post-colonialist farmers. Don't forget the Lulu trope: White people (e.g., Jews on Wall Street) caused the meltdown. Remember too the Morales/Chávez angle: Colonialists did all this to us mestizos.

THE RIGHT RELIGION
Don't shy away from the Arafat reinvention: The most devotedly atheistic Communist can still become a Muslim fundamentalist, if it's a matter of galvanizing anti-U.S. mobs. If you must kill a few hundred in Africa, make sure they are Christians. That way some nutty evangelical group from the U.S. will rally to their cause—and ensure that you win an exemption from the New York Times and NPR, which will talk more about Billy Graham and Rick Warren than about the mountain of corpses piling up. Islam is a win-win situation: You can play a victim of Islamophobia, or seem unhinged at perceived slights and whip up a Danish cartoon-like reaction.

NUKES
Invest in a few Pakistani or North Korean centrifuges. About every six months, go loony and talk about nuking Israel, Hawaii—almost anywhere there are Jews or at least a few white males. Don't worry about getting to the enrichment stage; just bluster and strut: You'll either get bribe money to stop or increased international stature.

Trot out one of your poor lackies educated at the Kennedy School and let him ramble about how unfair it is that Israel has a bomb and you don't. Under no circumstances, however, try this with the occasional wild-card American president like George W. Bush. You might end up like Saddam, or at least have to give up the game, as Qaddafi did.

FREE MONEY
Buy Chinese and Russian arms. They're cheaper, lend a revolutionary patina to your army, and may earn American bribe money later on. Egypt got $70 billion and American tanks not to repeat 1973. A few RPGs and suicide belts won the Palestinians billions of U.S. dollars. Arm to the teeth, talk up war—and then take cash to "stand down." One AK-47 with a big RPG attached shown on CNN is worth ten M-16s on Fox.

DRUGS
Under no circumstances fight drug cartels or talk tough about ending the marijuana, cocaine, or opium trade. These are legitimate sources of income for indigenous peoples, and their products often end up on

American college campuses anyway. What did all that DEA cooperation do for President Uribe in Colombia? If you use your ports and planes to smuggle drugs into the U.S., you could win three ways: The money is excellent, you are destroying bourgeois capitalist society, and the U.S. may give you a weird sort of pass out of respect for your act of revolutionary defiance and provocation. As a general rule neither Islamists nor Communists can be tagged as drug dealers, so it's pretty much a growth industry.

SEPTEMBER 2, 2009

From Preparedness to Appeasement

Grueling war, promises of peace, new attack— are we about to repeat a thrid cycle?

B y 1930 Verdun had been transmogrified almost into a dirty word in French schools. Throughout the late 1920s, the First World War was increasingly reinterpreted in the West as a futile bloodletting. International "Merchants of Death" and greedy capitalists, not the Kaiser's aggressive Prussian militarism, were now seen as the true causes of that recent horrific war. A punitive Versailles Treaty—and not the failure to invade, occupy, democratize, monitor, and transform a defeated Germany—was seen as the real mistake on the part of the victors.

Britain and France all but disarmed. The Maginot defensive line, England's island status, the new and welcomed art of appeasement (originally, lest we forget, a suitably liberal and humane idea), growing socialist movements, the League of Nations, and a new pacifism were all seen as substitutes for Neanderthal notions like deterrence and military preparedness. Perpetual peace was supposed to follow—and not another war with Germany a mere 20 years after the last one. Hitler, Mussolini, Tojo, and the rest begged to differ. After the Second World War, the United Kingdom and the United States once again disarmed at an astonishing rate. By June 1950, even tiny Communist North Korea had access to better tanks and jets than were available to nearby American occupation troops in Japan. Only the threat of a nuclear response kept Stalin's divisions from walking into postwar Western Europe—mostly disarmed despite efforts to forge a conventional NATO deterrent.

Louis Johnson, briefly Truman's secretary of defense, had sought to close down the Marine Corps altogether and dismantle as many army divisions as he could—all thought to be superfluous in the new postwar age of strategic air power and nuclear weapons following the defeat of the Axis powers. Admirals were up in arms over massive cancellations of shipbuilding and the mothballing of their fleets.

Then came the Communist-inspired effort to topple Greece and Turkey, the Communist takeover of China, the war in Korea, the brutal Soviet suppression of liberation movements in Eastern Europe, and the massive expansion of the Soviet Union's conventional and nuclear forces. Only the rearming of the United States in the early 1950s, along with the new policy of containment and foreign aid, stopped the Soviet advance and saved millions from Communist takeovers.

By the mid-1970s the United States was weary again. Vietnam had nearly wrecked the American military and had sent millions into the streets at home. Accommodation and détente—not the rollback of Communism—were the preferred way of dealing with an ascendant, but now supposedly more moderate, Soviet Union.

After the Nixon years and Watergate, the evangelical Jimmy Carter called for defense reductions and an end to our "inordinate" fear of Communism. He put confidence instead in the United Nations, good will among men, and a new emphasis on global human rights, rather than, yet again, reactionary deterrence.

But after the Soviet invasion of Afghanistan, Communist intrusions into Central America, the rise of radical Islam, and the takeover of the American embassy in Tehran, Carter ended his presidency in disillusionment about the efficacy of the United Nations, and about the supposedly benign intentions of the Soviet Union and radical Islam.

Nonetheless, Ronald Reagan was considered a cretin for once again massively rearming and waging an ideological war against the "evil empire" created by the Soviet Union, as well as for engaging in provocative acts like bombing Libya and invading Grenada. Reagan spent eight years enlarging all branches of the military, creating new strategic weapons, and opposing Soviet adventurism almost anywhere it was identified. Soon after he left office the Soviet Union collapsed and the Cold War ended.

George Bush continued these policies during the four years of his administration, but then, as if on cue, Bill Clinton reversed course and announced a "peace dividend." He reduced the number of army and marine divisions and of air wings. The military shrunk radically in size. New weapons programs were put on hold. We settled into the 1990s prosperity of the dot-com boom. The talk was all about twenty something college dropouts making millions in ground-floor stock options by brainstorming for brilliant new concerns like AskJeeves or America Online. Little Silicon Valleys were going to sprout up everywhere.

By 1999 Americans were focused on whether their president should be merely censured or impeached for engaging in sex acts with a White House intern in the Oval Office. Occasional radical Islamic attacks such as the World Trade Center bombing in 1993, the murder of U.S. servicemen in their Khobar Towers barracks in Saudi Arabia in 1996, the destruction of three of our East African embassies in 1998, and the assault on the U.S.S. Cole in 2000 were all considered police matters that did not warrant a full-fledged military response. It was the global American hegemony and support for Zionist Israel, not existential hatred for Western freedom and liberality, that provoked these outbursts from an exasperated radical Islam.

Then came 9/11, and the belated catch-up inevitably followed. A new Department of Homeland Security was created with bipartisan support. Both houses of Congress passed the Patriot Act. A majority of Democratic senators voted with the Republicans to authorize two wars, in Afghanistan and Iraq. President Bush enlarged the defense budget. In the dark days after 9/11, Americans praised the FBI, CIA, and armed forces for keeping us safe.

Indeed, for the next eight years there was no repetition of the September 11 massacres, despite terrible suicide bombings abroad. For all the tragedy of the occupations in Afghanistan and Iraq, both the

Taliban and Saddam Hussein were removed, and ensuing constitutional democracies continued to survive. Tens of thousands of al-Qaeda terrorists flocked to Iraq and were killed there. Their leadership remains attrited and scattered in the wilderness of Waziristan. Dozens of terrorist plots in America were broken up while still in the planning stages. The message went out that if another American city were to be attacked, an unpredictable but angry United States would go after any nation that had supported, housed, or subsidized the terrorists, even if only tangentially.

So here we are in yet the latest round of perpetual peace, this time overseen by a postnational, messianic Barack Obama. Serial apologies, engagement with dictators, the trashing of his predecessor, and calls for a newly empowered United Nations are all part of a sophisticated soft power that has replaced the old Bush "smoke 'em out," "dead or alive" reductionism.

We are more likely now to put CIA interrogators on trial than to arrest and berate new terrorists. Dick Cheney, not Osama bin Laden, has become the new national threat. George W. Bush has been reduced to Orwell's Emmanuel Goldstein, the "He did it" collective menace at whom we are supposed to yell out in hatred each morning. We now live in an era of renewed appeasement, faith in the United Nations, no "inordinate fear," and all the usual tired slogans.

Given the massive, nearly $2-trillion annual deficits, and the soon to be $9-trillion addition to the existing $11-trillion national debt, together with a new confidence in world governance, defense stagnation and cuts are not a matter of if, but only when.

So there is no need to mention what follows next in this tired old script. We may experience another attack like 9/11, given that many terrorists must now believe that the United States either cannot or will not go after them in the manner of the last eight years.

Many jihadists must feel that the new government in Washington is more likely to contextualize their hatred than ensure it does not spread or materialize into war. Regional bad actors—take your pick, from Ahmadinejad to Chávez to Kim to Putin –may feel it is about time to make regional adjustments in the balance of power, given their impressions that the United States is almost sympathetic to their frustrations and believes that Bush ineptness and bad faith, not the intrinsic agendas of such antidemocratic, ambitious powers, caused prior tension.

And once we experience such "adventurism," the reaction is just as scripted. We will want tougher CIA interrogators to ensure there is no more suicide mass murdering. Attorney General Eric Holder will go the way of Louis Johnson. Congress will hold hearings on who shut down Guantanamo and freed the terrorists. White papers will be issued detailing how the Obama administration curtailed proactive national-security measures. Committees will blast the creation of needless "firewalls" between agencies. Senators will call for more aid to Colombia or Georgia or South Korea or Israel or (fill in the blank). The cycle will play out as in the past, because, in this age of enlightenment, affluence, and leisure, we just cannot accept that human nature remains the same and thus predictable. It remains too depressing to concede that for a few evil opportunists good will is seen not as magnanimity to be appreciated, but as weakness to be tested. And who but a dunce would believe that continual military preparedness is far cheaper—and more humane—than the perpetual "peace dividend" and lowering of our defenses?

FEBRUARY 24, 2010

The 'I Am Not George Bush' Policy

What exactly are we doing with all the borrowing at home and the fighting abroad?

The first year of the Obama administration has been a vertiginous pile of confusions and contradictions. In hunting for a theme to its decision making, we might start with Obama's relation to his predecessor.

THE WORLD WAR II ANALOGY
George Bush, a purported conservative, ran up deficits reaching in

aggregate $2.5 trillion; therefore I, Barack Obama, a liberal, can legitimately exceed that figure by a factor of three or four. That seems to be the thinking of the present administration. And its common defense of the massive new deficit is the historical analogy that it will snap us out of the recession in the same way that deficit spending during World War II lifted us out of the Great Depression. Even many supporters of the new stimuli confess that the Depression was not cured by the New Deal, but rather by the strong demand in goods and services brought on by the war that followed. So the new mega-Keynesians describe their current remedies in terms not of 1933–39, but of 1941–45.

But even if one were to accept the questionable assumption that our current recession is anything like the downturn of the 1930s (10 percent unemployment versus 25 percent), we forget that what allowed us to manage the high levels of incurred debt was the rebound after 1945, when U.S. manufacturing, natural resources, and expertise met much of the industrialized world's postwar demand until the wrecked economies of Europe, Russia, and Japan rebounded. Yet in the current weak recovery, we certainly will not be paying back our borrowed trillions by exporting to a needy world already well supplied by Europe, Japan, Korea, and China. Bottom line: We have no easy means to create the wealth necessary to pay back the unprecedented trillions we now owe – and we have no accurate historical parallel to guide us through these upcoming years of unsustainable levels of indebtedness, other than perhaps a Greece or Argentina writ large.

WAR AS CRIMINALITY

The Obama administration may be right in the abstract that we can try in criminal courts individual terrorists who are apprehended here in the United States, on the assumption that they are not uniformed combatants of a declared enemy. But so far, in our post–9/11 world, the administration has offered no comprehensive exegesis concerning who the terrorist enemy is and how he is to be fought and defeated. Instead, Obama came into office with a generic mantra that "Bush did it" and therefore "it" was wrong—and apparently figured that a knee-jerk antithesis of any sort must therefore be right.

I used to think radical Islamic fundamentalists were the problem, but now I'm not quite sure whether our military is prepared for domestic guys mad at the IRS, natural disasters, anti-Muslim backlash, or poverty and hunger.

So we are not in a "war," we're in an "overseas contingency operation" (against whom?). Non-uniformed combatants are criminal suspects—sort of. If they try to blow up hundreds of people in our passenger jets we will arrest them, read them their Miranda rights, and try them in American civilian courts. But because we are terrified that one rogue juror might nullify an obvious verdict, edgy high-level administration officials will assure the public beforehand that the grotesquely misnamed "suspects" will be found guilty and either executed or imprisoned for life after their show trials. So prejudicial pre-trial publicity is now as acceptable as the absence of Miranda rights once was not.

We will also investigate former officials for waterboarding three confessed mass murderers in Guantanamo, but we will not investigate current officials for ordering dozens of assassinations in Pakistan as judge, jury, and executioner of suspected terrorists—and any living thing in their immediate environs. We adhere to the narrative that the prior War on Terror was flawed, and so either we will only very quietly embrace its protocols—tribunals, renditions, Predators, the Patriot Act, etc.—or we will embrace virtual changes, like the promise of closing Guantanamo within a year or trying Khalid Sheikh Mohammed in New York in a civilian court.

The apparent subtext is that the Left in the past really had no problems with renditions, targeted assassinations, Guantanamo, tribunals, Predators, or the wars in Iraq and Afghanistan—only that George Bush presided over them. Take the latter away, and so too vanishes criticism of the former. Bottom line: We have no systematic answer to whether we should try or summarily execute suspected terrorists, whether they are enemy combatants or felons, or whether it is more moral to waterboard known terrorists or to execute suspected ones.

IRAQ

Here is the Obama saga on Iraq: 2003: a mistaken war; 2004: "not much of a difference between my position on Iraq and George Bush's position at this stage"; 2005–07: voted each year to fund the war; 2007: all troops out by March 2008; 2008: the surge is not working; 2009: the status-of-forces agreement signed by Bush is adhered to; 2010: Iraq (according to Vice President Biden) might be the administration's greatest achievement—though it was, of course, not worth the cost. Factor in Bush's popularity rating at any one time, the relative ongoing level of violence in Iraq, and the proximity of Obama to an election, and one might predict his often-changing position on the war. So what exactly is Iraq now? Is it a brilliant effort by the U.S. military that removed Saddam, defeated an insurrection, helped to wipe out thousands of al-Qaeda terrorists, and birthed a viable consensual government? Or is it still "Bush's war," which somehow morphed into Obama's "greatest achievement" by some mysterious and yet unspoken process?

Bottom line: This administration, partly because of past declarations, partly because of its own innate confusion, cannot quite celebrate the success in Iraq and so settles on the confused notion that we nobly removed Saddam and fostered consensual government although we should never have tried to do either. Similar surreal examples could be found in matters of health care, global warming, partisan politics, and immigration. It seems reductionist to suggest that Obama came into office with little clue how to govern or to galvanize the country, but with one real assumption: He would simply advertise himself as not George Bush, and almost anything he subsequently did would be declared inspired by the enthralled media.

Keep that notion in mind, and the confusion over the last year makes a sort of sense.

MARCH 11, 2010

Resetting Our Reset Foreign Policy

Obama's old foreign policy wasn't working;
thank goodness he's hitting the reset button.

Almost every element of Barack Obama's once-heralded new "reset" foreign policy of a year ago either has been reset or likely soon will be. Consider Obama's approach to the eight-year-old War on Terror. Plans made more than a year ago to shut down the detention center at Guantanamo Bay by January 2010 have stalled. Despite loud proclamations about trying Khalid Sheikh Mohammed, the architect of 9/11, in a civilian court in New York, such an absurd pledge will probably never be kept.

Talk of trying our own former CIA interrogators for being too tough on terrorist suspects has also come to nothing. And why not put an end to the second-guessing of anti-terrorism protocols, since the Obama administration, in a single year, has quadrupled the number of assassinations by Predator drones of suspected Taliban and al-Qaeda operatives in Pakistan? After all, the targeted killing of hundreds of suspects is far more questionable than waterboarding three confessed killers.

The Obama administration seems to have embraced the once widely criticized Bush-Petraeus strategy in Iraq of gradual withdrawal in concert with Iraqi benchmarks. Indeed, Vice President Joe Biden in Orwellian fashion claims that our victory in Iraq may be one of the current administration's "greatest achievements." Was it not a defeatist Biden who not long ago advocated the trisection of Iraq into separate nations?

And after months of waiting, Obama finally sent more troops to Afghanistan, adopting a surge strategy that looks a lot like Bush's 2007 escalation in Iraq—this despite the fact that he once assured the country that Bush's surge, in a tactical sense, "wasn't working." Almost all of the once-derided Bush anti-terrorism protocols are still in place—wiretaps, intercepts, tribunals, and renditions. And given that there were more foiled radical-Islamic terrorist plots in 2009 than in any year since 2001, President Obama will probably stop his outreach speeches to the Islamic world and his serial recitations of American sins.

Our efforts to reach out and negotiate directly with Iran failed. Secretary of State Hillary Clinton effectively acknowledged the impasse, citing the unexpected de facto military coup by the Revolutionary Guard. In any case, does anyone believe that more Obama speeches, videos, new diplomacy, and imposed deadlines will halt an Iranian nuclear bomb?

President Obama was once a fierce critic of the former administration's Mideast policies. A year ago, he thought new outreach to the Palestinians and rebukes to the Israelis might lead to a breakthrough. They did not. In a Time magazine interview with Joe Klein, Obama confesses of the 70-year struggle: "I'll be honest with you. This is just really hard."

Obama assumed we could borrow a trillion dollars from the Communist Chinese and then turn around and lecture them on Tibet, human rights, and international trade and currency—sort of like a debtor admonishing his lender about his bank's shortcomings. Now the Chinese claim that their relations with America are "seriously disrupted," as they seek to dethrone the dollar as the global currency.

I don't think there will be any more grand deals with the Russians either, the sort that saw the United States withdraw anti-missile defense accords with Poland and the Czech Republic in hopes of halting the Iranian nuclear program. Instead, Russia and China are blocking American efforts to impose tougher sanctions on Iran. For all the outreach to Hugo Chávez, the Venezuelan strongman is still causing trouble in Latin America. So why is the "reset" foreign policy being reset?

First, too often Obama boxed himself into a corner by being against, in knee-jerk fashion, almost anything George Bush was for. Yet most of America's problems predated George Bush, who, especially in his second term, followed mostly centrist policies. Old enemies were enemies for a reason—and it had nothing to do with Bush.

Second, Obama's utopian rhetoric created impossible expectations of a new international brotherhood. So the disappointment became greater when nations simply acted like their usual self-interested selves instead of idealistic groupies at an Obama hope-and-change rally.

Third, the constant televised presence of Obama on his 24/7 bully pulpit has surely resulted in Obama fatigue. Most nations don't seem to fear any of his deadlines or appear mesmerized by his soaring rhetorical flourishes.

Fourth, the nearly $2 trillion annual deficit curbs both the moral and the material power of the United States, which has gone into hock to unsavory nations.

Fortunately for the country, Obama has not taken three years to reverse course—unlike Jimmy Carter, whose inaction led to a series of foreign-policy catastrophes like the 1979 Soviet invasion of Afghanistan and the storming of the U.S. embassy in Tehran.

By voluntarily backtracking—or being rebuffed—on almost all his initiatives, an idealistic Obama is reminding the world that anti-Americanism abroad is not caused so much by what the United States does, but largely by preconceived hostility to the values of liberty, free markets, and individual rights that the United States represents.

APRIL 28, 2010

Obama's Nuclear Naivety

The problem is not nuclear weapons per se, but who has them.

The Obama administration has celebrated its recent efforts to sign a nuclear-weapons accord with Russia and the hosting of a nuclear non-proliferation summit in Washington—all silhouetted against grandiose promises to seek the end of all nuclear weapons on the planet. But from all this, what real progress exactly have we made toward ensuring a world safer from the specter of nuclear annihilation? Aside from the wording of proposed treaties and proclamations, what are the larger philosophical assumptions behind the new utopian approach to non-proliferation?

First, nuclear weapons per se—regrettable though they may be—
are not exactly the problem. None of us is terrified that a democratic
Britain, France, Israel, or India possesses them. While we might prefer
that major autocracies like China and Russia were not nuclear, we do
not at present fret about a first strike from either, given that both are
invested in, and profit from, the global system of trade and commerce—and, in their more aggressive moments, are subject to classical
laws of deterrence.

Second, if any state is intent on mass murder, there are chemical
and biological mechanisms that might be cheaper and more accessible
than nuclear weapons. Far more people have been killed by machetes
since Hiroshima and Nagasaki than by nukes, but we could hardly have
stopped the violence in Rwanda by a worldwide ban on edged weapons.
The utopian wishes to ban the six-shooter; the realist, the gunslinger.

So the problem is not nuclear weapons, but who has them—in particular, the degree to which an autocratic, renegade country seeks them
either to threaten rivals, or to blackmail the world. We worry a lot about
a nuclear Pakistan, are especially disturbed over a nuclear North Korea,
and are terrified that Iran may well become nuclear. Their nuclear status earns them undue attention, money, and even deference from the
United States—which they might not have garnered had they not been
actual, or at least potential, nuclear powers.

So if we are to have a summit on non-proliferation, we should
either insist that Iran and North Korea are there, or ensure that their out-
lawry dominates the agenda. Anything else is merely a photo-op, the
equivalent of the grandstanding federal functionary citing the harmless,
mostly law-abiding citizen for his misdemeanor while he timidly
ignores the felonies of the dangerous hard-core criminal.

Third, an ancillary to nuclear non-proliferation should be strong
support for democratization. A world of 20 or so nuclear powers is
scary; a world of 20 or so dictatorial and autocratic nuclear powers is
terrifying. The Obama administration has loudly caricatured the supposed neoconservative fantasies of George W. Bush, but at least the
Bush administration grasped that the promotion of constitutional government was of value in discouraging first use of nuclear weapons.

In this context, it is especially regrettable that we have recently reached out to the dictatorship in Syria, despite its proven record of supporting terrorism and the spread of nuclear missiles while trying itself to obtain a nuclear program. President Obama's failure last spring and summer to support the Iranian dissidents was even more regrettable; the end of the theocracy is the only real way, short of the use of force, of increasing the likelihood either that Iran will not obtain a bomb, or that a future democratic government might, South African style, give up nukes that a prior regime had obtained.

Finally, the Obama administration is talking of eliminating nuclear weapons entirely. Unfortunately, I cannot think of a single deadly new weapon that ever disappeared by fiat. The Greeks at times tried to forbid the use of missile weapons; they later lamented the arrival of torsion artillery. Crossbows and then harquebuses were condemned by medieval and later European churchmen. Poison gas was supposedly never to reappear after its ghastly use in World War I.

All such utopian efforts failed for the simple reason that nations are sovereign entities and there has never been an effective international cop to enforce such well-meaning edicts. To expect nuclear weapons to vanish because of an international accord would be like supposing that the Articles of Confederation could bind and regulate the behavior of early American states, or that the League of Nations could save Abyssinia or Manchuria.

Instead, what restricts the use and effectiveness of deadly weapons systems historically has been both deterrence and new defensive technologies. If one state were to acquire an army of harquebusiers, they might be deterred from employing them in aggressive fashion, but only if convinced that their adversaries had an even larger army with better fiery weapons. Hitler refrained from using gas against enemy combatants because he feared reprisal in kind, not the long arm of the authorities in Geneva. And he most certainly did use Zyklon B against European Jewry because he felt neither fear nor shame in its usage.

What contributed to the ineffectiveness of catapults was not condemnation from infantry generals, but much broader, stone-faced, packed-earthen fortifications. In other words, given the general imperfectability of human nature, what will prevent a nuclear rogue state from annihilating its foes is either that it fears even greater retaliation, or, barring such deterrence, that an effective anti-ballistic missile system renders its arsenal nearly ineffective.

Any universal agreement barring the use of the bomb by existing nuclear powers is as likely to be honored by the majority of law-biding nations as it is to be broken by the minority of dangerous, lunatic states. True, international protocols could some day be collectively enforced by democratic states, but not through the promised participation of the world community at large, despite their protestations of global ecumenism. For confirmation of that pessimistic appraisal, simply review the membership rolls of the various U.N. commissions on human rights.

All that is not to say that the United States, either unilaterally or with its Western allies, should forswear the attempt, through force if need, to bar non-constitutional states from acquiring nuclear weapons at all costs. A nuclear Iran poses a myriad of dangers well beyond the specter of its first use of the bomb. More likely, Iran's agenda is to acquire nuclear weapons, and then increase the frequency of its promises to seek the annihilation of Israel—hoping insidiously and incrementally to wear down the Israelis to either appease Tehran or emigrate to safer places.

A nuclear Iran would be analogous to the lunatic homeowner with a huge personal arsenal who periodically threatens his neighbors with terrible retaliation should their leaves drift over his property—without necessarily intending to spray anyone with machine-gun fire. Who wishes to try to keep up property values, or even to live, in such a neighborhood?

This administration has developed a bad habit of talking tough and bullying friendly constitutional states while reaching out to hostile and bad-acting dictatorships. In general, that is unwise foreign policy. In terms of nuclear politics it is dangerous beyond belief.

JUNE 4, 2010

The Art of Seaborne Humiliation

There's just a chance that, if Israel doesn't lose its nerve, it could restore a climate of deterrence against seaborne provocations.

A tiny flotilla of "peace ships" sets out to run an Israeli blockade of the Gaza coast. The Israeli strategy in response is intended to ensure that neither weapons nor terrorists enter the Hamas-held territory, at a time when Hamas is in a virtual war with Israel.

Once the ships neared the coast, the choices were not good. Either the Israelis could allow the ships through, rendering the blockade irrelevant and permitting dozens of unknown persons to enter Gaza, along with unspecified cargos—or the Israelis had to intervene, ensuring that at some point they might have to use force, perhaps against some passengers who were not entirely unarmed.

And once things reached that point, the militarily dominant Israelis had lost the public-relations war—at least as conventional wisdom defines it. The Gaza flotilla, then, joins a long list of incidents— intifadas, kidnappings, rocket attacks—in which the provocation proves minor in comparison with the hoped-for response.

The aim of such provocations is to create over time a narrative in which the Israelis appear to be bullying aggressors not worthy of global, and perhaps not even of Western, support. As these incidents continue, Israel's enemies hope that at some point Israel will go too far, wear too thin the patience of the West, and finally lose the financial, military, and diplomatic support necessary for its very survival. That point has already been reached in Europe, and the Gaza-flotilla incident was aimed at doing the same within the United States—given the reset-button Middle East policy of President Obama.

As a general rule, nothing much good comes to a Western power when a rogue nation or anti-Western organization seeks confrontation on the seas. In such incidents, Iranians, Palestinians, North Koreans, and generic pirates are judged on an entirely different set of moral rules that tend to offer exemption for the weaker power (i.e., the victims of "disproportionate" force) or the crazier party (i.e., we expect provocation from them, but not retaliation from you).

In an unprovoked attack this past March, North Korea torpedoed a South Korean ship, killing 46 sailors. The general facts were clear enough, given torpedo fragments and the conclusions of an international body of experts who examined them.

But was South Korea going to risk a war—or even a small and temporary economic downturn—in any such period of heightened tensions? Would it restore deterrence if the South Korean navy sank the next North Korean ship that came its way?

Probably not. After all, there were neither worldwide demonstrations lamenting the killing of the South Korean sailors nor popular demands for retaliation against such naked aggression. But then, South Koreans are listening to iPods while not long ago North Koreans were eating grass.

China, nuclear North Korea's nuclear patron, was, of course, slightly miffed by the incident, given its commercial interest in keeping regional calm, but it was also slightly amused that states like South Korea, Taiwan, and Japan from time to time have to be reminded that power is not solely to be defined by GDP. As it is now, South Korea plays by the rules, convenes its expert panel to confirm what one already knew—and in the process humiliates itself by being presented with facts that, for a variety of reasons, it believes it cannot act upon.

When the Iranians hijacked a British patrol boat in March 2007 and took 15 sailors hostage for two weeks, the United Kingdom did little in response. Who wishes to go to war over a tiny spat like that? Meanwhile, Ahmadinejad paraded the sailors on television, fitted them out with Iranian dress, and thereby reminded the world that the navy of Nelson either cannot or will not protect its own personnel on the high seas. The message was clear to the nearby rich, but weak, Gulf oil exporters: Would you prefer to be allied with a brazen upstart that takes hostages from a supposedly stronger power, or with a hesitant power that begs to have them returned?

Over 1,000 pirates operate off the Somali coast. In 2009 they attempted 214 attacks on private shipping, well over twice the number tried in 2008. They remind ocean-goers that the world's great navies cannot ensure safe passage through the Gulf of Aden. And they count on Western publics' contextualizing their criminality—by adducing poverty, past exploitation, or lack of Western humanitarian aid—rather than demanding punishment for it.

Of course, the classical way of ending piracy—as Pompey demonstrated with the Cilician outlaws—is to combine naval interception with assaults against the criminals' home ports. But again, given the asymmetry involved in piracy—wealthy Western ship- or boat-owners versus desperate "others"—who wants to risk killing poor Third World civilians just to hit the pirates who live among them? The final scenes of Black Hawk Down give us a taste of what the shooting might look like on CNN.

Many other such incidents could be cited—think of the 1968 capture of the Pueblo by North Korea or the 1975 taking of the Mayaguez by the Khmer Rouge. While the details differ, the general playbook remains the same: Some sort of incident is staged at sea, where witnesses and boundaries are often nonexistent, in order to provoke a response that will work to the provoker's benefit.

In each of these cases, the instigator dares a powerful Western nation to retaliate and thereby stupidly endanger its collective good life over a small matter of 19th-century-style national pride. And if violence follows, the props almost always ensure that the Western nation is transmogrified in the blink of an eye into a bully, pushing around the Other where it has no business being in the first place. No wonder that the Western nation usually instead sends diplomats to work out some sort of restrained apology, which gives the provocateur stature and pours more humiliation upon the provoked—another milestone on a long road of weakening Western stature and influence.

What might change the rules of seaborne humiliation?

Perhaps the only remedy would be a new sort of public opinion that requires leaders to resist concessions. Such a tougher policy at first might mean some greater risk of violence, but standing up to Iranians, or North Koreans, or Somali pirates—or pro-Hamas activists—would, in the long run, reestablish deterrence and convince the aggressors that the last thing they wish to do is take on a Western ship.

In this regard, if Israel can make the case that it has a perfect right to inspect ships intending to bring supplies and persons into Gaza, then it should increase, not cease, such vigilance. What it would lose in public opinion in the short term would be more than outweighed in the long term by the establishment of a new scenario in which no ship, under any circumstances, wishes to confront an Israeli vessel at sea. But unless and until that happens, expect not only that the provocations of Hamas and its fellow travelers will increase, but also that regional powers from Iran to Turkey will take note of how staging confrontations with Israel results in strategic advantage—and favorable global press.

JUNE 18, 2010

The Great Anglo-American Spat

British public opinion was wildly in favor of candidate Obama. President Obama is proving to be something else again.

Various irate British observers—from columnists like Peter Hitchens and Geoffrey Wheatcroft to parliamentarians and former cabinet officials—have recently declared the "special relationship" with America to be over. The Anglo animus, perhaps brought to a boil by the World Cup soccer match and by President Obama's handling of the BP spill, has now reached comical levels. Everything from the War of 1812 to American neutrality in 1939 is evoked to prove that the present estrangement is more typical than aberrant in our post-1776 relations.

To be fair, the miffed British are reacting to two years of both perceived and real slights from the Obama administration. Who does not know the familiar litany? There was the rude return of the magnificent Churchill bust. The asymmetrical gift exchange with Gordon Brown—at the end of a visit in which the president repeatedly snubbed the prime minister—and the banal choice of gift for the queen the following month revealed a certain symbolic spite on the administration's part.

The State Department's suggestion that there was nothing particularly special about American-British relations did not help, especially given the feeling that America does not fully appreciate the singular British military contribution in Afghanistan—to be seen in the light of the meager European commitment.

Then there was Secretary Clinton's unnecessary preemptory announcement of American neutrality in the next round of disputes over the Falklands. All this is topped off by the constant presidential trashing of "British Petroleum" and its mess in the Gulf, with the implication that a foreign interest perhaps does not care too much for a former colony's ecology.

In reaction, polls reveal that a vast majority of British citizens believe that their relationship with America has worsened since 2009. Of course, we now show the same indifference to almost all our allies, such as the Colombians, Poles, and Israelis. Yet two ancillary considerations perhaps explain why the British are especially upset at these real and hyped slights.

One is embarrassment, and the second a sort of fear. First, in 2008 the British public heavily invested in candidate Obama as a long-awaited social-democratic anti-Bush. Four years earlier, in 2004, the British media had closely followed the American presidential election, with some commentators haughtily berating the voters of Ohio for giving Bush the margin of victory—as if one swing state that went conservative was responsible for ensuring a continuance of global discord. In this regard, the boorish and untrue slur against George Bush's supposed lack of interest in reading, offered earlier this month by the new court jester, Paul McCartney, as a sort of toady tip to a smiling Obama, is par for the course rather than a clumsy divot.

In 2008, the British public and press both bought, hook, line, and sinker, the reset-button promises of Barack Obama to be a listener. They welcomed a sort of elegant post-racial Wilsonian multilateralist—and, better yet, a progressive who did not drawl or offend like the pink, tongue-tied bore of old, Jimmy Carter. And so the damn-Bush/praise-Obama chorus sang on in Britain.

That the supposed yokel "Yo, Blair!" George W. Bush was strongly pro-British and that he cared deeply about his partnership with Tony Blair (who often had more influence on Bush than vice versa) were conveniently ignored. Indeed, the British were embarrassed by Bush's fondness for Blair and for the U.K. in general, as if he were some sort of Walmart Velcro that just wouldn't come unstuck.

Now, of course, the British have got what they wanted, and they are beginning to rue it. They fear that they have been had. And in a way, they most certainly have.

All of which brings us to our second consideration, the suspicion among some Brits that the Obama hostility is not so much the clumsiness of a raw rookie as it is the logical expression of our first "Pacific president," who feels no special affinity with Europe or reverence for the Western tradition—and thus especially no love for our colonial mother, Britain.

Indeed, we are getting yet another round of references in the British press to the passages in Dreams from My Father concerning the supposed maltreatment of Barack Obama's Kenyan grandfather for his anti-colonialist activities. When they are not doubting the truth of Obama's charges, British pundits express the fear that, in Aeschylean fashion, the sins of a pith-helmeted proconsul have earned them payback from a third-generation nemesis.

For some reason, the British—perhaps naïvely—believed that there was a universal brotherhood of progressives that transcended archaic national boundaries and so would trump any lingering animosity that Barack Obama picked up first from his family, and then during his odyssey from prep school in Hawaii, to Indonesia, to Occidental, Columbia, and Harvard Law, and to Chicago organizing, all of it amplified by close friendship with Bill Ayers and Rashid Khalidi, and, of course, dutiful attendance at Jeremiah Wright's Trinity United Church.

What these curiously assorted places and people have in common is disdain for the Western tradition and, again, an unspoken dislike of Britain in particular. In such a network, one might hear of the Raj, of Mossadegh, of the Mau Mau revolt, but nothing of Magna Carta, the Scottish Enlightenment, the effort to stop Bonaparte, the terrible costs of defending liberal values against Prussian nationalism, Nazism, fascism,

Japanese militarism, and Stalinism, or the largely peaceful withdrawal from empire—or the unmatched insight of Milton, Shakespeare, Gibbon, and Dickens, or the genius of Hobbes, Hume, Locke, and Burke.

In contrast, in the formative years of Barack Obama—and millions of others on the progressive Left—evocation of the evils of imperialism, colonialism, oppression, and exploitation were simply daily rituals. Names like Trafalgar, the Corn Laws, the British and Foreign Anti-Slavery Society, the Somme, the Battle of Britain, and El Alamein are, well, names of no particular significance. A president who thinks Americans liberated Auschwitz would hardly care to inquire about the RAF's "finest hour," or the contribution of a man like Field Marshall Alan Brooke to the winning of World War II.

In short, given the nature of American therapeutic education, the triumph of multiculturalism, and our own radically changing demography, if Barack Obama did not exist, one would have to invent him. What is strange, then, is not Obama's innate distrust of Britain, but the current surprise in Britain that someone like him is indifferent to what Britain stands for, past and present.

But note, when I said an Obama would have to be invented, I did not mean to imply that Obamaism is yet the norm—only that it is a strong current in American popular culture that at some point, if only for limited duration, was bound to find resonance at the highest level of government.

Obamaism is, however, not quite yet typical of American thinking.

Most Americans, across racial and cultural lines, still revere our British connection. It is what helps to explain why we are more like successful Canada than failing Mexico, why we look back at our own sacrifices at the side of Britain in two world wars with pride rather than regret, and why, for all the petty squabbling and rivalries, we usually think we are doing something wrong when Britain is not our partner.

What explains the way American Revolution unfolded and the success that followed is not just the courage and brilliance of our Founding Fathers but also the fact that we were revolting against Britain and not an Ottoman Empire, Russia, or China. Americans usually understand that, and so we blend our pride in American exceptionalism with acknowledgment that its font was British law, government, and culture.

Even as America becomes an increasingly diverse society, even as our schools turn away from traditional learning, nevertheless millions of Americans still grasp why we owe so much to Britain—and why we must never endanger our singular friendship with it, the cornerstone of American foreign policy. Our president's cavalier indifference to Britain reflects a strain in American life, but not American life per se. We may too often take Britain for granted, but we do so because our unspoken debt to it and our appreciation for it are part of our national fiber. Barack Obama cannot change that—as we will relearn either when he shows contrition, or at such time as he leaves office.

NOVEMBER 23, 2010

In Defense of Defense

From the November 29, 2010 issue of NR.

Two bedrock beliefs of traditional conservatism are fiscal discipline and strong national defense. Likewise, two general rules of budgetary reform in times of economic crisis are, first, to scale back expenditures rather than raise taxes, and, second, to look at defense for some of the deepest cuts. Something therefore will have to give.

In the last two years the United States has piled up record $1.3 trillion annual budget deficits. That red ink has pushed the national debt close to $14 trillion, approaching 98 percent of the nation's annual gross domestic product, a peacetime record. Worse still, there is no end in sight to this massive borrowing. Trillion-dollar budget deficits are scheduled at least through 2014 and will take our national debt beyond $18 trillion.

These staggering figures have caused near-panic throughout the world, as the Federal Reserve desperately prints $600 billion to monetize some of the huge debt, gold soars to over $1,400 an ounce, and Washington is chastised as profligate by everyone from Germany to

China, which worries about the solvency of its massive surplus dollar accounts. □□No wonder, then, that the quest for fiscal sanity became the signature of the Tea Party movement and fueled the general Republican political renaissance. But amid the talk of across-the-board budget freezes, radical entitlement reform, and elimination of entire programs, is it fair to spare defense from the anticipated 2011 slashing?

At first glance, clearly no. After all, the United States will spend over $680 billion on defense this year alone—slated to rise to $712 billion next year—and well over $1 trillion when you include defense-related expenses that are not counted in the official Pentagon budget. Depending on how one categorizes the figures, defense spending now represents over 19 percent of the federal budget and is nearing 5 percent of the nation's GDP. Over the last nine years, the Pentagon's budget has grown on average by about 9 percent each year, more than triple the rate of inflation—quite apart from the supplementary spending on the Afghanistan and Iraq wars.

Indeed, America now accounts for about 40 percent of the world's military spending. That is six times as much as its supposed chief rival, China. And when America's defense expenditure is added to the military budgets of Europe, as well as those of Australia, Canada, Japan, South Korea, and other allies, the Western alliance accounts for nearly three-fourths of all global outlay on defense. Why can't fiscal conservatives at least freeze Pentagon spending in an era of near–financial collapse?□ □In addition, national security and global influence are not always measured by arms alone. China, with an economy one-third the size of ours and a military budget one-sixth the size of ours, is increasing its profile in Africa and Latin America and is insidiously reminding Japan, the Philippines, South Korea, and Taiwan that the time is approaching when a near-bankrupt United States either cannot or will not support them in times of existential crisis. Flush with nearly $2.5 trillion in cash reserves (the result of huge ongoing trade surpluses and budgetary discipline), China reminds both neutrals and rivals that it has plenty of money to buy, bribe, or persuade its way with nations—and will have even more in the years ahead, even as its chief rival, the United States, will have less.

In Washington, meanwhile, the Democratic White House and

Senate are most likely to compromise on budget cuts if defense-spending freezes or reductions are on the table—concessions that might both preclude increases in income-tax rates and facilitate reductions in general social spending. No doubt the president's bipartisan deficit commission will include defense allocations among the cuts it recommends as necessary to balance the budget. After all, most government bureaucracies have plenty of waste, the Pentagon included—especially in a period of rapid expansion that saw the military budget double in less than ten years and consume $1 trillion in aggregate budget increases above the rate of inflation.

Yet there are also compelling reasons not to cut defense, and these are rarely discussed. The United States has an alarming record of courting danger when it has slashed defense, or even merely been perceived abroad to be pruning its military. In the 1930s the Germans and Japanese did not take the United States seriously as a deterrent power, and understandably so: It was not until 1943—after tens of thousands of American deaths—that the United States finally deployed planes, armor, and ships that were of rough parity in numbers and quality with those of its Axis enemies. □ □After World War II ended, America demobilized and returned to its parsimonious military ways. The result: By August 1950 an outnumbered and outclassed American army in South Korea was confined to the tiny Pusan perimeter. For the first six months of hard fighting in Korea, the military's obsolete tanks, anti-tank weapons, and planes proved no match for Soviet-supplied T-34 tanks and MiG-15 jets.

Three decades later, in April 1980, post-Vietnam budget cuts were the subtext of the humiliating failed mission (Operation Eagle Claw) to rescue the Iranian-held hostages. And the post–Cold War defense cuts of the 1990s may have made it far more difficult to pursue terrorists or fight in Iraq and Afghanistan in the new millennium. As Rudyard Kipling put in his poem "Tommy," the public demands a superb wartime military as much as it neglects it in peacetime—"For it's Tommy this, an' Tommy that, an' 'Chuck him out, the brute!' / But it's 'Saviour of 'is country' when the guns begin to shoot." □ □At present, the world is not tranquil. At least a half dozen countries, including Iran, North Korea, and Venezuela, have ratcheted up their bellicose rhetoric, spurned U.S. efforts at outreach, and either threatened or harassed their neighbors. Our future relations with China, Syria, and Turkey are at best problematic. Soon-to-be-nuclear Iran may start a new strategic-arms race in the Middle East, as Sunni Arab states seek to deter the Shiite Persian hegemon. Potentially more frightening are the increasing tensions between Japan and both China and Russia that stem from territorial disputes over islands near the Japanese mainland. It is almost a given that anytime the post-war United States cuts its military or tires of its global deterrent role, it will soon rue the effort and pay for its laxity with blood and treasure.

Second, the United States military keeps international peace in many quiet ways that transcend its more overt efforts to rid the world of assorted thugs, genocidal dictators, and terrorist sponsors such as Saddam Hussein, Slobodan Milosevic, Manuel Noriega, and the Taliban. NATO, which would be impossible without the United States, cools a number of traditional hot spots like Cyprus, the Aegean Sea between Greece and Turkey, and the historically vulnerable eastern-European borderlands that abut Russia. The U.S. military hunts down al-Qaeda from the horn of Africa to South America, fights the Somali pirates, organizes tsunami relief in Indonesia, facilitates aid to earthquake-stricken Haiti, and keeps sea lanes open from the China Sea to the Persian Gulf. These costly deterrent and humanitarian efforts save lives and build goodwill—and many of them either would not occur or would be taken up by less conciliatory powers should we cut back the current military budget. □□Third, much of the Pentagon budget is spent on military personnel—at least $150 billion—including college education and vocational training. After 20 years as a professor in the California State University system, I can attest that returning military veterans were more mature and responsible in general, and were better-motivated students, than my average undergraduates, who often expanded their college experience to six or eight years of on-again-off-again study. In short, the military was able to train 20-year-old signalmen on aircraft-carrier decks to park $150 million jet fighters wingtip to wingtip far more safely than college students zoom through campus parking lots.

Fourth, we are currently spending on defense (at least on average) one point of GDP less than we did during the Cold War in the 1980s—which ended with the implosion of a Soviet Union that simply could not produce a technologically sophisticated and disciplined military commensurate with America's re-equipped and expanded armed forces. When the George W. Bush administration entered office, we were spending only about 3 percent of GDP on defense, a historic low, and the figure did not exceed 4 percent until the latter half of Bush's second term. In other words, in terms of the overall economy, the present military budget is not historically high.

Fifth, the U.S. military is billions of dollars behind in repairing or replacing equipment worn out by years of fighting in Afghanistan and Iraq and by its increased responsibilities in the War on Terror. Indeed, we sometimes forget that we are in a global conflict with radical Islamists who most recently have attempted to kill thousands of Americans in the New York subway system, in Times Square, and on both passenger and freight planes.

The failures of these planned operations are attributable in part to stepped-up military intelligence, the elimination of thousands of terrorists in Afghanistan and Iraq, and the ongoing targeting of terrorists by drone attacks in the badlands of Pakistan, Somalia, Sudan, and Yemen. But this does not show that conventional weapons are unnecessary. As personnel costs and the prices of weapons systems skyrocket, we are forced to buy fewer planes and vehicles. Those economies increase both the per-unit cost of acquisition and the hours of usage per asset. The result, for example, is that in just 20 years the Air Force has gone from deploying over 4,000 fighter aircraft to scarcely 1,500. That means fewer and more costly planes than ever before, and more wear and tear on those that we can afford.

Of course it is salutary to review carefully all Pentagon expenditures, and to make sure we are not purchasing assets or fielding forces that we do not need, or that are not in line with our strategic goals and responsibilities. But we should also remember that near the end of the Cold War, in 1988, income taxes were lower (28 percent on top brackets), budget deficits were smaller (3 percent of GDP), and defense expenditures were proportionally greater (5.8 percent of GDP) than they are now—reminding us that the present budget meltdown reflects particular policies and priorities that transcend both tax rates and defense spending.

In the end, the problem of national security in a time of budget restraint is not so much about defense spending per se; instead, it lies in two other areas. First, we must establish our global responsibilities in the context of our fiscal limitations, and fund our military to fulfill the ensuing obligations. At present, defense spending is increasingly not synchronized with a clear and understandable strategic mission. Second, we must grow the economy. Our defense capability improved radically in the last 30 years without a great leap in expenditures as a percentage of GDP, simply because GDP grew at such a rapid clip. But unless we continue to expand the pie, there will be fights over the size of the slices. A healthy economy is the best national-security measure of all.

DECEMBER 3, 2010

Obama & Co., Growing Up Fast

Obama and his EU counterparts are learning that high-minded adolescence makes for bad governance. But it's an expensive lesson.

Old laws predicated on human nature cannot so easily be discarded—even by utopians who think they have the power to cool the planet and stop the rising seas. Borrowed money really has to be paid back. Governments cannot operate without confidentiality. Nations perish if they cannot protect themselves from existential threats. Watching a therapeutic Barack Obama grow up and learn these tragic lessons is as enlightening as it is sometimes scary.

When they are out of power, modern leftists advocate massive government spending and large deficits. They applaud when Republicans and conservatives sometimes prove as profligate as any big-government liberal. But when invested with the responsibility of governance, they come to understand that Keynesian "stimulus" must eventually cede to the same unhappy logic as the private household's indebtedness.

Maxing out credit cards does not exempt one from having to pay off the balance. Low or nonexistent interest on debt does not mean the principal vanishes. We are reminded that debt is real with the ongoing meltdown of the European Union, as a bloated public sector from the Atlantic to the Aegean demands that someone, somewhere cover its debts.

Here in America the same fiscal rules have not disappeared. In California, Governor-elect Jerry Brown will have few choices in January 2011. Since he cannot raise taxes much in a state that already has the nation's highest income and sales taxes, he can only find a way to cut expenditures. He must then either finesse such reductions with a sort of green philosophy of "small is better" or plead that his reactionary pre-decessor gave him, a compassionate liberal, no choice. Either way, the creditors and bondholders must be paid. Even Barack Obama, after spending $1.3 trillion more this year than the government took in, now seeks to save a few billion dollars by freezing federal wages.

In short, from Sacramento to Athens the world is reminded that obligations, despite in-vogue euphemisms like "stimulus" and "Keynesian," really do have to be met. There is an iron law that tran-scends politics and limits the application of fiscal liberalism: Print more money and money becomes less valuable; default just once and all future credit is lost or intolerably expensive.

In a similar way, the WikiLeaks mess reminds us of the adolescence of crusading freelance leakers and their enablers. This time the disclo-sures are not morality tales about Vietnam or Guantanamo. They con-cern a tough Hillary Clinton urging her State Department subordinates to spy on United Nations personnel. Barack Obama is not seen calling for the planet to cool, but is shown as so desperate to keep his promise to shut down Guantanamo that he is reduced, in tawdry fashion, to horse-trading photo-ops with the leader of any small country willing to take a detainee or two off his hands. In other words, those who once ser-monized about the morality of leaking the Pentagon Papers and details of U.S. policy in the war on terror are now seeing that a let-it-all-hang-out transparency can be nihilistic rather than liberating. Will Hollywood now follow Rendition, Redacted, and In the Valley of Elah with a hagiographic treatment of WikiLeaks?

Likewise, the notion that "civil liberties" were sacrificed in the effort to stop Islamist terrorism increasingly is shown to be a liberal talking point, not a serious criticism of responsible wartime government. Barack Obama conceded that argument when he flipped on every pre-presidential critique he had made of George W. Bush's protocols. At one time or another, Obama, as law professor, state legislator, senator, and presidential candidate, had ridiculed the Patriot Act, wiretaps, renditions, military tribunals, the Iraq War, Predator strikes, and Guantanamo.

He ended up as president embracing them all, and even expanding some. I think he was quite confident that his liberal base, outraged by Bush's supposed trashing of constitutional protections, would not much mind his own, inasmuch as civil-libertarian nitpicking was privately acknowledged as being as much of an advantage for outsiders as it was a liability for insiders. We live in an era, after all, where principled lawyer Howard Koh went from berating the U.S. for its use of renditions to now writing briefs empowering the U.S. government, for national-security reasons, to obliterate suspected terrorists in foreign countries by remote control. Surely one lesson is that when out of power one is not responsible for Americans' being murdered, and thus has the leeway to call for a sort of cosmic justice in a way one cannot when in power.

We have also come full circle with radical Islam. Critics found it easy to charge that the U.S. had unduly polarized the Islamic world. We know that narrative: Both past and recent sins of American foreign policy had tragically radicalized some Muslims. And because the United States was culpable for much of the hatred shown us by Islamists, so too that antipathy could be mitigated by unilateral outreach, reset diplomacy, and atonement through both the pathos of grand apology and the bathos of bowing and kowtowing.

So under a new charismatic, postnational President Obama, we tried the Al-Arabiya interview, the Cairo speech, the embarrassing euphemisms like "overseas contingency operations" and "man-made disasters," the description of Mr. Abdulmutallab as "allegedly" a terrorist, the promises to shut down Guantanamo and try KSM in a civilian court, the Ground Zero–mosque chest-thumping, the embarrassing NASA Islamic-outreach mission, the John Brennan outbursts against the Bush administration, the General Casey remorse over the fact that Major Hasan's mass murdering might imperil army diversity programs—and all the other nostrums that did little to convince the would-be Christmas bomber, the would-be Times Square bomber, the would-be subway bombers, and the would-be Portland bomber to pause, appreciate our good intentions, and so desist.

The WikiLeaks disclosures suggest that the Pakistanis in 2009 did not warm to such outreach. The Saudis did not suddenly clamp down on their funding of al-Qaeda. Syria was not won over. Iran did not think a new friend in Washington made the acquisition of nuclear weapons superfluous. The Arab world is more eager that we should show reckless abandon in taking out Iranian nukes than it is pleased when we calmly pressure Israel into granting concessions to the Palestinians. At best, these suspect nations were indifferent to our new magnanimity; at worst they interpreted it as waffling to be exploited rather than good intentions to be appreciated.

Finally, when we strip off the thin veneer of good-times talk about the European Union's being a cohesive community, and about a European continent of soft-power caring, we are left in the present recession with ancient squabbling nations, nationalist zeal, divisive cultures, differing religions, and antithetical customs—and, soon, the old remedies of diplomacy and alliances. Europeans chafe far more when their elites berate them as Neanderthals who were not up to their utopian dream than they do when their regional and national differences are honestly acknowledged and their disagreements recognized and dealt with diplomatically by sovereign nations with sovereign agendas.

What are we to make of this great history lesson of the last two years?

Behind the recent news of massive debt, looming defaults, WikiLeaks, the administration's about-face in the war on terror, and the implosion of the European Union is a reminder that progressivism, at least as it operates today, is a sort of high-minded adolescence, as sophisticated in faculty-lounge repartee as it is near-suicidal in its actual implementation.

DECEMBER 8, 2010

Julian Assange's EgoLeaks

WikiLeaks is the journalistic equivalent of the art world's Piss Christ—a product of the cynical postmodern West.

Julian Assange, the public face of WikiLeaks, is, among many things, cowardly. Courageousness would involve meeting with Iranian dissidents, Russian journalists, Pakistani Christians, or Chinese human-rights activists—and then releasing any confidential information that they might have about the torment institutionalized by their countries' authoritarian regimes. That would be risky to Assange, however, since such governments do not customarily go to court against their leakers; they gulag them—or liquidate them.

So, instead, Assange navigates through the European northwest among the good-life elites whose economic and security protocols he does so much to undermine. Being summoned to a trumped-up Swedish hearing for being an exploitative cad who fails to wear a condom in his ephemeral hook-ups is not the same thing as being dragged into the basement of the Pakistani intelligence service or appearing in an orange jumpsuit on an al-Qaeda execution video. Why does not the peripatetic Assange at least drive about, say, the back roads of the Middle East, Mexico, or Central Africa in his quest for conduits to spread cosmic truth and justice?

In truth, Assange is a sorry product of the postmodern West. He reminds us of the morality of Western shock artists who freely caricature Christianity on the hallowed principle of free speech, but, in a nano-second, censor themselves when Islam might provide an even larger target for their cynical secular disdain. WikiLeaks is the journalistic equivalent of a Piss Christ exhibition of the contemporary art world—a repellent reminder of the cowardly selectivity of the shock-jock huckster.

Julian Assange is without principles. He seems to think leaking confidential communications proves that the vast right-wing military-industrial-financial complex is harming either the most affluent, free Western population in the history of civilization or the globalized world itself—one that has done more to eliminate poverty and extend freedom in the last two decades than had been done at any other time in recorded history. We know from Climategate that the world's green scientists are every bit as conniving, petty, and mean-spirited as any American diplomat. I would like to see the secret communications that buzz back and forth among Hollywood agents, producers, and financiers to learn of the real criteria that led to box-office bombs like Redacted and Rendition being written, cast, financed, and made. Maybe to calibrate the level of sincerity and honesty among our movers and shakers, we can read the minutes of Harvard or Yale tenure committees, some correspondence from the minions of George Soros, or the communications of the U.N. secretary general—or, better yet, the encrypted e-mail transcripts of exchanges among the WikiLeaks board. Apparently Assange thinks that confidentiality is trafficked only among the suspicious Western ruling classes, while dissidents like himself are fueled instead by "truth." But if a man cannot be honest with a woman during intimacy, what can he be honest about?—whoops, one should not rush to an Assange-like judgment on the basis of gossip and innuendo; one should wait until the suspicious personage has had his day in court.

So Julian Assange is also a juvenile. Like some warmed-over let-it-all-hang-out Sixties loudmouth, he seems to think that transparency to the fullest is honesty, without a clue that truth is the final product that emerges from a combination of self-reflection, self-doubt, and introspection. These diplomatic cables contain raw gossip, half-baked impressions, innuendos, self-serving snideness, trial balloons, and witticisms among supposedly sober and judicious diplomats. Yet entering such confidential conversations in mediis rebus short-circuits, rather than enhances, the truth. In the adult world, venting to others does not necessarily translate into duplicity; actions are often a better indicator of veracity than rumblings and musings. Only a perpetual adolescent believes that one has to be perfect in word and thought to be good. The United States no doubt is told all the time by preening Gulf sheiks to hit Iran, but that does not mean that we or even they wish to reify such braggadocio. So far the real truth is our actions, which suggest that we do not think it is wise to bomb Iran.

Julian Assange is a narcissist. Like all self-absorbed egos who deny their selfishness, he protests that he wished WikiLeaks to remain an anonymously run, collective effort—while he ensured that it most certainly would not be, as he jetted the globe, giving dozens of media interviews, leveling threats, pontificating about world leaders who should resign, and promising to drop embarrassing megatonnage of gossip should he, Julian Assange, ever be charged.

Julian Assange has more or less ensured that WikiLeaks would be synonymous with Julian Assange and that he would be its man-of-the-year face on Time magazine. Like all narcissists, when reminded that his recklessness will lead to violence, mayhem, and deaths, he dismisses such dangers as insignificant in comparison to the benevolence that he bestows. Note how easily a computer hacker with a criminal record has established himself as judge, jury, and executioner on behalf of world truth. When he says, "I have become a lightning rod," he means, "I am the Lady Gaga of leaking."

His one mistake? Assange unfortunately got his sweepstakes trove from Bradley Manning during the Obama administration. Up until then, the global liberal media culture had less of a problem with WikiLeaks, since government disclosures only confirmed the nefarious nature of reactionaries like George W. Bush. But now in the age of progressive governance, we are learning that Secretary Clinton spies, that President Obama's diplomats are jaded and cynical, and that such disclosures have hurt the presidency of a liberal progressive. It is one thing to canonize a Daniel Ellsberg or transmogrify the serial deceiver Joe Wilson into a victim of Dick Cheney's dark plots, but quite another to deify a leaker whose machinations will serve to undermine the agenda of Barack Obama. To paraphrase George Orwell, Assange is learning that all leaks are essential—but some leaks are more essential than others.

CHAPTER SEVEN

THE BUSH AND PALIN DERANGEMENT SYNDROMES

SEPTEMBER 5, 2008

Sarah Palin and Her Discontents

Sneering power-women and the foul
whiff of aristocratic disdain.

Thomas here is something ignoble about these elite, affluent, and well-connected observers in smug fashion savaging Palin, when—especially in the case of the sneering power-women—we should all at least grant that Palin is intrinsically bright, energetic, savvy, and independent to have come this far at all, given the slanted and insider rules of the game she's in.

So pause to consider: If we wished to ensure that a bright, ambitious, and capable woman would not make it in contemporary national politics, as practiced by most successful contemporary office-holders and adjudicated by the New York-Washington media, then we would insist on the following ten requisites:

1. Ensure that she grew up in small-town America away from the centers of power and media influence;

2. Trump that by ensuring it was in rural Alaska;

3. Make sure she didn't go to the Ivy League—and especially an Ivy League law school in the paired Obama/Clinton tradition;

4. Require that she marry a non-metrosexual, one without money or influence or a fast-track job;

5. Trump that by assurance that her own family lacked capital, a brand name, or easy inside entry into regional politics;

6. Encourage her to have not one, but five, children;

7. Ensure that she was a conservative, pro-life, pro-gun, pro-religion, pro-drilling Republican;

8. Have her start a political career amid a hostile, entrenched ole-

257

boy, all-male, "you rub my back, I'll rub yours" corrupt Republican cloister like Alaska's;

9. If she did reach state or national attention, be sure it was during a downside cycle in times of an unpopular Republican administration;

10. Get her on video with a bloody moose, or on a loud snowmobile as proof of her savage affinity with guns and her gratuitously large carbon footprint.

When we consider, in contrast, the latticed background of careers of successful contemporary female role-model politicians, such as a Diane Feinstein, Nancy Pelosi, Mary Landrieu, or Hillary Clinton—or pundits like Sally Quinn, Eleanor Clift, Andrea Mitchell, Campbell Brown, Gail Collins (the list is depressingly endless, in which marriage or lineage provides either the necessary capital, contacts, or insider influence—or sometimes all three)—then surely, whatever one's politics, there should be some concession that what outsider Palin has accomplished, given where she began, is nothing short of remarkable.

In short, Sarah Palin is the emblem of what feminism was supposed to be all about: an unafraid, independent, audacious woman, who soared on her own merits without the aid of a patriarchal jumpstart, high-brow matrimonial tutelage and capital, and old-boy liaisons and networking.

Instead this entire sorry episode of personal invective against, and jealousy toward, Sarah Palin is surreal. Given the rising backlash, Palin Derangement Syndrome may prove to be the one thing, fairly or not, that sinks Barack Obama.

OCTOBER 2, 2008

Sarah Biden

Vice-Presidential meltdown.

J ournalists continue to ask, "What was John McCain thinking in selecting the gaffe-prone Gov. Sarah Palin?"

In what has now become a disturbing pattern, the Alaska gov ernor seems either unable or unwilling to avoid embarrassing state- ments that are often as untrue as they are outrageous. Recently, for example, in an exclusive interview with news anchor Katie Couric, Palin gushed, "When the stock market crashed, Franklin D. Roosevelt got on the television and didn't just talk about the, you know, princes of greed. He said, 'Look, here's what happened.' "

Apparently the former Alaskan beauty queen failed to realize that in 1929 there was neither widespread television nor was Franklin Roosevelt even President.

Sometimes the Idaho-native Palin seems to confuse and embarrass her own running mate. Shortly after her nomination, she introduced a "John McAmerica;" then she referred to the Republican ticket as the "Palin-McCain administration;" and finished by calling Sen. Obama, "Senator George Obama." The Palin gaffes seem to be endless: on her way to Washington to meet the national press corps, Palin, the mother of five, once again stumbled—this time characterizing Senator Biden as "Congressman Joe Biden," who, she chuckled, was "good looking."

But then Palin only compounded that growing image of shallow- ness when introducing her own snow-mobiling husband Todd, "as drop-dead gorgeous!" And when asked about the controversial McCain ad suggesting that Barack Obama had introduced explicit sex education classes to pre-teenagers, the Christian fundamentalist Palin scoffed that it was "terrible" and that she would have never had allowed such an unfair clip to run—before retracting that apology under pressure from the now exasperated McCain campaign staff. But then, according to press reports, wild Sarah only made things worse still by announcing that paying higher taxes was the "patriotic" thing for Americans to do.

This week, the gun-owning, moose-hunting Palin also promised blue-collar Virginians that she would protect their firearm rights— even, if need be, from her own running-mate: "I guarantee you, John McCain ain't taking my shotguns, so don't buy that malarkey. Don't buy that malarkey. They're going to start peddling that to you. I got two. If he tries to fool with my Beretta, he's got a problem. I like that little over and under, you know? I'm not bad with it. So give me a break. Give me a break."

Palin may have had some experience in Alaskan politics, but at times the former small-town mayor seems unaware of the pressures of running a national campaign in a diverse society. For example, Palin— who has had past associations with reactionary groups—caused a storm earlier when she characterized Democratic Presidential nominee Barack Obama in seemingly racialist terms: "I mean, you got the first mainstream African-American who is articulate and bright and clean and a nice-looking guy." Such stereotyping suggested that the Alaskan was not aware of the multiracial nature of American politics—an impression confirmed when in her earlier gubernatorial run, she had once suggested that to enter a donut shop was synonymous with meeting an Indian immigrant.

The recently-elected Governor Palin was further rattled by media scrutiny, when, in a moment of embarrassing candor, she confessed, "Mitt Romney is as qualified or more qualified than I am to be vice president of the United States of America. Quite frankly he might have been a better pick than me." That confession followed an earlier deer-in-the-headlights moment, when the nearly hysterical Palin urged a wheel-chair bound state legislator to rise: "Sally, stand up, let the people see you!"

The Palin gaffes are no surprise to those who have followed closely her previous races. They cite her aborted governor campaign, when she was forced to pull out after fraudulently claiming that her working-class family had been Idaho coal miners—in an apparent case of plagiarism of British Prime Minister candidate Neal Kinnock's stump speech. Palin once boasted: "I started thinking as I was coming over here, why is it that Sarah Palin's the first in his family ever to go to

University . . . is it because our fathers and mothers were not bright . . . who worked in the coal mines of Northeast Idaho and would come up after 12 hours and play volleyball?" It did not help Palin that reporters quickly discovered that while as a student at the University at Idaho she had been caught plagiarizing and also misrepresented her undergraduate transcript.

Most recently on the campaign trail, Governor Palin apparently promised a vocal supporter that the United States would certainly not burn coal to produce electricity—even though roughly half of current U.S. power production is coal-fired. The same uncertainty seems to extend to foreign policy. Under cross-examination, Palin appeared confused about her own recent trips abroad, first claiming that her helicopter had "been forced down" in Afghanistan, although other passengers suggested the landing was a routine cautionary measure to avoid a possible snowstorm. Palin likewise had alleged that she was shot at while in Baghdad's Green Zone, although there was no evidence from her security detail that she had, in fact, come under hostile fire.

Obama campaign has lost no time in hammering at the former hockey-mom Palin's foreign-policy judgment, alleging that shortly after September 11 she once suggested sending $200 billion to Iran as a "good will" gesture, and reminding journalists that in repeated interviews, Palin had called for dividing Iraq into three separate nations, despite Iraqi resistance to such outside interference. Palin, the nominal head of the Alaskan National Guard, has also falsely insisted that Chairman of the Joint Chiefs Admiral Mullen had once suggested that we were losing the war in Iraq and that the Bush administration had sent Undersecretary of State William Burns to Teheran to meet with Iranian officials.

In response to Palin's unbridled misstatements, journalists have coined the term "Palinism"—the serial voicing of sweeping declarations that are either insulting, or untrue—or both. No wonder rumors mount that Sen. McCain is now seeking a possible graceful exit for the gaffe-prone Palin, even as the Obama campaign continues to make the contrast with their own sober and circumspect Joe Biden.

OCTOBER 24, 2008

An Instructive Candidacy

What Sarah Palin taught us about ourselves.

S oon this depressing campaign will be over, and we can reflect on what we learned from our two-month introduction to Sarah Palin.

Clearly, it is more than we would have ever wished to know about ourselves.

First, there turns out to be no standard of objectivity in contemporary journalism. Palin's career as a city councilwoman, mayor, and governor of Alaska was never seen as comparable to, or—indeed, in terms of executive experience—more extensive than, Barack Obama's own legislative background in Illinois and Washington. Somehow we forgot that a mother of five taking on the Alaskan oil industry and the entrenched male hierarchy was somewhat more challenging than Barack Obama navigating the sympathetic left-wing identity politics of Chicago.

So we seem to have forgotten that the standards of censure of her vice-presidential candidacy were not applied equally to the presidential campaign of Barack Obama. The media at times seems unaware of this embarrassment, namely that their condemnation of Sarah Palin as inexperienced equally might apply to Barack Obama—and to such a degree that by default we were offered the lame apology (reiterated by Colin Powell himself) that Obama's current impressive campaigning, not his meager political accomplishments, was already an indication of a successful tenure as president. The result is that we now know more about the Palin pregnancies—both of mother and daughter—that we do the relationships of Tony Rezko, Bill Ayers, Reverend Wright, and Father Pfleger with our possible next president.

Indeed, the media itself—in private, I think—would admit that while have learned almost everything about Tasergate and the Bridge to Nowhere, we assume that at some future date a publicity-starved, megalomaniac Rev. Wright will soon offer his post-election memoirs, detailing just how close he and a President Obama were. Or we will learn Barack Obama and Bill Ayers, as long-time friends, in fact, did communicate via phone and e-mail well after Ayers had told the world, about the time of 9/11, that he, like our present-terrorist enemies, likewise wished he had engaged in more bombing attacks against the United States government. And the media never wondered whether a Palin's falling out with those who ran Alaska might have been more of a touchstone to character than Obama's own falling in with those who ran Chicago.

While Gov. Palin's frequent college transfers and Idaho degree are an item of snickering among pundits, none of them can claim to care much about Barack Obama's own undergraduate career. To suggest that he release his undergraduate transcript is near blasphemy; to scribble that Sarah Palin's Down Syndrome child was not her own is journalism as we now know it. To care that Joe Biden is vain, with bleached teeth, the apparent recipient of some sort of strange facial tightening tonic, and hair plugs is deservedly mean and petty; to sneer that the Alaskan mom of five bought a new wardrobe to run for Vice President is, of course, vital proof for the American voter of her vanity and shallowness.

Second, there does not seem to be much left of feminism any more. Of course, feminists once gave liberal pro-choice Bill Clinton a pass for his serial womanizing of vulnerable subordinates, and Oval Office antics with a young female intern. But they gave the game away entirely when they went after Gov. Palin for her looks, accent, pregnancies, and religion, culminating in assessments of her from being no real woman at all to an ingrate—piggy-backing on the pioneer work of self-acclaimed mavericks like themselves.

Feminism, it turns out, is no longer about equal opportunity and equal compensation, but, in fact, little more than a strain of contemporary elitist identity politics, and support for unquestioned abortion. Had Gov. Sarah Palin just been a mother of a single child at Vassar rather than of five in Alaska, married to a novelist rather than a snow-machiner, an advocate of pro-choice, who shot pictures of Alaskan ferns rather than shot moose—feminists would have hailed her as a principled kindred soul, and trumpeted her struggles against Alaskan male grandees.

So there was something creepy about droves of irate women, in lock-step blasting Sarah Palin from the corridors of New York and Washington, when most of them were the recipients of the traditional spoils of either family connections, inherited money, or the advantages that accrue from insider power marriages. Indeed, very few of Palin's critics on their own could have emerged from a small-town in Alaska, with an intact marriage and five children, to run the state of Alaska.

We have come to understand that—for a TV anchorwoman, op-ed columnist, or professor—it would be a nightmare to birth a Down Syndrome child in her mid-forties, or to have had her pregnant unwed teen actually deliver her baby. In the world outside Sarah Palin's Wasilla, these are career-ending blunders that abort the next job promotion or book tour—or the future career of a prepped young daughter on her way to the Ivy League.

Third, from the match-up of Joe Biden and Sarah Palin, we discovered that our media does not know anything about the nature of wisdom—how it is found or how it is to be adjudicated. For the last eight weeks, Palin has been demonized as a dunce because she did not, in the fashion of the class toady with his hand constantly up in the first row, impress in flash-card recall, the glasses-on-his-nose Charlie Gibson, or clinched-toothed Katie Couric.

Meanwhile Joe Biden has just been Ol' Joe Biden—which means not that he can get away with the occasional gaffe, but that can say things so outrageous, so silly, and so empty that, had they come out of the mouth of Sarah Palin, she would have long ago been forced to have stepped aside from the ticket.

Factual knowledge? Biden, in the midst of a financial meltdown on Wall Street, apparently thinks that the last time it happened in 1929, we heard FDR rally us on television. And such made-up nonsense came in the form, as many of Biden's gaffes do, of a rebuke to the supposedly obtuse George W. Bush.

Sobriety? Biden now admits that dangerous powers abroad will immediately test a President Obama. He warns that the results of such a crisis will be very disappointing to the American electorate, and thus Team Obama/Biden will need loyal supporters to rally as their polls sink. Yet remember that Biden himself has been a fierce and opportunistic critic of Bush, who despite a frenzy of congressional dema-goguery, initiated the successful surge and ignored the very polls that the for-the-war/against-the-war Biden so carefully tracked. More importantly, if an Ahmadinejad, Chavez, or Putin ever had any doubts about carving out new spheres of uncontested influence, they may entertain very few now.

Veracity? If one were to think that Biden's past brushes with pla-giarism, inflated bios, and falsehood were exceptional rather than char-acteristic, the last two months confirmed otherwise. For all the false recall, it is hard to remember anything he said in his Palin debate that was true, whether describing the status of Hezbollah in Lebanon or his own past remarks about the wisdom of burning coal.

Silliness? Imagine the following outbursts, mutatis mutandis, from the mouth of a Sarah Palin—"John McAmerica," "a Palin-McCain administration," "Senator George Obama," "Congressman Joe Biden," who is both "good looking," and "drop-dead gorgeous." Or "I guaran-tee you, John McCain ain't taking my shotguns. . . . If he tries to fool with my Beretta, he's got a problem. I like that little over and under, you know? I'm not bad with it. So give me a break."

Or "I mean, you got the first mainstream African-American who is articulate and bright and clean and a nice-looking guy." Or "Mitt Romney is as qualified or more qualified than I am to be vice president of the United States of America. Quite frankly he might have been a better pick than me."

The list could go on ad nauseam. But we got the picture. Biden has devolved from the ridiculous to the unhinged, confident that in-house journalism would understand that the law graduate with 36 years in the Senate was simply being Joe, while a Sarah Palin, who flinched when asked to parse the Bush Doctrine, was a Neanderthal creationist. I thought by now the You-tubed exchange of a Congressional Finance Committee hearing between the pompous Harvard Law School gradu-ate Barney Frank and the conniving Harvard Law School graduate Franklin Raines—at the proverbial moment of conception of the finan-cial meltdown—would have put to rest the notion that graduation from law school was any proof of either wisdom or morality.

I don't know whether Sarah Palin would make a great vice president. But I did learn that by the standard of John Kerry's pick of John Edwards, and now Barack Obama's choice of Joe Biden, as running mates, she is wise and ethical beyond their measure.

JANUARY 20, 2009

Bush Considered

*America is a safer place thanks
to his administration.*

A disinterested appraisal of Bush administration foreign policy will take years. For millions on the Left, events in Iraq, Guantánamo, and New Orleans rendered the 43rd president an ill-omened phantasma–omnipotent, ubiquitous, and responsible for all mischief big and small. "Bush Did It" soon became a sort of ritual throat-clearing that critics evoked at each new Florida hurricane, Israeli-Palestinian mini-war, or serial "revelation" from a Paul O'Neill, Richard Clarke, or Scott McClellan.

The fact remains, though, that most of the U.S. Senate and the House of Representatives shared Bush's desire to remove Saddam Hussein after 9/11. They patted the president on the back when he finally did so (after 16 months of acrimonious debate between the fall of the Taliban and the invasion of Iraq), abandoned him when the postbellum insurgency arose, opposed the surge when he nearly alone supported it, and gave him no credit for Iraq's eventual success. Now, in a sort of theater-of-the-absurd fashion, they claim Iraq worked largely because they once declared it lost and thereby prompted the necessary changes. The congressional opposition's record on Iraq is largely one of opportunism, his of principle–and that too will become part of the historical record.

Yet, strangest of all, well before even assuming office, the ever-flexible President-elect Obama has done much to prompt reassessment of Bush's tenure. He apparently has chosen to drop most of his primary-election rhetoric and instead intends to continue nearly all of the sitting president's anti-terrorism and foreign-policy initiatives–albeit cloaked in far-more-winning mantras of hope and change, energized by youthful charisma, and predicated on subtle appeals to multiracial fides.

The only discontinuity seems to be with the stance of the mainstream media. Without apology, journalists have already gone from the narrative of Bush, the destroyer of civil liberties, to Obama the continuer of "problematic" and "complex" measures. So just as Bush once eagerly licked his chops and salivated over Gulag Guantánamo, so Obama now with wrinkled brow and bitten lip is himself tortured that he has to sorta, kinda keep it open for a while longer.

Abroad, Bush has had three major successes.

We were not attacked after 9/11, despite serial warnings that such a comparable terrorist assault was inevitable. Bush created a new methodology of anti-terrorism. In magnitude and comprehensiveness (though unfortunately not in explication), it was analogous to Truman's similarly controversial promotion of anti-Soviet containment that proved successful for the subsequent near half-century.

For all the rhetoric about Bush's manufactured war on terror, today it is much more difficult–as the dozens of failed plots during the last seven years attest–to pull off a terrorist act inside the United States. War abroad and new anti-terrorism vigilance at home have decimated those who would wage such attacks.

Even Obama recognizes the success of these measures. We can see this well enough with the president-elect's shifting positions on FISA, renditions, the Patriot Act, Guantánamo, and withdrawal from Iraq (once envisioned by Obama to be completed by March 2008). Bob Gates II won't be that different from Bob Gates I at Defense; Hillary Clinton as Secretary of State will be far closer to Condoleezza Rice than to Howard Dean or Al Gore. Gen. James L. Jones could easily have served as national security adviser in the Bush administration. Hamas and other Palestinian groups will probably not get better actual treatment from Obama than they got from Bush–just some soothing rhetoric about dialogue and engagement rather than dead-or-alive, smoke-'em-out lingo.

Add all the foreign-policy alignments up, and either Bush was right then, or Obama is wrong now. The tired neocon slur has been that a secretive group of pro-Likud Jewish advisers of dual loyalties–Feith, Libby, Perle, Wolfowitz, Wurmser, etc.–convinced the clueless Bush to remove a largely harmless and irrelevant Saddam and, soon after, to consider further regime change for a host of other dictators (all to help Israel and steal the region's oil resources, of course). The truth was far different. Bush undertook just two operations to remove the two worst regimes in the region and, in a departure from Cold War–era policies, to encourage constitutional governments, not oligarchies, in their places.

The Taliban was a nightmarish Murder Inc. masquerading as a fundamentalist theocracy that rented its soil to al-Qaeda and other global terrorism networks. Saddam Hussein had been at war, in various manifestations, with the United States since 1991, using his oil to fund terrorists, build an arsenal, and attack his neighbors. Accordingly, the Clinton administration, when it was not bombing Iraq or taking over its air space, had passed legislation calling for regime change. Congress passed decrees citing 23 reasons why the United States president should be authorized to remove Saddam by force.

After a brilliant three-week victory, subsequent mistakes–to my mind the worst was the obsessive focus on WMD at the expense of the other Congressional articles authorizing the war, the reprieve given the Fallujah terrorists in April 2004, and the stand down accorded a trapped Muqtada al-Sadr–turned a temporary occupation into a counter-insurgency. That said, despite the great cost in blood and treasure, Bush's persistence, and the heroism and competence of the American soldier, finally ensured both the permanent end of a murderous tyranny and the survival of a constitutional government. The idea in 2001 that Sunni Iraqi Arabs in 2007–08 would have been fighting with Americans to destroy al-Qaeda terrorists would have seemed fantasy. By 2007, the popularity of both bin Laden and the tactic of suicide bombing had plummeted throughout the Arab Middle East.

The evacuation from Lebanon by the Syrian army, the surrender of Dr. A. Q. Khan's Pakistani nuclear franchise, and the shutdown of Libya's bomb-making program were results of the humiliation and fall of the Hussein dictatorship, and fears of a new no-nonsense American policy.

Aerial incursions into Pakistan have decimated al-Qaeda leaders–and Obama, who will largely continue existing policies in Afghanistan, won't stop them. In fact, Bush's support for democratization in the Middle East will allow Obama a far-wider range of choices than would have been the case if Bush had followed most conservative realists and simply extended blanket support for existing oligarchies. After Bush, there is no longer a simple calculus that liberals encourage democracy abroad, while conservatives don't.

Bush, it was alleged, foolishly empowered Iran. But that too is a premature conjecture. Iran is at present nearly bankrupt from the crash of oil prices. Despite being an oil-exporter, it is dependent on foreigners for much of its own gasoline supply. Its terrorist clients–Hezbollah and Hamas–have bad habits of provoking Israel, suffering tremendous damage, declaring premature victory by virtue that they survived the IDF, and then needing even more billions from Iran to replace terrible losses in men and materiel.

Because Iranian agents once nearly destroyed Iraqi democracy, the example of a constitutional Iraq may prove in the long run destabilizing to theocratic Iran. And with the demise of Saddam's lunatic regime, which once attacked both Kuwait and Saudi Arabia, the Sunni Arab nations can far more readily rally to isolate Iran. The truth is that, in the post-Saddam climate, a new reality is emerging in the Middle East, with Hamas, Hezbollah, and Iran isolated from, and hated and feared by, their Muslim brethren.

The media narrative is that President-elect Obama inherits a world turned upside down by George W. Bush. If so, where exactly will come the radical corrective changes, other than soaring (and let us hope effective) rhetoric about global hope and change? Will there be a new American relationship with China and India–both of which seem to appreciate the free-trade policies of the Bush administration?

Europe clearly favors Obama, but its two anti-Bush governments of Chirac and Schroeder are long gone, having given way to staunchly pro-American replacements. Apart from offering some soothing "We are the World" rhetoric of deference to the U.N. and multilateral dialogue, it is hard to determine exactly what the Europeans want Obama to do differently than Bush did. I doubt they look forward to true shoulder-to-shoulder, share-the-risk solidarity in Afghanistan. They talk grandly about Kyoto but have hardly reduced their own carbon footprints. If in times of crisis Obama invites them to multiparty talks with the Iranians or Russians, they will probably prefer old-style American leadership to "we are right behind you" assurances.

For all the talk about Guantánamo, European suspension of habeas corpus, summary deportations, and preventative detentions outstrip anything in Bush's America. So far, despite a larger economy, the European Union has not matched Bush's $15 billon commitment for HIV, and other infectious disease, relief in Africa.

There can be legitimate criticism of Bush's first-term spending spree and rising deficits, and his unwillingness to veto Congressional pork. He naively thought hard-core Congressional ideologues and partisans were analogous to the conservative Democrats with whom he had worked in Texas, and often appeased them so they wouldn't cut off support for the war.

Often, Bush's unnecessarily bellicose rhetoric was not commensurate with his tentative action. Too many of his closest associates were less than competent–the abject embarrassment of Scott McClellan is perhaps the best example of the apparent cronyism that hurt Bush terribly. There were too few in his circle willing or able to articulate in steady fashion exactly what our war against radical Islam was about–and how we could win it.

All that said, these are the debates that take place in times of relative peace and security–they would be impossible had we suffered a series of 9/11s. And it is largely to the honest and steady Bush's everlasting credit that we did not. The next president already appears to appreciate that as well as anyone.

MARCH 20, 2009

Bush Did It

What a difference an election makes.

President Bush was ridiculed today by critics of the Guantanamo Bay detention facility when he suggested that his administration no longer was incarcerating "unlawful combatants," but was instead in the process of renaming them as mere "detainees." The president also promised to close Guantanamo "within the year," and added that he had assigned a "special task force" to look into the matter.

"Orwellian," the New York Times fumed in an editorial entitled "Just Close It!": "If the President's Ministry of Truth thinks that his metamorphosing words change reality, then it is going to be a long four years. This latest Doublespeak comes on top of the President's ignoring his past assertions that 'signing statements are unacceptable' and continuing the policy unchanged from the Clinton administration." The Los Angeles Times joined in, adding, "Remember that Bush promise about posting pending legislation on his administration's website before signing it into law? Well, somehow several days' notice has evaporated into 24 hours, and now zilch."

Bush likewise ignored criticism that on the Patriot Act, FISA, and extraordinary rendition his current public positions were at odds with those that he ran on during the campaign. The Washington Post noted, "Here we go again with Karl Rove's daily machinations—it is the same old flip-flopping we saw last summer before the election, when an opportunistic Bush reversed himself on NAFTA, public campaign financing, Iraq, the surge, Iran, offshore oil, nuclear power, coal plants, capital punishment, gun control, and abortion. One would think the dignity of the office might nudge Mr. Bush away from his perpetual campaign trimming. But then we have a President who seems glued to his Teleprompter and the scripted message feeding in from the right-wing attack machine."

The Bush administration was further embarrassed when it boasted that the fundamentals of the economy were "sound"—although in its prior requests for bailout funds just a few weeks ago, it had ridiculed skeptics who countered that the economy's fundamentals were, in fact, "strong." Meanwhile, columnist Frank Rich complained that "In times of economic crisis here we go again with greedy and failed AIG execs—buddies of Bush's clueless Wall Street–retread treasury secretary—using federal money to pay themselves bonuses for their rampant failure. But what do you expect from revolving-door administration officials in bed with the very corporations they used to work for? Get used to more $100-a-pound beef at the 'let them eat cake' White House parties, lorded over by this AIG surrogate who took more than $100,000 in their money for who knows what? Maybe Speaker Hastert can let those GM execs on federal welfare piggy-back on his private jet next time they come to Washington to beg for more of our money. These people have no shame."

President Bush had warned the American people that the present recession could last "for years," and that it was analogous to the Great Depression. Yet today, after passage of his new stimulus bill, his team suddenly reversed course, reassuring the nation that we might see an end of the recession by year's end. Then Bush himself berated the American people, charging that they had become too pessimistic about the economy. Veteran journalist Bill Moyers sniffed, "These right-wing mythographers seem just to make this stuff up as they go along."

When critics pointed out that the president had once promised an end to earmarks, and yet had signed more than 8,000 into law, he countered by promising not to do it again in 2010. Yet more trouble ensued when Bush increased the budget's red ink from $500 billion to $1.7 trillion—after promising a new age of fiscal sobriety. "We inherited this recession from the Clinton administration," Bush countered, "and if we're going to offer real change, there is going to be some pain in order to get things right again. You have to borrow and spend to save and cut—anyone knows that."

Newsweek magazine offered a dry assessment of the by-now tiresome "Clinton did it" excuse: "At least students who lose term papers can claim the dog ate them; but this administration isn't even that clever. For them, it is 'Clinton did it'—yesterday, today, and tomorrow. Expect for the next four years to hear daily the tired refrain of Monica, serial appeasement of terrorists, Whitewater, Travelgate, Paula Jones, and the entire cargo of impeachment—anything other than Afghanistan, climbing unemployment, a crashing stock market, and soaring deficits."

Meanwhile, another Bush appointee withdrew his name from Cabinet consideration. An administration spokesman denied a "pattern of sleaze" and allegations of a "culture of corruption," brought about by the facts that Bush's treasury secretary had failed to pay sizable back federal taxes, that his labor secretary's husband had tax liens on their property, that his nominee for secretary of health and human services had withdrawn his name after admitting he had failed to pay thousands of dollars in income taxes for free corporate limousine service, and that his nominee for commerce secretary likewise bowed out pending the results of an FBI investigation into supposed "pay-to-play" favoritism. Late-night talk-show host David Letterman summed it up best: "If Bush nominates enough of his wayward tax-dodging cronies to the Cabinet, we might pay off the deficit yet."

When reminded by journalists that there were even more Bush appointees who either had withdrawn from consideration or were going to face tough hearings on past ethical violations, a defiant President Bush countered that he had established the "highest standards for public service in presidential history." Meanwhile, it was disclosed that ten corporate lobbyists had been appointed to administration posts, and that his Cabinet performance overseer herself had bowed out of Senate confirmation hearings because of unpaid tax bills.

An "exhausted" and "overwhelmed" Bush was reportedly "troubled" on hearing that his newly appointed attorney general had lambasted his fellow Americans as "cowards" for not addressing more forthrightly matters of reverse discrimination. Then controversy ensued when the Bush energy czar ridiculed environmentalists for stopping Western water projects, predicting that without more dams and canals, "California farms will dry up and blow away soon." Controversy did not end there, however, as Bush's head of veterans affairs suggested that veterans should start to "privatize"—i.e., to use their own private health insurance whenever they could, inasmuch as it would soon be taxed as normal income anyway. "Are these people nuts—or what?" fumed columnist David Brooks, who collated some of the more amazing assertions of newly appointed Bush officials, before concluding, "I'm really disappointed. I expected a lot better."

On matters of tax policy, the Bush administration fended off criticism that its change in the federal-income-tax code was not, as once promised, merely a small adjustment. Independent analysts reminded treasury officials that, in fact, Bush was offering radical new legislation, redefining tax policy on charitable deductions, private-health-care contributions, and income caps on payroll deductions. "Well," the president fumed, "we have to go after the 50 percent who pay no taxes and stay home in front of their TVs watching the Super Bowl and swigging beer."

In the face of such sustained criticism, it was leaked that once more Karl Rove, along with some former Reagan officials and prominent conservative bloggers, had orchestrated a campaign from the West Wing to go after Bill Maher, Michael Moore, Keith Olberman, and other prominent Bush critics in a strategy supposedly called "The New Face of the Democratic Party." Videotape of a recent interview belied Rove's repeated denial that he had boasted of "never wasting a good crisis." That brought a rebuke from veteran political observer David Gergen: "Here we are in Depression-like times, and all the Bushies can think of is how to use the ensuing fear to ram a right-wing social and economic agenda down the terrified throats of the American people. Shame on them!"

"Should we laugh or cry over this inept Texas bunch?" wrote the New York Times's Bob Herbert. "Let me get this straight: The British prime minister comes to Washington. Bush and his Texas yahoos haven't got a clue about protocol. They snub him at the airport, humiliate him while at the White House—and give him some cheap DVDs as a going-away present. So much for Texas hospitality!"

APRIL 27, 2009

Damnation of Memory

Persecuting his predecessors, Obama would establish a poisonous precedent.

T he Obama administration apparently is giving a green light for liberal zealots in Congress and in the Justice Department to go after former Bush-administration lawyers.

We are supposed to damn these out-of-office lawyers because, in a time of national crisis, they gave advice that was construed as permitting torture. In three exceptional cases, interrogators waterboarded terrorist detainees—at least one of them responsible for the murder of 3,000 Americans. I emphasize the adverb "apparently," because—as has been the case from campaign-finance reform to the imposition of the highest ethical standards in history for Cabinet nominations—with the Obama administration, any ethical proclamation is usually at odds with the unethical reality.

The administration should tread carefully, since it is about to embark on something nefarious that could tear apart the country.

POSTFACTO JUSTICE?

First, remember that the Constitution already permits ongoing audit of the executive branch. Watergate prompted Nixon's resignation in face of impending impeachment. Iran-Contra almost destroyed the Reagan administration. President Clinton's sexual antics with a female subordinate, and lying about it subsequently (speaking no truth to those without power), prompted his impeachment. Nancy Pelosi, who was briefed on the options of waterboarding in the dark days following 9/11, had ample opportunity to hold congressional hearings on Bush's overemphasis on homeland security. Her outrage now rings false, an unseemly ploy to hide her complicity in what she once thought was responsible governance.

Such ongoing audit is not just the purview of congressional committee hearings. Between 2001 and 2008, Congress could easily have forced the appointment of a special ethics prosecutor, or even a torture prosecutor. Indeed, we have the frightening precedent of Mr. Fitzgerald's convicting Scooter Libby, in which the supposedly covert Ms. Plame was not covert, and the supposed initial leaker was not the targeted Cheneyist, Mr. Libby, but the protected Powellist, Mr. Armitage.

In other words, Americans deal with perceived executive abuses, both effectively and clumsily, as they transpire. Such contemporary audit avoids the sort of postfacto, partisan damnation of former leaders so common in unstable dictatorships. Prior to President Obama, Americans did not go in for this sort of thing, because we knew where it led.

Politics and conditions change. What a conservative administration does at a time of national crisis to protect the public may subsequently, in the calm of an eighth consecutive year of safety, seem in retrospect illiberal to a new liberal government.

Dwight Eisenhower did not open hearings to pave the way for indictment of federal officials of the Roosevelt administration or California lawyers working for Gov. Earl Warren, who in concert planned and carried out the forced internment of American citizens into camps. Much less did he bring Truman & Co. up on charges of using nuclear weapons to incinerate Japanese civilians.

Warren Harding and Calvin Coolidge did not seek indictment of Woodrow Wilson's Justice Department, which did everything from strengthening segregation to jailing war critics and helping foster the odious vigilantes of the American Protective League. No subsequent administration tried to arrest Lincoln's Cabinet members for signing off on the suspension of habeas corpus after Fort Sumter—unconstitutional decrees that eventually would mean some 15,000 Americans were held without charges for indeterminate length.

President Obama would not a want a putative President Palin to begin hearings on who ordered the targeted executions of two suspected Somali pirates, taken out in the middle of protracted negotiations. He would not wish the next president one day to indict those Obama officials who approved the assassination-by-Predator-missile of suspected terrorists and their families in Pakistan—without habeas corpus, Miranda rights, or avenues of appeal. He would not enjoy a future President Giuliani's bringing indictments of Obama officials over the NSA's exceeding its allotted e-mail intercepts, or the CIA's conducting overseas renditions of suspected terrorists without providing them the benefits of U.S. law.

DAMNATIO MEMORIAE

Second, Americans also do not Trotskyize our public sphere, in the manner of trying to erase memory itself—so familiar from the Soviet Union and the works of George Orwell. The Romans called this practice damnatio memoriae, "damnation of memory," in which the new emperor, to prove that he had "reset" the government, and that the present ills were all the fault of his odious predecessor (e.g., "Domitian did it"), simply erased the memory of the prior ruler—even chiseling off imperial names from statues and decrees.

Yet Obama officials can hardly begin a foreign-policy address without either trashing the Bush administration or giving it no credit whatsoever for policies that continue today, with the Obama administration's blessing. From current Democratic proclamations, no one is supposed to remember or even read memos circa 2001–03. We are supposed to forget that Democrats were chest-thumping their national-security bona fides—giving soapbox speeches about going into Iraq, leaking their worries about raw intelligence over WMD threats, and green-lighting coercive interrogation techniques to prevent another 9/11.

Be careful of fostering animus against well-intentioned American officials for the sake of short-term partisan advantage. Sharks smell blood. Now enters one Austrian professor, Manfred Nowak, the "U.N. special rapporteur" for torture who hails from a country that routinely sells Iran everything from sniper rifles to nuclear technology. Professor Nowak informs the world that the Bush officials must be punished. He is eager to please the Obamians, but not so eager to displease the Chinese, Russians, Libyans, Iranians, Saudis, and most of the rest of the world, where torture is as commonplace as its investigation is futile— if not dangerous.

ENDLESS CYCLES OF BLAME

Third, once we start this tit-for-tat cycle of adoration and damnation, there is no end—because it is based not on principle, but abject expediency. We saw such contortions in the Iraqi War. Once upon a time, many liberal columnists and Democratic congressional leaders praised the pre-war notion of preemption. Public intellectuals wrote letters to then-president Clinton demanding that he preempt and remove Saddam Hussein. Some even castigated a hesitant Bush with charges that he resembled his timid father. One or two went on to demand consideration of nuclear strikes against Iraq should it be associated with the anthrax attacks of 2001.

Then came the insurgency. Not only did such braggadocio cease, but embarrassed liberal hawks suddenly reinvented themselves as long-suffering, anguished, and principled doves. They now felt betrayed by "phony intelligence" as they bought into the cheap rhetoric of "Bush lied, thousands died."

Yet we all know their conversions into moralists were predicated entirely on the escalation of the insurgency. Only then did their inspired and perfect three-week victory become outsourced as someone else's fouled-up occupation. And we all know that 20 of the 23 original congressional writs to go the war were as unchanged by the absence of WMD stockpiles as they were forgotten when the conflict became unpopular.

So we know this predictable pattern of flexibility and accommodation. From 2001 to 2003, Bush officials were deemed serious and sober, and reformed the intelligence agencies to stop the incompetence that led to 9/11. By consensus, they took decisive measures to stop new enemies in a new sort of war—in which terrorists out of uniform, blending in with civilians, had devised ways of infiltrating the United States to murder thousands. And that consensus kept us safe.

Then, in the luxury of that very safety, and with the recrudescence of partisanship, from 2004 to 2009, our once-praised guardians were redefined by their Democratic critics as Gestapo-like torturers who created a Stalag in Cuba. And the terrorists, this new story went, were unfortunates bundled away for being in the wrong place at the wrong time, in the vicinity of bin Laden's Hindu Kush compounds.

And we know in advance the dénouement of this tragicomedy. Should we lose another 3,000 in a morning, and should the attackers have appeared earlier on wire-taps, been released from Guantanamo, or escaped notice due to new "firewalls," then once more we will go into the cycle of recrimination.

The only constant is that those who are most loudly screaming for the heads of the Bush officials will be silent should the carnage return—or perhaps they will be the most vocal in allotting blame to the Obama administration, which listened to them. No doubt they will demand postfacto hearings on topics such as "Who let him out of Guantanamo?" as they chant, "Obama slept, we wept!"

MAY 15, 2009

President Palin's First Hundred Days

A near disaster.

WASHINGTON (AP)—The first 100 days of the Palin presidency, according to a consensus of media commentators, have proven a near disaster. Perhaps it was Palin's scant two years' experience in a major government position that has eroded her gravitas, or maybe it was her flirty reliance on looks and informal chit-chat. In any case, the press has had a field day, and it is hard to see how President Palin can ever recover from the Quayle/potatoe syndrome. Here is a roundup of this week's pundit mockery.

LET THEM EAT MOOSE
"Ted Stevens may have gotten off," wrote Bob Herbert in the New York Times, "but he taught our Sarah something first—like using $100-a-pound beef for her state dinners. And what's this $50 mil for her inauguration gala? Since when do you fly in your favorite pizza-maker from across the country on our dime? Or send the presidential 747 for a spin over the Big Apple for a third-of-a-million-dollar joyride? Does Palin

think she's still in Alaska and has to have everything flown in from the South 48 by jumbo jet?"

WASILLA CHIC

Also in the Times, Gail Collins weighed in on the already-tired yoke-lism of the new commander in chief. "What we're getting is Wasilla chic. That's what we're getting. She arrives in the Oval Office, and first thing sends back Blair's gift of the Churchill bust as if it's a once-worn Penney's outfit. Then she gives the Brits some unwatchable DVDs as a booby prize—as if she idled the old Yukon and ran into Target's sale aisle. Did Sarah send Bristol into Wal-Mart back in Anchorage for that 'engraved' iPod for the queen? And what's this don't-bow-to-the-queen stuff, but curtsy for a Saudi sheik? Maybe that explains why she brags to Stephanopoulos about her 'Muslim faith.' So far, the best things going for her are Todd's biceps."

IT'S THE MATH, STUPID!

"Well," lectured Paul Krugman, again in the Times, "we were worried that they didn't teach math at Idaho U., and now we know for sure they don't. Is it $1.6 trillion, $1.7 trillion, or $2 trillion in red ink this year? Are we supposed to be impressed that she offers 'fiscal sobriety' by cutting 0.003 percent of the budget? She gives out money to those who don't pay taxes and calls it a tax cut. And now Queen Sarah tells us that in four years she'll 'halve' the deficit, as if she hasn't borrowed another $5 trillion in the meantime. Does she think we're morons? How many 'Drill, baby, drill!' oil wells can she tap into up there in Alaska to pay for the extra $11 trillion in debt she's saddling us with?"

WORSE THAN 'NUCULAR'

ABC's Katie Couric summed up the general disappointment with the president's communication skills. "I tried to warn the American people in that interview a few years back what they would get if they voted for her. Let's face it: She's a walking embarrassment. I mean just count 'em up: The mayor of Wasilla thinks Austrians speak some lingo called 'Austrian.' Then she tries her hand at Spanish and comes up with some concoction, 'Cinco de Cuatro.' Next thing she'll walk into the window of the Oval Office and expect it to open—oops, she's already done that. No wonder that when her Teleprompter stalls, she shuts her mouth until it catches up. I'm surprised she managed to get sworn in. And did she think that tasteless 'Special Olympics' slur was funny? Or making fun of octogenarian Nancy Reagan's séances? No wonder Wanda Sykes feels at home."

ANCHORAGE STYLE

A "dragon lady in heels" is what President Palin is, according to the NYT's Frank Rich. "Don't fall for this pageant nice-girl stuff. Our former beauty queen is a ward hack. Look at her nominations. Can't Palin find anyone who has paid his taxes—or do they simply ignore that stuff in no-tax Alaska? Does 'No more lobbyists' mean 'More lobbyists than ever'? Her chief performance overseer doesn't perform too well herself—and, like Daschle, Geithner, and the rest, skips out on her taxes. When Palin brags about fiscal sobriety, it really means record deficits. In Sarahland, not wanting to take over banks and car companies translates into, 'She already has.' Highest ethical standards equates to 'There are none.' Calling herself the VA president means she's just told vets to use their own health insurance."

GUTTER TRASH

"Pretty crude, pretty petty," Sally Quinn sighed in the Washington Post. "No manners at all. Does our new mom in chief think it's neat to laugh when her court jester at the correspondents' dinner calls Michael Moore a traitor and a terrorist—and hopes he dies of kidney failure? Is that funny? Ask those on dialysis. Is that what Alaskan hockey moms do—scream out at every talk-show host who hurts their itty-bitty feelings? Limbaugh, Hannity—who will it will be next? Poor old Jim Cramer?"

NEOCON CON

"She's a Bush clone," the Times's Maureen Dowd chimed in. "Bush is out, Palin is in—but we keep getting renditions, military tribunals, wiretaps, e-mail intercepts, Predator drone executions over Pakistan, the same in Iraq, and even more of the same in Afghanistan—all retrofitted with new 'hope and change' banalities. I mean, who's putting Mommy Dearest up to this—Wolfie, Perlie, Cheney?"

TINGLE FOR HUGO?

"There is no foreign policy," Chris Matthews said on Hardball, his voice dripping with scorn. "She just tours the world and nods, as if her good looks and serial apologies are going to win us a collective tingle abroad. I don't think Hugo Chávez and Mahmoud Ahmadinejad care much that she's got great legs and a nice wink. How many times can Ms. Vapid say, 'We're sorry' and 'Hit that old reset button' and expect thugs to make nice?"

RACE, ALL THE TIME

Eugene Robinson worried in the Washington Post about Palin's emphasis on race. "Look, she gets 95 percent of the working-class white vote. She promises next month to talk to the 'Christian world' from Estonia, of all places. Hello? She goes to the Summit of the Americas and immediately puts race on the table—as if we are supposed to separate those with European heritage from those without. Then she tells al Arabiyya that she hopes to heal the rift with Europe 'because of my own shared European heritage that seems to resonate in ways I hadn't imagined throughout the EU.' I guess we're learning that those 'gaffes' last year on the campaign trail, like her 'typical black person' remark and Todd's 'I am finally proud of my country again' nonsense were not gaffes at all."

WHERE IS THE PRESS?

Howard Kurtz summed up the press cynicism the best in his Washington Post column. "How long does she think she can keep picking on her right-wing plants in the audience for these softball Q-and-A sessions? I mean, there are only so many pukey 'What has surprised you the most about this office? What has enchanted you the most about serving in this office?' questions you can lob."

MAY 29, 2009

Bush Obsessive-Compulsive Disorder

*Obama continues to trash Bush in
words—but his actions speak louder.*

L ast July I wrote a column entitled "Barack W. Bush" outlining
how candidate Barack Obama was strangely emulating Bush
policies—even as he was trashing the president.

Nearly a year later, President Obama has continued that schizo-
phrenia, criticizing Bush while keeping in place Bush's anti-terrorism
protocols. The result of this Bush Obsessive-Compulsive Disorder is
that, thanks to Obama, history will soon begin reassessing George W.
Bush's presidency in a more positive light.

Why? Because the more Obama feels compelled to trash Bush, the
more he draws attention to the fact that he is copying—or in some cases
falling short of—his predecessor. He seems to wish to frame his presidency in terms of the Bush years, even though such constant evocation
is serving his predecessor more than it is serving Obama himself.

For eight years conservatives whined—and Democrats railed—at
the Bush deficits. In the aggregate over eight years they exceeded $2
trillion. The administration's excuses—the 2000 recession; 9/11; two
wars, in Afghanistan and Iraq; Katrina; and two massive new programs,
No Child Left Behind and Medicare Prescription Drug—fell on deaf
ears.

Between 2001 and 2008 we still spoke of annual budget shortfalls
in billions of dollars. But an early effect of the Obama administration is
that it has already made the Bush administration's reckless spending
seem almost incidental. In the first 100 days of this government we
have learned to speak of yearly red ink in terms of Obama's trillions,
not Bush's mere billions. Indeed, compared to Obama, Bush looks like
a fiscal conservative.

Another complaint was the so-called culture of corruption in the
Republican Congress—and the inability, or unwillingness, of the Bush

administration to address party impropriety. Jack Abramoff, Larry Craig, Duke Cunningham, Tom DeLay, and Mark Foley were each involved in some sort of fiscal or moral turpitude that—according to critics—was never convincingly condemned by the Bush administration.

But compared to some of the present Democratic headline-makers, those were relatively small potatoes. Speaker Nancy Pelosi has slurred the CIA and accused it of habitually lying to Congress. Rep. Charles Rangel has not paid his income taxes fully, and has improperly used his influence to lobby corporations for donations; he has also violated rent-stabilization laws in New York. Sen. Chris Dodd has received discounts and gifts from shady corporate insiders in clear quid-pro-quo influence peddling. Rep. Barney Frank got campaign money from Fannie Mae before it imploded, despite the fact he was charged with regulating the quasi-governmental agency—which at one time hired his boyfriend as a top executive. Former Rep. William Jefferson, an outright crook, is about to go on trial in federal court.

As for other prominent Democrats, the sins of Blago and Eliot Spitzer bordered on buffoonery. A series of Obama cabinet nominations—Daschle, Geithner, Richardson, Solis—were marred by admissions of tax evasion and the suspicion of scandal. In other words, should either the Democratic leadership or President Obama now rail about a "Culture of Corruption"—and neither unfortunately has—the public would naturally assume a reference to Democratic misdeeds.

For the last eight years, a sort of parlor game has been played listing the various ways the Bush anti-terror policies supposedly destroyed the Constitution. Liberal opponents—prominent among them Sen. Barack Obama—railed against elements of the Patriot Act, military tribunals, rendition, wiretaps, email intercepts, and Predator drone attacks. These supposedly unnecessary measures, plus Bush's policies in postwar Iraq, were said to be proof, on Bush's part, of either paranoia or blatantly partisan efforts to scare us into supporting his unconstitutional agenda.

Now, thanks to President Obama, the verdict is in: All of the Bush protocols turned out to reflect a bipartisan national consensus that has kept us safe from another 9/11-style attack.

How do we know that?

Because President Obama—despite earlier opposition and current name changes and nuancing—has kept intact the entire Bush anti-terrorism program. Apparently President Obama has kept these protocols because he suspects that they help to explain why his first few months in office have been free of successful terrorist attacks—witness the foiled plot earlier this month to murder Jews in New York City and shoot down military planes in upstate New York.

There are only two exceptions to Obama's new Bushism. Both are revealing. The president says he wishes to shut down Guantanamo in a year, after careful study. But so far no one has come up with an alternative plan for dealing with out-of-uniform terrorists caught on the battlefield plotting harm to the United States. That's why Obama himself did not close the facility immediately upon entering office, and why the Democratic Congress has just cut off funding to close it. So we are left with the weird paradox that Obama hit hard against his predecessor for opening Guantanamo, while members of his own party are doing their best to keep it open.

Obama says he opposes waterboarding and calls it torture. Many of us tend to agree. But despite the partisan rhetoric of endemic cruelty, we now learn that the tactic was used on only three extraordinarily bad detainees.

Furthermore, the administration that disclosed the once-classified technique to the public now refuses to elaborate on whether valuable information that saved lives emerged from such coerced interrogations.

Meanwhile, liberal congressional icons like Jay Rockefeller and Nancy Pelosi are on record as being briefed about the technique—and, by their apparent silence as overseers, de facto approving it. Senator Schumer, remember, all but said that we must not rule out the resort to torture in the case of terrorist suspects.

Mini-histories have already been written blasting Bush for unprecedented deficits, for being in bed with a sometimes corrupt Republican Congress, and for weakening our civil liberties. Now the historians will have to begin over again and see Bush as a mere prelude to a far more profligate, and ethically suspect, administration.

More important, President Bush bequeathed to President Obama a successful anti-terrorism template that the latter has embraced and believes will keep the nation safe for another eight years. And, oddly, we are the more certain that is what he believes, the more a now obsessive-compulsive President Obama attacks none other than former President Bush.

CHAPTER EIGHT

OBAMA, DREAM, AND REALITY

MARCH 18, 2008

An Elegant Farce

Obama's 'conversation' about moral equivalence.

B arack Obama's Tuesday sermon was a well-crafted, well-delivered, postmodern review of race that had little to do with the poor judgment revealed in Obama's relationship with the hateful Rev. Wright, much less the damage that he does both to African Americans and to the country in general.

Obama chose not to review what Wright, now deemed the "occasionally fierce critic." said in detail, condemn it unequivocally, apologize, and then resign from such a Sunday venue of intolerance—the now accustomed American remedy to racism in the public realm that we saw in the Imus and other recent controversies.

Instead, to Obama, the postmodernist, context is everything. We all have eccentric and flamboyant pastors like Wright with whom we disagree. And words, in his case, don't quite mean what we think; unspoken intent and angst, not voiced hatred, are what matters more.

Rather than account for his relationship with a hate-monger, Obama will enlighten you, as your teacher, why you are either confused or too ill-intended to ask him to disassociate himself from Wright.

The Obama apologia was a "conversation" about moral equivalence. So the Wright hatred must be contextualized and understood in several ways that only the unusually gifted Obama can instruct us about:

1) The good that Rev. Wright and Trinity Church did far outweighs his controversial comments, which were taken out of context as "snippets" and aired in the "endless loop" on conservative outlets.

2) We are all at times racists and the uniquely qualified Obama is our valuable mirror of that ugliness: Wright may say things like "God

damn America" or "Dirty Word" Israel or "Clarence Colon," but then it must be balanced by other truths like Obama's own grandmother who also expresses fear of black males (his grandmother's private angst is thus of the same magnitude as Wright's outbursts broadcast to tens of thousands).

3) We don't understand Wright's history and personal narrative. But as someone who grew up in the hate-filled and racist 1960s, it was understandable that he was bound to mature into his present angry anti-American, anti-Israel, anti-white mentality. (As if all blacks did?)

4) Indeed, Wright does nothing that much different from radio-talk show hosts and those of the Reagan Coalition who thrive on racial resentments. But whereas Wright has cause as a victim, his counterparts are opportunists who play on white fears.

5) And if we wish to continue to express worries about Obama's past relationships with Wright—never delineated, never explained in detail—in trite and mean-spirited ways such as replaying the Wright tapes, then we have lost a rare opportunity to follow Obama into a post-racial America.

6) We, both black and white alike, are victims, victims of an insensitive system, a shapeless, anonymous "it" that brings out the worst in all of us—but it will at last end with an Obama candidacy.

The message? Some of us are never quite responsible for what we say. And Obama has no responsibility to explain the inexplicable of how he closely tied himself to someone of such repugnant and racist views. We will never hear "It's time for Rev. Wright and me to part our separate ways, and here's why."

Instead, the entire Wright controversy evolved due to America's failure to understand the Wright's past and the present status of race. No doubt, the next time some public figure utters a racist comment—and it will happen—we will then expect to hear about context that explains and excuses such an apparent hurtful outburst.

Obama is right about one thing: We are losing yet another opportunity to talk honestly about race, to hold all Americans to the same standards of public ethics and morality, and to emphasize that no one gets a pass peddling vulgar racism, or enabling it by failing to disassociate himself from its source—not Rev. Wright, not even the eloquent, but now vapid, Barack Obama.

MARCH 24, 2008

The Obama Crash and Burn

If he acts as if the Wright controversy is behind him, it's over for Obama.

The latest polls reflecting Obama's near-collapse should serve as a morality tale of John Edwards's two Americas—the political obtuseness of the intellectual elite juxtaposed to the common sense of the working classes.

For some bizarre reason, Obama aimed his speech at winning praise from National Public Radio, the New York Times, and Harvard, and solidifying an already 90-percent solid African-American base—while apparently insulting the intelligence of everyone else.

Indeed, the more op-eds and pundits praised the courage of Barack Obama, the more the polls showed that there was a growing distrust that the eloquent and inspirational candidate has used his great gifts, in the end, to excuse the inexcusable.

The speech and Obama's subsequent interviews neither explained his disastrous association with Wright, nor dared open up a true discussion of race—which by needs would have to include, in addition to white racism, taboo subjects ranging from disproportionate illegitimacy and drug usage to higher-than-average criminality to disturbing values espoused in rap music and unaddressed anti-Semitism. We learn now that Obama is the last person who wants to end the establishment notion that a few elite African Americans negotiate with liberal white America over the terms of grievance and entitlement—without which all of us really would be transracial persons, in which happiness and gloom hinge, and are seen to do so, on one's own individual success or failure.

Instead there were the tired platitudes, evasions, and politicking. The intelligentsia is well aware of how postmodern cultural equivalence, black liberation theory, and moral relativism seeped into Obama's speech, and thus was not offended by an "everybody does it" and "who's to judge?/eye of the beholder" defense. But to most others the effect was Clintonian. Somehow Obama could not just say:

There is nothing to be offered for Rev. Wright except my deepest apologies for not speaking out against his venom far earlier. We in the African-American community know better than anyone the deleterious effects of racist speech, and so it is time for Rev. Wright and myself to part company, since we have profoundly different views of both present- and future-day America.

The more the pundits gushed about the speech, the more the average Americans thought, "Wait a minute—did he just say what I thought he said?" It's not lost on Joe Q. Public that Obama justified Wright's racism by offering us a "landmark" speech on race that:

1.   Compared Wright's felony to the misdemeanors of his grandmother, Geraldine Ferraro, the Reagan Coalition, corporate culture, and the kitchen sink.

2.   Established the precedent that context excuses everything, in the sense that what good a Wright did (or an Imus did) in the past outweighs any racist outburst of the present.

3.   Claimed that the voice of the oppressed is not to be judged by the same rules of censure as the dominant majority that has no similar claim on victim status.

What is happening, ever so slowly, is that the public is beginning to realize that it knows even less after the speech than it did before about what exactly Obama knew (and when) about Wright's racism and hatred.

Even elites will wake up to the fact that they've been had, in a sense, once they deconstruct the speech carefully and fathom that their utopian candidate just may have managed to destroy what was once a near-certain Democratic sweep in the fall. And a number of African-Americans will come to resent that they are being lumped into a majority akin to the Rev. Wright, millions of whom the majestic Sen. Obama has nobly chosen not to "disown," despite their apparently similar embarrassing racialism.

Over the past four days, I asked seven or eight random (Asian, Mexican-American, and working-class white) Americans in southern California what they thought of Obama's candidacy—and framed the question with, "Don't you think that was a good speech?" The answers, without exception, were essentially: "Forget the speech. I would never vote for Obama after listening to Wright." In some cases, the reaction was not mild disappointment, but unprintable outrage.

The blame, such as it is, for all this goes to the Obama campaign "pros," who, in their apparent arrogance over Obamania (a phenomenon due to the candidate's charisma, not their own savvy), simply went to sleep and let the senator and his wife resort to their natural self-indulgence—itself the offspring of the Obamas' privilege and insularity. Any amateur handler could have scanned that speech and taken out just 8-10 phrases, called for a tougher stance on Wright, a genuine apology, and put the issue behind them.

Now it's too late. Like Hillary's tear, one only gets a single chance at mea culpa and staged vulnerability—and he blew it.

Where are we now? At the most fascinating juncture in the last 50 years of primary-election history. Super delegates can't "steal" the election from Obama's lock on the delegate count. And they can't easily debase themselves by abandoning Obama after their recent televised confessionals about abandoning Hillary.

But they can count and compute—and must try to deal with these facts:

1.   Obama is crashing in all the polls, especially against McCain, against whom he doesn't stack up well, given McCain's heroic narrative, the upswing in Iraq, and the past distance between McCain and the Bush administration;

2.   Hillary may not just win, but win big in Pennsylvania (and maybe the other states as well), buttressing her suddenly not-so-tired argument about her success in the mega-, in-play purple states. Michigan and Florida that once would have been lost by Hillary in a

fair election, now would be fairly won—and Clinton is as willing to replay both as Obama suddenly is not;

3. The sure thing of Democrats winning big in the House and Senate is now in danger of a scenario in which a would-be Senator or Representative explains all autumn long that the party masthead really does not like Rev. Wright, whose massive corpus of buffoonery no doubt is still to be mined. (The problem was never "snippets," but entire speeches devoted to hatred and anger, often carefully outlined in a point-by-point format).

What is the remedy?

I would go buy about 10,000 American flags to blanket every Obama appearance, have a 4×4 lapel-button flag custom-made for the senator, have Michelle finish every appearance by leading a chorus of "God Bless America," draft every middle-of-the-road crusty drawling Democratic veteran (the knightly Harris Wofford doesn't cut it) to criss-cross the country—and try to Trotskyize Rev. Wright from the campaign.

Oh, and no need for any more Obama half-conversations about race and "typical white person" clarifications. All that does far more damage to the country than even to Obama himself.

APRIL 8, 2008

An Elegant Farce

How Obama will restore America's standing in the world.

We know the critique of present American foreign policy under George W. Bush—unilateralist and preemptive—and to some extent we know Sen. Obama's promised corrective—multilateral and reflective. So let's take a serious look at what exactly is wrong with the former, and how things would substantially improve under the latter.

Let's start with India. Indians poll pro-American by wide margins—due no doubt to America's unnecessary coddling of the world's largest democracy. If Sen. Obama acts on his complaints about the outsourcing of U.S. jobs to India and institutes his anti-NAFTA preferences in U.S. trade relations, India may finally receive the tough love it has been needing. After all, didn't President Bush give away the nuclear game with India? Perhaps a President Obama will back out of existing agreements in order to ensure that India does not receive advanced nuclear technology. (In recompense, they'll have little reason to complain, relatively speaking: Sen. Obama has suggested the U.S. should preemptively invade our ally Pakistan in order to hunt down Osama bin Laden.)

And China—what are we doing wrong there? Its increasing appetite for world resources means it cares not a whit what happens in the Sudan, as long as it gets its oil. Some Chinese products, as Sen. Obama rightly reminds us, are shoddy and sometimes dangerous—no doubt a result of our indiscriminate free-trade policy. The way China treats Tibetans and Uyghur Muslims violates canons of human decency. Will a President Obama protect American jobs, champion human rights, and ensure fair and safe trade by redefining our relationship with China—which holds a trillion dollars in U.S. government bonds?

Anti-Americanism runs rampant in Europe. Under an Obama administration, should we expect friendlier governments than Sarkozy's France or Merkel's Germany? Perhaps Obama might cancel that provocative missile-defense system in Eastern Europe designed to stop an Iranian nuclear guided missile—a welcome end to the saber-rattling of George W. Bush's cowboy diplomacy.

Or will Sen. Obama try to save American jobs by nullifying contracts with the European Aeronautic Defence and Space Co. to provide refueling tankers to the U.S. Air Force? We can be sure that he will embrace the emissions-reduction targets set in the Kyoto accords—in that way, he will encourage Europeans to do the same, since their repeated failures in meeting their promised reductions must surely be laid at Mr. Bush's feet: the EU has been waiting for America to show the way. Perhaps Sen. Obama could regain EU goodwill by pressuring Europeans to drop agricultural subsidies—and eliminate our own—and so give former third-world farmers a break. That would be liberal change I could believe in.

Then there is Russia. Surely Obama will do something about Putin, who seemed too cozy with Bush while he hijacked Russian democracy and used his oil to bully Europe. Perhaps Obama can craft an ingenious speech that will persuade the Kremlin's ex-KGB kleptocrats to act more civilly in the world, especially concerning their trafficking with the likes of Iran and Syria?

Speaking of the Middle East, how will Obama restore American prestige there and ameliorate the damage done in the Bush years? Perhaps he could send Nancy Pelosi back to Syria to engage Mr. Assad? Or ask the Democratic Congress to condemn Turkey for the Armenian genocide?

Will Obama's fast-track pullout of Iraq—and his willingness to sit down, without preconditions, with the mullahs of Iran—assure stability in the region, and win the confidence of our Arab allies? Sens. Obama and Clinton have both written epitaphs for the surge: Why, then, continue a failed policy? Once Americans are out of Iraq by mid-2009, Iraqis themselves—as Afghans, Cambodians, Somalis, Rwandans, and Yugoslavs have done before them—can work out their differences on their own. And since we were always the gratuitous targets that created terrorists ex nihilo, no doubt Dr. Zawahiri and President Ahmadinejad will move on to other Great Satans, once they see that those provocative American GIs have turned tail and fled their neighborhoods.

Since it is self-evident that the absence of another 9/11-like attack here at home was a fluke—and had nothing to do either with Guantamo, the Patriot Act, wiretaps, the destruction of al Qaeda bases in Afghanistan, or the annihilation of Wahhabi terrorists in Iraq—President Obama will be free to shut down all such legally dubious homeland-security measures. All that will reassure Americans and Europeans that those efforts were both unnecessary and antithetical to our values. There never was, and won't be, any danger of another 9/11.

Since NAFTA was a sell-out of American workers, President Obama can, as he seems to promise, withdraw from the association and restore tariffs on Canadian and Mexican goods, while ending our xenophobic paranoia about "secure borders"—especially silly ideas like fences and walls. There would be no need to extend NAFTA-like accords to Colombia, and we should also reexamine sweetheart deals with Middle-Eastern countries like Jordan.

The world between 1992-2000 is the model we are to emulate, it seems. The world was much safer then—before George W. Bush's indiscriminate wars—and it can be so again. In those golden days, the U.S. rightly contextualized "random" terrorist acts—making the proper distinctions between war and "police matters." Yes, it's true that thousands of American soldiers died in those peaceful days—about 7,500 between 1993-2000—but they did so in noncombatant-related operations. Back then, our experts appreciated the hard lines and firewalls that separated Hezbollah from Iran, Sunni terrorists from Shiite killers, and were always careful not to overreact and turn mere responses into needless wars. In extremis, we can employ tried-and-true tools like no-fly zones, oil-for-food embargoes, U.N. sanctions, and the occasional cruise missile—avoiding the mess of President Karzai's Afghanistan or President Maliki's Iraq, and the peripheral blowback involving a jittery Libya, Syria, and Pakistan's Dr. A. Q. Khan.

Presently the United States does the world's heavy lifting under a Texan who says "nucular." But soon it may well be charmed and mesmerized by a smooth-talking icon who raises trade barriers, leaves the Middle East to the Middle East, gets tough on China and India, relaxes relations with Iran, Syria, Cuba, and Venezuela, while redefining existing ones with Pakistan—and says to Europe, "We're right behind you!" Let's hope it will be as pleasant to see the results as it has been to listen to the utopian rhetoric.

APRIL 25, 2008

Who Is 'They'?

Inside the Obama mind.

"They"? Who in the hell is "they"?
—Lyle Gorch in *The Wild Bunch*

Recently Barack Obama got into trouble by explaining to an affluent San Francisco audience why the cash-strapped, mostly white, working classes in Pennsylvania and the Midwest do not logically vote for his brand of economic populism, but instead cling to issues that sophisticates can see are extraneous to their economic plight.

And it's not surprising then they get bitter, they cling to guns or religion or antipathy to people who aren't like them or anti-immigrant sentiment or anti-trade sentiment as a way to explain their frustrations.

That sentence has been analyzed to death. But a single word struck me—who are Obama's distant they?

Are they basically decent people, without a lot of education, who turn to religious and national superstitions like guns and church, or to primordial passions like racism and xenophobia, in lieu of Obama's nostrum of "hope" and "change"? "They," then, turn out to be the nice, but deluded folk—and yet sometimes dangerous people when riled by immigrants and other races that don't look like them?

But the bitter, they can't be the same they that Obama also said are jacking up the cost of his condiments in the store?

"Anybody gone into Whole Foods lately and see what they charge for arugula? I mean, they're charging a lot of money for this stuff."

Perhaps this nebulous and ever changing they evokes the same forces that Michelle Obama says are now thwarting her husband's phenomenally successful campaign. Sometime they seem to be politicos, or media pundits, or hostile rule keepers who do all they can to sabotage the Obamas: "They tell you to raise money, you raise money. "They tell you to build an organization, and you build an organization."

But at other times they for Michelle Obama can apparently also mean faceless government officials who likewise conspire against the American public as soon as it makes any progress—perhaps like achieving the Obama's 2007 $4 million annual income, or $1.6 million home: "We live in a nation where they set the bar and you try to get over the bar and they move the bar."

On rarer occasions, Michelle Obama becomes somewhat more specific with her they, and so names them as "folks." But who and where these folks are, we are never told: "Folks set the bar, and then you work hard and you reach the bar—sometimes you surpass the bar—and then they move the bar!"

The multifarious use of they tells us a great deal about the Obamas. In one of the many manifestations of they, there is a sort of resentment here, the evocation of someone or something to blame when it is time to buy high-priced arugula or send the kids to summer camp or explain why you will lose Pennsylvania. This whiny they serves a psychological need, and relieves them of any introspection like, "Buy lettuce at Safeway instead of arugula at Whole Foods." Or "Try harder to appeal to the working classes of Iowa and Pennsylvania by spending more time out of, rather than in, Whole Foods and San Francisco mansions."

There is, as has been pointed out, also condescension aplenty. The unsympathetic hoi polloi they is not the powerful, but the impotent—not those who know everything about the arugula price-gougers that thwart the fast-rising Obamas, but those who know nothing and ignore the Obamas' wisdom. Or as Michelle puts it, "The question is not whether Barack Obama is ready. The question is, are we ready for him?"

There is also a closely related conspiratorial they. If the Obama campaign hits a rough patch, they changed the rules. If the Obamas find that their own appetites have increased with their incomes, and the higher they live, the greater the debt they accrue, then someone or something—more powerful, more wealthy—has surely changed the rules of finance and economics to do in the Obamas.

The conspiratorial they is far more worrisome than the elite liberal's condescending they or the nouveau riche's whiny they, since it seems to evoke the dark forces that Rev. Wright articulated, the "white folks' greed" that is responsible for everything from bombs on poor

Japanese and weapons that target Arabs and blacks to planting AIDs viruses and holding the black man down by three-strikes laws.

The Obamas are not that crude in the Wright sense ("typical white person" is not quite "rich white people"). But when they talk of a self-serving, paranoid Middle American as they, or an all-powerful government as they, or manipulative financial forces as they, then the Obamas evoke the same sense of conspiratorial resentment and scapegoating as does a Wright.

From time to time, all Americans, of course, blame they who raised the price of gas, or started a war, or jacked up their taxes, or ruined their schools and neighborhoods.

But the next stage in the public evolution of the use of they is critical: The demagogue takes they up even more promiscuously to fire the passions of the crowd, thereby alleviating it of any responsibility for its own unhappiness. To the hothouse intellectual they are either the unwashed, or the more evil and powerful that only the learned and sophisticated can understand and mock, but ultimately navigate around.

Yet for the true statesman, they is rarely used, since the interest is not in finding generic culprits for the past problem, but in offering specifics for the future solution—requiring the use of the now rare "we" and "us."

MAY 19, 2008

Appeasement and Its Discontents

Obama and Dubya.

S ome seem to believe we should negotiate with terrorists and radicals, as if some ingenious argument will persuade them they have been wrong all along. We have heard this foolish delusion before. As Nazi tanks crossed into Poland in 1939, an American senator declared: 'Lord, if only I could have talked to Hitler, all of this might have been avoided.' We have an obligation to call this what it is—the false comfort of appeasement, which has been repeatedly discredited by history.

So spoke President's Bush to the Israeli Knesset on the 60th anniversary of the birth of the Jewish state last week. Ostensibly the president's historical references made perfect sense for a variety of reasons. First, the state of Israel is inextricably a result of the Holocaust—a genocide that was in itself the logical consequence of an ascendant Nazi state, whose industry of death might could been circumvented by concerted action earlier in the late 1930s by the then stronger liberal democracies.

Bush was assuring the Israelis that the United States would not, in contrast to liberal democracies of the past, appease states and organizations intent on killing Jews by the millions.

Second, Bush's warning came in a climate of fear and weariness in the West, in which calls to meet without preconditions with both Iran and Hamas—the former state whose president has forecast the impending destruction of Israel, the latter terrorist organization whose charter hinges on the end of the Jewish state—have been voiced by several public figures, most prominently in recent days by former President Carter.

Third, the warning about appeasement comes not just after, and in implied defense, of military action in both Afghanistan and Iraq, but in the case of the United States, also after the September 11 catastrophe, which itself followed a decade of bipartisan inability to confront and respond to a number of al-Qaeda serial provocations.

The speech caused outrage among Democrats who insisted that it was "appalling" and a "smear" on Barack Obama, who has advocated talks, without preconditions, with Iran, and who had been informally endorsed by a Hamas official, and who had recently fired a Middle Eastern adviser, Robert Malley, for meeting with Hamas leaders. Obama fired off the following reply:

It is sad that President Bush would use a speech to the Knesset on the 60th anniversary of Israel's independence to launch a false political attack…It is time to turn the page on eight years of policies that have strengthened Iran and failed to secure America or our ally Israel . . . George Bush knows that I have never supported engagement with ter-

rorists, and the president's extraordinary politicization of foreign policy and the politics of fear do nothing to secure the American people or
our stalwart ally Israel.

Three questions are raised by this controversy. First: What consti-
tutes appeasement in the 21st-century age of globalization? Second: If
President Bush had wished to imply a connection with the unnamed
Barack Obama, how fair would such a charge have been? Third: Has
President Bush himself followed his own advice and shunned the
appeasement of "with terrorists and radicals"?

Most define appeasement not by the mere willingness on occasion
to negotiate with enemies (i.e., the heads of nation states rather than
criminal terrorist cliques). Rather, appeasement is an overriding desire
to avoid war or confrontation to such a degree so as to engage in a serial pattern of behavior that results in an accommodation of an enemy's
demands—and ultimately the inadvertent enhancement of its agendas.
Key here is the caveat that there must muscular alternatives to appeasement, as was true with a rather weak 1936 Nazi Germany or a non-
nuclear theocratic Iran.

Talking with an Iranian theocrat like Mahmoud Ahmadinejad per se
might not necessarily constitute appeasement. But continuing such
talks without preconditions that made no progress in curbing Iranian
nuclear agendas, or support for Hezbollah terrorists and Shiite militias
in Iraq would not only be futile, but encourage further Iranian adventurism—by the assurance that negotiations were infinite and there
would be few lines in the sand and little chance of military opposition
to follow. In our era, the locus classicus of appeasement is the near
decade of negotiations, empty threats, and drawn-out diplomacy with
Slobodan Milosevic, in which with virtual impunity he butchered thousands of Croats, Kosovars, and Bosnians—until a belated bombing war
forced him to capitulate.

Bush in his Knesset address may have acknowledged that expansive notion of appeasement when he elaborated on his "negotiate with
terrorists and radicals" line, with the proviso of futility—namely that
such talking assumed an "ingenious argument will persuade them they
have been wrong all along." In addition, Bush's example—that when
"Nazi tanks crossed into Poland in 1939, an American senator declared:

"Lord, if only I could have talked to Hitler, all of this might have been avoided"—suggests that his reference to appeasement meant not just one-time talking, but delusional and persistent engagement that is oblivious to facts on the ground.

If the president also meant to include Obama among those who would engage in such appeasement, would there be any evidence for such a view? Obama himself has never been in a position of exercising executive judgments, so we have only his campaign statements from which to surmise. In this regard, we certainly know that Obama is willing to meet any and all our enemies without preconditions. During a televised debate he was asked directly whether he would agree "to meet separately, without precondition . . . with the leaders of Iran, Syria, Venezuela, Cuba, and North Korea," Obama replied: "I would."

His website amplifies that answer with the boast that "Obama is the only major candidate who supports tough, direct presidential diplomacy with Iran without preconditions." The problem here would not be in theory talking with an Iran or Syria—Sec. of Defense Gates on numerous occasions has advocated negotiations with Teheran—but in a priori signaling to tyrants such an eagerness to elevate their grievances to head-of-state diplomacy. Under what conditions, how long, and to what degree Obama would be willing to exercise non-diplomatic options when talks proved futile would adjudicate whether his preference for unconditional talks devolved from diplomacy to appeasement.

If a President Obama were to enter into multiple negotiations with Iran, and if Iran were to continue to subvert the Lebanese government and threaten Israel through its surrogate Hezbollah, and continue to develop a nuclear arsenal while promising the destruction of Israel, at what point would he be willing not merely to cease talking, but to accept that his negotiations had done more harm than good and thus required a radical change of course—and would it be in time?

Given President Bush's admonitions about appeasement, does the president practice what he preaches?

That depends on a variety of factors such as whether enemies are nuclear or not, whom exactly we define as adversaries—Saudi Arabia, Pakistan, the Sudan, Libya?—and to what degree our existing negotiations are proving not only futile, but emboldening our enemies by the assurance that we will neither cease diplomacy nor threaten the use of force.

Both the president and Obama, in arguing abstractly over appeasement, do not factor in such realist concerns of leverage that govern decisions to negotiate, such as exporting ten million barrels a day of scarce oil (Saudi Arabia), the possession of nuclear weapons in the hands of an unstable government (Pakistan and North Korea), or the unwillingness of American public opinion to support an armed intervention (Darfur).

In that regard, Barack Obama shows his own inexperience when he evokes past summits that a John Kennedy or Ronald Reagan conducted with the nuclear Soviets—contemporary rivalries in which escalation to nuclear annihilation was a real worry, and at the time Soviet combatants (as is true in Iraq) were not killing our own soldiers.

In short, nothing in the president's speech was inaccurate, inflammatory, or hypocritical. Whether Barack Obama believes he was a target of the president's rhetoric, or whether he would engage in appeasement, hinges on whether his over eagerness to talk without preconditions to the world's thugs and rogues would persist in the face of unpleasant facts—and so make the likelihood of eventual military action more, rather than less, likely.

JUNE 10, 2008

Gone, but Not Forgotten

Barack Obama and Rev. Wright.

There is a general sense—after Texas, Ohio, Pennsylvania, West Virginia, Kentucky, and Indiana—that the white working class is somehow illiberal, and so now the Obamians discuss, ponder, and fret over the "race question" ahead. But the problem is not, and has never really been, race, at least any more than it was in having a black secretary of state or Supreme Court justice or chairman of the Joint Chiefs, but simply the question of grievance.

When Obama bought stock in the Trinity race industry, he sent a message that grievance-blaming America, the country's past, whites, and present bias—not behavior or values of a black underclass—explains almost all problems in the black community. That deeply offended poor whites who haven't had anything handed to them, recent immigrants whose ancestors had nothing to do with Wright's rogue's gallery of evil white men, and Hillary's women supporters whose glass-ceiling argument was out-victimized (cf. Bill's rant about Trinitites cheering as Fr. Pfleger caricatured Hillary as a racist).

When pundits say that Obama "must define himself" or "introduce himself to the American people" they are on to something they don't fully understand. Better to define his problem as this: Each time he soars with his lofty utopian rhetoric, the not-so-amnesiac voter frowns, and then remembers Wright's hatred, Obama's former investment in it, and the abject absence of a truly honest and principled discussion of his disturbing past subsidy of it.

A more honest candidate might have explained why a future president of the United States should never have abetted the racialist mentality, by encouraging, by his presence and purse at Trinity, some to blame others for their problems (increasingly silly in a multiracial society of various contending groups), and why as people first we cannot advance our own careers and agendas by investing in the tribe rather than in transcendent ideas and values.

So here we have the Obama paradox: The more he poses, and is praised, as the post-racial healer, the more 25 years of his career belie the rhetoric. In short, he now talks far more humanely than most about race, but the way in which he started and nourished his career proves that he was also far more cynical and divisive than most.

As far as the rest of the campaign goes, I think we pretty much know the script and the Obama rules to come: as long as Obama stays ahead by 3-5 points, race will be framed in optimistic terms as irrelevant, or proof of Obama's racial transcendence and statesmanship. But if the race becomes dead even or Obama falls increasingly behind for questions having to do with inexperience or serial gaffes or fears over

Carteresque doctrinaire liberalism, then we will hear that race, racial fears, etc. are largely to blame.

All that is the legacy of Obama's long ago Faustian bargain with Rev. Wright.

JUNE 30, 2008

Dreams from His Grandmother

Ten general-election strategies Obama can use to disguise his hard-left views.

I think we are beginning to see the full measure of the Obama general campaign strategy, framed along ten or so key directives that can allow the election of the most leftward candidate in American political history.

So far the candidate himself needs no coaching, inasmuch he has proved to be one of the most pragmatic, flexible, and ambitious figures in recent memory, with superb handlers who understand the challenge of getting such a hard leftist past the suspicious American electorate.

1. "Maturing" Views. Move to the center on as many problematic issues as possible—whether FISA, NAFTA, talking to dictators, the death penalty, etc. Disguise blatant flip-flops by talking about McCain's changes of heart—such as his opposition to tax cuts eight years ago. And just as dreams of Obama's father were once essential in cementing his questionable racial bona fides in Chicago, now the thing to do is drop most mention of the African connection, and instead resurrect his grandparents as proof of his more influential Midwestern, working-class Americana credentials. Think "Dreams from My Grandmother."

2. Resort to "Sorta." Avoid details on any current hot-button issues (so sort of be open to discussion of nuclear and clean coal, and sort of not, sort of getting out pronto from Iraq and sort of not, sort of

against gun control and sort of not, etc.). It is always better to "hope and change" an issue, than to get bogged down in details of a topic—such as evoking the banalities "wind, solar and green" than counting barrels of oil saved or produced when talking of the current energy meltdown.

3. "Hope and Change." Keep to teleprompted set speeches in front of enthusiastic crowds, avoiding as much as possible press conferences, off-the-cuff venting with donors, interviews with neutral correspondents, town halls, and one-on-ones with McCain. These forums only showcase Obama's inexperience and hubris, and consistently lead to deer-in-the-headlights-pauses, embarrassing "48-states" bloopers, and the voicing of left-wing nostrums—as well as sudden loss of the mellifluous "hope and change" sound patterns, with their Reverend Wright-lite cadences and studied pauses.

4. Outsourcing. Let the sympathetic media defend the more blatant flips like public campaign financing or boasts of meeting McCain "anytime, anywhere." Outsourced pundits can do a far better job of explaining inconsistencies and placating the net roots than Obama himself. Trust that, for all the left-wing shrillness on the blogs and cable shows, the hungry zealots will prove far more pragmatic than expected—on the unspoken assumption (cf. the inoperative rust-belt populist speeches, the now ancient Rev. Wright contortions, and the long forgotten Gettysburg Race Address) that, once elected, Obama will veer back to the hard left.

5. No Lecturing. Ensure at all costs that Michelle avoids Phil Donahue—like, walk-into-the-crowd, unscripted lectures in front of sympathetic audiences. These are unguarded moments in which her long accustomed and familiar ideological and educational referents, in Pavlovian-style, spontaneously begin to surface. The public is only one "raise the bar" and "no pride" moment away from a complete turn-off.

6. Lock the Closet Door. Make sure that surrogate watchdogs keep a tight lid on Wright, Pfleger, Rezco, Ayers, and all the other embarrassing Chicago intimates of the last two decades. They are now

to be as expendable and irrelevant as they once were central and involved. In case of unforeseen outbursts, adopt the vocabulary of hurt—like "disappointed in" or "disrespected me."

7. "Politics as Usual." Raise tons of private money at record levels, whether bundled or not, while talking of the evils of politics, lobbyists, and same old, same old big money in Washington.

8. Corral the Mustangs. Weed out or temporarily muzzle hard-left advisers, former generals, professors, and future appointees, occasionally with the qualifier that an aide erred, or the person who sounded off is not the same sober voice Obama once knew.

9. Play the Victim. From time to time, hint about or make explicit mention of race, the exotic middle name, etc., as a way of reminding audiences of the illiberal and racialist mentality of all those who would will surely stoop to such tactics in future attacks.

10. Cue the Swift-Boats. Egg on the 527 third-party hit-men on the Left, like Moveon.org, while preemptively decrying the "swift-boat" tactics to come from non-liberal enemies.

In defense of Obama, his campaign has little choice, and can hardly debate the issues in any depth. While the electorate is tired of two decades of Bush/Clinton and the sleaze of the past Republican spendthrift Congress, it is even more wary of the recent hard-left, do-nothing Democratic congressional majorities and their Carteresque liberal agendas.

In other words, to defend a 60-percent tax bite on top incomes, trillion-dollar new government subsidies and programs, open borders, rejection of the successful anti-terror, post-9/11 protocols, trade protectionism, U.N./EU deference in foreign policy, and stasis on coal, nuclear, and oil drilling, is not necessarily to win a U.S. presidential election—even with a candidate as gifted in set-speeches and as malleable as Barack Obama.

MAY 19, 2008

Obama: The Great American Hope?

Optimism over our president-elect's foreign policy derives from four rosy, unquestioned assumptions.

T here is great hope that President-elect Obama will change the course of U.S. foreign policy, create far greater goodwill toward America, and thereby ease world tensions. Such optimism is not based on former Sen. Obama's foreign-policy experience. In essence, he has none.

Nor does improvement hinge on Obama's past career in Chicago politics or his U.S. Senate tenure—the former was problematic at best, the latter cursory.

Instead, our great expectations derive from four rosy, but heretofore unquestioned assumptions:

1. Most of the current Bush policies are not merely wrong, but inflammatory: ipsis factis being against them is wise and will bring dividends overseas;

2. Obama's singular eloquence, youth, charisma, and "presence" will win over the world in the manner it swept the American electorate, providing a welcome change from the "smoke 'em out" Texas global turn-off of the past;

3. Obama's exotic name, his multiracial background, the Muslim faith of his father, and his dalliance with hard-left politics as a student and community-organizer will all coalesce to sort of "flip" the image (if not the reality) of the U.S., as the world's superpower transmogrifies from an oppressive to a sympathetic international player;

4. The reemergence of Clintonites such as Hillary, Emanuel, Panetta, Podesta, Susan Rice, and others will bring back successful

advocates of "soft power," "multilateralism," and "engagement," who reflect Obama's worldview, but bring a gritty realism to the implementation of an often heretofore utopian rhetoric.

Let us for the sake of the country hope that such expectations prove absolutely true. But until they do, I worry that there are problems with all four assumptions. First, as we have seen, Bush's policy during 2004—8 was very different from the now ossified acrimony over the removal of Saddam Hussein of autumn 2002—spring 2003—when Villepin, Chirac, Schröder, Arafat, etc. took turns on the world media stage delivering boilerplate invective of "hyperpower" and "The German Way."

But since then, governments in France, Germany, Italy, and much of Eastern Europe have proven as pro-American as they could be given the realities of EU culture. It is hard to see many Obama alternatives to the EU3/multilateral Bush approaches to preventing nuclear proliferation in Iran. Few have any new ideas about improving existing relatively good relations with China and India, given the liberal trade and outsourcing policies of the Bush administration. Russia is, well, Russia—an authoritarian petrol state that demands visible signs of American goodwill even as it interprets them when given as weakness.

Senate Democrats seem to be aping Bush's Middle East policies; their only difference on Iraq now is a weird sort of revisionism in which a Harry Reid's once serial declamations about the war being lost and a surge as lunatic are now reformulated as invaluable criticism that alone forced Bush to adopt the necessary Democratic changes that saved Iraq.

Obama himself on matters as diverse as the Patriot Act, FISA, NAFTA, Iran, Iraq, missile defense, and the surge seems to have gravitated away from his early Moveon.org/ANSWR campaign rhetoric to positions almost indistinguishable from those of the present Bush administration—as the appointments of centrists like Bush veteran Robert Gates at Defense and Gen. Jones as National Security Advisor attest.

Second, Obama's rhetorical skills will help, especially with world opinion. We've already seen the American media re-characterize issues such as preventative detentions, renditions, the treatment of enemy combatants, and Guantánamo from "Bush shredding the Constitution," to "problematic and complex inherited dilemmas that defy easy solutions, as Obama will tragically learn."

There is reason to believe that the world likewise—especially the international media, at least for a while—will simply about-face and assume that Obama's brand on Bush's policies makes them less objectionable. All that said, it is not clear that the likes of Ahmadinejad, Chavez, Kim Jong Il, Putin, and the rest of the world's cabal of thugs who are the likely suspects in future crises either care much for what their own people think or care whether Obama's is young, glib, and vigorous or senile, inarticulate, and decrepit. Instead, they simply have agendas that are not our own: liberal or conservative America is still America, and therefore something to challenge and test rather than cooperate with.

Third, Obama himself has suggested his nontraditional pedigree offers America advantages abroad. And he's right. In almost Orwellian fashion, we have seen—in the feigned outrage to past references to the tripartite Barrack Hussein Obama—that here at home to emphasize Obama's Arab/Islamic resonance is taboo, but to emphasize it abroad to win multicultural fides is indeed welcome.

The problem once again, however, is that many of those who may give Obama wide latitude for his apparent more sympathetic American profile will do so for less than welcome reasons. A confounded Iran may find it harder to manufacture mass rallies with Barack Hussein Obama burning in effigy, but won't cease proliferation on that account. A Hamas, Hezbollah, Iran, or Syria that instinctively might seek closer relations with an Obama will do so under the assumption that their, rather than our, agenda, might better prevail—and that poses all sorts of both foreign and domestic problems ahead. If creepy thugs abroad express hope for better relations with Obama or, contrarily, if they feel "betrayed" by his surprising continuance of Bush policies, neither reaction is necessarily welcome.

Fourth, it is true that talented Clintonites who have experience from 1993—2000 will hit the ground running. That said, the world may also remember that during those eight years the United States either could not or would not reply to serial provocations—the World Trade Center Bombing of 1993, the murdering of American soldiers in their Khobar quarters, the attacks on our East African embassies and diplomats, or the bombing of the U.S.S. Cole—ensuring that 9/11 was the logical rather than aberrant denouement.

Risks now seen by terrorists and rogue states as unwise during the cowboyish Bush administration may once again seem worth reconsideration in a manner reminiscent of the Clinton years. Talking of soft power, multilateralism, the U.N., dialogue, and restoring our image abroad are all salutary and resonate well in Europe; but to others more nefarious, such calming assurances may send the opposite message that the U.S. is now predictable—and predictably not going to hit hard back when provoked. Deterrence is earned with difficulty and over many years, but it is easily lost in seconds.

What should we then expect? As some point, perhaps in his first few months in office, President Obama, as Joe Biden predicted, will be tested by the rogue oil-producing states. Most—like Iran, Russia, and Venezuela—will soon be facing bankruptcy if oil prices stay flat, as their only source of foreign exchange largely vanishes.

Expect all in multifarious ways to test America, in part to humiliate the United States, but more likely simply to cause enough tension to create panic among speculators and restore their windfall profits. Anyone can dream up scenarios—a move on Georgia, a cutoff of natural gas entirely to Europe, a brazen announcement of an Iranian bomb with a dare to Israel to stop it, a suicide attack on a tanker or warship in the Straits of Hormuz, flagrant violation of the Monroe Doctrine by home porting Russian vessels in Venezuela, simultaneous rocket barrages from Lebanon, Gaza, and Syria, etc. For such countries, any disruption is good in the sense that it creates panic, and panic in turn spikes oil prices.

Expect Pakistani-based terrorists to renew terrorist assaults on India, on the premise that Pakistan enjoys both nuclear exemption and deniability of culpability. In the multilateral world to come, European NATO countries may praise Obama to the skies as they quietly begin to leave Afghanistan. Al-Qaeda remnants in Iraq may think even a tenth of its former suicide attacks could now pay real dividends, on the assumption that once U.S. troops leave Iraq, under no circumstances will they ever come back.

All Americans in bipartisan fashion should hope that Obama will get though successfully the perilous first six months at a time when the U.S. economy is shaky, the Commander-in-chief unproven, and our enemies eager to test our president's mettle. Yet I suspect that conservatives will more likely than liberals forgive the fact that Obama's governance at times will come to resemble just what he used to caricature in George W. Bush.

JANUARY 29, 2009

Time To Beam Down to Earth, President Obama

Bad and worse choices of governance.

L ast week the United States got lucky again and took out several suspected terrorists by Predator drone attacks over Pakistan. Anti-war critics prior to Jan. 20 used to decry "collateral damage" from such controversial strikes. But there was a weird silence here about the Obama administration's successful first attack—despite the usual complaints from abroad that several civilians perished.

President Barack Obama just announced, to great applause, that he wants to close Guantanamo right away—sort of. But in the meantime he rightly worried over the immediate consequences. So, instead, in circumspect fashion, he appointed a "task force" to prepare for such closure within a year.

We forget that a less politically adept George Bush years ago conceded that he likewise wanted Guantanamo closed at some future date. But the media then, unlike now, largely ridiculed such pedestrian worries over what to do with unlawful wartime combatants who would either have to be released or tried as criminals in U.S. courts.

A saintly Obama upon entering the presidency announced to great fanfare that he would once and for all stop revolving-door lobbyists and end shady business as usual in Washington. But during the transition and the first two weeks of governance, Obama's team has already experienced a number of ethical problems of the sort that often plague incoming administrations. Obama's commerce secretary nominee, Gov. Bill Richardson, of New Mexico, has been under federal investigation and withdrew from consideration.

Attorney General designate Eric Holder, as Bill Clinton's deputy attorney general, helped pardon a fugitive on the FBI's Most Wanted list who was a big Clinton campaign donor.

Timothy Geithner, just confirmed as secretary of the Treasury, cannot adequately explain why he didn't pay thousands of dollars in Social Security and Medicare taxes and took illegal tax deductions.

Obama's staff already has already waived its new ethics rules for former Raytheon lobbyist William Lynn, who was nominated for deputy defense secretary.

Such embarrassments sometime happen in politics—but to humans, not gods—and they often create media firestorms, not a mere flicker or two. Throughout the campaign and after the inauguration, Obama also talked grandly of bipartisanship. The fact that he once had the most partisan record in the U.S. Senate, played tough Chicago-style politics to win elections, and toed a strict liberal line in the Illinois legislature caused few in the media to wonder about such promises. Yet despite aspiring to be an Olympian president, Obama just warned Republicans not to listen to earthly Rush Limbaugh. In words more like those of George Bush than of Mahatma Gandhi, Obama privately rubbed it in with, "I won."

Despite the near-evangelical sermons, Obama, like most savvy presidents, assumes bipartisanship is the art of persuading—and coercing—the opposition into following his polices. George Bush likewise called for an end to acrimony while he pushed his agenda. The only difference is that the media mocked the "divider" Bush's clumsy talk of bipartisanship but so far is still hypnotized by the "uniter" Obama.

Why is Obama's grand talk already at odds with his actions?

For one reason, he is unduly empowered by a media that too often roots for him, rather than reporting critically about his actions.

Second, in the last two years, Obama and his supporters advanced two general gospels that are coming back to haunt him:

First, that George W. Bush was a terrible president, and that his toxic policies had done irreparable damage to the United States. Second, and in contrast, that Obama was an entirely novel candidate with fresh hope-and-change ideas that would bring a renaissance to the United States and the world. Bush's Texas twang and occasionally tongue-tied expressions strengthened the first supposition. Obama's youth, charm, and multiracial background enhanced the second. But we are already seeing that simplistic polarity was infantile—even if the enthralled media desperately wanted to believe in the mythology.

In truth, Bush, after the left-wing hysteria over the 2003 invasion of Iraq, governed mostly as a traditional conservative rather than a reactionary extremist. Meanwhile, newcomer candidate Obama predictably embraced old-style and well-known liberal orthodoxy.

The result is that President Obama is quickly discovering that many of those easy Bush-blew-it issues of the campaign really involved only bad and worse choices of governance. Most solutions now call for realism instead of doctrinaire leftwing bromides and catchy speechmaking.

Obama should decide quickly whether to beam back down to earth. If he doesn't, at some point even a sympathetic media won't be able to warn him that his all-too-human actions are beginning to make a mockery of his all too holy sermons.

JANUARY 29, 2009

President Hamlet

It's 'to be or not to be' time for Obama.

Instead of Scott McClellan, who was inept and disingenuous as White House spokesman, we now get Robert Gibbs, a nicer sort— who is likewise inept and disingenuous. For all the promises of a revolution in ethics, President Obama has created a new syndrome: The well-off can be made to stop evading their taxes by nominating them for cabinet posts. In any case, compare Bush's cabinet picks with

Daschle, Geithner, Holder, Lynn, and Richardson—and discover that there is no empirical evidence of any higher ethical standard for public office in the Obama era.

George Bush called for unity, passed some bipartisan legislation on prescription drugs and education, and appointed a few Democrats to his administration. Barack Obama appointed a few Republicans to his administration, but so far has not mapped out areas for bipartisan law-making. Despite his legendary cool and gravitas, he has scoffed "I won" (in the manner of Bush's "I'm the decider"). The uniter went after Rush Limbaugh in a way that Bush never quite took on Keith Olberman or Chris Matthews.

Bush bumps into doors; so does Obama. Bush swaggered; so does Obama (often in a swimming suit). Not much difference there, either.

Bush said Iran was part of an axis of evil. Outraged media insisted that his braggadocio was unwise and gratuitously alienated Tehran. Obama said he wanted to talk to the theocracy without preconditions and improve on the mistakes of our past. Iran answered back: "This request means Western ideology has become passive, that capitalist thought and the system of domination have failed. . . . Negotiation is secondary, the main issue is that there is no way but for (the United States) to change." So, like Bush's, Obama's words incurred Iranian disdain—but won some humiliation as dessert.

On other issues as well—the withdrawal plan from Iraq, the Patriot Act, FISA—Obama is Bush II. Your counterexample is Guantanamo? But Obama has not closed Guantanamo, which has mysteriously become complex and problematic, and therefore has disappeared as the Gulag and Stalag of the op-ed pages. Bush said in 2006 that he wanted to close it; Obama echoed that in 2009, but promised a task force to study how to do it within a year. So is Obama Bush redux? Not quite.

The comparisons are simply to point out that Obama can pick and choose to do what Bush did, without worrying over press censure or consistency with his past protestations. Remember, there is no press now, at least as we have known it since Watergate. Sometime around mid-2007, during its coverage of the Democratic primary, it ceased to be investigatory and chose to become an adulatory megaphone. A news story on the front pages of the *New York Times* or *Washington Post*, or a piece aired on NPR, or a feature in Time or Newsweek, is simply a disguised op-ed on yet another underappreciated moral or intellectual gift of Barack Obama. He has transcended the traditional doctrinaire support for liberal governance and become a sort of talisman that offers exemption to our elite from all sorts of guilt and anguish in matters ranging from race at home to multicultural sensitivity abroad.

Obama, unlike Bush, is an adherent of the therapeutic mindset. The recession was caused by "them"—Wall Street greed mostly—and never "us," we who borrowed too much for houses we could not afford and things we did not need. The solution will be the European socialist model, in which a few thousand well-trained elites, educated at our best Ivy League law and business schools, will form partnerships with private enterprise. These Guardians will make major economic decisions and redistribute wealth through high taxes and massive entitlements—albeit with the understanding that the managerial class in both business and government will enjoy lifestyles similar to those they led in the past.

The tragedy in all this—aside from the manifest hypocrisy of the first two weeks of the Obama administration—is that Obama is uniquely positioned to do things no other president could accomplish. He need not vote "present" or offer mere hope and change or continue to play Hamlet. He could, for example, raise the age eligibility of Social Security benefits, cut back on the rates of annual increase, save the system—and hear little of the invective that would greet any other who tried it.

He could call for utopian pacifism, praise the U.N. to the skies, talk up the EU at every turn—but nonetheless allow Hillary Clinton, Robert Gates, Richard Holbrook, and James Jones to play a morose Shane to his noble-sounding Joe Starrett when the creepy Rykers and the bloodthirsty Wilsons of the world begin to cause trouble. We remember Bill Clinton not for all his bite-the-lip nonsense and therapeutic bromides, but largely for two major achievements: stopping the holocaust in the Balkans and ending government welfare as we knew it.

Obama could radically revise the tax code, not by mega-increases, but by simplification and transition to a flat-tax formula. We are beginning to suspect that the government's revenue problem follows not from the percentages we pay, but from the fact that millions of

Americans—from the lowly who take their wages in cash to the most exalted at the Treasury Department—too often cheat.

In the next year Obama can continue to run against George Bush and whine about the "mess" that "they" left him as he tries to turn the U.S. economy and government into copies of those in Spain and Greece. He can print money and label as "stimulus" a pork plan that is designed to empower Democratic constituencies at the price of leaving generations to come with decades of debt. He can use his formidable powers of rhetoric to talk of ethical progress while he allows Clintonian ethical regress. He can hope-and-change the world—and learn to his dismay that its thugs take such magnanimity for weakness to be ridiculed and indecision to be exploited. And he can end up a mediocre president who counts on historians to whitewash his presidency just as the media once ensured it.

Or President Obama can decline to be worshiped and instead stop the monstrous borrowing, unsustainable debt, and endless expansion of an increasingly incompetent government. And as solace, he can remember that his idol, Lincoln, was as hated by his contemporaries as he was worshiped by posterity—and that the latter is often predicated on the former.

JANUARY 29, 2009

The Audacity of Irony

'Hope and change' meet reality. The ironies bring us back to the unlamented days of Jimmy Carter.

We have seen irony before, when the moralist Jimmy Carter chastised us with sermons about our paranoid, inordinate fear of Communism and our amoral unconcern with human rights, even as the dividends of his policies were the Soviets in Afghanistan and the Ayatollah Khomeini in Iran—and even greater global misery than before.

For the last 24 months a youthful Barack Obama has daily offered unspecified "hope and change" idealism—all set against the supposed cynical wrongdoing of the tired Bush administration. In the unhinged manner in which his supporters turned a center-right president like George Bush into some sort of sinister reactionary, so too they deified a rookie senator as the long-awaited liberal messiah.

How could irony not follow from all that?

For the past seven years the United States has seen no repeat of 9/11, although plots were uncovered and threats from radical Islam were leveled in serial fashion. The ability to intercept and hold terrorists overseas, to tap into cell-phone calls abroad, to detain terrorists caught on the field of battle, and to ensure that intelligence agencies freely swapped information was critical to our unexpected salvation.

Like Lincoln, Wilson, FDR, Truman, and other wartime presidents (though none of the above witnessed 3,000 Americans butchered on the soil of the United States by foreign agents), George Bush, with strong bipartisan support, enacted new wartime protocols in the effort to protect the security of the United States. Only a fool would suggest that these homeland-security efforts were unnecessary, or that, in unprecedented fashion, they shredded the Constitution.

But such foolish criticism was exactly the sort leveled against the Bush security protocols by candidate Obama. And so almost at the minute he assumed governance, the now President Obama discovered that his Bush the Constitution-shredder had been a clumsy caricature of Bush the sober commander-in-chief. For Obama on the stump, the choices were endless; in the Oval Office suddenly only bad and worse. So the new president, the favorite of the ACLU, is now in the ironic position of maintaining the hated Foreign Intelligence Surveillance Act reforms, keeping the repugnant Patriot Act, retaining "extraordinary renditions," and continuing—task forces and promises aside—operation of the Gulag at Guantanamo.

There were many legitimate critiques of the Iraq war. But insisting, as Barack Obama did, that we invaded recklessly and in haste was not one of them. From the fall of the Taliban in December 2001 to the invasion of Iraq in March 2003, the Bush administration deliberately and in public fashion sought debate in the Congress for over a year, received bipartisan authorization, and tried for months to win sanction from the United Nations.

In contrast, Barack Obama immediately upon entering office demanded the largest government expansion in the history of the nation. The staggering debt program will require nearly a trillion dollars in borrowing to fund all sorts of entitlements and redistributive efforts, and in revolutionary fashion redefine the role of government itself. Obama pronounced the current economic crisis the moral equivalent of war, and he wanted a national mobilization to meet it—pronto.

But unlike the Bush administration, which took 15 months to prepare the country for a real war in Iraq, the Obama administration gave the public only a few hours to read the final draft of the legislation before it was made into law. Where the polarizing partisan George Bush managed to obtain the vote of majorities in both parties to remove Saddam Hussein, the healing bipartisan Barack Obama lacked the support of even a single Republican in the House and won over a mere three Republicans in the Senate.

Liberals who once screamed that congressional opponents of the Iraq war were being unfairly tagged as unpatriotic by the Bush administration now yelled louder that the opponents of the Obama debt program were, in fact, unpatriotic.

Bush was pilloried for supposedly hyping al-Qaeda in order to create a security state. Obama trumped that by proclaiming that the present recession is a catastrophe, a disaster, a Great Depression. He ceased his scare-mongering only when he had exhausted the vocabulary of doom. "You never want a serious crisis to go to waste," bragged Rahm Emanuel, reminding us that the envisioned Obama socialism could take root only if a climate of fear was created.

In foreign policy the irony is more telling still. Obama on the campaign trail either did not grasp that Bush's second-term foreign policy was largely centrist—or found it politically advantageous to ignore that fact. Either way, irony followed. The problem with Europe's failing to get tough with Iran, or failing to fight in Afghanistan, or appeasing Russia, was not George Bush, but the nature of Europe. Bush inherited, he did not create, Osama bin Laden, Putin's authoritarianism,

Ahmadinejad's Iran, Chávez's Venezuela, Kim Jong Il's North Korea, Qaddafi's Libya, or the Dr. A. Q. Khan laboratory.

More often, Bush ameliorated, rather than exacerbated, these problems, by being both tough and, yes, multilateral—as friendly governments in the United Kingdom, France, Germany, Italy, and India attested. Yet by demonizing George Bush—and that is how Team Obama prefaces each announcement of a new initiative—Obama has only set himself up for more irony. He can continue his first few weeks of damning Bush and emulating Jimmy Carter. But if he does, he will soon see another 9/11-like strike, more Russian pressure on Europe, more North Korean missiles, a bomb in Iran, the restarting of Dr. Khan's nuclear franchise and its appendages in Libya and Syria, and a theocratic nuclear Pakistan.

One can make many criticisms of the Bush administration—occasional hubris, an inability to communicate its ideas, excessive federal spending, unnecessary bellicose rhetoric not matched always by commensurate action—but corruption is not really one of them. While the Republican Congress gave us Duke Cunningham, Larry Craig, and Mark Foley, the Bush administration itself was one of the most corruption-free in recent memory—no Monicas, no serial Clintongates, no pay-to-play presidential pardons, no shaking down donors for a library and a spousal Senate campaign.

So when Barack Obama of Chicago lineage—with former associates like Tony Rezko, Gov. Rod Blagojevich, Mayor Richard Daley, and the Rev. Jeremiah Wright—began offering moral platitudes about his soon-to-be-enacted revolutionary ethics, we expected the irony that always follows such hubris and brings in its wake nemesis.

Now we are witnessing one of the most scandal-plagued incipient administrations of the last half-century. And these ethical embarrassments are doubly ironic. The Treasury secretary and nominal head of the IRS is a tax dodger. The egalitarian liberal Tom Daschle, who was going to make health care accessible for the masses, was caught hiding from the tax man tens of thousands of dollars in free limousine service. Reformist cabinet nominees like Bill Richardson (who has already withdrawn) and Hilda Solis cannot themselves follow the laws they were asked to enforce. The would-be performance czar, Nancy Killefer, did not perform on her taxes. We are now awaiting a third try for commerce secretary. The more Obama railed about his new no-lobbyist policies, the more he issued exemptions for the dozen or more insider lobbyists he hired.

The list of ironies could be expanded. Reps. Maxine Waters, Barney Frank, and Gregory Meeks—infamous for their Fannie Mae laxity—now interrogate supposedly incompetent or greedy bank CEOs. Nancy Pelosi, who demanded that the Speaker of the House in novel fashion receive a government-financed private jet, rails against government-enabled private jets. Bush supposedly politicized the White House, so in reaction Obama moves control of the census—the very linchpin of the American political system—for the first time into the White House. Big Brother comes not through tapping a terrorist's phone, but, perhaps soon, through having the state collect and centralize everyone's medical records or monitor the content of talk radio.

Why again the audacious irony of Barack Obama?

First, George Bush was not Judas Iscariot nor was Obama Jesus Christ. In the vast abyss between those two caricatures was plenty of room for hypocrisy. The more Obama claimed moral culpability on the part of the sober Bush, the more he proved his own—either by ratifying in hypocritical fashion many of the Bush policies or by reminding the public that if Texas perennially gives us spurs, six-guns, and bring-'em-on lingo, Chicago entertains us with the likes of Tony Rezko, the Daley machine, Rahm Emanuel, and Blago.

Second, Obama did not duly appreciate the sort of pernicious culture that permeates Washington in general, and the Democratic Congress in particular. While it was easy to say that Jack Abramoff and Duke Cunningham typified a culture of Republican corruption, the truth was always that they were just the flip side to Sen. Chris Dodd and Rep. Barney Frank taking cash from Fannie Mae as it exploded, or Rep. Charles Rangel overseeing the tax code that he serially ignored, or Rep. William Jefferson stashing payoff cash in his fridge. A true messiah would have lamented the bipartisan rot in Washington, and then in Lincolnesque fashion figured out a way to clean up his own party first, and the opposition second.

The truth is that Americans don't take well to self-appointed holy men like Woodrow Wilson or Jimmy Carter. Yes, we've had our rare saints, but they were reluctant moralists like Washington and Lincoln, who were recognized as such only after they had saved the nation and stoically endured slander by enemies in war and at home.

Obama can end his irony only when he accepts that he and his supporters were never saints, and his predecessor not a notable sinner, and then accepts that history will judge him on what he does rather than what he says he might do.

APRIL 1, 2009

President Obama's First 70 Days

It really all does make sense.

I n just the first 70 days of the new administration, a number of Obama supporters have expressed some dismay at their new president. Some find his ethically challenged appointments at odds with his soaring moral rhetoric. Others lament his apparent inability to stir up supporters in impromptu speeches, at least in the manner he did with set oratory on the campaign trail. And they worry about his occasionally insensitive remark. Many cannot quite figure out why, after lambasting George W. Bush for running a $500-billion deficit, Obama has outlined eight years of budgetary red ink that would nearly match the debt run up by all previous U.S. presidents combined.

But such disappointments should be tempered. Not only is Obama simply drawing on his past 30 years of education, writing, work, and associations, but he is also properly reflecting the worldview of many of those working for him.

What, then, is the mindset behind America's new approach to domestic policy and foreign affairs? If you believed that average Americans are not well educated, do not think in sophisticated and rational ways, and cannot be trusted to make good decisions, whether for themselves or for their nation, then you would expand the power of better-educated and wiser government overseers. This would ensure that, instead of millions of private agendas that lead individuals improperly, and at times recklessly, to acquire and consume, we would have benevolent and far-sighted powers directing our lives in ways that benefit the environment, the economy—and themselves.

If you believed that highly educated and sometimes distracted liberals occasionally slip on rather mundane questions of taxes, lobbying, and conflict of interest—but not at all in the felonious, premeditated manner of the corporate hierarchy—then it would be necessary to overlook such minor lapses for the greater good of marshaling talented and well-disposed experts into progressive government.

If you believed that socially minded liberals are tolerant and extraordinarily empathetic, then their rather impolite speech is not at all offensive. Constant disparagement of the previous administration, and jokes about fellow Americans—ranging from the physically or mentally impaired, to Nancy Reagan and her séances, to the stereotyped religion and culture of a clinging middle America, to the purported prejudices of a "typical white person"—are not insensitive, let alone callous. No, the evocation of these occasional infelicities reflects the tally-sheet of nitpicking right-wing agitators, keen to bring down a hard-working progressive sacrificing for the people.

If you believed that compensation in this country was intrinsically unfair—that income is arbitrary and quite capriciously rewards some while unjustly shortchanging others—then you would wish to hike income and payroll taxes on high earners to reach confiscatory levels so that a fairer government could correct the errors of an unfair market for the benefit of the many. Higher taxes on some, then, are not just a means of raising revenue, but an important redistributive tool of government to spread the wealth around.

If you believed that government does too little for the average citizen—that at present, with its unnecessary wars and perks for the wealthy, it cannot ensure everyone lifelong entitlement—then you would wish to double, even triple present federal expenditures. The key would be to borrow enough now to provide relief to the people first, and only afterwards to worry how to pay off the resulting deficit of $1.7 trillion. Once people are accustomed to the services they deserve, they will ensure that their representatives find the right revenue mechanisms to guarantee that such necessary benefactions continue. If you build programs to help the people now, the necessary taxing and borrowing for a $3.6-trillion budget will come.

If you had little idea of how businesses are created, how they are run, and why they sometimes go broke, and if you thought that the truly talented and sophisticated never go into business but instead gravitate to the Ivy League to be trained as lawyers, professors, writers, and organizers, then you would assume that our present problems are largely the fault of the former, and can best be addressed by putting as many of the latter in your government as possible.

If you believed that Main Street and Wall Street have little, if anything, to do with why publishers can afford to extend million-dollar book advances, or why the Ivy League has millions in scholarships for students, or why foundations, universities, and governments can afford to hire so many advisors, consultants, administrators, lawyers, and professors, then you would never really connect the conditions that promote good business with those that allow intellectuals, technocrats, and bureaucrats to thrive.

If you believed that those with capital have had an unfortunate head start, or have done dubious things that others less fortunate would not, then you would seek ways to forgive loans, to allow the indebted to start over with a clean slate, to ensure new borrowing with record-low interest rates, to lower or eliminate taxes on most people, and to expand in turn the financial help from the government—and not worry that stocks are down, dividends are nearly nonexistent, interest on deposits is at a record low, equity in real property has often disappeared, and accumulated capital is itself often diminished or insecure.

If you believed that the story of the United States is more a narrative of gender, race, and class oppression than of brave souls promoting liberty and trying to reify the promise of the Constitution, then you would have empathy for fellow victims of such endemic Western oppression. The cries from the heart we are hearing from Bolivia and Cuba, from Iran, Syria, and the West Bank, are not anti-American, much less illiberal: they are efforts to articulate the oppression that the people in those places have suffered at the hands of others.

While in the short run the once-victimized may need to be deterred in their anger from harming the United States or themselves, in the long run their legitimate grievances must be addressed through a variety of concessions, apologies, or dialogues in order to promote the general peace. That a Hugo Chávez calls Americans "gringos," or Brazil's President Luiz Inácio Lula da Silva blames "white, blue-eyed" bankers for the financial mess, or that state-run Palestinian papers refer to Jews as "pigs and apes," or that the Iranian president serially claims the Holocaust is a concoction of Zionists, is all an unfortunate rhetoric of the oppressed (in the same way Reverend Wright once referred to Italians as "garlic noses"), brought on by colonization and exploitation, rather than proof that a large portion of the world beyond our shores is run by racist—and rather loony—people.

If you believed that the traditions and customs of the United States are largely a story of the oppressed overcoming the perniciousness of the privileged, rather than the collective efforts of the many to stop tyranny, then you would talk about past oppression, past victimization, and past unfairness far more than you would evoke Shiloh, the Meuse-Argonne, or Iwo Jima.

If you believed that the United States is hardly exceptional, but merely one nation not all that different from others, then you would have confidence in the aggregate wisdom of the United Nations, and the cultural and economic paradigms provided by the nations of the European Union.

If you believed that wars, crises, and international tensions are brought about by miscommunications, misunderstandings, and Western insensitivity, rather than by despots trying to advance illiberal agendas whenever and wherever they sense an opening, then you would blame past administrations for our present ills, with all their bellicose and retrograde talk of preparedness, deterrence, and pre-emption. You would grandly proclaim a new age of harmonious relations, and count on your rhetorical abilities and charisma to persuade past rivals and mischaracterized enemies that, at this rare but opportune moment, there are no real differences between us—and thus no reasons for future disputes.

In other words, if you believed as President Obama and many of his advisors do, then you would do what Obama and his advisors are now doing.

JUNE 12, 2009

Just Make Stuff Up

President Obama's war on the truth.

I n the first six months of the Obama administration, we have witnessed an assault on the truth of a magnitude not seen since the Nixon Watergate years. The prevarication is ironic given the Obama campaign's accusations that the Bush years were not transparent and that Hillary Clinton, like her husband, was a chronic fabricator. Remember Obama's own assertions that he was a "student of history" and that "words mean something. You can't just make stuff up." Yet Obama's war against veracity is multifaceted.

Trotskyization. Sometimes the past is simply airbrushed away. Barack Obama has a disturbing habit of contradicting his past declarations as if spoken words did not mean much at all. The problem is not just that once-memorable statements about everything from NAFTA to public campaign financing were contradicted by his subsequent actions. Rather, these pronouncements simply were ignored to the point of making it seem they were never really uttered at all.

What is stunning about Obama's hostile demagoguery about Bush's War on Terror is not that he has now contradicted himself on one or two particulars. Instead, he has reversed himself on every major issue—renditions, military tribunals, intercepts, wiretaps, Predator drone attacks, the release of interrogation photos, Iraq (and, I think, soon Guantanamo Bay)—and yet never acknowledged these reversals.

Are we supposed to think that Obama was never against these protocols at all? Or that he still remains opposed to them even as he keeps them in place? Meanwhile, his attorney general, Eric Holder, is as voluble on the excesses of the Bush War on Terror as he is silent about his own earlier declarations that detainees in this war were not entitled to the protections of the Geneva Convention.

Politicians often go back on earlier promises, and they often exaggerate (remember Obama's "10,000" who died in a Kansas tornado [12 perished], or his belief that properly inflating tires saves as much energy as offshore drilling can produce?). But the extent of Obama's distortions suggests that he has complete confidence that observers in the media do not care—or at least do not care enough to inform the public.

The "Big Lie." Team Obama says that Judge Sotomayor misspoke when she asserted that Latinas were inherently better judges than white males. Yet the people around Obama knew before Sotomayor was nominated that she has reiterated such racialist sentiments repeatedly over many years. Obama complained that his deficits were largely inherited—even though his newly projected annual deficit and aggregate increase in the national debt may well, if they are not circumvented, equal all the deficit spending compiled by all previous administrations combined.

The president lectures Congress on its financial excesses. He advocates "pay as you go" budgeting. But he remains silent about the unfunded liabilities involved in his own proposals for cap-and-trade, universal health care, and education reform, which will in aggregate require well over a trillion dollars in new spending on top of existing deficits—but without any "pay as you go" proposals to fund them.

By the same token, his promise that 95 percent of Americans will receive an Obama "tax cut" is impossible. Remember, almost 40 percent of households currently pay no income taxes at all—and the $1.7-trillion annual deficit will necessitate a broad array of taxes well beyond those assessed on incomes above $250,000.

Obama talks about cutting federal outlays by eliminating $17 billion in expenditures—one-half of one percent of a $3.4-trillion budget. Here the gap between rhetoric and reality is already so wide that it simply makes no difference whether one goes completely beyond the limits of belief. Why would a liberal "budget hawk" go through the trouble of trying to cut 10 or 20 percent of the budget when he might as well celebrate a 0.5 percent cut and receive the same amount of credit or disdain? If one is going to distort, one might as well distort whole-hog.

Outright historical dissimulation. On matters of history, we now know that much of what President Obama says is either not factual or at least misleading. He predictably errs on the side of political correctness. During the campaign, there was his inaccurate account of his great-uncle's role in liberating Auschwitz. In Berlin, he asserted that the world—rather than the American and British air forces—came together to pull off the Berlin Airlift.

In the Cairo speech, nearly every historical allusion was nonfactual or inexact: the fraudulent claims that Muslims were responsible for European, Chinese, and Hindu discoveries; the notion that a Christian Córdoba was an example of Islamic tolerance during the Inquisition; the politically correct canard that the Renaissance and Enlightenment were fueled by Arab learning; the idea that abolition and civil rights in the United States were accomplished without violence—as if 600,000 did not die in the Civil War, or entire swaths of Detroit, Gary, Newark, and Los Angeles did not go up in flames in the 1960s.

Here we see the omnipotent influence of Obama's multicultural creed: Western civilization is unexceptional in comparison with other cultures, and history must be the story of an ecumenical, global shared brotherhood.

The half-, and less-than-half, truth. At other times, Obama throws out historical references that are deliberately incomplete. To placate critical hosts, he evokes the American dropping of the bomb. But he is silent about the impossible choices for the Allies—after Japanese atrocities in Manchuria, Korea, the Philippines, Iwo Jima, and Okinawa—facing the necessity of stopping a Japanese imperial killing machine, determined to fight to the death.

He lectures about equivalent culpability between Muslims and Americans without mentioning American largess to Egypt, Jordan, and the Palestinians. He mostly ignores American military efforts to save Muslims in Afghanistan, Bosnia, Kosovo, Kuwait, and Somalia—and American criticism of Russia's and China's treatment of their own persecuted Muslim minorities.

When Obama contextualizes the United States' treatment of Muslims, does he do so in comparison to the Chinese treatment of the Uighurs, the Russians in Chechnya and Afghanistan, or the European colonial experience in North Africa?

When he cites European colonialism's pernicious role in the Middle East, does he mention nearly 400 years of Ottoman Muslim colonial rule in the Arab-speaking world? Or the Muslim world's own role in sending several million sub-Saharan Africans to the Middle East as slaves? By no stretch of the imagination is purported Western bias against Islam commensurate with the Islamic threats that have been issued to Danish cartoonists, British novelists, the pope, or German opera producers.

Obama surely knows that a mosque is acceptable in America and Europe in a way that a church is not in most of the Gulf States, or that Muslims freely voice their beliefs in Rotterdam and Dearborn in a way Westerners dare not in Tehran, Damascus, or Riyadh.

Here we see the classic notion of the "noble lie," or the assumption that facts are to be cited or ignored in accordance with the intended aim: Interfaith reconciliation means downplaying Muslim excesses, or treating Islamic felonies as equivalent with Western misdemeanors.

Why has President Obama developed a general disregard for the truth, in a manner far beyond typical politicians who run one way and govern another, or hide failures and broadcast successes?

First, he has confidence that the media will not be censorious and will simply accept his fiction as fact. A satirist, after all, could not make up anything to match the obsequious journalists who bow to their president, proclaim him a god, and receive sexual-like tingles up their appendages.

Second, Obama is a postmodernist. He believes that all truth is relative, and that assertions gain or lose credibility depending on the race, class, and gender of the speaker. In Obama's case, his misleading narrative is intended for higher purposes. Thus it is truthful in a way that accurate facts offered by someone of a different, more privileged class and race might not be.

Third, Obama talks more than almost any prior president, weighing in on issues from Stephen Colbert's haircut, to Sean Hannity's hostility, to the need to wash our hands. In Obama's way of thinking, his receptive youthful audiences are proof of his righteousness and wisdom—and empower him to pontificate on matters he knows nothing about.

Finally, our president is a product of a multicultural education: Facts either cannot be ascertained or do not matter, given that the overriding concern is to promote an equality of result among various contending groups. That is best done by inflating the aspirations of those without power, and deflating the "dominant narratives" of those with it.

The problem in the next four years will be not just that the president of the United States serially does not tell the truth. Instead, the real crisis in our brave new relativist world will be that those who demonstrate that he is untruthful will themselves be accused of lying.

JUNE 19, 2009

Obama's New Liberal Realism

Obama abandoned Wilsonianism just in time to avoid supporting Iranian democracy.

President Obama has largely drawn praise for his tepid response to the mass uprisings in Iran challenging the reelection of Mahmoud Ahmadinejad. In general, Obama has offered three justifications for his tentativeness—and they have strangely been accepted by his supporters, who almost immediately evolved in lockstep from liberal Wilsonians to hardcore realists.

Here are Obama's three justifications:

1.   Given the historical record of U.S. intervention in Iran, we do not wish either to perpetuate that shameful record, or to hang on the necks of the dissidents the smelly albatross of U.S. support.

2.   We don't know which side will emerge triumphant. Supporting losers in the street will only antagonize the Ahmadinejad regime and render Obama's ongoing diplomatic overtures null and void.

3.   There is not much difference anyway between the agendas of Mahmoud Ahmadinejad and those of his challengers, led by Mir-Hossein Mousavi Khameneh. No matter who wins, Iran will still have an overtly anti-American government bent on acquiring nuclear

weapons. Why then incur further hostility for a response that would bring no advantage anyway?

There are a number of things wrong with all this—well aside from the strange spectacle of seeing once-fervent liberal critics of old-style Kissingerian realism suddenly espousing Barack Obama's kinder, gentler version of it.

The coup that unseated Mohammad Mossadeq was in 1953—nearly six decades ago. Its details are still controversial: the proportional degree of CIA intervention compared to that of the British, the role of fundamentalist clerics in the opposition, the degree to which Mossadeq himself entertained authoritarian measures, and so on. What Kermit Roosevelt Jr. did or did not do as the CIA officer in charge, what were the actual intentions of the Mossadeq government in the Soviet-American Cold War rivalry—all of that is all now in the distant past.

Blaming America for undermining Mossadeq but not blaming it for later undermining the Shah is about as logical as claiming we must hold the current generations of Japanese accountable for Pearl Harbor, or that German actions in World War II permanently warped the American psyche, or that the Chinese Communists' butchering thousands of Americans in Korea must be held against current generations of Chinese. At some point, all nations, big and small, need to get a life and move on. Of course, when one rushes in and blabbers out apologies without context, then one becomes a prisoner of those past actions—we are to be sorry about Iran then and so must be sorry ever after.

Iran, remember, has no such reluctance about meddling. It endorsed Bush in the 2004 presidential race—to the delight of the Kerry campaign. For six years, it has tried to murder Americans in Iraq and destabilize the Iraqi democracy. It has killed Americans in Lebanon and Saudi Arabia, and done its best to thwart democratic government in Afghanistan, Lebanon, and Iraq. How odd that Iranian theocrats have no worries about violently overthrowing democracy abroad, while we are terrified of supporting democracy by words alone.

Criticizing the Ahmadinejad government for its election fraud and its response to peaceful demonstrations is not synonymous with crudely egging on street demonstrations. Reagan found a way to voice support for the Polish resistance to Soviet thuggery. Kennedy made sure that the Berliners knew that we believed they were right and the Soviet-sponsored East German Communists wrong.

In contrast, Ford's calculated snub of Solzhenitsyn brought no gratitude from the Soviets, but plenty of shame to America. The elder Bush's allegiance to Gorbachev over Yeltsin was finally embarrassing, and was rendered obsolete almost before it was embraced. To the extent that George W. Bush spoke out against autocracy in the Gulf and Egypt, he was to be praised, and some liberalization followed; but to the extent that he grew quiet in his second term, we were branded as hypocrites for supporting freedom in Iraq but not elsewhere in the Arab world.

Support for the reformers can be framed in terms of shared criticism of what we and they oppose, rather than clumsy cheering for their own agenda. Voicing careful and wise support for the challenge to Ahmadinejad's thuggery can influence events. That's why the European Union is well ahead of us in its condemnation of the Iranian election fraud and subsequent crackdown. Ahmadinejad is going to blame the U.S. whatever it does. He rightly sized up the new administration and realized there is now an American government that will apologize for the CIA's actions in 1953, but not ask Iran to apologize for its deplorable record in Iraq from 2003 to 2009. So it is a one-way street with Iran, and it's better to be damned for voicing criticism than for being afraid to voice criticism.

The Iranian theocrats are realists par excellence; they do not give a damn about ideals or morality, and will deal with us in the future on their perception of their own self-interest: whether or not we "meddle" now, if they find it useful to talk in the future, they will; if they find it of no value to talk in the future, they won't.

Obama's third assumption makes even less sense than the first two. Mousavi may be a past supporter of Khomeinism, as are ostensibly all Iranian politicians. But he is not on a moral or even a practical par with Ahmadinejad. He has already voiced criticism of Holocaust denial, and has called for freer expression and communication, and for liberalization of Iranian theocratic law. In other words, he is a type of multicultural "other" who is a rational opponent of U.S. policy, but whom Obama actually could court.

Furthermore, the crowds seem already to have transcended Mousavi, seeing in him more a tool than a totem, hoping that his election would lead to far more liberalization than even he intended. One of the reasons Gorbachev was welcomed by Reagan was that he began to initiate change that would soon render Gorbachev himself obsolete. The same may well be true with Mousavi.

In conclusion, we are seeing a new multicultural realism in American foreign policy—the result of a number of currents in our popular culture. We do not judge the authoritarian "other" in the same way in which we judge authoritarian conservatives abroad who ape Westernism.

There is also a weird sort of multicultural fantasy about cleric-ruled Iran, fueled by the non-Western dress of its elites, the constant evocation of 1953 (ironically by fundamentalists whose forefathers approved of Mossadeq's removal), and its serial Hollywood-like denunciation of America. Ahmadinejad brilliantly ties into the Che effect, which makes his blood-curdling remarks about Israel's end about as disturbing to American public opinion as the fact that Che himself was a cold-blooded killer who executed the innocent with his own hands. Add it all up and we get a reprise of Bill Clinton at Davos in 2005 gushing on about Iranian democracy and its progressives, as if a rigged plebiscite overseen by a group of unshaven dictators in Nehru-like coats is somehow neat.

Iraq explains a lot—and provides the greatest irony of all. We wish not to meddle in Iran in order to encourage real democracy there, but we accept Iranian meddling intended to destroy Iraqi democracy. We reach out to the Shiite thug Ahmadinejad in Iran, but not to the Shiite moderate Maliki in Iraq. We feel so guilty about promoting Iraqi democracy that we won't aid its budding counterpart in nearby Iran. We are so wedded to the canard that the removal of Saddam removed the counterweight to Iran and empowered the clerics that we cannot see the existence of Iraqi democracy as a great catalyst to the democratic forces in Iran, undermining the theocracy more with words than Iran could undermine the Iraqi democracy with guns.

Then, of course, there is Obama and his quest for a global messianic rather than an American presidential role. So far it pays to be

Hamas and the Palestine Authority rather than Israel, Chávez rather than Uribe, Ahmadinejad rather than Maliki, Putin rather than an Eastern European elected prime minister, a Turkish Islamist rather than a Greek elected prime minister. The former all gain attention by their hostility, the latter earn neglect by their moderation and generally pro-American views. Praising Islam abroad is a lot more catchy than praising democracy—one boldly inspires Bush's critics, the other sheepishly dovetails with Bush's agenda. All that, in varying degrees, also explains the troubling neglect of the Iranians in the street.

One mystery remains: Does Obama do this because the squeaky problem gets the attention, or does he really empathize with the tired anti-colonial, anti-imperialist, and anti-capitalist refrain of those who used to be considered hostile?

JANUARY 29, 2009

Obama and the 'Noble Lie'

Our philosopher-king prevaricates on behalf of us all.

For much of the Bush administration, the media splashed stories of neoconservative conspiracies and cabals. Exposés about mostly Jewish liberals-turned-conservatives charged that they were adherents of the philosopher Leo Strauss and embraced the Platonic notion of the "noble lie."

In his Republic, Plato outlined an elaborate, ranked utopia, a good city ("Kallipolis") run by a sort of benign natural selection. The philosopher-kings sat atop hierarchies in which occupations were assigned for the citizenry. To justify arbitrary selections, the rulers would make up "noble lies" about divine edicts, making clear that the occupations chosen for lesser folk were God-given.

Once the inferiors understood that there were divine sanctions behind their lot in life, they would feel happier. And society at large would benefit by each worker's having the proper aptitude for his occupation. The larger point Plato was making was simply that sometimes an all-knowing elite must hedge on the truth to convince the ignorant public what is good for it.

Other Greek authors likewise were willing to give an educated elite wide latitude. Many aristocrats, such as the historian Thucydides, felt that religion was a sort of superstition of the ignorant masses. But he tolerated it as something deserving support by rational leaders, inasmuch as it provided a valuable bridle on the dangerous appetites of the mob. Some of our own Founding Fathers were deists—rationalists who may have believed in a creator, but believed even more that adherence to religious ritual among the more ignorant and potentially dangerous classes was critical for a good society.

The Left charged that President Bush was surrounded by wannabe Guardians who, via the work of Leo Strauss, bought into Plato's argument. Therefore, according to their critics, they played fast and loose with the truth (Saddam's ties with al-Qaeda, WMD in Iraq, etc.) in order to scare clueless Americans into accepting the invasion of Iraq and waging a war on terror. These "noble lies" were deemed necessary, since the authoritarian threats from the Middle East after 9/11 were, in fact, real, and the public otherwise would never have appreciated the mortal danger to our country.

No accuser, however, was ever able to demonstrate a pattern of sustained, premeditated prevarication on the part of neoconservatives. How, after all, had Platonic Straussians taken over the government from WASP or African-American realists like Bush, Cheney, Powell, Rice, and Rumsfeld? In most cases, "neo-con" ended up simply as an acceptable anti-Semitic slur to describe Jewish intellectuals who supposedly put Israel's national security on a par with, or above, our own.

The irony is that during the Obama administration's first six months, we have seen ample evidence of noble lies. The first category is the historically inaccurate statement designed to bolster the spirits of the Islamic world. This type of lie offers proof of Obama's noble intentions and conduces to the greater good. Obama, of course, seems to know little history. And to the degree he is interested in the past, history becomes largely a melodramatic, rather than tragic, story, in which we are to distinguish victims and oppressors based on modern moral standards, and allot sympathy and blame accordingly.

That said, I still cannot quite believe Obama thinks that chattel slavery in America was ended without violence. Or that Islam was responsible for unprecedented breakthroughs in advanced math, sophisticated medicine, and printing, let alone that it served as a catalyst for the Renaissance and the Enlightenment. Instead, Obama seems to believe that fudging on facts is not fudging, but simply offers a competing narrative that gains validity by its good intentions. Most Americans, Obama further believes, are either too dense or too uneducated to discern his misinformation. But they will at some future date appreciate the global good will that results from his feel-good mytho-history.

No one in the Arab street is going to object when Obama assures us all that Islamic felonies—religious intolerance, gender apartheid, coercive government—are equivalent to American religious and gender misdemeanors. Hitler made up stories about World War I and German minorities in Eastern Europe for murderous racist reasons. His ignoble lies are in no way similar to present-day noble lies that are offered for exactly the opposite goal of promoting religious tolerance and global brotherhood.

A second type of noble lie is more personal. Obama as a Platonic philosopher-king advocates all sorts of exalted aims that he himself will probably never fulfill. That he is hypocritical matters little, given the fact that his bromides are unquestionably for the public good. Obama apparently speaks no foreign language, yet he deplores the lack of foreign-language fluency on the part of less sophisticated Americans. He is unable to quit smoking entirely, but emphasizes the role of preventive medicine and healthy lifestyles in his radical health-care reform initiatives.

He wisely calls for racial transcendence and an end to racial identities—even as he excuses Judge Sotomayor's clearly racialist belief that race and gender inherently make one a better or worse judge. Obama, the healer, jumpstarted his own political career through religiously listening to and subsidizing the racist hate-speech offered by the charlatan Reverend Wright.

Obama deplores Wall Street greed and CEOs who take junkets to the Super Bowl and Las Vegas, even as he serves $100-a-pound beef, flies in his favorite pizza maker from St. Louis, and goes on a lavish "date" with Michelle to New York. Philosopher-kings accept certain protocols for themselves, others for the less sophisticated—knowing that if most people tighten their belts in time of recession such parsimony is good for the country, but it is irrelevant to the occasional indulgences by an all-knowing elite.

We saw earlier examples of such elite personal exemptions with an array of Obama's appointees. The most brazen called for higher taxes while, as gifted technocrats, they obviously felt that such taxation did not, and should not, apply to their own exalted 1040s.

The third sort of noble lie is the deliberately incomplete truth. Obama sincerely believes that "stimuli" and vast new budget-breaking programs are critical for the welfare of hoi polloi, but he also knows that the mob is suspicious of record-breaking deficits. So he signs the record-breaking deficits into law, while promising to be a deficit hawk—by cutting one half of one percent of the federal budget. In his Platonic mind, the mindless public is both pacified and shepherded in the right direction.

Obama knows that our country needs to be protected from radical Islam by renditions, tribunals, wiretaps, intercepts, Predator assassinations, and persistence in Iraq and Afghanistan. But he also knows the public feels bad when some (like an earlier Obama himself) demagogue the issue, alleging a war against constitutional rights.

So he offers the noble lie of denouncing these Bush protocols that his antiwar base abhors—even as he maintains or expands them. He is certain that the average Joe cannot quite figure out what is going on, and would never suspect that a charismatic, postracial Guardian would ever deceive the people.

Obama plants soft questions at news conferences, lies about earlier promises of posting pending legislation on government websites for public perusal, feigns populist unease with his radical government expansion, fires public auditors who uncover liberal transgressions, and in general adopts a hardball politics that the Left claimed was innate to George W. Bush. These again are lies that are noble, in that they facilitate progressive politics that help the people—and they are presumably indiscernible by a fawning media and an unaware electorate.

So why does President Obama so often get history wrong, so often call for utopian schemes he would hardly adopt for himself, and so often distort by misinformation and incomplete disclosure? Partly the culprit is administrative inexperience, partly historical ignorance. But mostly the disconnect comes because Barack Obama believes he is a philosopher-king, whose exalted ends more than justify his mendacious means.

In other words, Obama is our first truly postmodern president. And the Guardians who form his elite circle—in the very manner that they once falsely accused neo-cons of doing—deliberately, but "nobly," distort the truth on behalf of us all.

SEPTEMBER 8, 2009

Once Upon a Time . . .

Whatever happened to the old Barack Obama?

Once upon a time, a fresh new politician, Barack Obama—black, young, eloquent, and hip—soared with rhetoric about hope and change. The people were mesmerized. What a contrast with the tongue-tied outgoing president, George W. Bush, and his unpopular wars in Iraq and Afghanistan!

Presidential Candidate Obama sensed their ecstasy, and so he made two great promises: Whatever Bush was, he would not be, and despite the right-wing slander about his former intimacy with Bill Ayers, the Reverend Wright, Father Pfleger, Rashid Khalidi, and all his other old Chicago radical friends, Obama would be a centrist, a cooler version of Bill Clinton. There were to be no more red/blue state divides. The most partisan politician in the Senate promised a new era of bipartisanship. He who had profited from identity politics would suddenly be beyond race.

The people were considering voting for this unknown, fresh, hope-and-change candidate—a decision made easier after the financial meltdown of mid-September 2008. They decided then that they wanted a new-frontier moderate, a JFK for the 21st century, who would put competence and style over ideology—and clean up the financial mess left by Wall Street and the greedy Republicans.

Obama also promised that he would craft a foreign policy from the bipartisan center, while making us liked abroad once more. During the campaign, to reassure the doubtful, he name-dropped at length Republicans with whom he would consult: old centrist pros like Dick Lugar and Bob Gates, as well as four-star generals.

But having been elected, President Obama sensed that, just maybe, the United States was part of the problem rather than the solution. So he shunned Israel and warmed up to Syria and the Palestinians. He cut off relations with Honduras. He ignored our ally Colombia while reaching out to Castro, Chavez, and Ortega. Putin's Russia received more deference than did most of Russia's old vassals in Eastern Europe. The British were snubbed in gratuitous fashion.

When hundreds of thousands of Iranian dissidents went out in the streets to protest their theocracy's rigged voting, Obama voted present—or perhaps accepted beforehand that the reformers would fail. After all, dealing with a lunatic revolutionary Iranian government would showcase far better his own singular multicultural finesse.

Meanwhile, Obama went on an apology tour abroad. He inflated the accomplishments of the Islamic world, magnified his own country's sins, and once again blamed Bush for America's global unpopularity. In short, it was not intrinsic differences in ideology and objectives, but the prior president, that explained the tension with Europe, Iran, North Korea, and Russia.

A common theme was that the new president, Barack Obama—suddenly referencing his family's Muslim roots and his African lineage in a way that others dared not during the campaign—was as skeptical of America's history as were its critics, who likewise doubted there was anything "exceptional" about American democracy.

During the campaign, Nominee Obama talked of fiscal sobriety. He damned the Bush deficits. And he warned voters that his comprehensive agenda might have to wait a bit while we put our financial house in order. From time to time, Obama brought old Paul Volcker out of the closet and proclaimed him a key adviser—the subtext being that Obama, too, was an inflation fighter, a budget balancer, and a fiscal hawk of the first order. The likes of Warren Buffett assured us that all this fiscal seriousness was authentic. So the people were relieved and found another reason to vote for the moderate—only to be shocked when he submitted a budget nearly $2 trillion in the red, with plans to add $9 trillion more to the soaring national debt.

In the spring and summer of 2008, when gas soared and right-wingers started chanting "Drill, baby, drill," Barack Obama replied to his rival, John McCain, that all America's energy cards would be on the table—oil, gas, nuclear, and new sources of petroleum in tar and shale. The wavering voters were once more relieved, and encouraged that their would-be president was an American nationalist who wanted to use our own energy as we transitioned to wind and solar.

But then gas prices dropped. Obama was elected—and there would be no new offshore drilling after all, no promise to use clean coal, and little if anything planned about nuclear power. Instead, Americans got one Van Jones, some sort of environmental "czar," who had a long history of ritually trashing the American economy, American agriculture, and American coal producers—while derogating George W. Bush as a "crack-head" oilman as addicted to petroleum as an addict is to cocaine. (Presumably Mr. Jones does not fly to his many conferences on carbon-spewing jets and is not picked up by gasoline-burning taxis.)

"Distortions!" Candidate Obama screamed, when charged with wanting a Canadian-style health-care system. All he wanted to do, Obama swore, was lower our costs and insure the uninsured. But then President Obama somehow demanded that a 1,000-page blueprint of a proposed government takeover of the nation's health care be voted on before August recess—as if even one more month of treating patients the way we have for the last 100 years simply would be too much.

Once upon a time, Candidate Obama also assured skeptical voters that he would show us how to transcend race. He was no Al Sharpton or Jesse Jackson, who used skin color and white guilt for careerist purposes. The Reverend Wright, "typical white person," Michelle Obama's "downright mean country," and the Pennsylvania "clingers" remark were mere aberrations of the exhausting campaign, hyped by the shameless right wing.

But soon the people got the attorney general of the United States calling them racial cowards and dismissing voter-intimidation suits against club-wielding Black Panthers who had swarmed voting booths. Cambridge police were relegated to Neanderthal profilers who stereotyped the innocent, such as Harvard professor Henry Louis Gates. Environment czar Van Jones warned of white conspiracies to pollute the ghetto and bragged that blacks, unlike whites, did not go on public-school shooting sprees. The nation's most powerful politicians, like House Ways and Means chairman Charlie Rangel and New York governor David Paterson, for some strange reason, were suddenly victims of racial bias, which alone explained their travails. All this was not supposed to happen in the age of Obama.

Bush trampled on the Constitution, Candidate Obama alleged. Without a major terrorist attack against the homeland in seven years, the voters had the luxury to consider those charges. They seemed to agree that Bush and Cheney were nearly as much a threat to our freedoms as was Osama bin Laden. But soon President Obama read the classified intelligence briefings. Suddenly military tribunals, renditions, the PATRIOT Act, Predator assassinations, and the wars in Afghanistan and Iraq were not just Bush conspiracies after all, but serious, necessary tools of American overseas contingency operations to thwart real man-caused disasters. The media, Hollywood, and the intelligentsia agreed, and thus Code Pink, Michael Moore, and a screaming Al Gore either quieted down or dropped out the news.

No lobbyists, Obama thundered during the campaign—not one!— would serve in his administration. Impending legislation would appear on government web sites for the people's perusal. White House logs would be available from Day One to enlighten the voters about who did and did not enter the people's house.

Cabinet nominees and officials would be beyond ethical reproach. Speaker Pelosi would "drain the swamp," end the "culture of corruption," and ensure the "the most ethical Congress ever." There would be no more plants at news conference; no staged questions from administration hacks; no serial presidential addresses hogging the airways at prime time; no constant press conferences of a media-hungry president; no direct talks to school kids on state television screens.

Barack Obama, you see, had felt the pulse of the people. He was an old-pro community organizer, a street-savvy politician who had encouraged dissent and vocal protest.

But then President Obama appointed lobbyists. For months he forgot all about the White House logs and websites. His cabinet nominees had strange habits, such as not paying their taxes despite advocating higher rates for everyone else. Obama's face was everywhere; he held more press conferences in eight months than did Bush in eight years. Questions and questioners were on occasion planted or staged.

The community organizing and protests of others now became regrettable, even unpatriotic. Criticism of the establishment was the work of brownshirts, mobs, Nazis, and the selfish, who had no moral or religious concern about the health of others and were envious of the success of their president. Insurance companies wanted even more astronomical profits. Doctors were greedy and took out tonsils needlessly for profit. Surgeons rushed to lop off diabetics' limbs for princely sums of $50,000 and more.

The new town-hallers and tea-partiers who went to meetings and press conferences and protested their government were not Chicago-style hoi polloi, but counterrevolutionaries or insurance toadies who feared real reformers. The dissidents were, of course, also racists. These inauthentic Astroturfers simply could not tolerate a black president and so, like the doomed dinosaurs, they mindlessly bellowed out at the new landscape that they could not live within.

Once upon a time the people deluded themselves into thinking a suave extremist was to be their nuts-and-bolts centrist. Now they don't know whether to be mad at him or themselves—or both.

SEPTEMBER 18, 2009

Dr. Barack and Mr. Obama

The backlash is sharp as voters learn that
Obama is not the man they thought he was.

No one imagined that Barack Obama, during his first nine months in office, would be falling in the polls even faster than George W. Bush did prior to 9/11. We all knew what Obama's weaknesses were as he came into office—a lack of experience in foreign affairs, little knowledge of how private business works, and poor judgment concerning the extremist company he had kept in the past.

But given the unhappiness over the war, the September 2008 financial meltdown, the animosity toward Bush, and the lackluster Republican campaign, millions of moderates and conservative Democrats were willing to give the unconventional Obama a chance.

Voters wanted political change—anything other than the status quo. They warmed to the idea that in their generation America would elect its first black president. When the most partisan member of the U.S. Senate started sounding like the least partisan, they believed him. There was a sense of reassurance that Obama was a healer. He was a transcendent figure that would bring us together at home and make us better liked, and perhaps thereby more secure, abroad. People assumed that his easy rhetoric was not a result of studied preparation or superficial style, but a natural reflection of honesty and sincerity. So Obama was elected and enjoyed quite a 90-day honeymoon in an atmosphere of promised transparency and togetherness. A "god," a Newsweek editor called him.

Now nearly half the country is not merely distrustful of him, but increasingly viscerally angry at him as well. Actually, "him" is a construct: At times there seems to be no "him." Instead, the people don't know whether the kindly Dr. Barack is their president, or his unpredictable double, Mr. Obama.

They never expected the president to show mastery of economic affairs or reveal much expertise in matters abroad, and accordingly were not disappointed when he did not. His critics concede that he inherited two wars and a dismal economy, though they argue that he may be making these bad situations far worse.

Instead, the real anger from independents arises over disappointment, false merchandising, and hypocrisy. It is real and deep—as is true of any animosity that arises from a sense of betrayal of former trust. You see, it took millions of Americans months of fair and judicious examination to conclude that Obama's real weaknesses were his once-advertised strengths: He seems not a healer at all; he is not particularly sincere; and he is not especially veracious. Someone other than the man who ran for president is sometimes occupying the Oval Office: The present Mr. Obama looks and sounds like the old Dr. Barack, but he surely does not act anything like the candidate who persuaded America.

When thousands of loud protesters went to tea parties and town halls, the people wanted the self-advertised purple-state Obama, the old organizer, in good nature to laugh that he was being out-organized—not to unleash lackeys to call the concerned activists mobs and brownshirts. When the crude Rep. Joe Wilson shouted, "You lie!" the people wanted their transcendent Obama to remind us all that we should not sound off like either a Joe Wilson or a Van Jones, if we wish to engage in responsible debate. Instead, Obama went back into campaign mode, alleging fabrication on the part of his opponents, even as he fabricated many of his own talking points.

Health care would prove to be Obama's perfect storm, bringing out all of these disturbing revelations at once. In serial fashion, Obama has accused his opponents of lying and distortion—and yet himself still cannot clearly demonstrate in detail whether our existing health plans will change, whether illegal aliens will be included in his reform, how we are to pay for this new entitlement, and why there is need for revolutionary change in the next 60 days.

Obama has given us several figures on the number of uninsured; they change weekly. There was to be a public option; now there is not; and then there is sort of not one. He knows no more than we do what exactly lies hidden in a 1,000-page plan.

Tort reform? Perhaps; but not likely; or is it suddenly kind of? A bigger deficit? Not by a dime—as if more people can get better coverage (remember no rationing!) at less cost. Billions in waste and fraud will soon be saved to pay the costs—if so, why not right now and banked instead?

In almost every statement on health care, Obama uses the conditional or optative mood (may, could, would, should, etc.). And for good reason: When he resorts to the indicative mood of fact he is rarely being fully truthful. The problem is existential: The American people like their health-care system and want it at most only tweaked. All the invocations of God, threats, distortion, and assigning of guilt over the dead to come cannot make them accept in a democracy what they do not trust or want.

Obama worked hard abroad to be liked, but it was a funny sort of charm offensive. He insulted the British in a variety of gratuitous and trivial ways, from poor gift giving to sending the bust of Churchill unceremoniously home. Democratic Israel is hardly an ally any longer. The constitutional government of Honduras is bullied, apparently because it acted in a constitutionally sober, but conservative, manner. The Eastern Europeans, traditionally among America's staunchest friends, were strangely shorted in order to curry favor with the thuggish Vladimir Putin.

To soothe the anger of the Islamic world, our sins were magnified, those of the Muslim world understated—and over 1,400 years, no less. The new president defamed his predecessor so often and to such a degree that even Obama's supporters politely urged that he move on and get a life. When the ahistorical president indulged in historical reference, the result was analogous to a George W. Bush offering tutorials on rhetoric and oratory.

All this, the American people put up with on the expectation that Obama's new directions, his stately apologies, and his airing of American sins and blunders would win over our enemies. Yet the exact opposite has followed.

Iran is more bellicose than ever. It is emboldened by its unchecked progress in getting the bomb and by the ease with which it strangled a democratic reform movement, ignored by Obama himself. What ally wishes to join risky embargos and boycotts when at any moment

Obama might cut their legs out from under them with yet another video or valentine sent to Tehran?

Hugo Chávez is following suit. He grasps that the nuclear finagling that works for Iran can serve another dictatorial oil exporter just as well. If Iran is going to be the regional nuclear hegemon of the Persian Gulf, why not its friend Venezuela in Latin America?

No one knows what is going on with North Korea. But we assume that it is not disappointed with America's move away from missile defense or with a new trade war with our creditor China. It is not clear that the key governments of Britain, France, Germany, and Japan are any more pro-American now than they were in the days of Bush. Many may privately have preferred to safely caricature reliable old "smoke 'em out" and "dead or alive" George W. Bush than run the present risk of soaring along with "hope and change" and "this is our moment" Obama among the Iranians, Koreans, Syrians, and Venezuelans. In other words, Obama the healer has in kindly fashion estranged many of our friends and, by intent or not, encouraged our enemies.

Did Obama at least achieve togetherness on matters of race? A year ago most Americans thought his long association with the Reverend Jeremiah Wright, his "typical white person" slur, and his crude stereo-typing of rural Pennsylvanians were understandable aberrations, not revelations into the candidate's inner character. Indeed, they expected the soft-spoken Obama to be a liberal version of Condoleezza Rice or Colin Powell: Matters racial would be incidental, not essential to the presidential worldview.

But the president, in just nine months, has managed to ensure that race is on the verge of becoming more problematic than at any time in the last twenty years. As the president's polls dip, his supporters—scan the week's network news shows—cry out "racism" on spec, although empirically they have not made the case that the opposition to Obama is any more virulent than what was unleashed against Bush. Most, in fact, assume that what the Left did to Bush—mainstreaming hatred in respectable venues like Hollywood, The New Republic, Alfred Knopf, or MSNBC—the Right has not even approximated. I do not recall any-one suggesting that the Left's often visceral anger at Condoleezza Rice revealed its own racism.

Instead, through a series of incidents, Obama himself has alienated—perhaps permanently—millions of swing voters. He need not have commented on a minor incident involving Professor Gates at Harvard. Instead, the president pontificated on racial stereotyping and accused the local police of acting stupidly. Most people of all races disagreed, and felt that Obama's friend had himself gratuitously insulted the officer and played on his position and contacts to construct a dramatic and self-serving "teachable moment." Would the president now editorialize on all, some, or no more publicized racial confrontations?

Obama appointed a racialist to a White House position. When it was revealed that Van Jones had alleged that white people were racial polluters and were more likely to commit Columbine-like massacres in schools, Obama said not a word in opposition to his venom—akin to his initial ambiguity over the revelations about his own crude pastor.

When the New York governor and a number of prominent House Democrats—most notoriously the ethically challenged Rep. Charles Rangel—played the race card, Obama voted present and said not a word. Obama's attorney general, Eric Holder, accused his fellow countrymen of being cowards, because of their alleged reluctance to discuss race under the only conditions that Holder would consider fair. None of these incidents alone was important; but collectively they confirmed doubts from last year's campaign.

So now we are reduced to a new polarization in which African-American elites are portrayed as more racially sensitive than ever, and quicker to allege bias as the first explanation of discontent. Indeed, a melodramatic congressman has now charged that we are back to the days of night riders in sheets harassing African Americans.

In turn, there is a new simmering on the part of the working classes, as they hear ad nauseam replays of the vulgar Van Jones anti-white accusations, and as they wonder whether the unseemly outbursts—splashed 24/7 on the Internet—of the prominent and successful Serena Williams and Kanye West (who has a history of racial polarization) are emblems of America's new racial anger and coarseness. All that leaves them confused—and increasingly angry themselves that their healer is more part of the problem than the solution.

Why is Barack Obama sinking in the polls in a fashion beyond the easy remedy of more hope-and-change elixirs? The people were willing to overlook his weaknesses, given his obvious strengths. But when after months of fair examination they concluded his purported plusses were even greater liabilities than his flaws, they began to see him not merely as unimpressive, but perhaps even as unappealing—to a degree we have not seen often during the first year of a presidency.

Obama's real problem is not conservative rabble-rousers at town halls or Republican activists. Rather, it is the Democratic rank and file. They may rewarm with an improving economy, but for now they are discovering that just as Obama could take them individually to great heights last fall, so too he could soon bring them down collectively to unprecedented depths.

SEPTEMBER 23, 2009

Barack Obama, College Administrator

Our commander-in-chief seems to think he's president of the University of America.

I f you are confused by the first nine months of the Obama administration, take solace that there is at least a pattern. The president, you see, thinks America is a university and that he is our campus president. Keep that in mind, and almost everything else makes sense.

Obama went to Occidental, Columbia, and Harvard without much of a break, taught at the University of Chicago, and then surrounded himself with academics, first in his stint at community organizing and then when he went into politics. It shows. In his limited experience, those who went to Yale or Harvard are special people, and the Ivy League environment has been replicated in the culture of the White House.

Note how baffled the administration is by sinking polls, tea parties, town halls, and, in general, "them"—the vast middle class, which, as we learned during the campaign, clings to guns and Bibles, and which has now been written off as blinkered, racist, and xenophobic. The earlier characterization of rural Pennsylvania has been expanded to include all of Middle America.

For many in the academic community who have not worked with their hands, run businesses, or ventured far off campus, Middle America is an exotic place inhabited by aborigines who bowl, don't eat arugula, and need to be reminded to inflate their tires. They are an emotional lot, of some value on campus for their ability to "fix" broken things like pipes and windows, but otherwise wisely ignored. Professor Chu, Obama's energy secretary, summed up the sense of academic disdain that permeates this administration with his recent sniffing about the childish polloi: "The American people . . . just like your teenage kids, aren't acting in a way that they should act." Earlier, remember, Dr. Chu had scoffed from his perch that California farms were environmentally unsound and would soon disappear altogether, "We're looking at a scenario where there's no more agriculture in California."

It is the role of the university, from a proper distance, to help them, by making sophisticated, selfless decisions on health care and the environment that the unwashed cannot grasp are really in their own interest—deluded as they are by Wal-Mart consumerism, Elmer Gantry evangelicalism, and Sarah Palin momism. The tragic burden of an academic is to help the oppressed, but blind, majority.

In the world of the university, a Van Jones—fake name, fake accent, fake underclass pedigree, fake almost everything—is a dime a dozen. Ward Churchill fabricated everything from his degree to his ancestry, and was given tenure, high pay, and awards for his beads, buckskin, and Native American—like locks. The "authentic" outbursts of Van Jones about white polluters and white mass-murderers are standard campus fare. In universities, such over-the-top rhetoric and pseudo-Marxist histrionics are simply career moves, used to scare timid academics and win release time, faculty-adjudicated grants, or exemption from normal tenure scrutiny. Skip Gates's fussy little theatrical fit at a Middle American was not his first and will not be his last.

Obama did not vet Jones before hiring him because he saw nothing unusual (much less offensive) about him, in the way that Bill Ayers likewise was typical, not an aberration, on a campus. Just as there are few conservatives, so too there are felt to be few who should be considered radicals in universities. Instead everyone is considered properly left, and even fringe expressions are considered normal calibrations within a shared spectrum. The proper question is not "Why are there so many extremists in the administration?" but rather "What's so extreme?"

Some people are surprised that the administration is hardly transparent and, in fact, downright intolerant of dissent. Critics are slurred as racists and Nazis—usually without the fingerprints of those who orchestrated the smear campaign from higher up. The NEA seems to want to dish out federal money to "artists" on the basis of liberal obsequiousness. The president tells the nation that his wonderful programs are met with distortion and right-wing lies, and that the time for talking is over—no more partisan, divisive bickering in endless debate.

That reluctance to engage in truly diverse argumentation again reveals the influence of the academic world on Team Obama. We can have an Eric Holder—type "conversation" (a good campusese word), but only if held on the basis of the attorney general's one-way notion of racial redress.

On most campuses, referenda in the academic senate ("votes of conscience") on gay marriage or the war in Iraq are as lopsided as Saddam's old plebiscites. Speech codes curb free expression. Groupthink is the norm. Dissent on tenure decisions, questioning of diversity, or skepticism about the devolution in the definition of sexual harassment—all that can be met with defamation. The wolf cry of "racist" is a standard careerist gambit. Given the exalted liberal ends, why quibble over the means?

Some wonder where Obama got the idea that constant exposure results in persuasion. But that too comes from the talk-is-everything mindset of a university president. Faculties are swamped with memos from deans, provosts, and presidents, reiterating their own "commitment to diversity," reminding how they would not "tolerate hate speech," and in general blathering about the "campus community." University administrators instruct faculty on everything from getting a flu shot, to covering up when coughing, to how to make a syllabus and avoid incorrect words.

Usually the frequency of such communiqués spikes when administrators are looking for a job elsewhere and want to establish a fresh paper trail so that their potential new employers can be reminded of their ongoing progressive credentials.

Obama has simply emulated the worldview and style of a college administrator. So he thinks that reframing the same old empty banalities with new rhetorical flourishes and signs of fresh commitment and empathy will automatically result in new faculty converts. There is no there there in health-care reform, but opponents can be either bullied, shamed, or mesmerized into thinking there is.

Czars are a university favorite. Among the frequent topics of the daily university executive communiqués are the formulaic "My team now includes . . . ," "I have just appointed . . . ," "Under my direction . . . " (that first-person overload is, of course, another Obama characteristic), followed by announcement of a new "special" appointment: "special assistant to the president for diversity," "acting assistant provost for community affairs and external relations," "associate dean for curriculum enhancement and development."

Most of these tasks are either unnecessary or amply covered by existing faculty, department chairs, and deans. Czars, however, proliferated on campuses for fairly obvious reasons. First, they are spotlights illuminating the university administration's commitment to a particular fashionable cause by the showy creation of a high-profile, highly remunerative new job. When loud protests meet the university's inability to create a new department or fund a trendy but costly special program, administrators often take their loudest critics and make them czars— satisfying the "base" without substantial policy changes.

Second, czars are a way to circumvent the usual workings of the university, especially faculty committees in which there is an outside chance of some marginalized conservative voting against putting "Race, Class, and Gender in the Latina Cinema" into the general-education curriculum.

Special assistants for and associates of something or other are not vetted. Czars create an alternative university administration that can create special billets, hire adjuncts (with de facto security), and obtain budgeting without faculty oversight. The special assistant or associate rarely is hired through a normal search process open to the campus community, but rather is simply selected and promoted by administrative fiat.

One of the most disturbing characteristics of the new administration is a particular sort of whining or petulance. Dissatisfaction arises over even favorable press coverage—as we saw last weekend, when Obama serially trashed the obsequious media that he had hogged all day.

Feelings of being underappreciated by the public for all one's self-sacrificial efforts are common university traits. We've seen in the past a certain love/hate relationship of Professor Obama with wealthy people—at first a Tony Rezko, but now refined and evolved much higher to those on Wall Street that the administration in schizophrenic fashion both damns and worships.

Michelle Obama during the campaign summed up best her husband's wounded-fawn sense of sacrifice when she said, "Barack is one of the smartest people you will ever encounter who will deign to enter this messy thing called politics." Academic culture also promotes this idea that highly educated professionals deigned to give up their best years for arduous academic work and chose to be above the messy rat race. Although supposedly far better educated, smarter (or rather the "smartest"), and more morally sound than lawyers, CEOs, and doctors, academics gripe that they, unfairly, are far worse paid. And they lack the status that should accrue to those who teach the nation's youth, correct their papers, and labor over lesson plans. Obama reminded us ad nauseam of all the lucre he passed up on Wall Street in order to return to the noble pursuit of organizing and teaching in Chicago.

In short, campus people have had the bar raised on themselves at every avenue. Suggest to an academic that university pay is not bad for ninth months' work, often consisting of an actual six to nine hours a week in class, and you will be considered guilty of heresy if not defamation.

University administrators worship private money, and then among themselves scoff at the capitalism that created it. Campus elites, looking at a benefactor, are fascinated how someone—no brighter than they are—made so much money, even as they are repelled by a system that allows those other than themselves to have pulled it off. No wonder that Obama seems enchanted by a Warren Buffett, even as he trashes the very landscape that created Berkshire Hathaway's riches. No president has raised more money from Wall Street or has given it more protection from accountability—while at the same time demagoguing it as selfish and greedy.

Many of the former Professor Obama's problems so far hinge on his administration's inability to judge public opinion, its own self-righteous sense of self, its non-stop sermonizing, and its suspicion of sincere dissent. In other words, the United States is now a campus, we are the students, and Obama is our university president.

OCTOBER 6, 2009

The Buck Passes Here

According to Obama's chorus of whiners, nothing is ever his fault.

Meet the Obama whiners. "They did it" is the new administration's credo when things go wrong. Most often, the culprit for disappointment in Obama's hope-and-change agenda remains George W. Bush—a sort of modern-day fallen angel Azael, whose wickedness is persistent and omnipresent.

Nine months after his departure, the former president insidiously still has his hand in almost everything that seems to plague Barack Obama's utopian plans. At other times "the Republicans," "the far Right," "conservatives," or even the "mob" have kept America from getting the future it deserves. One would never guess that the Democrats have held the Senate and the House since 2006, own the executive branch, and enjoy the support of the ever-obsequious media.

Instead, demons everywhere are busy at work to stall Obamism.

Civil-rights problems? "Cowards!" Attorney General Eric Holder yells at his countrymen. Energy stasis? "Teenagers!" we Americans are, Energy Secretary Steven Chu sermonizes about the ill-informed electorate. More problems with terrorists? The old bogeyman Bush created a "global war" mindset that served only to "validate al-Qaeda's twisted worldview"—or so insists the new terrorism czar, John Brennan.

Persistent joblessness? It can only be the aftereffect of the Bush-induced financial panic of over a year ago—not past bipartisan criminality at Freddie Mac and Fannie Mae, or present failed stimuli, or massive deficits, or the current climate of chronic uncertainty, given that business has no idea of the cost of promised high taxes to come, health-care reform to come, cap-and-trade to come, or anything else to come. We have forgotten that John Kerry ran in 2004 on the notion of a Bush-induced "jobless recovery"—when unemployment was at 5.4 percent, just a little more than half of what it is currently.

Obama's signature health-care reform is being stalled by mob-like right-wing tea parties and town-hall racists who have mysteriously nullified Democratic majorities in Congress. Few fault Obama's insane idea of outsourcing the reform bill to the Democratic House and Senate, which cobbled together an unreadable 1,000-page free-for-all spending mess at a time of a $2 trillion deficit.

The failure to charm Russia, denuclearize Iran, or commit to Afghanistan? All these problems likewise persist because of George W. Bush, who antagonized the misunderstood Putin, wanted to "wage war" against a troubled Ahmadinejad, and "took his eye off the ball" in regard to the "necessary war" against the Taliban. Even when we push the reset button, Bush still manages somehow to confound the new diplomacy and prevents the Russians from helping with a mysteriously stubborn Iran.

Supposedly outspoken generals like Stanley McChrystal are fouling up administration policies in Afghanistan, getting dangerously close to tipping the balance between civilian and military authority—not at all like the noble "revolt of the generals" during the Bush-era controversy over the surge, when dozens of high-ranking officers, present and past, took turns, candidly or stealthily, trashing the chief executive.

Obama jetted in to Copenhagen to lobby for a Chicago Olympics. He spent a little over an hour there. Both he and Michelle wowed Europeans with inspirational stories from their Chicago neighborhoods. Most of the anecdotes proved implausible or inane: Michelle sitting on her father's knee (at 20?) watching Carl Lewis, or learning from her dad to throw a right hook (at a time when the world was watching YouTube snippets of a wild Chicago street slugfest). Obama found himself playing the role of a 19th-century Irish pol finagling for the home tribe—at a time when the natural consequence of his serial apologies and post-modern transnational rhetoric would be the selection of Rio as host to the 2016 games.

No matter. It was Bush who lost Chicago its sure-thing bid—literally, according to Illinois senator Roland Burris. He claimed that the judges were still angry at Bush's America, rather than peeved that Europeans were being treated by Barack and Michelle almost like teeny-boppers at a Beatles concert who were supposed to weep in adulation and seek autographs.

State Rep. Susana Mendoza (D., Chicago) added, "I feel in my gut that this vote today was political and mean-spirited. I travel a lot. . . . I thought we had really turned a corner with the election of President Obama. People are so much more welcoming of Americans now. But this isn't the people of those countries. This is the leaders still living with outdated impressions of Americans."

The president unwisely boasted upon coming into office that he would close Guantanamo within a year. He apparently forgot that Bush had wanted to phase out the detention center since 2006, but faced a bad/worse choice of having to put unrepentant out-of-uniform terrorists somewhere else.

So when Obama soon discovered the same existential challenges that had plagued his predecessor, his administration immediately came up with a "Bush did it" excuse. Here is Obama's Guantanamo czar, Greg Craig: "I thought there was, in fact, and I may have been wrong, a broad consensus about the importance to our national security objectives to close Guantanamo and how keeping Guantanamo open actually did damage to our national-security objectives." Craig still has not fathomed that it was a Congress controlled by the Democrats that balked at the administration's promise.

Throughout the campaign Barack Obama called for an end to the "Don't ask, don't tell" policy on gays in the military. That won him ample support from the homosexual community. And now? The two Bush wars apparently prevent him from following through on that promise as well. The national-security adviser, Gen. James Jones, complains that there is "an awful lot on his desk. I know this is an issue that he intends to take on at the appropriate time." Apparently we were not fighting in Iraq and Afghanistan when Obama made his grandiose campaign pledge.

There is a growing credibility problem with this young administration. When Barack Obama promises a public option in health-care reform, or the passage of such legislation before the August break, or a renewed commitment to the necessary war in Afghanistan, or an end to lobbyists in government, or a new transparency, no one believes any of it anymore. Even worse, we know that the broken promises and policy mishaps will always be someone else's fault.

The problem with all this is that while Americans may tire of duplicity, they hate whining with a passion. Harry Truman became a folk hero for not blaming others for the myriad of crises that he inherited. In contrast, Barack Obama's legacy is shaping up as "The Buck Passes Here."

OCTOBER 16, 2009

Obama's Theorems

The people don't believe any more.

Part of the problem with the president's agenda is that it is predicated on a number of radical ideas that are asserted, rather than proven. His experts and the elites assure us of a reality that most people in their own more mundane lives have not found to be true. In short, they may find Obama personally engaging, but they no longer believe what he says.

Take cap-and-trade legislation. We are asked to endanger an already-weak U.S. economy with a series of incentives and punishments to discourage the use of carbon-based fuels, with which—whether shale, natural gas, coal, or petroleum—America is rather well endowed.

A number of eminent scientists, along with environmental advocates such as Mr. Gore, lecture us that global warming as a manmade phenomenon is unimpeachable. But this month Americans are shivering through one of the coldest Octobers in memory, whether in Idaho, Colorado, or Michigan. They understand that over the last decade average global temperatures did not spike; in fact, they slightly decreased.

We are advised, of course, to look at larger trends to grasp the full extent of the looming disaster. But again, that is a more abstract proposition. And it is not one that is enhanced by elite condescension. In the here and now, the weather seems cooler, and it has for a decade. Voters, unless convinced otherwise, are not about to invest trillions on a theorem.

If borrowing money is the right way to get us out of the recession, the public wants to know why we do not call it "borrowing," rather than "stimulus." If well over a trillion dollars in new debt was supposedly essential to restarting the economy, why not three, four, or five trillion more to make recovery a sure thing? And if Americans know from firsthand experience that charging purchases on their credit cards is optional, quick, easy, and fun, but that paying them off is necessary, slow, difficult, and unpleasant, why would they think their government's charges would be any different?

We are in a terrible energy crisis, we are told: Petroleum supplies have spiked, and we must immediately convert to mass transit, hybrids, biofuels, and electric cars. Such concern is wise, since oil is indeed a finite product. And while this recession has unexpectedly given us a reprieve from crippling oil prices, it is only a reprieve.

But be that as it may, the public sees no reason why it should not hedge its bets. Why not keep frantically searching for oil and gas, both to avoid going broke by buying expensive imported fuels, and to ensure America's political autonomy from the likes of Chávez, Putin, and the Saudis?

The annual World Gas Association conference in Argentina just announced that new finds—many of them in North America—have pushed natural-gas reserves up to 1.2 trillion oil-equivalent barrels. Recent discoveries of huge fields in the Dakotas, the Gulf of Mexico, and the interior of California remind the public that there are still enormous domestic resources, which, if tapped, could tide us over until solar power, windmills, and biofuels become more economical.

Developing all our energy resources, rather than using often-changing parameters to brand some sources environmentally incorrect (is nuclear power still taboo, sort of okay, or acceptable in terms of global warming?), seems far wiser to voters.

Health-care reform presents the same disconnect. The public is told the president's radical overhaul of American medicine will save trillions of dollars. But the public wonders how that could be when more people are to be covered, with greater government intrusion.

They do not believe that the government—given vast unfunded liabilities from Medicare, Social Security, and the Postal Service—is particularly efficient. Or that all those who do not purchase private medical insurance are indigent or being "murdered" in a "holocaust," rather than, in at least a few cases, simply gambling that they will stay healthy and preferring to spend their cash on other things.

If ridding Medicare of waste and fraud will help pay for nationalized health care, why have we waited this long to realize such economies? And if Medicare is admittedly rife with abuse, why would an even larger government-run program be singularly exempt from the same inherent dangers?

Abroad, there is the same commonsense intuition that something about the president's talk does not quite seem right. One or two apologies might convey magnanimity; three or more reveal obsequiousness. Apologizing to a cranky neighbor for mowing on a Sunday morning is wise; apologizing to the entire block for an array of past sins does not just ensure ridicule, but could prove downright dangerous.

There is a reason why previous presidents were skeptical of Ahmadinejad, Assad, Castro, Chávez, Morales, and Putin, and it had nothing to do with Bush's strut or twang. When Obama acts as if these rogues have been misunderstood, he might be right about one of them but not all of them—and it would not be because they were collectively and gratuitously alienated by the United States.

When told that Obama's resonance abroad and forthright candor about what America has done wrong should be welcomed, since it makes us better liked, not all the public agrees. Some prefer not to be liked by some abroad; others wonder whether the president wants himself or the United States in general to be the more popular. If Obama can be quite detailed about all the things America has done wrong in the past, could he just once offer the same specificity about what we've done right—especially since America seems a far more prosperous and successful country today than, say, Egypt, Kenya, or India?

Something is also not quite right about Afghanistan. We are lectured ad nauseam that Bush took his eye off the good war to fight the optional and hopeless one in Iraq, while Obama for years has promised to reset priorities by finishing off the Taliban and bin Laden.

But that narrative troubles the public. If we neglected the war in Afghanistan, why were almost no Americans dying there between 2001 and 2006? In some years of war, fewer perished in twelve months in Afghanistan than in a single month in Iraq. Either both sides went into an agreed-on remission, or both sides simultaneously escalated elsewhere, turning to the hotter theater in Iraq. If we took our eye off the ball, did not radical Islam as well, when it called forth thousands to flock to Anbar Province?

If Bush was crazy to think that an oil-rich Sunni Arab kleptocracy on the Gulf—with a long history of genocide, sponsorship of terror, and war with the United States—needed a long-overdue reckoning after 19 Sunni Arab terrorists slaughtered 3,000 Americans, were his enemies even crazier to agree that Iraq was indeed now the central front in radical Islam's war against the infidel?

Other questions arise. If Obama long ago wanted to finish off the Afghan war, why doesn't he do it now when Iraq is not the distraction that it was under Bush? Why, after a victory in Iraq, should we be discouraged, while radical Islam, coming off a defeat in Anbar Province, should be eager to escalate in Afghanistan? And if General Petraeus was right about the surge in Iraq, and candidate Obama, who wanted to clear the country of American combat forces by March 2008, was quite wrong ("the surge is not working"), then why would we assume that Petraeus is now wrong on Afghanistan and Obama right? After all, the former has been proven wise and consistent, and the latter wrong in the past and erratic in the present.

Americans want out of the recession and wish long-term problems of war, energy, and health care to be solved. They welcomed a young, charismatic president who seems eager to tackle these challenges head-on. The problem, however, is that they are not convinced that he understands the challenges, let alone that he offers the right solutions. In short, what Obama says seems pleasant to the ear, but an increasing number of Americans believe that his answers are not just unlikely, but perhaps not even possible.

OCTOBER 23, 2009

America's Obama Obsession

Anatomy of a passing hysteria.

For 30 months the nation has been in the grip of a certain Obama obsession, immune to countervailing facts, unwilling to face reality, and loath to break the spell. But like all trances, the fit is passing, and we the patient are beginning to appreciate how the stupor came upon us, why it lifted, and what its consequences have been.

HOW OBAMA WON
Barack Obama was elected rather easily because, in perfect-storm fashion, five separate trends coalesced last autumn.

1.   Obama was eloquent, young, charismatic—and African-American. He thus offered voters a sense of personal and collective redemption, as well as appealing to the longing for another JFK New Frontier figure. An image, not necessarily reality, trumped all.

2.   After the normal weariness with eight years of an incumbent party and the particular unhappiness with Bush, the public was amenable to an antithesis. Bush was to be scapegoat, and Obama the beginning of the catharsis.

3.   Obama ran as both a Clintonite centrist and a no-red-state/no-blue-state healer who had transcended bitter partisanship. That assurance allowed voters to believe that his occasional talk of big change was more cosmetic than radical.

4.   John McCain ran a weak campaign that neither energized his base nor appealed to crossover independents. McCain turned off conservatives; many failed to give money, and some even stayed home on election day. Meanwhile, the media and centrists who used to idolize McCain's non-conservative, maverick status found Obama the more endearing non-conservative maverick.

5.   The September 2008 financial panic turned voters off Wall Street and the wealthy, and allowed them to connect unemployment and their depleted home equity and 401(k) retirement plans with incumbent Republicans. In contrast, they assumed that Obama, as the anti-Bush, would not do more bailouts, more stimuli, and more big borrowing.

Take away any one of those factors, and Obama might well have lost. Imagine what might have happened had Obama been a dreary old white guy like John Kerry; or had Bush's approvals been over 50 percent; or had Obama run on the platform he is now governing on; or had McCain crafted a dynamic campaign; or had the panic occurred in January 2009 rather than September 2008. Then the trance would have passed, and Obama, the Chicago community organizer and three-year veteran of the U.S. Senate, would have probably lost his chance at remaking America.

OBAMA'S ASSUMPTIONS
I note all this at length because Obama seems to act as if this right-center country—one that polls oppositely to his positions on most of the major issues (deficits, spending, nationalized health care, homeland security, Guantanamo, cap-and-trade, etc.)—has given him a mandate for a degree of change not seen in nearly 80 years.

Apparently, Team Obama figured that with sizable majorities in both the House and the Senate, Obama would snap his fingers, Congress daily would pass bills redefining America, and Obama would stay in perpetual campaign mode to hope and change the country to accept his agenda. Governing would be like campaigning, as audiences fainted hearing the details of a 1,500-page health-care bill or of ever more sins from America's past.

But, after just a few months in office, that proved not to be the case. Just as a number of planets had to line up precisely to allow an inexperienced hard-left ideologue to be elected president, so there would have had to be a similar configuration to allow him to govern successfully.

BITTER TRUTHS

Obama had to match his unity rhetoric with brotherly action. In fact, he has done the opposite. At one time or another, Obama and his supporters have, rather scurrilously, insulted doctors, insurers, the police, tea-partiers and town-hallers, opponents of his health-care plan, non-compliant members of the media, and a host of other groups as either greedy, dishonest, treasonous, unpatriotic, moblike, racist, or in general worthy of disrespect.

Fewer and fewer Americans now believe that Obama—after just nine months of governance—is a uniter. In Obama's world, doctors carve out children's tonsils for profit, racist morons rant at legislators about losing their private health care, and trillions in borrowed money must be paid back by the greedy rich whose capital was unearned in the first place.

When his base supporters lambaste him for softness, they are lamenting his inability to become an effective partisan—not a lack of partisanship in general. In surreal fashion, liberals demand that the ideologue Obama become more ideological precisely at the time his ideologically driven agenda is souring millions of non-ideological Americans.

His opposition is no longer ossified, but decentralized and grass roots. One of the oddest proofs of that statement is the sudden leftist furor at tea parties, town halls, the media, dissent, and free speech. As long as Obama was opposed by calcified Republicans in Congress, there was no real danger to him. But once the opposition proved populist, panicked liberal elites started demonizing populism—and Obama now finds himself opposed to the popular grievance-mongering that was once the mother's milk of our Chicago organizer's existence.

Obama campaigned on the notion that even if voters might not like his policies, they most assuredly would like him. Even that spell is now lifting. The more the American public gets to know Barack Obama, the less they find him appealing.

On matters racial, their campaign-season unease with his connection to the Rev. Jeremiah Wright, his toss-offs like "typical white person," and his stereotyping of rural Pennsylvanians has not been allayed; rather, it has been amplified by Eric Holder's Justice Department, Obama's own statement that the Cambridge police acted "stupidly" in arresting Professor Gates, and the use of the race card by prominent Democrats from the likes of Rep. Charles Rangel to Gov. David Paterson of New York.

Much of the newly stirred public suddenly assumes two things from the Obama administration: that the president himself will periodically say something racially insensitive or unwise; and that his supporters will call opponents of his policies racist. If we have wearied of all that in nine months, think what four years of it will do to the public mood.

In just nine months the phrase "Chicago style" has gone from something old-time that evokes Al Capone or Mayor Daley to something very real, contemporary, and scary—as David Axelrod, Rahm Emanuel, Valerie Jarrett, and others try to strong-arm the opposition, demonize the media, and manipulate government largesse to either penalize or reward recipients on the basis of their degree of support for Obama.

Could the most imaginative right-wing political operative have invented the idea of a National Endowment for the Arts official gleefully considering quid pro quo grants, administration officials trying to persuade other media outlets that a network critical of Obama is "not a news organization," or an administration communications director bragging about how her team sandbagged the American media and took them to the cleaners? We can believe there might be one statement like Van Jones's slander of "white people," or Sonia Sotomayor's "wise Latina" boast, or Anita Dunn's lengthy praise of the mass-murdering Mao, but not an entire series of them. At some point, the American public snaps out of it, and sighs, "Wow, these people really are nuts!"

"Bush Did it" was the IV drip of the Obama campaign, always there to infuse a fresh life-saving excuse into every Obama fainting spell. But the problem now is that it has been more than nine months since Bush left office, and Obama's "mop up" metaphors are getting stale. Worse still, the reasons the public soured on Bush are precisely the reasons it may well sour more on Obama, inasmuch as he took Bush's problems like deficits, soaring federal spending, bailouts, and unemployment and made them far worse.

Yet Obama has given no credit for the good that Bush did, and therefore must remain mum about the other "Bush Did It"s, like quiet in Iraq; the homeland-security protocols, from renditions and tribunals to wiretaps and intercepts; AIDS relief for Africa; friendly governments in Britain, France, Germany, India, and Italy; and domestic safety since 9/11. If Bush is at least partly responsible for all these things as well, were they therefore bad?

NOW WHAT?

Obama very soon is going to have to make a tough choice, far tougher than his current "present" votes on the option of sending additional troops to Afghanistan.

As the midterm elections near, and his popularity bobs up and down around 50 percent, Obama can do one of two things.

He could imitate Bill Clinton's 1995 Dick Morris remake. In Obama's case, that would mean, abroad, cutting out the now laughable apologies for his country, ceasing to court thugs like Ahmadinejad, Chávez, and Putin, keeping some distance from the U.N., and paying closer attention to our allies like Britain and Israel. At home, he could declare victory on his sidetracked agenda and then start over by holding spending in line, curbing the deficit, stopping the lunatic Van Jones—style czar appointments, courting the opposition, and tabling cap-and-trade. I think there is very little chance of any of the above, whatever voters may have thought during the campaign.

Or, instead, Obama could hold the pedal to the floor on the theory that, as a proven ideologue, he must move the country far left before the voters catch on and stop him in his tracks in November 2010. That would mean more of the "gorge the beast" effort to spend and borrow so much that taxes have to soar, and thus redistribution of income will be institutionalized for a generation. He would push liberal proposals no matter how narrow the margin in the Senate. He would keep demonizing Fox News. In Nixonian fashion he might continue to hit the stump, ratcheting up his current "they're lying" message and energizing his left-wing base by catering to the unions, gays, minorities—and liberal Wall Street special interests.

If he chooses the former, he might well be a more successful version of Bill Clinton given that his appetites are far more in check. But if, as is likely, he chooses the latter, he will polarize the country in a way not seen since 1968, set back racial relations to the 1960s, do to the reputation of big government what LBJ did from 1964 to 1968, and, in the manner of what Jimmy Carter wrought, turn voters off liberal foreign policy for a generation.

OCTOBER 28, 2009

Guantanamo Laureate

Barack Obama threw many stones at George W. Bush, and now lives in a glass house.

O ver the last decade Barack Obama—in campaign mode for various state and federal offices—repeatedly denounced the Bush-era security protocols as either unlawful or of little utility. Indeed, few political figures made the case so unremittingly that the United States had gone rogue in its zealotry to fight terror.

To perpetual candidate Obama, there were no tragic choices, no hazy areas of human frailty, no recognition that well-intentioned public servants were doing their best under trying circumstances to keep Americans safe, and to do so as humanely as possible. Instead, the so-called "war on terror" became an easy target for a demagogue worried more about scoring political points than about understanding the plight of his country at war.

Rendition? Obama once called that "shipping away prisoners in the dead of night."

Military tribunals? They were nothing more than a "flawed military commission system."

Preventive detention of terrorists? To Obama that was "detaining thousands without charge or trial."

How about the surge of troops into Iraq? "Not working."

And the Patriot Act? "Shoddy and dangerous."

But nothing so roused candidate Obama's scorn as the detention facility at Guantanamo Bay. To him, it was a "sad chapter in American history"; "a legal black hole"; "a false choice between fighting terrorism and respecting habeas corpus"; etc. On the stump he serially caricatured it before cheering audiences as some sort of Soviet-style gulag. Not once but in succession he vowed to close it down by January 2010, to mark a symbolic year's period of change in the era of Obama.

But that might not happen quite so easily. Around 50 to 60 prisoners who have been released have returned to some sort of terrorist activity—most recently the Guantanamo alumnus Yousef Mohammed al-Shihri, who was repatriated to Saudi Arabia in 2007 and was killed earlier this month in a terrorist operation at the Saudi-Yemeni border.

Apparently few foreign governments want back their own home-grown terrorists who have been caught on the battlefield—unless we pay huge bribes and quit worrying whether the released prisoners might be tortured or summarily executed upon their arrival home.

Indeed, many nations may have put themselves in a rough spot: If it was rather easy to slur the cowboy Bush as a Nazi-like jailer who wouldn't close down his shop of horrors and release innocent suspects, it is harder to deal with a kinder, gentler Obama who wants to release terrorist-killers into their care.

Candidate Obama often sounded as if he had always assumed that Bush first created Guantanamo as a monument to his Constitution-shredding paranoia, and only later filled it with largely innocent prisoners. At one point Obama offered his Senate office to help lawyers sue on behalf of Guantanamo prisoners.

But as President Obama has discovered—just as he has dropped his campaign talk of ending renditions, tribunals, wiretaps, and intercepts, and of rapidly withdrawing from Iraq—Guantanamo is a bad choice among a number of worse ones.

In declared wars against uniformed enemies, we might—as we did during World War II—build POW camps and detain captured enemies until the peace was ratified. Even in nebulous wars like the Korean and Vietnamese conflicts, there were most often uniformed fighters, and formal written intentions, armistices, and declarations that marked the beginning or ending of hostilities.

But after 9/11, we faced an enemy that had attacked the continental United States in a deadly fashion beyond the ability of the Nazis, imperial Japanese, and Soviets, but without uniforms—or even conventional military forces as we had known them in the past. Yet al-Qaeda and its Taliban sympathizers were not quite a handful of criminals who could be individually tried and convicted for terrorist acts, given that there were thousands of radical Islamists along the Afghanistan-Pakistan border who had committed mayhem—both on the field of battle as combatants, and in foreign sanctuaries as architects of terrorism.

The ad hoc solution at Guantanamo sprang up, in other words, for want of a better idea of what to do with hundreds of such captured monsters. Were we to put them all on much-celebrated trials, with public defenders or publicity-seeking radical pro bono lawyers, with changes of venue to fairer jury pools in Berkeley or Madison, and with intricate legal disputes over contaminated evidence in Waziristan and lack of Miranda warnings in Kandahar?

The problems of Guantanamo's existence transcend George W. Bush. That truth is evidenced by the reluctance of Obama himself to summarily close it down, and of his aficionados abroad to make his task easier by accepting their own detained nationals, and of his liberal supporters to extend the same sort of invective to him as they did to Bush for not shutting it down.

But there is one other problem with closing Guantanamo—perhaps the greatest of the paradoxes that will plague Obama. Since he took office, there has been a marked increase in Predator assassination strikes, both inside Pakistan and on its borders. Indeed, in just nine months Obama has approved more Predator strikes than did George Bush in three years. By some accounts, dozens, maybe hundreds, of terrorist suspects and their families have been obliterated from the air since January 2009. In a few cases, women and children near the intended targets have also gone up in the Hellfire-induced smoke; in others we have tragically hit the wrong targets and executed the innocent.

Yet once the Obama administration went down the path of redefining war as courtroom procedure, and assuming that the United States was somehow amoral in not extending habeas corpus and American jurisprudence to captured terrorists, then almost everything the United States does in our newly dubbed "overseas contingency operations" is ripe for legal scrutiny.

Personally, if I were a terrorist suspect, I'd rather be picked up by a Special Forces team in the Hindu Kush, be shipped to Cuba, have my case reviewed by military lawyers, be allowed a Middle Eastern diet, and be provided with a Koran and arrows pointing to Mecca than simply wait to have my head exploded without warning by a Hellfire missile, while sitting inside my mud-brick hideout in Waziristan alongside my soon-to-be-incinerated family.

When Bush ordered such Predator attacks, it was seen as part of a brutal war, in which the United States had few options to stop terrorists from committing another 9/11. In such a messy, horrific struggle, Predators—like Guantanamo—were seen as terrible choices amid more terrible alternatives.

But not now. An administration that wants to investigate former CIA officials for their part in Guantanamo, assures the Europeans and the UN that "Bush did it," and has made the case that America's name was sullied through unnecessary and cruel detentions, surely cannot become investigator, prosecutor, judge, jury, and executioner in one millisecond from the skies over Pakistan. Sorry, no such leeway is allowed messianic moralists.

Even the charismatic Barack Obama cannot convince his liberal base for long that it is horribly wrong to waterboard Khalid Sheik Mohammed, the planner of the mass-murdering on 9/11, but perfectly fine to incinerate an al-Qaeda suspect along with noncombatants in his general vicinity.

In short, Nobel Peace Prizes are awarded for those who loudly promise to undo George Bush's work, not to trump him.

NOVEMBER 9, 2009

Who Are 'They'?

To Obama, 'they' are responsible for all troubles.
Problem is, 'they' are most of us.

B arack Obama ran a healing campaign. He offered sonorous
themes of a country no longer to be divided by blue-state/red-
state animosities, by race, by income—or by much of anything.

In turn, we were to suspend disbelief over his past hardball campaigns for the state senate and the U.S. Senate. The young, charismatic, post-racial, post-political inheritor of Camelot could not really have
compiled the most partisan record in the Senate. We were to think away
his tough-guy Chicago-style associates. His pastor at the time, the venomous Rev. Jeremiah Wright, was an aberration. And when candidate
Obama occasionally derided George W. Bush, it was considered rough,
but deserved.

Alas, the first nine months of this administration have proven the
most polarizing in memory. Polls show a 61 percent partisan gap.
Obama is now rated as the most divisive first-year president in the past
four decades. As this week's elections suggest, even in liberal New
Jersey and moderate Virginia, voters are becoming tired of being caricatured as either saints or sinners, depending on the degree to which
they embrace the Obama vision. No wonder. As a Manichean, he
increasingly envisions the world as "us" versus "them."

Who are "they," who have raised the bar on everyone else?

First, of course, "they" are the rich in perpetual war against the
poor. "They" made out like bandits under Bush, so "they" should have
their federal income taxes raised to make "them" "pay their fair share"
in "patriotic" fashion. Forget that currently about 5 percent of taxpayers shoulders nearly half the federal income-tax burden. It matters little
that a greater percentage of households (well over 40 percent) now pays
no federal income tax whatsoever.

On the Obamist reading, the record federal deficits are not due to waste and fraud. Nor are unnecessary government spending and excessive entitlements the culprits. A bankrupt Medicare and soon-to-be-bankrupt Social Security, congressional pork-barrel projects, and interest due on past profligate spending did not cause our budget crisis. Instead, the red ink is almost entirely due to a shortage of revenue, and brought on by the greedy who have the capacity, but not the caring, to fork over more.

"They" should be targeted as well by the states, many of which have rightly raised their tax rates—in California, to over 10 percent. "They" are easily able to pay a new health-care surcharge, the greedy few lending a helping hand to the virtuous many. "They" surely have enough to pay the full 15.3 percent FICA tax on most of their income over the current $106,000 cap. Add it up, and soon state, federal, FICA, property, and sales taxes will reach 60 to 70 percent of "their" incomes.

But that is a tolerable bite since income is now seen as inherently arbitrary and rigged. How compensation is calibrated is somehow illegitimate in the first place—and thus it cannot properly belong entirely to the earner. At least, I think that conjecture reflects the president's own past unguarded references concerning the need for "redistributive" change and his exhortations to "spread the wealth."

Who exactly are "they"? The selfish Chamber of Commerce. The profit-driven doctors who cut out tonsils unnecessarily. The rapacious insurance companies, which jack up health-care costs. Wall Street, of course, which ruined the economy. Those who do not have overdue accounts on their credit cards, who pay their taxes in full, and who meet their mortgage payments do so not because they live by a particular code and forgo some discretionary spending, but only because "they" somehow have more income than others.

"They," however, are not always quite defined by income alone. Barack Obama himself lived in a spacious home. His populist advisers David Axelrod and Rahm Emanuel have used their insider contacts to make millions. So has a surprising number of other high-ranking administration officials, from Larry Summers to Timothy Geithner. Populist Obama supporters Charles Rangel and Chris Dodd both found sweetheart deals to finagle vacation homes. Compliance with the tax code is not a characteristic of an Obama cabinet appointee, or of a liberal congressman who lobbies for higher tax rates. "They," in other words, means every American who makes over $250,000 (or is it $200,000? or really $150,000?)—but does not support Barack Obama.

In this world of "them" versus "us," an individual is not so responsible for his own circumstances. All those without health insurance, but who have money for cell phones or plasma televisions, nonetheless face a veritable "murder" by the neglect of the affluent. Illegal aliens, who choose to send $50 billion annually back to Latin America, are forced to live in the shadows without adequate federal entitlements. The young over 23, who choose to spend some of their disposable income on cars, plasma TVs, or cell phones, obviously don't have a dime for a catastrophic insurance plan. In this new world, wealth and poverty are judged in relative fashion—to be impoverished is not to have as much as "they."

A second binary is the vicious and cruel political opposition. Fox News is not a news organization at all: It is "opinion journalism" like "talk radio"—and thus to be ostracized at all costs. The White House communications director said nicer things about mass-murdering Chairman Mao than anyone in the administration has said about Rush Limbaugh. To Barack Obama, the opposition "does what they're told." To his former green czar, Republicans are "a——s." If you rally or protest, you become the mob, Nazi-like and astroturf-like. Town-hall protesters are to be derided by the media with the graphic sexual slur "teabaggers."

Abroad, good things happen because of Obama's inspiration, bad things are the residue of George W. Bush. To be an Obama diplomat is to start a speech by trashing the prior president of the United States. There is no sense of decades of a unified foreign policy, and no memory that Democrats during the Bush administration authorized everything from two wars to the Patriot Act.

Unfortunately, race is also an Obama-administration binary. The telltale symptoms of the campaign have now grown into a clear pathology. In a moment, white police can become stereotypers who act "stupidly." America suddenly is "cowardly" on matters of race. Black congressmen or state governors who are unhappy with their political fortunes take their cue from the Obama administration and cite "racism" for their troubles.

If protesters at town halls are not proportionally representative in racial terms, they are of course "racists." In the world of Obama favorite Van Jones, whites steer pollution into black communities, and white suburban kids are more likely than black urban kids to commit mass murders. Valerie Jarrett, arguably one of the most powerful women in the world by virtue of her access to the president of the United States, in her war against Fox News resorts to the coded civil-rights trope of "speaking truth to power." Apparently, in this cosmic struggle, by virtue of her race and her anointed vision she has perpetual truth on her side, while others, less saintly, have perpetual power, which is to be assailed.

When 97 percent of African-American voters preferred Obama to a liberal Hillary Clinton in the primaries, that does not suggest racialism, but a modest majority of whites voting for John McCain likely does. Racism, cited during the last weeks of the campaign as the only reason why an otherwise shoo-in Obama might lose, now often explains Obama's falling popularity. Indeed, to the degree that Barack Obama gets what he wishes, the country is deemed to be on racial probation; to the degree he does not, it is considered recidivist and back to Jim Crow days.

But race, wealth, and politics are not the only good-guy/bad-guy dichotomies. Obama has somehow managed to inject divides even into the most mundane things we do. Buy a car? Purchasing a Ford now means something politically different from buying a Chevy. Get an NEA grant? If so, you are part of the solution; if not, you're not. If you're behind the DMV counter wearing a purple union T-shirt, you're a progressive and for the "people"—even if you care little about the long lines of waiting customers. An oilman who finds precious natural gas to fuel an energy-starving America is not of the same moral sort as a "green" visionary who garners federal subsidies for an inefficient solar-panel project.

One America, now out of power, did all sorts of terrible things that require atonement and apology overseas; another America, now in power, did all sorts of good things that explain our current status and influence. In the age of Obama's apologetics, innocence would require a plea like, "But my family was from the North. But I wasn't alive in August 1945. But my grandmother was 1/16 Cherokee. But I voted for Al Gore and John Kerry."

As we saw in the elections in purple state Virginia and blue state New Jersey, the problem with Obama's various binaries is that they are beginning to overlap. In short, those finding themselves on the bad "them" side of the equation are growing in number, while the anointed "us" shrinks.

NOVEMBER 18, 2009

Obama's Prissy America

Why does Obama tolerant, apologetic America seem so very self-centered?

T he liberal writ was that a strutting "bring 'em on" George W. Bush for eight years did what he pleased on the international scene. His "unilateral" America supposedly did not consult with either allies or international organizations, as he rammed through democracy in Iraq and Afghanistan. President Bush's "my way or the highway" personal credo resulted in an America alone.

Obama, of course, was hailed as the multifaceted antidote to all that. The new nontraditional America would reach out to the world. We would now listen rather than lecture. This was a welcome reflection of Barack Obama's own cool and tolerant approach to politics, learned as a seasoned community organizer in Chicago.

But things have not quite worked out as planned. Barack Obama to all appearances is certainly more relaxed than Bush. And he resonates abroad as a nontraditional American. Indeed, Obama is now the paradigm of America's ongoing metamorphosis into something more like the rest of the planet.

Yet in his own way Obama projects a far more prissy, self-indulgent

America than we had under Bush. And that self-centeredness seems a logical extension of the new commander-in-chief himself.

How can that be, given Obama's well-known apologies—for everything from slavery and our treatment of Native Americans to being imperious toward Europeans and Muslims? In obsequious fashion, we have sought to assure the Russians that we won't deploy antiballistic missile defenses in Poland and the Czech Republic. Obama has reminded the Chinese that they enjoy sovereignty over Taiwan. Mahmoud Ahmadinejad, Bashar al-Assad, the Castro brothers, Hugo Chávez, and assorted other old enemies of the United States are suddenly considered either neutrals or friends. It seems counterintuitive, then, to suggest that Obama's America is increasingly self-absorbed.

GLOBAL PENITENT

But consider first the nature of his apologies. America deigns to apologize to Muslims without much mention of a murderous Islamic radicalism that almost daily fuels a terrorist attack on some portion of the world's civilian population.

Left unsaid by the global penitent is that Russia flattened Grozny and butchered hundreds of thousands of Chechens in serial wars. No need to talk of the absorption of Tibet by China or of the 70 million Chinese who were killed or starved to death under Mao. Will the adjudicator Obama not say who was at fault in Rwanda, who needs to apologize—and how?

Obama is conflicted over Hiroshima, but not so much over the millions of Chinese, Koreans, Australians, British, and Americans who were slaughtered by the legions of the Co-Prosperity Sphere—and were desperate to find a way to stop Japanese militarism.

The point is this: When Obama takes it upon himself to adjudicate, in quite ahistorical fashion, who is culpable and who not, the resulting verdicts are consistent only in terms of the president's own Chicago-style race/class/gender politics.

Detention in Guantanamo is Bush's transgression against the Constitution, but the incineration of terrorists and their families by judge/jury/executioner Predator drones in Waziristan is Eric Holder's approved cosmic justice.

The New York trial of Khalid Sheikh Mohammed, the architect of mass murder, proves to the world that war can become a refined legal matter in the prissy new age of Obama. But there is no need to go into the morality of blowing apart the head of a negotiating Somali pirate with sniper fire, since the killing had a presidential seal of approval.

What is lost in all this "Bush did it" moral posturing is any sense of American humility, of tragic acceptance that in bad/worse alternatives there is no good choice.

Instead, Obama's America arrogantly sermonizes to the world that it alone, in its singular wisdom and morality, has redefined war as a courtroom drama—but not quite when it is a matter of what America wants.

Just wait: If a few unhinged jury members, ACLU lawyers, and showboating judges collude to acquit KSM as only 99 percent guilty, then Obama will, for 2010 political purposes alone, connive to find a way to keep the acquitted killer in prison.

Obama lectures the world on new American values, and then does pretty much what he pleases—whether it is not quite "shutting Guantanamo down" in a year, or not quite ushering in a new global age of his radical cap-and-trade environmentalism.

The more Obama confesses to America's shortcomings, the more his bored hosts abroad sense that such loud self-righteousness is psychodrama—Obama's angst about his own country. The world has a lot on its plate—hunger, war, plague, poverty, histories of mass murdering—without adding yet another private sermon by Obama about how his own miraculous presidency is moral redemption for an array of past American sins.

GIVE ME YOUR CASH

Consider next the matter of debt. Obama inherited the Bush budget deficits—and then drove them through the roof. Indeed, he is on schedule not only to run up consecutive trillion-dollar-plus annual shortfalls, but also in his tenure nearly to match the aggregate debt piled up by all previous administrations combined.

A large portion of the new Obama borrowing has to be covered abroad, mostly through Chinese and Japanese purchase of U.S. government bonds.

The Obama administration expects to borrow yearly hundreds of billions of dollars from the Chinese to expand American health care. In some sense, therefore, 400 to 500 million Chinese—most of them without much access to even rudimentary medicine, doctors, and hospitals—will be working overtime to loan Americans enough money to ensure universal access to hip replacements, gastric bypasses, and flu shots.

Cut through the soaring rhetoric: We are left with an America that assumes the world's less well-off will directly subsidize our own better-off.

No wonder that Obama has cooled his rhetoric on Chinese smoky coal plants, Tibet, mercantile trade policies, and human rights. All such idealism falls before America's voracious appetite for borrowed cash.

For Obama to fulfill his grand visions of expansionary American entitlements in health, education, and welfare, he must jettison the idealistic international rhetoric, and instead concentrate on the money. We want dollars that we haven't earned. And, like a grasping heir, we will do or say almost anything to get them.

I NEED YOUR OIL

Our energy policy reveals the same prissy sense of self. For all the campaign rhetoric about using all America's energy resources, the administration seems focused on subsidizing relatively small amounts of wind and solar power. Green talk is preferable to encouraging American industry to exploit our sizable gas, oil, shale, tar sands, and nuclear resources. Apparently, we want to boast to the world about our new solar farms, while quietly continuing to import Hugo Chávez's messy goo.

Since American consumption of gasoline and traditional generation of electricity remains steady even in the new age of wind and solar power, Obama's message is, again, hardly subtle: The rest of the world is supposed to keep drilling in the ecologically fragile Persian Gulf, tap the tundra of Siberia, and pump out of the Latin American jungle—while we pay for it with borrowed Japanese and Chinese money.

That way we are assured that the California coast, the Alaskan frontier, and much of the American West stay off limits from exploitation—in accordance with our ever more refined environmental and aesthetic sensibilities.

OUR EXCEPTIONAL PRESIDENT

Again, much of this disconnect between utopian rhetoric and national selfishness reflects Obama's own conflicted persona. When the common man Obama travels abroad, foreigners witness the strange spectacle of soothing "We are the world" sloganeering, coupled with an imperial entourage of jumbo jets, caravans of SUVs, and an array of flacks who allot precious seconds of face time with Him. During the campaign there was Obama the Humble, offering creepy messianic rhetoric about subsiding seas and cooling temperatures, in a mise-en-scène of faux-Greek temple convention sets, Latin mottos and the Obama "seal," schoolchildren singing Obama songs, and the staged Victory Column backdrops. All that led right into ten months of an even more megalomaniac climate in which dissent—whether from Fox News, the Tea Party protests, or the Chamber of Commerce—was seen as blasphemous.

We have now hit bottom with government requests to report "fishy" critics. The NEA schemes to advance the agenda of the new Caesar. And official communiqués announce fictitious jobs in fictitious congressional districts "saved" by more quite real government borrowing.

The net result of all this is that America is becoming as self-righteous, self-centered, and prissy as its president is himself.

NOVEMBER 25, 2009

The New War Against Reason

Medieval heretic-hunters had nothing on Obama when it comes to close-mindedness

Barack Obama promised us not only transparency, but also a new respect for science. In soothing tones, he asserted that his administration was "restoring scientific integrity to government decision-making."

In our new Enlightenment of Ivy League Guardians, we were to return to the rule of reason and logic. Obama would lead us away from the superstitious world of Bush's evangelical Christianity, "intelligent design," and Neanderthal moral opposition to human-embryo stem-cell research. Instead, we are seeing an unprecedented distortion of science—indeed, an attack on the inductive method itself. Facts and reason are trumped by Chicago-style politics, politically correct dogma, and postmodern relativism.

MYTHICAL JOBS

For decades, the government's Bureau of Labor Statistics has maintained a rational, scientifically based, and nonpartisan system of reporting the nation's "seasonally adjusted unemployment rate." Presidents of both parties respected its metrics. Their own popularity sunk or soared on the basis of officially released jobless numbers, as tabulated and computed by the nonpartisan Bureau. The public trusted in a common standard of assessing presidential job performance.

The BLS is still releasing its monthly report, but alongside it the Obama administration has created a new postmodern barometer called jobs "created or saved."

Over the last nine months, the official government website Recovery.gov has informed us how the stimulus has saved jobs—even as hard data reflected the unpleasant truth of massive and spiraling job losses.

In other words, not the real number of jobs lost, but rather the supposed number of jobs saved by Barack Obama's vast dispersion of borrowed money, was to be the correct indicator of employment.

The message? In superstitious fashion, the public is to ignore what statistics say, and trust instead in the Obama administration's hypotheses. And if pesky doubters still want "facts," and if there are not enough supporting data for such speculation, then why not simply fabricate them out of thin air? Thus mythical congressional districts were posted on an official government website with more fanciful data of "jobs saved." Just as creationists insist that the world was made 6,000 years ago, so too the Obamians believe that joblessness must show a decline because their messianic leader says it's so—bothersome facts be damned. In this current Orwellian climate, a scientific document listing the latest unemployment figures is the equivalent of a stegosaurus foot-print—an inconvenient truth for the upbeat employment gospel according to St. Barack.

THE ENVIRONMENTAL INQUISITION
Obama also campaigned on the "fact" that the planet was heating up, and that it was because of man-made carbon emissions. In fact, in messianic fashion he promised that his ascension would mark the moment when the rising seas receded and the warming planet cooled.

In response, we would have to do our own part to cool down civilization's imprint, by turning to wind and solar energy, and taxing oil and gas so as to vastly reduce their usage.

The fact that nuclear power could give us plentiful electrical energy and autonomy from foreign imports—and without the release of hot carbon gases—was ignored. Instead, by fiat, nuclear power was deemed a politically incorrect fuel source, somehow tainted by memories of everything from Hiroshima to Three Mile Island.

That nuclear plants are now safe, as we see from long experience in Europe and from their operation here at home; that we have spent billions to find a solution to the problem of their wastes; that they do not heat or pollute the atmosphere, or add to our quarterly trade deficit—all this is simultaneously substantiated by facts, and yet refuted by superstition and hysteria.

In contrast, government-subsidized windmills and solar panels, which give us little energy—and only on breezy or sunny days—are "rational" sources of power for 300 million consumers. There are other problems of logic with the global-warming industry.

First, the public does not, by and large, see a heating planet. Average global temperatures over the last decade have, in fact, cooled. Some of us recall the media-driven worry in the 1970s over a new ice age—a dubious conclusion based on data from many of the same supposedly cool past decades that are now reinvented as warm to provide a case for decades-long patterns of dangerous planet heating.

These controversies could be adjudicated through substantive debate, but instead politically correct hysteria again has followed. "Good" informed people—like those who adhered to every doctrine of the medieval church—"know" the planet is heating up, thanks to the greed of carbon-based industry. "Bad" heretics challenge official environmental dogma and exegesis. In such an anti-empirical age, if the "truther" Van Jones had not been there, ready for Obama to tap as green czar, he would have had to be invented.

Even skeptics are surprised at just how cynical some global-warming "scientists" have been in their efforts to stifle dissent and fudge unwelcome data. Recently, for example, computer hackers released confidential communications from a leading global-warming research institute in the United Kingdom—the University of East Anglia's Climate Research Unit—that gave the game away.

In their private e-mail correspondence, these "scientists," like clerics squabbling over religious schisms, scheme to explain away and cover up unpleasant evidence. They dream of injuring heretics; they connive to get more money for their own pet projects; and they are terrified that increasingly the data seem to support public doubts—and therefore must be subjected to unscientific, but morally superior, efforts to undo unsettling results.

The second problem with the global-warming movement is the age-old problem of human greed. If the billions of people on planet earth can be convinced that they are doomed without new paradigms of energy use, then those who are ready to provide us with green elixirs can become fabulously wealthy.

Such a one is Al Gore, who left the vice presidency in 2001 worth under $5 million and is now said to be a magnate with a net fortune of over $100 million.

Gore, the green populist, has mastered a scam worthy of Bernie Madoff—based on a brilliant three-step business strategy:

1. Write, speak, and produce movies as a disinterested public intellectual to bring "research" to the public's attention. Demonize skeptics through suggestions that they are either stupid, cold-hearted, or greedy.

2. Meanwhile, create all sorts of green companies designed to offer wind and solar technologies—and even stranger services like

"carbon offsets." The latter is a medieval concept in which rich carbon sinners can continue to satisfy their lust for cars, big homes, and airplanes. The trick is to hire out green priests who take carbon confession, and then offer the sinner a way back into earth-first heaven— through the commensurate penance of planting trees or building windmills somewhere else as divine compensation.

3   When the rationally minded complain of this scam, Gore's lieutenants proclaim that he is not a hypocrite, much less a scheming businessman, because he invests in "what he believes in."

Ponder that twisted logic: You circle the globe proselytizing that Earth will soon resemble the planet Mercury. But that's okay, because you make your millions by offering products to alleviate the subsequent induced fears. The rationalization is akin to the financial manipulator who claims that he has done nothing wrong, because he reinvests his insider profits back into the Wall Street he helped to panic.

POLITICALLY CORRECT BLINDNESS
Then we come to radical Islam and a series of both formal and ad hoc Islamist terrorist attacks on American civilians. There have been over 40 such incidents since the mass murdering of 9/11.

Western inductive thinking used to teach us to look at facts and collate symptoms. (E.g., we have observed a number of killers evoking Islam, yelling out "Allahu Akbar!" at the moment of their murdering, or post facto, bragging unrepentantly of murdering Jews and infidels.)

Then one makes a diagnosis based on such empirical findings. (E.g., unlike the case with radical anti-abortionists or violent environmentalists, in the last eight years we have witnessed a series of unhinged Muslim males who have justified their violent actions through affinities with, or promotion of, radical Islam.)

All those data lead to a scientific conclusion and prognosis. (E.g., while only a small proportion of Muslims have committed violent attacks, over the past eight years there have been dozens of cases in which angry Muslim males have attacked Jewish centers or U.S. military personnel, and have shot or deliberately run over individual

Americans. Therefore, there is a danger that a subset of young Muslims is disproportionately committing terrorist acts. Furthermore, the combination of disaffected Muslim males and ubiquitous jihadist propaganda, together with Western denial, will logically lead both to more formal plots and to more lone-wolf attacks.)

But not so fast: Remember, we are now in an age of superstition, not rationalism, in which utopian ends justify unscientific means.

And so, quite logically, we got the Fort Hood massacre. Major Hasan, the perpetrator, gave ample indication that he favored the tactics of suicide bombing and empathized with radical Muslim enemies of the United States. He went so far as to print business cards proclaiming himself a "soldier of Allah"—while he tried to convert his trauma patients to Islam and sought guidance from a radical imam in Yemen.

No matter. For an Army officer to have preempted Hasan's jihadism would have meant incurring a charge of politically incorrect anti-Muslim bias. Inductive reasoning was thus abrogated, and the world of touchy-feely make-believe took over.

Even as Hasan shot the innocent and yelled out to Allah in adoration, media talking heads were still insisting that Islam had nothing to do with either his anger or its dénouement in murder. Such an unscientific belief system was best illustrated by the FBI agent who announced that Hasan's intercepted e-mails sent to radical cleric Anwar al-Awlaki—detailing his jihadist sympathies and desire to join Awlaki "in the afterlife"—were "benign."

In short, we are witnessing the rise of a new deductive, anti-scientific age.

Instead of Christian, southern-twanged fundamentalists, we see instead kinder, gentler federal bureaucrats, globetrotting Ph.D.s, liberal hucksters, and politically correct diversity officers.

All are committed to the medieval fallacy that exalted theoretical ends justify very real tawdry means. The result is the triumph of superstition, and the dethronement of science.

DECEMBER 4, 2009

Resetting the Reset Button

Obama wanted to set our diplomacy on a new track. And that's just what he has done.

A fter ten months of "Bush did it" diplomacy, the Obama administration needs to reset its reset button.

EUROPE

On substantial issues, relations with Europe have not improved. The governments in France, Germany, Italy, and, soon, Great Britain are conservative, and increasingly skeptical of Obama's diplomacy.

Germany bowed out on further stimulus. Sarkozy lectured us about utopian rhetoric without action on Iran's nuclear ambitions. The British press is collating a daily litany of our snubs and slights—and is beginning to conclude that, in Obama's eyes, the British are not centuries-long invaluable American allies, but pesky, bothersome has-beens, forever culpable for colonial imperialism. If only their queen were a royal Saudi theocrat or a deified Asian emperor, she'd win an Obama kowtow.

The Czechs and Poles will never again rely on a distant ally in confrontation with a proximate enemy; they do not need to relearn the lessons of 1939. Autonomous former Soviet republics understand that Russia's Putin has a de facto green light to "readjust" their present-day, "ad hoc" borders—with President Obama about as clear on any future dispute as candidate Obama was about Georgia.

Don't expect more European troops in Afghanistan. The NATO allies believe that our hearts aren't in the war, and they fear being part of a humiliating Suez-like defeat. And after preening for a "green" American president, half of Europe is angry that Obama's soaring hope-and-change rhetoric will not be followed by any concrete cap-and-trade commitment; while the other half is scared that Obama really believes the hocus-pocus science that the world got a recent glimpse of from the corpus of East Anglian e-mails.

ASIA

India and China—one-third of the world's population—have not fallen for the hope-and-change trope. China won't hear our sermons on Tibet, human rights, carbon imprints, or Taiwan—not with new American hyper-deficits that will lead us to ask China to cough up trillions in capital to finance new entitlements for Americans that are not accorded to the Chinese people.

India wants to ensure that the Bush administration's support for outsourcing, free trade, nuclear development, and India's position in Kashmir is not replaced by a moral equivalence in which a democratic English-speaking India is simply unexceptional, and thus indistinguishable from an Islamic, bellicose, and unstable Pakistan.

But didn't Obama's new Middle East outreach—stamped with Bush culpability, recognition of Islam's brilliance, monotonous promises of friendship, and emphasis on Obama's unique name, heritage, and patrimony—at least bring political dividends?

Hardly. Iran has announced an expansion, not the cessation, of its nuclear-enrichment program. We have achieved the paradoxical result of having polarized our democratic ally Israel without winning over the autocratic Palestinians. The Sunni Arab world assumes that a Shiite Persia will go nuclear, and in response the Arabs will probably seek their own deterrent. Obama's cozying up to Syria has achieved nothing other than bolstering Damascus's confidence about re-entering Lebanon and copycatting the Iranian model of nuclear acquisition.

In general, the Arab world is suspicious of those who trash their own. Its leaders interpret Obama's apologies for his own country as being as much a character defect as proof of any new accommodation. And while Obama repents for America's misdemeanors, most leaders in the Middle East have no intention of apologizing for their countries' felonies.

LATIN AMERICA

After the loud outreach to Castro, Chávez, Morales, Ortega, and Zelaya, Latin America may truly believe that we have flipped. Imagine! America is now more on the side of socialist, non-democratic leaders who agitate for radical social and economic changes.

But that about-face only means more turmoil, not less, as

Venezuela's Chávez weighs the pros and cons of a border dispute with Colombia and leaders in Ecuador and Peru see the tangible advantages of shutting down the opposition, as Chávez has done.

In other words, we will return to the polarization of the 1960s and '70s, when Communist takeovers brought on reaction from right-wing caudillos, now that the United States has withdrawn its accustomed moral support for democratic, free-market reformers and sided more with the foreign practitioners of the same sort of statist, soak-the-rich efforts that are beginning here at home.

A KINDER, GENTLER DIPLOMACY?

But at least our president and his diplomats are showing a kinder, gentler side of American diplomacy? Not really. Messianic moralists and the loudly self-righteous—whether a Woodrow Wilson, a Jimmy Carter, or a Barack Obama—are seldom tolerant of mere mortals.

Hillary alienated the Pakistanis by lecturing them on everything from catching Osama bin Laden to taxing their own people. Richard Holbrooke hectored the Karzai government, to no avail. George Mitchell has done very little other than to convince the Israelis that America is no longer their ally and that he is George Mitchell, Mideast Czar.

The supposed "bad" war in Iraq is essentially won and the country quiet; the much-ballyhooed "good" war in Afghanistan is heating up, with a split-the-difference American battle plan focused more on exit strategies than on victory.

Radical Islam looks forward to a show trial in New York, in which its self-confessed mass-murdering heroes will tell the world why America deserved what it got on 9/11. Meanwhile, for the two years of the presidential campaign, terrorists heard from candidate Obama that the Americans' tribunals, renditions, wiretaps, intercepts, drone attacks, and Guantanamo were as illegal and unfair to them as they are still open for business under President Obama. And what a message that is: You Islamists were right that we shredded our Constitution to go after you, but we are going to continue to shred it anyway!

GOOD FOR THEE, NOT FOR ME

The image abroad was supposed to be a new hope-and-change multilateral deference. Instead, there is a new whiny, self-indulgent, and loquacious America, as mixed up and inconsistent in its sermonizing message as it is consistently self-righteous in tone.

We want to protect our new state-run industries—at others' expense. We want the world's available capital to finance ever more government entitlements for our own comparatively well-off citizens. We want you to drill for oil and natural gas in terrain we would never consider here in the United States. We want to apologize for the old America, but in the bargain expect the world to listen to our new sermons. We want you to seek democratic reform, but don't ask us to say a word on your behalf when your own thugs push back.

Old friends of America from Colombia to Israel are getting the message that they did something wrong in befriending pre-Obama America; while old enemies like Ahmadinejad and Chávez gloat that at last America understands why they were so hostile in their prior serial trashing of America.

DEAN OBAMA

Ronald Reagan told the world that he would side with freedom against Communist aggression and autocracy. George Bush the elder told the world that its borders would stay sacrosanct, and one country could not swallow another. Bill Clinton finally showed that a genocidal dictator could not practice mass murder in the heart of Europe and get away with it. George Bush the younger removed two of the worst terrorist regimes on the planet, the Taliban's and Saddam Hussein's, and replaced them with constitutional systems, while keeping the U.S. homeland free from another 9/11 attack.

Barack Obama is telling the world that all of the above was far too complex—and characteristic of an America that was not listening, but dictating.

Instead, like any good college dean, Obama is now running a faculty seminar on a global scale. We listen to everyone's gripes, add in our own personal angst, draw up pros and cons, offer polite, non-judgmental suggestions to all sides, and recommend 50-50 solutions that can be ratified by the newly revitalized U.N.—all to be summed up by a bow or two and a soaring address touting our own wisdom and success.

We may hope that some old wise men are now whispering to the Obamians to reset their reset button. You see, it's doubtful that the world can take another three years of this.

DECEMBER 11, 2009

Obama's Wheel of Fortune

The president's luck has changed—
and he doesn't seem to have noticed.

N o one in the Obama throng has ever believed much in the Roman concept of a "wheel of fortune"—rota fortunae—so often alluded to by the likes of Cicero and Boethius.

But that metaphor for changeable fortune reminds us that at times we all enjoy inexplicable good luck—and therefore must brace for the moment when the wheel turns, and inevitable adversity follows.

Of course, the downturn is always worse for those who were flippant on the upturn—or so medieval moralists reminded haughty royalty. All cultures are aware of the fickleness of fortune—whether exemplified through the morality tale of Job, the polarities of hubris/nemesis, or the notion of karma.

Any student of the 2008 campaign could have seen that Obama's messianic persona would not last—given the human propensity to tire of flashy neon signs that advertise empty trifles. Candidate Obama said nothing of real substance—even as he advised the wowed crowds that there were first-aid provisions for those who would soon faint in ecstasy at his very words.

That his platform was vague and disingenuous, contradicted much of what he had said in the past, and remained inconsistent mattered little. Any suspicions of the inexperienced community organizer from Chicago were trumped by popular fury at the Wall Street meltdown, weariness with eight years of the Bush administration, and the promise that the ascension of Obama would, on the cheap, wash away the guilt of the American suburbanite.

Remember his energy policy, such as it was?

When candidate Obama was pressed, he reluctantly mentioned nuclear energy, coal, oil, and natural gas. But these were castoff concessions. They were offered as sops until the popular anger over gas-price hikes subsided—and they were to become no more than mere bookends to soaring rhetoric about "millions of new green jobs."

Infatuated voters apparently bought this fantasy. Our deserts and mountain passes would be scarred with ugly panels, turbines, and access roads, as millions of newly hired government construction workers rushed out to ensure that we could obtain 5 percent of our current power needs from such green salvations.

A charlatan like Van Jones (cf. the remarks of Valerie Jarrett, "Oooh. Van Jones, all right! So, Van Jones. We were so delighted to be able to recruit him into the White House. We were watching him . . . ") surely knew more about America's energy needs than did the CEO of Exxon.

But now, on the wheel's downturn, President Obama must brace for spiraling energy costs when the world economy rebounds. Soon the sobering electorate will turn and ask why Obama did not push for nuclear power and encourage more exploitation of newly discovered natural-gas fields.

Ditto the war. For much of 2007—2009, "hope and change" masked the absurdity of Obama's "I'm for the good war/Bush did the bad war" dichotomy. So now the wheel turns again, and hokey rhetoric cannot mask reality.

The bad war is relatively quiet. The good war has heated up—more Americans were killed in Afghanistan in Obama's first ten months than in any of the Bush years. And the good-war president now addresses the nation with the look of "This is really not supposed to happen to Nobel Peace Prize winners!" and "Remember, Bush did it!" and "Where are the American people who used to support the Afghan war?" Had candidate Obama empathized with bad/worse choices in every war, rather than simplistically demonizing his predecessor, the public might be more sympathetic to his present plight.

Candidate Obama did not worry much about a creepy cast of characters that kept surfacing around him—Bill Ayers, Rashid Khalidi, Father Pfleger, Tony Rezko, the Rev. Jeremiah Wright. In the aggregate, they appeared as a coterie of unhinged, anti-American, and quite unpleasant people. Someone should have reminded Obama that he was running to be president, not a Chicago ward boss.

The lesson went unlearned. And so the cast was updated with the likes of Van Jones, Anita Dunn, and Kevin Jennings. Instead of "God d*** America," we got George Bush was in on 9/11, the mass-murdering Chairman Mao was an inspirational political thinker, and homosexuality is merely an alternative lifestyle choice for our teens. The revolving planets change, but the pull of their sun remains the same. On fiscal policy, candidate Obama could not quite explain who "they" were, who were to be skinned for the sins of Wall Street. Those who made over $150,000? Or was it $250,000, or perhaps $200,000?

In Obama's never-never land, these amorphous "they" had all sorts of money from stealing bonuses, getting exorbitant tax cuts, or unnecessarily taking out tonsils or cutting off limbs. What was so hard about having "them" cash out a few of their hidden bank accounts to pay for green jobs and comprehensive health care?

So President Obama went on demonizing the productive classes, promising more taxes, gratuitously slurring the Chamber of Commerce and the town-hallers. And now suddenly there is surprise on the downturn that we are on the verge of what John Kerry once said of a 5.3 percent unemployment rate under George W. Bush—"a jobless recovery."

"Bush did it" was the repeated campaign message. Those soaring cadences of castigation silenced worries that a first-term senator and former Chicago community organizer did not know much about the world around us.

Apparently, Obama was convinced that apologies, bows, concessions to Iran, Putin, Latin American Marxists, and the Arab world would wow them all the way his tropes had mesmerized upscale suburbanites in Palo Alto and Greenwich. After all, Obama had as many suspicions about America's past as did our enemies and rivals whom he courted.

But then Obama learned that—unlike professors, stockbrokers, lawyers, and teachers—the likes of Ahmadinejad and Putin did not care about his Kenyan father. They had not read his Dreams from My Father. Their names are even more exotic than his. Instead such thugs interpret his showy magnanimity as innate weakness, and men like these will manipulate it rather than show deference.

Soon Putin will flex his muscles in Russia's backyard. In a year or two Iran will announce that it has the bomb. And we will witness more anguished debates over the motives of the next Major Hasan, more Khalid Sheik Mohammeds contextualizing their mass murders live from New York, and more terrorist plotting on the assumption that the new administration is more interested in shutting down Guantanamo Bay than putting the fear of God into radical Islamists bent on our destruction.

So the wheel turned, and now most of the country disapproves of President Obama—in the greatest crash of approval ratings of any first-year-presidency in recent history. Will the wheel turn again? Not for a while, given Obama's reaction to his downturn. Foreign policy? It is still "Bush did it," not reflection on his own rookie errors.

The economy? Jobs saved by borrowing are better metrics than the old unemployment statistics. Blame Bush again, tinker with the stats, and print more money.

Small businesses? Employers are still "they," who must and will pay higher income and payroll taxes, and higher premiums for medical insurance. They won't be thanked for their greater contributions; rather, they owe a sort of penance for doing well and creating the nation's wealth.

Energy? President Obama is on his way to Copenhagen—oblivious to Climategate. He ignores the paradoxes of a planet the last decade slighting cooling, when it is supposed to be radically heating. And he does not worry at all about the effects of new green taxes on the country—when the productive classes may soon be paying 65 percent of their incomes in state and federal taxes and increased insurance premiums.

Spending? Obama, if given his way, will run up debts to match the aggregate red ink of all prior presidents combined. So far, "Never let a serious crisis go to waste" has not been repudiated. Instead, Obama continues to blame Bush and the Republicans for causing the recession, rather than wondering whether his massive borrowing and disbursement are making things far worse.

In other words, a very human President Obama still does not grasp that events are catching up to him and that even his empyrean rhetoric cannot allow him to escape. For now, the wheel has turned, and it is still heading downward. If he does not change, his luck won't either.

DECEMBER 16, 2009

Obama and the Malleability of History

In pursuit of noble goals, Obama
ignobly twists the truth.

President Obama has given a number of major speeches touching on world affairs since he announced his bid for the presidency. All have invoked historical examples—usually for moral purposes, but often at the expense of both literal and figurative truth.

THE VICTORY COLUMN SPEECH

Candidate Barack Obama had supposedly made a presumptuous request to speak at the Berlin Wall and been denied (the Germans might later have regretted that turndown, since a year later Obama, tit-for-tat, declined an invitation to speak there on the 20th anniversary of the wall's fall), and so he chose the Victory Column as his backdrop instead.

It was an ironic setting for a historic speech on global peace, since the monument is formed of gun barrels taken from conquered enemies, and it commemorates defeats of the Danish, Austrians, and French—as well as Nazi chest-thumping over the annexation of Austria. The monument is an icon to aggressive nationalism, which is why the French wished to destroy it after World War II.

The speech's noble—and utopian—motif was that the "world" ("a world that stands as one") was responsible for saving Berlin during the airlift and can come together to achieve such noble things again. Not mentioned was the fact that it was the United States Air Force, with help from Britain, that fed Berlin. Most of our other allies thought the airlift was either impossible or counterproductive. As for the Russians whose blockade had made the airlift necessary, they predicted failure in days. The airlift was a testament to unilateral American-British action, and to the failure of the U.N. or any other world body to save the Berliners.

Obama warned in that speech, "As we speak, cars in Boston and factories in Beijing are melting the ice caps in the Arctic, shrinking coastlines in the Atlantic, and bringing drought to farms from Kansas to Kenya." This Gore-like motif is controversial to say the least. I don't think it is a historical fact that periodic droughts in Kansas have been proven to be due to global warming. "Shrinking coastlines" I think refers to mathematical projections, and is an overstatement concerning a possibly greater-than-average two-millimeter change during the 20th century. As to cars in Boston melting the Arctic ice caps, that too is unproven, as we witnessed this week with Al Gore's various exaggerations about human activity as a cause of rapid polar melting.

THE CAIRO SPEECH

The following can be said of Obama's Islamic mythography: a) Islam did not pave "the way for Europe's Renaissance and Enlightenment." To the extent Islam was involved at all, it was Greek scholars fleeing Ottoman pressure at Byzantium who sparked the Western Renaissance, while the Enlightenment's Romantic movements proclaimed a desire to free classical lands from supposed Ottoman backwardness. b) Breakthroughs in navigation, pens, printing, medicine, etc. were largely Western or Chinese innovations. c) "Islam has a proud tradition of tolerance. We see it in the history of Andalusia and Córdoba during the Inquisition." Córdoba had few Muslims when the Inquisition began in 1478, having been reconquered by the Christians well over two centuries earlier. d) Left unsaid was that the great colonizers of the Middle East were not the Europeans, but the Ottoman Muslims, who were far harsher and ruled far longer.

"No system of government can or should be imposed upon one nation by any other." Would that include postwar Japan, Italy, and Germany? Should we not have attempted to impose a system of government in Iraq or Afghanistan?

"For centuries, black people in America suffered the lash of the whip as slaves and the humiliation of segregation. But it was not violence that won full and equal rights." During the 1860s, more than 600,000 Americans died over slavery in America's bloodiest war, which resulted in universal citizenship; during the 1960s and 1970s, racial turmoil over matters of racial equality was not nonviolent.

THE WEST POINT SPEECH

1) "Commanders in Afghanistan repeatedly asked for support to deal with the reemergence of the Taliban, but these reinforcements did not arrive." Obama did not cite a single specific request for more troops that was denied by the Pentagon during Bush's time in office. One might fault the Bush administration's strategy in Afghanistan and Iraq, but the problem was largely a command theory of "light footprint," which sought not to alienate indigenous populations through a large, obtrusive American presence. So far there is no evidence of a denied troop request between 2001 and 2009.

2) "I then announced a strategy recognizing the fundamental connection between our war effort in Afghanistan, and the extremist safe-havens in Pakistan." That obvious strategy predated Obama, who inherited from his predecessor everything from Predator drone attacks to carrot-and-stick diplomacy with the Pakistanis.

3) "This is the epicenter of the violent extremism practiced by al-Qaeda. It is from here that we were attacked on 9/11, and it is from here that new attacks are being plotted as I speak." This is, of course, true, but leaves out the inconvenient fact that the 19 hijackers of 9/11 were—like most al-Qaeda operatives—Sunni Arabs who came to the borderlands from somewhere else, supported by Gulf private money and energized by radical teaching that emanates from Gulf and Cairo Wahhabi mosques. The epicenter of radical Islam is not Waziristan. Rather, it is

found at the nexus between petro-money and radical Islamic teaching in the Arab world.

4) "In the past, we too often defined our relationship with Pakistan narrowly." That may be true of the Carter and Reagan administrations, or the Clinton tolerance for a nuclear Pakistan, but it is hard to accept as a description of the Bush administration's eight years of ongoing massive American military and economic aid, public pressure for democratic reform, and close consultation with India and Pakistan about regional disagreements. The logical corollary should have been praise for the Bush administration's holistic engagement and rebuke for the Carter-era policy (continued under Reagan) that armed Islamic fundamentalists to fight the Soviets without much worry over the blowback in either Afghanistan or Pakistan.

5) "As a country, we are not as young—and perhaps not as innocent—as we were when Roosevelt was president." In fact, American diplomacy is far more transparent than it ever was during the Roosevelt administration, which engaged in all sorts of secret accords affecting millions, including the future of most of Eastern Europe.

THE NOBEL PRIZE SPEECH

1) Obama suggested that "In some countries, the failure to uphold human rights is excused by the false suggestion that these are Western principles." Bush made an analogous argument that the desire for freedom is innate in the heart of everyone as a result of being human. Nevertheless, the formal articulation of human rights is an entirely Western concept—as Obama inadvertently acknowledged earlier by citing the "Universal Declaration of Human Rights." This is a U.N. proclamation that was drafted by Westerners and based on ideas found in the Magna Carta (1215), the English Bill of Rights (1689), the French Declaration on the Rights of Man and Citizen (1789), and the U.S. Constitution (1788) and Bill of Rights (1791), and which is still opposed by many Islamic countries because of its secularism. It is true, not false, that upholding human rights is a Western principle, one lam-

entably not shared by most people on the globe, particularly among present members of the United Nations Human Rights Council.

2) "These extremists are not the first to kill in the name of God; the cruelties of the Crusades are amply recorded." The Crusades, in terms of history's catalogue of bloody wars and deaths, were a minor affair, especially in comparison to the turmoil of the much earlier Islamic expansions through North Africa and Iberia, or the later savage Ottoman inroads into Asia Minor and Eastern Europe.

3) "Only when Europe became free did it finally find peace." Not exactly. "Finally," I think, is not an accurate adverb for a mere 60-some years of peace in Europe (excluding things like Milosevic's war against the Croatians, Bosnians, and Kosovars). So far, Europeans haven't even matched the prior, century-long achievement of the Congress of Vienna (1815—1914).

THE OBAMA FORMULA

In these minor and major historical distortions, there are two recurrent themes. The most obvious is that George W. Bush has been culpable, and that a far more sensitive and astute Obama is here to set things right. Historical citations will be crafted, in deductive fashion, to support that thesis.

But there is a second sort in which the self-proclaimed global healer Obama marshals history for noble purposes. And in service to his inspirational global ecumenism, the president apparently feels free to twist and fudge the past in order to suggest that our cultures are all roughly equal, with pasts that are likewise both good and bad, and thus we now need to bond and unify with appreciation of one another's differences.

Obama feels that reverence for both the facts and spirit of history is not as important as that noble aim. If, for example, Muslims can be assured that the West has been just as culpable as they have been, and if they can be praised by unduly exaggerating their past cultural achievements, then perhaps the Islamic world will see that the United States is a broker of good will.

The alternatives to Obama's constant historical revisionism would be to be quiet about history's often disturbing truths—or to admit that the present globalization, in terms of economics, politics, culture, and military affairs, is largely an embrace of Westernization and the result of the unique dynamism and morality of Western culture itself.

To articulate the latter truth abroad would be chauvinistic and impolitic. To be quiet about it would be diplomatic. But to distort it for noble intentions has been nevertheless ignoble.

DECEMBER 30, 2009

Our Year of Obama

Obama is in a great race: Can he remake
America before the next elections?

A merica is at a day of reckoning that it never quite expected to face.

Not long ago, tired of eight years of Republican rule, terrified by the September 2008 financial panic, unimpressed by the campaign of John McCain, and mesmerized by the hope-and-change elixirs and landmark candidacy of Barack Obama, the American people voted for change.

But change of what sort?

I think voters wanted an end to the Bush deficits. Big government and Wall Street insiders sickened them. They were tired of the expense of two wars. By 2006, the scandals of the Republican Congress had turned them off. But mostly voters just wanted an end to the shrill politics that had torn the country in two.

Barack Obama saw all that. So he gave the crowds what they wanted: promises of vetoes of wasteful spending, no more lobbyists, an honest Congress for once, financial sobriety, and no more red-state/blue-state, at-your-throat politics. For millions of believers, Obama was to be our version of Truman or Eisenhower—centrist competence, but spiced up with 21st-century postracial pizzazz.

The people took Obama at his word, and here we are a year later with the largest drop in popularity of a first-year president in poll-taking history. A clear majority of the country is now opposed to almost all of the Obama program—more stimuli, bailouts, deficits, and takeovers; statist health care; cap-and-trade; and therapeutic-apology/reset-button diplomacy abroad.

I think it is a fair generalization to say that both the Right and the Left agree that Obama ran as a moderate in order to move America sharply to the left. The former calls it perfidy; the latter, necessary politics to achieve the desired ends. So what we now have is a progressive, grass-roots populist who is doing his best to obfuscate his own goals and ignore the desires of the great majority of the people.

BREAD AND CIRCUSES

Despite his obfuscation, the American people are starting to see a common thread in almost everything Obama does, from the significant to the trivial. The purpose of health-care reform was not really to lower medical costs and broaden access. The current system could have been tweaked to do just that with more intrastate insurance competition, tax credits, modest state grants, and tort reform.

Instead, the real aim was to create a vast new trillion-dollar bureaucracy, staffed by hundreds of thousands of new government auditors and clerks, and necessitating new redistributive taxes to pay for it. The more numerous such government workers, the more plentiful the loyal constituents who receive and hand out more government entitlements—look at the public-employee unions, higher taxes, and resulting financial implosion in California. And the more the "good" people receive, the more the other, "bad" people must pay—and that way we can remedy the unfair and arbitrary nature of individual compensation.

Cap-and-trade proposals are similar. We could have had an honest debate on both the nature of climate change and the catalysts for it. The public could have been apprised by our leaders about the Climategate scandal. Concerns could have been aired about the disturbing conflict-of-interest pattern of international green advocates like Al Gore, who are increasingly combining doomsday sermonizing with old-style multimillion-dollar profit-making. The trade-off of higher carbon taxes in a recessionary economy should have been explored.

Instead, the Obama administration has asserted, not explained, climate change. It has even hinted that if future green legislation is blocked in Congress, then some of it may be implemented by executive fiat through the Environmental Protection Agency. Once again, we should expect new government agencies and thousands more government employees—all working in concert with their foreign counterparts to monitor American energy use.

On the dubious claims that man himself is alone responsible for any heating of the planet and alone can stop such change with radical changes in his daily lifestyle, the Obama administration wants to see to it that the average consumer will have less disposable income and less choice—but we will have more government elites sermonizing about what is deemed correct and tolerable.

THE CHICAGO WAY

On the trivial side, the exhortations of many of Obama's appointees reflect this world-view—which is innately unpopular with the American people, but nonetheless felt necessary for their well-being.

Former communications director Anita Dunn praises not just any mass murderer, but the greatest and most statist of them all, Mao Zedong. Van Jones, the Truther, talks proudly of his Communist past and the need to castigate whites for their assorted illiberal sins. At the National Endowment for the Arts, where good politics is now equated with good art, Obama is to be an iron-fisted populist Caesar whose intellectual and political powers are put to the service of the populus. Rahm Emanuel plays the enforcer and threatens the unbelieving with warnings that Obama will have a long memory, and that none of these crises will go to waste.

Like the rejection of public campaign financing last summer, almost all of Obama's promises of reforms—no more lobbyists, healthcare debates aired on C-SPAN, legislation posted on the Internet—have been ignored as impediments on the path to a universal equality of result. Obama's various assertions are as much to be believed as were his supposed deadlines on the closing of Guantanamo, Iran's nuclear compliance, and health-care reform.

The old congressional "culture of corruption" has been replaced by the well-meaning efforts of Charlie Rangel, Chris being Chris Dodd, and cranky uncle John Murtha. Controversial decisions are quietly announced late on Friday afternoons. Congressional debates and votes on controversial legislation happen on weekends and holidays—all the better to ensure that the American people won't tune in to see the making of what they don't want but must have. Chicago-style bribery buys the votes of senators like Ben Nelson and Mary Landrieu with tens of millions of taxpayers' dollars.

OBAMA'S GUARDIANS

Here we are one year later in a great race. By almost any means necessary, Barack Obama is trying to remake America at home and abroad before he is stopped by the 2010 and 2012 elections. He knows that his agenda is not what he ran on, and not what the American people want, but it is one nevertheless achievable by majorities in both houses of Congress, despite his own waning popularity.

Obama quite simply believes that those like himself—Ivy League—trained, having spent their lifetimes on government payrolls, untainted by private-enterprise entrepreneurship—not only know best what is good for America, but understand how to implement it through redistributive taxation and vastly expanded entitlements.

In such a vision of the blessed, a Platonic guardian class—so much better educated, better intentioned, better motivated than the rest of us—will direct our lives and yet be exempt from the constraints they place on the less capable.

Our Al Gores to come will still fly on private jets. The next progressive John Edwards, of two-nations fame, and more Tom Friedmans, of hot-and-flat warnings, will appear, still living in carbon-spewing mansions.

More well-meaning Timothy Geithners will dodge their taxes. The Larry Summerses and Robert Rubins of the brave new world will still make millions in a year for their Wall Street expertise while damning fat-cat bankers. Bill Clinton will reemerge to make tens of millions more while talking up his global initiatives.

The wealthiest man on the planet—and the man with the biggest tax-exempt foundation—will support more inheritance taxes, as Bill Gates has been advocating. The second wealthiest, the Warren Buffett of the future, will want higher taxes, whose steep rates the actual Mr. Buffett has so successfully managed thus far to avoid. Such is always the way of the guardian class, from Platonic fantasy to its darker manifestations as so aptly depicted by Orwell.

THE OLD AMERICA

And what will be lost if this race is won by the Obamians?

Consider: The reason that Obama himself enjoys such international stature, such ability to weigh in on matters insignificant and monumental, is not his teleprompted rhetoric nor his utopian world-view. Instead, Obama's own singularity is tied to an exceptional United States that has always been different and, in the end, far more moral and powerful than the alternatives.

Almost alone in the world, America has never had a command or socialist economy. Its old creed was merit, and confidence in the freedom of the individual to run his own life rather than being told what to do by the state apparat. Its Constitution was antithetical not only to monarchy, but also to Enlightenment statism of the European 18th-century brand.

Freedom of the individual explained not only why America became wealthy and the world's dispossessed flocked to our shores, but also why it had a moral sense about the world in its willingness to confront, rather than appease and apologize to, thugs and totalitarians. Everything that the United Nations Human Rights Council is now for, we used to be against. "Give Me Liberty or Give Me Death" has now been replaced by égalité and fraternité.

The final irony is that should Obama and his revolutionaries prevail in their remaking of America, their own progeny will not enjoy the opportunity and affluence that they so cavalierly take to be their birthright, which was bequeathed to them by less liberal others.

Mr. President, Words Matter

Obama, the rhetorician, forgot that people might actually take seriously what he said.

W hat is Barack Obama's real problem? Too many people here and abroad took him at his word, and he now seems quite angry at that.

For two years Obama serially damned the entrepreneurial classes. They should "spread the wealth," be "patriotic," and pay "their fair share." They should be paying more income, payroll, and inheritance taxes. They could not be trusted with health care, student loans, high finance, or auto manufacturing. Their lifestyles of private jets and Super Bowl junkets came at the expense of the downtrodden. The would-be rich who made just over $200,000 were indiscriminately lumped together with the elite rich on Wall Street—who ironically contributed inordinately to Barack Obama's non—publicly financed campaign coffers.

Apparently, the small-business classes took Obama's writs seriously, and for the foreseeable future they have shut down—they have quit hiring and buying, and are riding out the "recovery." In response, a frantic Obama suddenly began talking about balanced budgets, tax cuts, and tax credits, and praising the private sector. Too late: Too many entrepreneurs took him at his original word.

Then there was the constant partisanship, the "never let a crisis go to waste" Chicago hardball. Never has a president talked so much about reaching across the aisle and done so little of it. During the campaign, the Senate's most partisan member claimed he was its least. That same deception characterized most of his first year in the White House. He promised C-SPAN coverage of bipartisan give-and-take, while actually holding the health-care debate behind Democratic congressional doors to offer bribes and insider deals in exchange for votes. "Let's end the bickering" was usually the preface to "Bush did it, not me." Absolute

Democratic control of Washington—both Congress and the White House—meant that Republicans had "played Washington politics" to stop grass-roots governance.

Then Scott Brown won the Senate seat long occupied by the late liberal lion Ted Kennedy, and Obama's polls dived below 50 percent. Soon even New York Times columnists began listing all sorts of reservations about Obama that they had long entertained but mysteriously only now voiced. In response, a frantic Obama is suddenly talking about reaching out, meeting with Republicans, and drafting bipartisan legislation. Too late: Too many Republicans took him at his original word.

In his dealings abroad, remember "hope and change," the "reset button," and all the grandiose promises of a year ago? Barack Obama assured our critics that he would have the dreadful Bush Guantanamo Bay detention center closed by now. But then the reality that most of the detainees were cold-blooded killers who would revert to terrorism upon release—and many were Yemenis eager to join up with al-Qaeda at home—made those repeated boasts inoperative. I will be surprised if Obama ever closes Guantanamo.

The architect of 9/11 and self-confessed beheader, Khalid Sheikh Mohammed, was supposed to be accorded a big public civilian trial a couple of thousand yards away from the scene of his mass-murdering. There, his attorneys could plead that the Bush-Cheney nexus had waterboarded him, as he voiced to the world all his grievances against a purported neo-imperialist, colonialist, and racist Bush America—hoping that at least one sympathetic juror might fall for his "America made me do it" defense.

That too seems now to be history. Sometime around Christmas, Obama discovered that al-Qaeda both still wishes to kill us and does not appreciate that we give Miranda rights to our would-be killers. I would be surprised if KSM is ever tried in a civilian court in the United States.

Iran was to be wowed and charmed by Barack Hussein Obama, who would distance himself from America's past sins, dating all the way back to the coup against Mossadegh in 1953. Ahmadinejad would faint in ecstasy like the 2008 campaign crowds, as he gave up his nuclear-weapon plans and fell in love with the new postnational

America. And now? Iran does the same old, same old—"Israel must be destroyed," and no one dare tell us to stop our nuclear program. The latest theocratic communiqué promised the "end of American civilization"—as we rush anti-missile batteries to the Gulf. I would not be surprised to see Iran set off a bomb this year or next.

This scenario has been replayed all over the globe. Thousands of Japanese hit the streets, echoing Obama's signature "Change!"—but as in "Change U.S.-Japanese Relations." And why not, if we are to take on another $9 trillion in debt during this administration, much of it from Japan and China? And how dare we base our troops on Japanese soil—especially in a postnational age, when alliances, and a world divided into good guys and bad guys, are, well, so passé?

Russia still bullies its neighbors and tries to embarrass the United States. China still threatens to take over Taiwan. North Korea still tries to shake us down for cash by stirring up trouble with Seoul. Chávez is as buffoonish as ever, and has only been empowered by our recent "outreach."

In short, throughout the campaign and during the first months of his presidency, Obama globally made the argument that George Bush's America had done wrong and was part of the world's problem rather than its solution. But the world garbled Obama's message, and instead came away with the distinct impression that America itself—whether Bush's or Obama's—was the problem. One cannot spend two years blaming America under Bush, and then suddenly claim, "That was then, this is now," and expect the world to rally to the godhead of Barack Obama and his new, improved America.

How odd that Obama, the rhetorician, forgot that words matter—and that the truth is not a trifle, a mere construct predicated on the particular situation at the moment it is voiced.

Too many people, here and abroad, took Barack Obama at his word. And right now—drifting amid high unemployment, mounting domestic opposition, and energized enemies abroad—he sorely wishes that they had not.

MAY 5, 2010

Good and Bad Words

A rose by any other name might smell as sweet, but an 'undocumented worker' sounds much more sympathetic than an 'illegal alien.'

B arack Obama once warned, "Don't tell me words don't matter!" He was right. They do.

These days, financiers and investors are a "bunch" of "fat-cat bankers." When your 401(k) tanks, surely a "bunch" of "fat-cat" miscreants who run a "bank" did it. I have a fat cat—and nothing is more unpleasant than to see this lazy pet sleep all day, yawn, and then turn over on his rolls of fat.

"I make a lot more money if I take this kid's tonsils out," the president also warned, speaking in the voice of an unscrupulous pediatric surgeon. Note the use of "take out" instead of "operate." Obama preferred also "kid's" for "patient's." Presto—a surgeon performing a carefully considered tonsillectomy becomes a swaggering chopper who carves out a tonsil or two from an unlucky child for an exorbitant profit.

Note a similar reference: "If that same diabetic ends up getting their foot amputated, that's 30,000, 40, 50,000 dollars immediately the surgeon is reimbursed." In the dysphemic ("speaking with bad words") world of Barack Obama, profiteering surgeons also waltz into operating rooms, needlessly lop off a slightly infected foot or two—and within hours (i.e., "immediately") a check for $30,000 to $50,000 is in the mail.

In the health-care debate, insurers were "filling the airwaves with deceptive and dishonest ads" and "funding studies designed to mislead the American people." I think that means they ran advertisements to counter pro-administration advertisements, and that they fund research as their opponents do.

Recently, new government estimates suggested that the health-care-reform bill will cost more money, not less. Yet the president, on the eve of its passage, blasted opponents with more dysphemism: "It's smoke and mirrors. It's bogus. And it's all too familiar. Every time we get close to passing reform, the insurance companies produce these phony studies as a prescription." Opposition is "smoke," "mirrors," "bogus," "all too familiar," "phony"—and never worthy of legitimate debate and counterpoint.

Las Vegas is a favorite tar-and-feather term. Big companies blew our money, but they will not be able to do this any longer, in the Age of Obama, "You can't go take that trip to Las Vegas or go down to the Super Bowl on the taxpayers' dime." And later: "You don't blow a bunch of cash on Vegas when you're trying to save for college."

According to one participant in closed-door health-care meetings, Obama warned Democratic fence-sitters, "Does anybody think that the teabag, anti-government people are going to support them if they bring down health care?" Americans who are worried about deficits and who evoke the events leading up to 1776 are "anti-government" and reduced to the moral equivalent of the sexually adventurous.

If a news organization is often critical, then it is not "legitimate"— as in the denunciation of Fox News by former White House communications director Anita Dunn: "We don't need to pretend that this is the way that legitimate news organizations behave." The president himself added, "I've got one television station that is entirely devoted to attacking my administration."

Note again the language: "I've got," suggesting a simple bipolar client relationship between Fox and President Obama. "Entirely devoted" implies that every show on Fox News on any topic attacks the president. But Obama is also fond of using good expressions. Euphemism ("speaking with good words"), of course, is the opposite of dysphemism, and yet it similarly distorts realty.

For example, once supporters of big-government cap-and-trade programs changed the term "global warming" to "climate change," we knew that everything from the Indonesian tsunami to the Haitian earthquake could be chalked up to human sin. Furthermore, "climate change" might resonate in a way that "global warming" would not to people freezing through the coldest winter in recent memory. Whether you are roasting or shivering, no matter—"they" caused both, and everything in between.

Consider the more general way dysphemism and euphemism interact in discussions of some of the nation's most pressing problems, such as spiraling illegal immigration, terrorism, and the national debt. The majority of Americans worry about porous borders and illegal immigration in ways our elites find illiberal. So they are demonized as "anti-immigrant." That's personal; they don't like Juan or Herlinda, rather than not liking the Mexican government's following a safety-valve policy that will lead to more remittances for Mexico City, fewer dissidents, and a large expatriate community; or not liking employers' using cheap labor to undercut American workers' wages; or not liking millions of people ignoring U.S. law as they see fit.

"Illegal aliens" is an accurate descriptive term for foreigners who cross the border unlawfully. So, naturally, we hear instead of "undocumented workers." In this formulation, you see, the newcomers are all employed, and they merely forget to bring their documents. Thus the problem in the Southwest is one of memory, not legality.

"Comprehensive immigration reform" has nothing to do with rewriting the immigration laws. Indeed, to close the border we need only enforce existing laws; we do not need to make new ones. Instead, this is a euphemism for a politically toxic idea: a blanket amnesty.

Who can be against "comprehensive" anything (think "comprehensive health-care reform" versus "socialized medicine"), or "immigration" per se (as in the law-abiding recent immigrant Ph.D. in computer science from Taiwan), or "reform" (as in changing something that is bad)? Put the three together, and the resulting whole is greater than the sum of its parts—so how could anyone understand "comprehensive immigration reform" as meaning to deem what is illegal legal?

Many of our policymakers also flinch at the notion that the United States is still in a war against Islamic extremists nine years after the September 11 attacks. In the last 15 months, the Obama administration had scrapped the terms "Islamic extremism," "Islamic radicalism," and "jihad."

Instead of real enemies, we are mobilized against "man-caused disasters"; now we can hate oil slicks and Congolese famines rather than the misunderstood and underprivileged from the Middle East. "Overseas contingency operations" means that all those carrier groups are really intended for tsunami relief.

After all, there are no longer threatening "rogue states," but only "outliers." The problem is not that some nations act in dangerous ways, but just that they lie somewhere out there beyond Australia.

We need worry no more about another Major Hasan or Christmas Day panty-bomber, or the would-be Times Square bomber, than we fret about our noble fight against climate change. And once the "detainees" at the "closed within a year" Guantanamo Bay detention center were no longer called "unlawful combatants" (i.e., enemy soldiers without uniforms caught on the battlefield), we knew there was no longer a war. Who, after all, worries about "detainees" any more than we do about the DUI suspects held in the drunk tank on Saturday night?

Barack Obama, in just 15 months, has turned George W. Bush's financial misdemeanors into felonies. If unchecked, his grand eight-year plan will almost double the national debt, to almost $20 trillion. Rather than freeze or cut government outlays—which would involve scaling back his ideological agenda—President Obama here too prefers a linguistic cop-out.

Obama did not invent "stimulus," but he has used the nice word as never before to cloak reality. We do not hear that we are borrowing $3 trillion from Japanese, Chinese, and American bondholders to bail out the auto unions, or to offer sweetheart deals to crony banks and investment companies. Instead, we are "stimulating" the economy.

"Fiscal responsibility" means an occasional speech or two about the unmentionable unsustainable borrowing. It most certainly does not mean spending only what we take in.

Better yet is a "jobs bill." Who is against "jobs"? And "bill" sounds like something out of the 1930s, when no-nonsense congressmen smoked cigars and brought home the bacon to out-of-work constituents. A congressman can now put his name on any building or bridge he wants. That is hardly a "pork-barrel" project: It is an "earmark" that "creates jobs."

More important, who wants to hear about the "unemployment rate"? Aren't more people working than not? So let's look positively at the effects of "stimulus" and count instead "jobs saved" or, better yet, "jobs created." Is anyone against "saving" or "creating" anything? I know I am irked by "unemployment" and anything to do with the word "rate."

What are we to make of the new dysphemism and euphemism?

Note the pattern. Americans who are successful are reduced to limb-loppers, fat cats, and phonies; they enjoy jetting to Vegas and the Super Bowl at our expense, and they seem to be "anti-immigrant" and eager to lock up Muslims—as opposed to those who wish to save children's tonsils, save jobs, save the economy, save the Mexican poor, and save the planet.

True, on rarer occasions, the president has dropped the demonizing and whitewashing and simply spoken from his heart. Earlier he once talked of "redistributive change" and "spreading the wealth around." More recently, he remarked, "I do think at a certain point you've made enough money."

But don't misunderstand. That is not "socialist" talk, but merely the language of "community organizing."

JULY 7, 20109

Obama's New Take on Partisanship

President Obama's worst nightmare?
A conservative Senator Obama.

One of President Obama's strangest complaints is that there are too many in Congress who act, well, like former senator Obama.

In his recent speech on the question of comprehensive immigration reform, President Obama once again blasted Republican political opportunism that opposes his initiatives for partisan, rather than principled, reasons. Indeed, Obama regularly criticizes as disingenuous those conservative politicos in Congress who mindlessly thwart his every move on health care, foreign policy, cap-and-trade, illegal immigration—you name it.

Consider the present confirmation examination of Obama nominee Elena Kagan to the Supreme Court. Clearly Obama thinks that she is a centrist whose record as a law-school dean in unimpeachable. A no vote, in his view, would only reveal rank partisanship—in the style of Sen. Barack Obama.

Remember, he not only opposed Justice Alito, but also joined with other senators to try to filibuster the nomination in hopes that Alito would not be accorded a simple up-or-down vote. (Note in passing that President Obama in the last year has repeatedly criticized the filibuster as partisan and obstructionist in diminishing the influence of the Democratic majority in the Senate.) In the case of his no vote against Justice Roberts, Senator Obama admitted that Roberts had shown the necessary "adherence to legal precedent and rules of statutory or constitutional construction." But there was a problem regarding "empathy." Roberts, you see, did not show the sort of empathy that Obama thought Supreme Court justices should embrace. Yet imagine if a Republican senator now said of Elena Kagan that he believed she would follow the law, but should nevertheless be rejected because she had not shown enough "empathy" toward conservative interests.

President Obama is now calling for a surge in troops into Afghanistan to restore an unstable front, to be overseen by Gen. David Petraeus. He expects both Congress and the public to rally around that common effort. Both should. But Senator Obama once grilled the same Gen. David Petraeus and ridiculed his notion of surging into Iraq at a time when the military desperately needed public support to salvage the situation there. Senator Obama gave a speech rather than asked questions, as was expected in Senate hearings, and suggested that Petraeus had "punted" on telling the truth about the broader strategy in Iraq, and therefore had made it difficult to grant his request for more troops on a bipartisan basis.

President Obama now hopes that when senators examine the Petraeus appointment and the administration's request to surge into Afghanistan, they will not act in partisan fashion, in the manner of Senator Obama. In January President Obama blasted the Supreme

Court's reversal of elements of the McCain-Feingold act barring certain types of private political contributions. He saw it as an attack on the public financing of presidential campaigns and encouragement for big money to influence political decision-making: "It is a major victory for big oil, Wall Street banks, health-insurance companies, and the other powerful interests that marshal their power every day in Washington to drown out the voices of everyday Americans."

It was just two years ago that Senator Obama became the first presidential candidate since public financing was instituted to renounce such funding in the presidential general election, and he went on to amass a record amount of corporate cash—becoming both Goldman Sachs's and BP's largest recipient of money.

In his recent immigration speech, President Obama lamented, "Now, under the pressures of partisanship and election-year politics, many of the eleven Republican senators who voted for reform in the past have now backed away from their previous support."

Yet Obama himself in 2007 did not quite go along with the bipartisan effort by Senator Kennedy and President Bush to enact the same comprehensive immigration reform. Instead, he held out for provisions that would help to doom the bipartisan effort to enact almost the identical legislation that President Obama has now taken up.

Nothing was more difficult to enact than controversial legislation aimed at preventing another 9/11 and launching an offensive against the Taliban and their Islamic terrorist allies in Afghanistan. Yet here is what Barack Obama had to say—first as a state legislator and then as a U.S. senator—about such anti-terrorism protocols. Renditions: "shipping away prisoners in the dead of night." Military tribunals: "a flawed military commission system that has failed to convict anyone of a terrorist act." Guantanamo Bay: "a tremendous recruiting tool for al-Qaeda." Preventive detention: "detaining thousands without charge or trial." The surge of troops into Iraq: "not working." The Patriot Act: "shoddy and dangerous."

President Obama has tripled the annual number of targeted assassinations from Predator drones in the Pakistani borderlands. Yet here is how candidate Obama characterized airborne attacks under the Bush administration, when they were far less frequent: "We've got to get the job done there and that requires us to have enough troops so that we're not just air-raiding villages and killing civilians, which is causing enormous pressure over there."

If a Republican senator behaved today as Senator Obama did then, he would hammer away at the president's continued adherence to tribunals, renditions, wiretaps, intercepts, the continued use of Guantanamo, the use of Predators, and the surge into Afghanistan simply to score political points and to jockey for position in the next presidential race—without consideration of the responsibility of governance, when there are so often only bad and worse choices.

During the health-care debacle, President Obama frequently lamented that he was reduced to ramming through the legislation without a single Republican vote in the Senate—as part of a larger complaint about the unwillingness to step across the aisle and put principle above partisanship.

Yet in 2007, when National Journal tallied the voting records of then-serving U.S. senators, it ranked Barack Obama as the most partisan senator of either party, voting along straight party lines over 95 percent of the time. Even the most conservative current Republican senator, Jim DeMint of South Carolina, a frequent target of the Obama administration for his lockstep opposition to the administration's agenda, has compiled a 93 percent partisan voting record.

What can we make of all this?

President Obama wants us to believe that too many in the conservative opposition simply vote in knee-jerk partisan opposition to his liberal agenda. He declares that what America needs is more congressional bipartisanship of the sort that would give Supreme Court nominees a fair hearing; that would provide support to generals who are trying to bring in more resources to save a failing theater; that would not endanger comprehensive immigration reform by playing to narrow political constituencies; that would cut off corporate campaign cash; and that would understand that our far-from-perfect anti-terrorism protocols may in fact be necessary to keep us safe.

All of this is a fine and noble thing to say, and much of it is quite true. But the problem remains that a President Obama cannot expect complete amnesia on the part of the American people—especially when they suspect that his present calls for bipartisanship in word are in direct proportion to his past rejection of it in deed.

In sum, President Obama's worst nightmare would be a conservative incarnation of a Senator Obama who in Pavlovian fashion would reject almost all executive initiatives on a strictly political basis—on his way to compiling the most partisan record in the entire U.S. Senate.

Finally, all this is doubly odd in that President Obama is a self-described student of philosophy. So he must know that a theme from Thucydides to Burke is the timeless sanctity of law, custom, and tradition—that one cannot expect, as an insider, to count on the very same protocols that, as an outsider, one once helped to tear apart. Quite simply, for President Obama to restore his presidency, he must now persuade Congress not to act in the fashion that he once found so conducive to his upward career as a senator and presidential candidate.

President Obama's falling approval ratings are not just due to ineptness on the Gulf oil spill, the economy, and the war, but also to a growing perception of abject hypocrisy and lack of character. The disjunction between Senator Obama and President Obama explains a great deal of why he cannot convince either his opposition or the public as a whole that he will ever quite be sincere about anything.

JULY 28, 2009

Obama's Real Problem

Why the president's poll numbers have declined.

A ccording to a popular myth, President Obama's declining poll numbers are a consequence of his failure to be liberal enough. On race, in the wake of the Shirley Sherrod mess, we are told he needs to appoint more African Americans and bring in more advisers from the black community. On the economy, liberal economists decry his unwillingness to borrow and stimulate more.

This is lunatic in political terms.

Obama's poll numbers are falling for three reasons clear to any amateur student of politics. First, the voters in 2008 did not vote for liberal change, but for change from the costly and lengthy Bush wars, deficits, spending policies, and immigration proposals. Obama voters were also motivated by a desire to elect our first African-American president, fear over the September 2008 financial meltdown, a lackluster McCain campaign, and the strange perception that Obama was a centrist.

Since his election, Obama has outdone the average Bush deficits by a factor of four or five. His brief "stimulus" became the prelude to a gorge-the-beast reordering of American society. Meanwhile, after demagoguing as a candidate everything from Guantanamo to Iraq, Obama in office has kept in place almost every major security protocol that Bush had established. He has broken his promises to close Guantanamo, try Khalid Sheikh Mohammed in New York, and pull out of Iraq. This has meant alienating his shrinking base while being exposed as a hypocrite to suddenly wiser and less forgiving independents.

Second, after ramming through his health-care bill without either bipartisan support or public approval, Obama is polling badly on just about every hot-button issue. The electorate simply does not want cap-and-trade, amnesty, more deficits, and higher taxes. Rather, it prefers to produce more oil and gas, and more hydroelectric and nuclear power; it wants to follow the Arizona immigration model; it wants to cut spending; and it wants to balance the budget.

The Left may be disheartened that Obama has not borrowed more for green-energy subsidies, has not yet rammed through an amnesty for illegal immigrants, and has not spent more money trying to stimulate the economy. But these are not the reasons that Obama is sinking in the polls. Indeed, a good way for Democrats to lose both the House and the Senate would be to use the health-care model to push through amnesty and cap-and-trade legislation before November.

Third, the problem is not that Obama is insufficiently attuned to race, but that he is perceived (fairly or unfairly) to be obsessed with it. Since 2008, both Barack and Michelle Obama have committed a series of gaffes that appeared to reflect an attachment to identity politics.

Taken together, these divisive musings have fostered the impression that the first couple is excessively concerned with racial issues.

In terms of Obama's appointees, no one forced Van Jones to brag of his earlier Communist sympathies; to get involved, even tangentially, with the 9/11 "truthers"; or to say that white teens are more likely than black teens to be mass murderers, and white adults more likely to be polluters. The Left may see Jones as a sacrificial lamb, perhaps deserving of an Ivy League sinecure; but the public was glad to see him go, and even more relieved to see him stay away. Beyond Jones, the comments made by Anita Dunn, NASA chief Charles Bolden, "documented or not" Hilda Solis, and Donald Berwick certainly have not made the case that Obama needs to bring in more hard-core liberal ideologues.

Indeed, to use a rather brutal metaphor, Obama has planted throughout his administration a number of far-left time bombs. On any given day, one of them can go off. A dozen or more may very well implode before the November elections.

By the time the public learned that Shirley Sherrod had really delivered a speech about class divisions and the culpability of the rich rather than a racist diatribe about the culpability of whites, she had managed to evoke slavery in Jesse Jackson fashion. As the week ended, her husband was on YouTube peddling the same old tired racist cant with a very thin progressive veneer.

One unmentioned lesson from the Sherrod saga is that the public does not want to hear federal agricultural officials weigh in on either racial or class activism in front of national advocacy groups. If Obama appoints more advisers and officials primarily on the basis of race, he surely will not see a sudden rise in his approval rating among independent voters. A talking head on MSNBC may be outraged that we did not initially hear Sherrod expand on why she is no longer a racist in sincere and conciliatory terms. But the public might wonder why she admitted to being one in the first place—and how dividing people on the basis of class rather than race represents a significant moral evolution.

In terms of poll ratings, Obama is in poor shape, but not necessarily in poorer shape than various past presidents who eventually were reelected. His problem is not, as he alleges, that he inherited a worse mess from Bush than Reagan did from Carter or Bush did from Clinton.

Nor is his problem that he slightly deviated from his left-wing hope-and-change rhetoric and disappointed his base. His problem is more fundamental: It is one of self-knowledge.

Obama and his supporters have somehow convinced themselves that 2008 was the result either of (1) a left-wing American majority that finally came out of the shadows, or (2) a mesmerizing personality that by sheer force of rhetoric and charisma could take America where it otherwise did not wish to go. Neither is true. America remains a center-right country, and Obama, the teleprompted messiah, has grown tiresome. If the president wishes to recovery politically, he must embrace a responsible, workmanlike centrist agenda, just as Bill Clinton did between 1994 and 1996.

Obama can choose to be a successful triangulating Clinton, or he can insist on being a failed ideological Carter. As the November election draws closer, those bad and worse choices will become even clearer to the president and his liberal supporters.

DECEMBER 30, 2009

Obama: Not the Great Stone Face

Obama could still restore his standing with the American people if he copied the Clinton of 1995 and abandoned his unpopular agenda. But he won't.

In 1850 Nathaniel Hawthorne wrote an allegory about a series of small-town would-be heroes who the gullible public claimed resembled the Great Stone Face on the side of a New Hampshire mountain. The citizens assumed that these men would have a granite-like ability to stand firm against whatever dangers the people faced. ("About this time there went a rumor throughout the valley, that the great man, foretold from ages long ago, who was to bear a resemblance to the Great Stone Face, had appeared at last.") The most confident and charismatic of these quick-fix characters—Mr. Gathergold, Old Blood-and-Thunder, and Old Stony Phiz—always in the end proved failures, as the people finally learned that they did not have the qualities they ascribed to the face on mountain.

When a once widely popular George W. Bush left office, he was polling about 35 percent approval and 60 percent disapproval. The country had two years earlier turned out the Republican Congress—to the tune of promises from Nancy Pelosi (in the pre-transcontinental-jet days) to end the wars, end the culture of corruption, and end the power of special interests.

In 2008 Barack Obama ran as a moderate liberal, offering assurances on instituting sound financial governance, getting out of Iraq, repealing the Bush anti-terrorism protocols, and making government work for the little guy by taking over some private enterprise—that is, offering government-run health care, subsidized student loans, and new and extended entitlements. A Newsweek grandee, Evan Thomas, declared Him "sort of God." He caused another pundit, Chris Matthews, to experience leg tingles. And the world anointed Him a Nobel laureate for good intentions.

After 19 months, a once cool, laid-back Barack Obama—beloved by Oprah in his mesmerizing ability to make the enraptured faint at his sermons—now polls about 45 percent approval and 50 percent disapproval—nearly a 20-point swing in less than two years. Currently, a generic Republican challenger enjoys on average a six-point edge in the polls—quite a turnabout from the twelve-point spread that Democrats mounted in January 2009. Public approval of Congress ranges from about 10 to 20 percent—the Democratic-led Congress getting even lower marks than the pre-2006 Republican one.

One might say the public has changed its opinion of Obama, but it seems more likely that the public is beginning to see Obama as it finally did Bush. The hard Right always felt about Obama as the hard Left did about Bush, but now independents seem simply to have rechanneled their Bush anger to Obama anger—something that has bewildered Team Obama, who cannot gain any traction by blaming the current malaise on the Bush legacy. Voters apparently don't see the corrective to Bush's deficit budgeting in Obama's yet higher spending and larger government.

When the economy under Bush was good, the public was more worried about Iraq. When Iraq became quiet as Obama entered office, it turned its furor on him for the recession. Obama thought his popularity and charm could win the public over to his unpopular agenda; now he worries that his own growing unpopularity and lack of charm may make any agenda unpalatable. Any more "successes" in enacting a widely unpopular agenda, and Obama's approvals will be in the teens.

What can we learn from all this?

There is a growing desperation among politicians that the populace perceives them as pretty much alike—alike in the sense of not being appealing. In Obama's case, the charge is doubly serious, because he made extravagant claims that our first community organizer and our first African-American to become president—and our most purely liberal president in a generation—would be different, as in bringing a new humility and competence to the office.

Instead, over half the electorate sees only hypocrisy. Obama initially called for understanding and patience with the BP spill, in a way he had not when demagoguing Katrina. He suddenly found Guantanamo, renditions, military tribunals, Predator assassinations, and Iraq to be complex issues, after assuring us that they were open-and-shut cases of simple morality. Bush's deficit misdemeanors suddenly became Obama's felonies—after he ran on the theme that Bush had recklessly run up the debt. The 2008 campaign to highlight racial harmony by electing the symbolic postracial Obama has become a sort of nightmare in which the old, tired identity politics of the 1980s rage as never before, fanned by an unpopular president desperate to rev up his base.

The common denominator here is that a largely conservative electorate has always wanted lower taxes, smaller but more competent government, fewer overseas commitments, honest government, and officials who live like the public they represent—and it can't seem to find that package in any party or candidate being presented to it. Indeed, the Obama medicine is now seen as worse than the Bush disease, in that he less competently oversaw the war in Afghanistan, blew apart the budget, and lives more royally than any Republican.

The obsequious media have been left scrambling to explain this new Orwellian barn wall: Bush's aristocratic golf is now Obama's needed relaxation; Bush's bumbling press conferences might explain why Obama wisely doesn't hold many at all; Republican congressional corruption simply led to a "They all do it, even Democrats" narrative; Bush's failure to articulate how and why we would win in Iraq suddenly morphs into Afghanistan as a baffling experience that confuses all of us. Obviously, even the most adept public-relations-minded journalist could not pull all that off, and so we are left with media now as discredited as they are loathed.

And where does all that leave us?

The public is waiting for an articulate conservative reformer who will quietly keep promises to balance the budget more through spending cuts than taxes, close the border to illegal immigration, either win or get out of long wars abroad, respect federal law and apply it equally, and restore a sense of American confidence and American exceptionalism.

The odd thing is that the entire country senses how Obama could restore his ratings to over 50 percent in the same way Clinton did in 1995. He would simply call in Republicans to work out a deal to balance the budget, quit his two-year "Bush did it" whine, stop suing the states, reassure business that there will be no more tax hikes, praise the private sector for its ingenuity and competence, stop trying to appeal to his base through race and ethnicity, and get engaged on Afghanistan.

Because there is no chance that Obama will or can do that, we are witnessing another Greek tragedy as our chief executive slowly implodes.

So we, the American public, have become something like the anxious townspeople of Hawthorne's morality tale. We keep claiming that our next national leader is some sort of monumental icon who will magically solve our crises, only to learn that in the flesh he turns out not to be the Great Stone Face on the mountain at all. (The Obama euphoria of 2008 was not unlike the Bush worship for a short while between September 2001 and early 2003.)

In the end, if we are lucky, we will end up with a workmanlike candidate similar to the Ernest of Hawthorne's short story, someone nondescript from the community, someone like the rest of America, who through humility and competence avoids the vanity of high office, balances budgets, wins wars, cuts spending, restores American confidence, finesses the partisan rancor, and restores our global stature and competitiveness—and slowly grows to resemble the visage on the side of the mountain.

AUGUST 13, 2010

Obama: Fighting the Yuppie Factor

From the price of arugala to vacations in Malibu, the Obamas are the perfect yuppie couple.

In October 1987, *Newsweek* ran a cover story on would-be presidential candidate George H. W. Bush with the blaring headline "Fighting the Wimp Factor."

That Bush was a World War II combat pilot, well over six feet, athletic, and a genuinely nice guy mattered little. Apparently, the fact that he had been Reagan's subordinate for eight years, sounded nasal at times, and lapsed into occasional stuffy metaphors created an impression—fueled by everyone from the Newsweek editors to Jimmy Carter—that Bush was a wimp. He dispelled that for a time in 1988 (opponent Michael Dukakis, awkwardly perched in an Abrams tank, helped), but down-home good ol' boy Bill Clinton exploited the preppy charge again in 1992, to some effect. Stereotypes, in other words, die hard.

For Obama, the stereotype is one of a distant, cool, rather narcissistic yuppie.

Yuppism, remember, is not definable entirely by income or class. Rather, it is a late-twentieth-century cultural phenomenon of self-absorbed young professionals, earning good pay, enjoying the cultural attractions of sophisticated urban life and thought, and generally out of touch with, indeed antithetical to, most of the challenges and concerns of a far less well-off and more parochial Middle America.

For the yuppie male, a well-paying job in law, finance, academia, or consulting in a cultural hub, hip fashion, cool appearance, studied poise, elite education, proper recreation and fitness, and general proximity to liberal-thinking elites, especially of the more rarefied sort in the arts, are the mark of a real man.

For Obama, all the self-referencing about his black heritage and his tough community organizing, the publicly shared confessions about his absent father, the Chicago "bring a gun to a knife fight" tough talk, and the "cool" manner of shooting hoops cannot quite erase the image of an aloof, whiny urban professional of the sort who likes having nice things and kicking back, has not a clue about the lives of the middle and working classes, and heretofore has worried mostly about his own upward mobility.

In that context, for the Obamas, if there were not a Martha's Vineyard or Costa del Sol, such places would probably have to be invented. Barack Obama—the son of a Ph.D. and a Harvard-educated economist, graduate of a Hawaii prep school, replete with Ivy League education, stylish digs in a good Chicago neighborhood, properly tamed and presentable radical social circles, and the requisite power-couple marriage—appreciates the ambience of a vacation spot: Who goes there and why, and what others will say and think, alone matter. Otherwise, the sun and surf at Pismo Beach would do just as well.

During the campaign, numerous critics highlighted what we can legitimately call Obama's yuppie problem—especially after the good times ended with the September 2008 meltdown, and a frazzled public wanted a president who would symbolically appreciate their ordeal. Instead, Obama wondered out loud about the price of arugula. He could not bowl a lick (but foolishly tried), and he scoffed at the gun-owning, white churchgoers of rural Pennsylvania as hopeless clingers, just the sort you would not want to meet at a Bill Ayers book-signing party in Hyde Park.

Michelle Obama, for her part, seemed incapable of giving an impromptu speech without the characteristic yuppie whining. Those damn student loans. And sky-high piano lessons to boot—not to mention the cost of the right camp and private-school tuition! How is a family of four to survive these days?

Oblivious to her privilege and perks, Michelle lectured working-class America that she felt their pain in such a "downright mean country." You see, each time the Obamas got raises, a cruel America "raised the bar," and so the two had to pay even more for their incessant upward mobility. Of course, the insular hip urban professional never realizes how ridiculous complaints about the price of arugula or piano lessons sound to most Americans. But to the Obamas, a cruel world was inherently unfair in demanding that the two pay back a $50,000-a-year tab at Harvard Law School.

There was never any thought of choosing a cheaper Penn State rather than Harvard, or skipping Marbella for Galveston. Instead, there is always the unfairness of the fact that Harvard costs so much—or that clueless people can be so silly as to criticize necessary downtime in southern Spain. Professor, legislator, and candidate Barack Obama was never going to climb into his Winnebago and, in the manner of Supreme Court Justice Clarence Thomas, drive off to tour rural Midwestern America.

So the Obamas, like all insular yuppies, were oblivious to their choice lot, always assessing their social and financial position in terms of lamentation for what they lacked in comparison to the capriciously better off—never in terms of appreciation for their benefactions in relation to the understandably less blessed 99 percent of Americans.

The media were of no help. So desperate were most reporters and commentators for an Obama presidency (and so insular themselves, as yuppies par excellence) that they naïvely assumed that being half black ipso facto gave one street cred—race alone in some warped sense providing working-class authenticity. After all, how could anyone who mimicked the Rev. Jeremiah Wright's hood cadences be tagged as a yuppie?

The media labored mightily to ignore Obama's inability to incite passion and to "connect" with the American people. Golfing, complete with polo shirt and shades, was no longer an aristocratic distraction, but now something analogous to the fellas shooting baskets. Celebrity nights at the White House were really the cultured return of a dignified Camelot. Vacations at the in-spots were authentic antidotes to presidential stress, unlike the staged "down on the ranch" chain sawing of

Ronald Reagan or George W. Bush. (The media were wise enough not to expect Barack Obama to try a photo-op chain sawing some limbs.)

All in vain. It has been 19 months now, and a NASCAR-savvy public knows a yuppie when it sees and hears one. Obama has never lived in the path of unchecked illegal immigration, with all its attendant social and cultural ripples; instead, he has lived where even murmuring "Close the borders" is considered Neanderthal. So he foolishly sues Arizona when 70 percent of America wants to emulate the state.

Typical of the yuppie elite, Obama judges administrative talent by Ivy League certification, not business or entrepreneurial experience in the school of hard knocks. A Harvard Ph.D. is always worth far more than an autodidact, jack-of-all trades entrepreneur who created a successful company from scratch. And that shows.

"Green"—as in the now-worn trope "millions of green jobs"— becomes almost a religious mantra, divorced from practical worries during a recession. For a jet-setting Obama, the idea, even the symbolism, of cap-and-trade, not its messy details amid a recession and national insolvency, is what counts.

Hypocrisy is an important attribute of yuppies, safe in the "right" urban and suburban enclaves, and thus free to pontificate in the abstract about the sort of life they studiously avoid in the concrete. Yuppies like teachers' unions for our children; but they send their own children to charter, private, or prep schools where teaching excellence and results (defined by getting kids into the top private universities) matter.

Yuppies preach racial and class ecumenicalism, but they usually associate with their own kind. Yuppies compensate for their lack of physicality through hyper-expressions of gym- and sport-induced fitness. Put Obama in a pickup truck scrounging for voters, and in comparison Dukakis's tank ride would seem like George Patton in a Sherman. Reagan knew how to use a Weed Eater; Obama would worry about machine-induced allergies and cite studies on hearing damage.

The earthier David Axelrod and Rahm Emanuel are in a dilemma. They know now that the public has caught on, and that they must manufacture an empathetic First Couple, who in times of severe recession understand what the middle and working classes are going through. But they also know that nothing in Obama's own prep-school, Occidental,

Columbia, Harvard, Chicago Law School, Annenberg Foundation past would have imparted such a feel for blue-collar folks. (He is no Bill Clinton, whose studied yuppism was an escape from, and a conscious veneer over, a real trailer-park genesis.)

After 2004 we thought that John Kerry—spandex-clad, wind-surfing, at home with the good mansion life, stiff, pontificating, and passionless—had proven that yuppism was a career-ender for a presidential candidate. So it was not easy just four years later to sell a kindred yuppie, but centrist-talking, Obama to the public, as an antidote to George Bush's Iraq and Katrina—even after the worst financial panic in modern memory, and as a sort of collective penance for past real and purported racial sins.

But those planets will not line up again in our lifetime. And so a country that is deep in a stalled economy and tired of elite bromides is left with our first metrosexual president, Barack Obama. Both the man and the agenda, after nearly two years, are yuppie still to the core.

And it shows.

SEPTEMBER 8, 2010

Our Waning Obama Worship

We Americans know not what we do.

I n just 20 months, President Obama's polls have crashed. From near 70 percent approval, they have fallen to well below 50 percent. Over 70 percent of the public disapproves of the Democratically controlled Congress. Hundreds of thousands of angry voters flocked to hear Glenn Beck & Co. on the Washington Mall. Indeed, things have gotten so bad that the cherubic Mormon Beck might outdraw Barack Obama himself on any given Sunday.

All this was not supposed to be—and it has evoked a lot of anger.

Washington Post columnist Eugene Robinson thunders, "The American people are acting like a bunch of spoiled brats."

You see, hoi polloi want "easy solutions"—like trying to close an open border, cut federal spending, and balance the budget. Instead, they should be manning up to pay more for gas, more in taxes, and more for entitlements for more to come across the border.

Worse still, the uninformed voter cannot seem to appreciate the brilliance of Barack Obama, who has deigned to suffer on our behalf, in offering only unpopular but necessary solutions. Obama has tried his best to prepare an immature nation for amnesty, borrowing at record levels, cap and trade, and additional trillions of national debt—the castor oil that the obese and now constipated public for some reason just won't swallow.

Cynthia Tucker of the Atlanta Journal-Constitution chimes in with the thought that Neanderthal Americans can't really distinguish between cause and effect. So in clueless fashion, they blame big deficits, big spending, and high unemployment on Obama, when what they're really afraid of is the "browning of America." In other words, we remain a nation of primitives resisting the future. "Successful black and brown professionals have had to learn to be comfortable in a sea of white faces, but most white Americans have not experienced the reverse. And many are not eager to have that experience. While some prognosticators were naïve enough to believe that Obama's election signaled the beginning of a post-racial era, it prompted something altogether different: a backlash against the browning of America."

Vanity Fair just ran yet another hit piece on the now-worn subject of the ogre Sarah Palin. Uppity Sarah, you see, is still on her hind legs—even after the 2008 swat from the Katie Couric set, the jogging-suit photos, and the true-story revelations from the philosopher Levi Johnston.

Worse still, Sarah is no longer quite the white-trash yokel with the snowmobiling husband and pregnant teenage daughter that so appealed to Cynthia Tucker's backlash America. Instead, Palin has had the gall to have devolved into a fake yokel, with Michelle Obama—like fashion pretensions. So Vanity Fair shocks us with the dirt that the now-clothes-hungry former mayor of Wasilla is making some money speaking. She is not the sandwich-making mom of five that she used to be. And she doesn't really do the moose-and-fish thing any more.

Still, in reading *Vanity Fair*'s bill of particulars, we wonder, "Compared to what?" Is Ms. Palin making any more money than the aggregate $100 million collected by good ol' boy Bill Clinton—as he jetted his way around the globe between 2001 and 2009, offering his "aw shucks" global initiatives to any creepy foreign thug who would pony up the near-million-dollar fee? Are the now-orphaned Palin children missing their careerist mother more than, say, the Obama children missed their absentee father huckstering on the campaign trail for two years in 2007—2008? And is Ms. Palin really less of a game-eating shooter than the duck-hunting camouflaged John Kerry was in 2004?

The New York Times is just as let down with the volatile American mob that has stormed out in the middle of the sermon on the mount—after once so bravely thronging to the "god" who assured us that he would stop the flooding and cool the planet. Vero possumus indeed.

Americans, and even liberal New Yorkers, poll over 70 percent opposed to the so-called Ground Zero mosque—even after our president gave a courageous standing-ovation pep talk to a group of anguished Muslims at a White House Ramadan dinner. "New Yorkers," the Times scoffed, "like other Americans, have a way to go." My god, you would have thought that we had given a discount to moveon.org to run a slanderous "General Betray Us" ad, as an American general came back from the front to Washington to save a war.

The president himself is grieved by these polls and the Beck-led protests. Indeed, he derides it all as the "silly season." He does not mean "silly" as in Michelle Obama's Marbella—to—Martha's Vineyard odyssey, or his own mini-recession summits on the golf links. Instead, like Robinson and Tucker, he is bewildered that millions don't appreciate that our godhead is "making decisions that are not necessarily good for the nightly news and not good for the next election, but for the next generations." I suppose here the president means that he is on schedule to add more debt than all previous presidents combined—just the sort of bravery that the "next generations" who will pay for it will appreciate.

In the case of Obama worship, the tone is always set at the top. So we are back to 2008, when candidate Obama likewise attributed any rejection to the inability of yokel America to appreciate his inspired leadership—"it's not surprising then they get bitter, they cling to guns or religion or antipathy to people who aren't like them or anti-immigrant sentiment or anti-trade sentiment as a way to explain their frustrations."

In short, a frustrated America has let the liberal elite down. And it is all the more disheartening when you think that just two years ago we proved sort of redeemable by electing Barack Obama—amid the hysteria following the financial panic of September 2008, the lackluster campaign of John McCain, Obama's own faux-centrist veneer, the glow of electing America's first African-American president, and the first orphaned election since 1952 when no incumbent of either party was running.

Apparently the liberal elite did not consider that perfect storm of events that elected a northern liberal in a way that had been impossible with George McGovern, Walter Mondale, Michael Dukakis, and John Kerry. Instead, they really believed that Obama's election was proof that at last America had shed its odious -isms and -ologies. America was now ready for an updated FDR New Deal—as if, after seven decades, America had never tasted Social Security, unemployment and disability insurance, a 40-hour work week, and trillions in unfunded pensions and entitlements. In this "never let a crisis go to waste" teachable moment, the cognitive elite was convinced that America had at last crossed the liberal threshold and so evolved from the passé equality of opportunity to the promised equality of result.

But now a grouchy elite and a petulant president see that they were sorely mistaken about us, and Mr. Obama's election was more flukish than predestined. Americans were given government takeovers of business, multi-trillion-dollar deficits, promised higher taxes, a path to socialized medicine, and an end to building the odious border fence—with, to top it all off, accusations from the likes of Van Jones and Eric Holder, apologies and bows abroad, and the beer summit. And yet the rustic ingrates are rejecting both the benefactor and his munificence.

Forgive us, Barack Obama, for we know not what we do.

AUGUST 5, 2010

The Great American Debt

We are committing national suicide by debt addiction, as the Chinese rake in our IOUs.

With our national debt at $11 trillion and climbing at a projected rate of $1 to $2 trillion a year, examine the brilliant manner in which Americans justify borrowing much of this money from abroad, particularly from the Chinese.

Precise figures on how much the United States owes China are hard to come by. China is secretive about where it invests its vast surpluses, and even about how gargantuan they have become. Perhaps they are afraid that if such data become widely known, Chinese reformers will start questioning state financial policy—and specifically how, why, and where such national wealth is banked.

But for now, many observers believe the figure may have reached $1.4 trillion. On a per-capita basis, this means that each affluent American has borrowed well over $4,000 from the rather poor Chinese. We have excused our indebtedness in a variety of insidious ways. We say that our annual deficits and aggregate debt stimulate the U.S. consumer demand that is so essential to the Chinese export market. By buying and borrowing from China, we have jumpstarted its transformation from rogue nation to member of the responsible capitalist world—with benefits for the planet at large.

We go on to say that cheap Chinese goods keep consumer costs down in the U.S., increase the purchasing power of a weak currency, and maintain constant pressure on American competitors to maximize efficiency, lower prices, and cut costs. If real earnings have remained stagnant for the middle class, their purchasing power has increased, thanks in part to reduced prices at Wal-Mart and other mass retailers of Chinese goods.

And we've thought up even more justifications. Some argue that this debtor/creditor relationship is analogous to the federal government's tangled no-divorce involvement with AIG or Citibank: The U.S. is simply "too big to fail," and so we have more leverage over the Chinese than they have over us. They stop lending, we stop buying— and soon their factories shut down. And by the way, we pay low interest at fixed rates on their billions, and plan to pay them back with inflated dollars that will translate in the end into negative-interest loans.

Others point out that China has few options as to where to park its surpluses. Even in the era of Bernie Madoff and Lehman Brothers, what other country is so transparent and committed to protecting capital from arbitrary confiscation or government manipulation? And if China were to tap its vast cash reserves and begin a domestic shopping spree, it might create a consumer revolution at home, in which ever-increasing expectations would fuel ever-rising discretionary spending. If one billion Chinese started investing in three-bedroom homes, SUVs, and power boats, would the Chinese environment support it? Would China's labor remain competitive? Could the government still control public discourse and expression?

Besides the strange ways in which we addicts justify our borrowing habit vis-à-vis China, such huge sums have also warped politics at home. Republicans have not balanced a budget since the latter days of the Eisenhower presidency. We are supposed to nod and smile when they talk about financial responsibility, like the crowds at the naked emperor's procession. Nixon, Reagan, and the two Bushes all employed varying exegeses to justify red ink—Keynes, supply side, tapering deficits, a balanced budget by 2010, etc. Clinton, in contrast, was the last president to actually balance a budget—thanks mostly to a Republican Congress.

The recent Republican-Democratic symbiosis about borrowing is bizarre: Democrats in Congress run up debts like teenagers, enabled by the fact that their Republican parents in the White House never call in their credit cards. Republicans, in turn, started calibrating debts and deficits as percentages of GDP, not in real dollars, once hundreds of billions had metamorphosed into tens of trillions.

Liberals privately talked about "gorging the beast," hoping that their out-of-control spending would force higher taxes, and with them a long-awaited redistribution of income and government-mandated equality of result. Conservatives have talked of "starving the beast," by voting in tax cuts that would dry up government revenues and therefore force an end to huge federal expenditures. In the end, we got only higher taxes and higher spending and higher deficits and more debt. Republicans now say of Obama's fantasyland deficits, "He's gone way beyond Bush." Democrats reply, "But Bush did it first."

Both parties privately know that financial physics will take care of the problem in Californian or Icelandic fashion: Lenders abroad and at home will cut off our supply of money; conservatives will have to agree to even more tax increases; liberals will have to agree to some modest spending cuts; and the voters will be told that neither side had any choice. Unless we change our habits, that rendezvous is as inevitable as the sun's rising. The only mysteries are the approximate date of its arrival, and whether we will call federal pay cuts and layoffs "furloughs," massive income-tax hikes "surcharges," and a new blanket federal sales tax an innocuously European-sounding "value-added tax."

In the meantime, we might begin to look at federal expenditure in terms of where the money is borrowed. Cash-for-clunkers sounds like a great stimulus. But in terms of debt, we are borrowing a few billions from the Japanese and Chinese so that we can rent-to-own new fuel-efficient cars largely from the Japanese and Koreans. At some point, an economist will show us that the savings in fuel efficiency per clunker removed are overmatched by the interest on the money we borrowed for an imported replacement.

I support the conservative argument for a strong next-generation fighter component for national defense. But in acquiring more $177-million F-22 Raptors in our present financial circumstances, we should at least be honest enough to admit that we are renting the planes, not buying them. We are borrowing billions of dollars from the Chinese to protect against future threats from the Chinese. That may sound neat, but at some point the Chinese will not be amused.

When we talk of trillion-dollar health-care initiatives and universal coverage, we fool ourselves again. In essence, we are borrowing hundreds of billions from the Chinese, who do not have adequate health care, in order to give millions of our own citizens what the Chinese lack. Rationed health care is indeed a scary thought, but so is the idea that at age 85, I will have my government Medicare plan borrow $250,000 from the Chinese for my artificial hips and knees while my 50-year-old counterpart from rural China goes without annual check-ups or necessary medications.

Imagine instead an America in which we were obsessed with paying for things rather than borrowing, especially abroad. A senator might pontificate, "I propose purchasing another 100 F-22s, and so advocate cutting the national bike-path program." Or a congressman would bellow, "I demand universal health care and will force the average rich person to give the government another $25,000 a year to pay for it." Populists could cry out, "We need interest-free student loans, so I urge that those who make $10 million a year give us another $1 million as a surtax." Conservatives could counter, "We need a supplemental appropriation for Afghanistan, so we have to cut $200 billion from agricultural subsidies."

In short order, the entire way we think would be turned upside down, from buying votes with freebies to losing them by demanding payment up front. It all reminds me of the ancient world of my grandfather, who would point to a used tractor he had purchased (and paid for in cash) and sigh, "That cost me 20 tons of raisins"; or would look at the living-room floor and say with a shrug, "It took an acre of Santa Rosa plums to pay for that rug."

Instead, today we charge it, pay the 19 percent interest on our credit cards, get behind, and then applaud as a Sen. Chris Dodd rails that we were tricked, snookered, and victimized by evil usurers as we justifiably renege on the debt.

It will be interesting when America tries all that with the Chinese.

AUGUST 17, 2009

What Went Wrong

Piling up debt, gaffes, and hypocrisy, Obama & Co. are sinking.

We are witnessing one of the more rapid turnabouts in recent American political history. President Obama's popularity has plummeted to 50 percent and lower in some polls, while the public expresses even less confidence in the Democratic-led Congress and the direction of the country at large. Yet, just eight months ago, liberals were talking in Rovian style about a new generation to come of progressive politics—and the end of both the Republican party and the legacy of Reaganism itself. Barack Obama was to be the new FDR and his radical agenda an even better New Deal.

What happened, other than the usual hubris of the party in power?

First, voters had legitimate worries about health care, global warming, immigration, energy, and inefficient government. But it turns out that they are more anxious about the new radical remedies than the old nagging problems. They wanted federal support for wind and solar, but not at the expense of neglecting new sources of gas, oil, coal, and nuclear power. They were worried about high-cost health care, the uninsured, redundant procedures, and tort reform, but not ready for socialized medicine. They wanted better government, not bigger, DMV-style government. There is a growing realization that Obama enticed voters last summer with the flashy lure of discontent. But now that they are hooked, he is reeling them in to an entirely different—and, for many a frightening—agenda. Nothing is worse for a president than a growing belief among the public that it has been had.

Second, Americans were at first merely scared about the growing collective debt. But by June they became outraged that Obama has quadrupled the annual deficit in proposing all sorts of new federal programs at a time when most finally had acknowledged that the U.S. has lived beyond its means for years. They elected Obama, in part, out of anger at George W. Bush for multi-billion dollar shortfalls—and yet as a remedy for that red ink got Obama's novel multi-trillion-dollar deficits.

Third, many voters really believed in the "no more red/blue state America" healing rhetoric. Instead, polls show they got the most polarizing president in recent history—both in his radical programs and in the manner in which he has demonized the opposition to ram them through without bipartisan support. "Punch back harder" has replaced "Yes, we can."

Fourth, Americans wanted a new brand—youthful, postracial, mesmerizing abroad. At first they got that, too. But after eight months, their president has proven not so postracial, but instead hyper-racially conscious. Compare the Holder "cowards" outburst, the Sotomayor riff on innate racial and gender judicial superiority, and the president's Cambridge police comments. All that sounds more like Jesse Jackson than Martin Luther King Jr. Demagogues, not healers, trash their predecessors at the beginning of every speech. When a once-eloquent president now goes off teleprompter, the question is not whether he will say something that is either untruthful or silly, but simply how many times he might do so at one outing. Some once worried that George W. Bush could not articulate our goals in Iraq; far more now sense that Obama is even less able to outline his own health-care reform.

Fifth, even skeptics are surprised at the partisan cynicism. A year ago, Democratic leaders such as Nancy Pelosi, Harry Reid, and Barack Obama praised organizing, dissidents, and protest. Today they have become near-Nixonian in demonizing popular resistance to their collectivized health-care plans as mob-like, inauthentic, scripted, Nazi-like, and un-American. There are still ex-lobbyists in the government. High officials still cheat on their taxes. Hacks in the Congress still profit from their office. The public is sensing not only that Obama has failed to run the most ethically clean government, as promised, but indeed that he is not running as ethically clean a government as the predecessor whom he so assiduously ridiculed.

Sixth, there is a growing fear that Obamism is becoming cult-like and Orwellian. Almost on script, Hollywood ceased all its Rendition/Redacted—style films. Iraq—once the new Vietnam—is out of the news. Afghanistan is "problematic," not a "blunder." Tribunals, renditions, the Patriot Act, and Predators are no longer proof of a Seven Days in May coup, but legitimate tools to keep us safe. Words change meanings as acts of terror become "man-caused disasters." Hunting down jihadists is really an "overseas contingency operation." Media sycophants do not merely parrot Obama, but now proclaim him a "god." New York Times columnists who once assured us that Bush's dastardly behavior was proof of American pathology now sound like Pravda apologists in explaining the "real" Obama is not what he is beginning to seem like.

Seventh, the Obama cabinet is sounding downright uncouth and boorish. The tax-challenged Treasury secretary, Tim Geithner, unleashed a profanity-laced diatribe against bank regulators. Hillary Clinton's recent outburst in the Congo, captured on YouTube, was something out of Days of Our Lives. Joe Biden cannot speak extemporaneously without causing an incident with the Russians or misleading the public about swine flu. Attorney General Holder sounds like a tired scold, only to be overshadowed by the president's off-the-cuff cuts about the Special Olympics, Las Vegas, and the Cambridge police. Press Secretary Robert Gibbs makes Scott McClellan sound like a Cicero by comparison.

Eighth, we were all appalled by Wall Street greed and the notion that an individual could take $100 million rather than one or two million as a bonus. But the Obama remedy for that obscenity was to conflate Goldman Sachs or AIG with the family orthodontist or local asphalt contractor whose 80-hour weeks might result in an annual $250,000 income. Worse still, the public impression is that while small entrepreneurs may pay up to 65 percent of their income in new state and federal income taxes, payroll taxes, and surcharges, those on Wall Street have been bailed out and have cut various deals with upscale liberals in government.

Ninth, Democratic populism turned out to be largely aristocratic elitism. Obama spends more money on himself than did Bush. The liberal Congress has a strange fondness for pricy private jets. Those environmentalists and racialists who lecture us about our ecological and ethical shortcomings prefer Martha's Vineyard and country estates to Dayton and Bakersfield. Offering left-wing populist sermonizing for others while enjoying the high life oneself is never a winning combination.

Tenth, Americans no longer believe this is our moment when the seas stop rising and the planet ceases warming. Instead, there is a growing hopelessness that despite all the new proposed income taxes, payroll taxes, and surtaxes, the deficit will skyrocket, not shrink. There is foreboding that while apologies abroad are nice in the short term, they will soon earn a reckoning. And while the productive classes pay more of their income, and while government grows and entitlement expands, there is a sense that what follows will not be thanks for either taxes paid or benefits received, but even more anger that neither is enough and that much more is owed.

Obama's popularity might rebound with a natural upturn in the economy, continued low energy prices, and good will for our first multiracial president. But then again, it could get even worse if the recovery turns into stagflation, gas prices soar, and the identity-politics lectures amplify. The next six months should be interesting.

AUGUST 26, 20090

Obama and 'Redistributive Change'

Forget the recession and the 'uninsured.'
Obama has bigger fish to fry.

The first seven months of the Obama administration seemingly make no sense. Why squander public approval by running up astronomical deficits in a time of pre-existing staggering national debt?

Why polarize opponents after promising bipartisan transcendence?

Why create vast new programs when the efficacy of big government is already seen as dubious?

But that is exactly the wrong way to look at these first seven months of Obamist policy-making.

Take increased federal spending and the growing government absorption of GDP. Given the resiliency of the U.S. economy, it would have been easy to ride out the recession. In that case we would still have had to deal with a burgeoning and unsustainable annual federal deficit that would have approached $1 trillion.

Instead, Obama may nearly double that amount of annual indebtedness with more federal stimuli and bailouts, newly envisioned cap-and-trade legislation, and a variety of fresh entitlements. Was that fiscally irresponsible? Yes, of course.

But I think the key was not so much the spending excess or new entitlements. The point instead was the consequence of the resulting deficits, which will require radically new taxation for generations. If on April 15 the federal and state governments, local entities, the Social Security system, and the new health-care programs can claim 70 percent of the income of the top 5 percent of taxpayers, then that is considered a public good—every bit as valuable as funding new programs, and one worth risking insolvency.

Individual compensation is now seen as arbitrary and, by extension, inherently unfair. A high income is now rationalized as having less to do with market-driven needs, acquired skills, a higher level of education, innate intelligence, inheritance, hard work, or accepting risk. Rather income is seen more as luck-driven, cruelly capricious, unfair—even immoral, in that some are rewarded arbitrarily on the basis of race, class, and gender advantages, others for their overweening greed and ambition, and still more for their quasi-criminality.

"Patriotic" federal healers must then step in to "spread the wealth." Through redistributive tax rates, they can "treat" the illness that the private sector has caused. After all, there is no intrinsic reason why an auto fabricator makes $60 in hourly wages and benefits, while a young investment banker finagles $500.

Or, in the president's own language, the government must equalize the circumstances of the "waitress" with those of the "lucky." It is thus a fitting and proper role of the new federal government to rectify imbalances of compensation—at least for those outside the anointed Guardian class. In a 2001 interview Obama in fact outlined the desirable political circumstances that would lead government to enforce equality of results when he elaborated on what he called an "actual coalition of powers through which you bring about redistributive change."

Still, why would intelligent politicians try to ram through, in mere weeks, a thousand pages of health-care gibberish—its details outsourced to far-left elements in the Congress (and their staffers)—that few in the cabinet had ever read or even knew much about?

Once again, I don't think health care per se was ever really the issue. When pressed, no one in the administration seemed to know whether illegal aliens were covered. Few cared why young people do not divert some of their entertainment expenditures to a modest investment in private catastrophic coverage.

Warnings that Canadians already have their health care rationed, wait in long lines, and are denied timely and critical procedures also did not seem to matter. And no attention was paid to statistics suggesting that, if we exclude homicides and auto accidents, Americans live as long on average as anyone in the industrial world, and have better chances of surviving longer with heart disease and cancer. That the average American did not wish to radically alter his existing plan, and that he understood that the uninsured really did have access to health care, albeit in a wasteful manner at the emergency room, was likewise of no concern.

The issue again was larger, and involved a vast reinterpretation of how America receives health care. Whether more or fewer Americans would get better or worse access and cheaper or more expensive care, or whether the government can or cannot afford such new entitlements, oddly seemed largely secondary to the crux of the debate.

Instead, the notion that the state will assume control, in Canada-like fashion, and level the health-care playing field was the real concern. "They" (the few) will now have the same care as "we" (the many). Whether the result is worse or better for everyone involved is extraneous, since sameness is the overarching principle.

We can discern this same mandated egalitarianism beneath many of the administration's recent policy initiatives. Obama is not a pragmatist, as he insisted, nor even a liberal, as charged.

Rather, he is a statist. The president believes that a select group of affluent, highly educated technocrats—cosmopolitan, noble-minded, and properly progressive—supported by a phalanx of whiz-kids fresh out of blue-chip universities with little or no experience in the market-place, can direct our lives far better than we can ourselves. By "better" I do not mean in a fashion that, measured by disinterested criteria, makes us necessarily wealthier, happier, more productive, or freer.

Instead, "better" means "fairer," or more "equal." We may "make" different amounts of money, but we will end up with more or less similar net incomes. We may know friendly doctors, be aware of the latest procedures, and have the capital to buy blue-chip health insurance, but no matter. Now we will all alike queue up with our government-issued insurance cards to wait our turn at the ubiquitous corner clinic.

None of this equality-of-results thinking is new.

When radical leaders over the last 2,500 years have sought to enforce equality of results, their prescriptions were usually predictable: redistribution of property; cancellation of debts; incentives to bring out the vote and increase political participation among the poor; stigmatizing of the wealthy, whether through the extreme measure of ostracism or the more mundane forced liturgies; use of the court system to even the playing field by targeting the more prominent citizens; radical growth in government and government employment; the use of state employees as defenders of the egalitarian faith; bread-and-circus entitlements; inflation of the currency and greater national debt to lessen the power of accumulated capital; and radical sloganeering about reactionary enemies of the new state.

The modern versions of much of the above already seem to be guiding the Obama administration—evident each time we hear of another proposal to make it easier to renounce personal debt; federal action to curtail property or water rights; efforts to make voter registration and vote casting easier; radically higher taxes on the top 5 percent; takeover of private business; expansion of the federal government and an increase in government employees; or massive inflationary borrowing. The current class-warfare "them/us" rhetoric was predictable.

Usually such ideologies do not take hold in America, given its tradition of liberty, frontier self-reliance, and emphasis on personal freedom rather than mandated fraternity and egalitarianism. At times, however, the stars line up, when a national catastrophe, like war or depression, coincides with the appearance of an unusually gifted, highly polished, and eloquent populist. But the anointed one must be savvy enough to run first as a centrist in order later to govern as a statist.

Given the September 2008 financial meltdown, the unhappiness over the war, the ongoing recession, and Barack Obama's postracial claims and singular hope-and-change rhetoric, we found ourselves in just such a situation. For one of the rare times in American history, statism could take hold, and the country could be pushed far to the left.

That goal is the touchstone that explains the seemingly inexplicable—and explains also why, when Obama is losing independents, conservative Democrats, and moderate Republicans, his anxious base nevertheless keeps pushing him to become even more partisan, more left-wing, angrier, and more in a hurry to rush things through. They understand the unpopularity of the agenda and the brief shelf life of the president's charm. One term may be enough to establish lasting institutional change.

Obama and his supporters at times are quite candid about such a radical spread-the-wealth agenda, voiced best by Rahm Emanuel—"You don't ever want a crisis to go to waste; it's an opportunity to do important things that you would otherwise avoid"—or more casually by Obama himself—"My attitude is that if the economy's good for folks from the bottom up, it's gonna be good for everybody. I think when you spread the wealth around, it's good for everybody."

So we move at breakneck speed in order not to miss this rare opportunity when the radical leadership of the Congress and the White House for a brief moment clinch the reins of power. By the time a shell-shocked public wakes up and realizes that the prescribed chemotherapy is far worse than the existing illness, it should be too late to revive the old-style American patient.

JANUARY 20, 2010

Why the Great and Growing Backlash?

What Scott Brown's election portends for the Obama agenda.

Dream up a gargantuan backlash against Barack Obama's left-wing gospel, and you still could not invent the notion of a relatively unknown, conservative Scott Brown knocking off an Obama-endorsed, liberal, female attorney in liberal Massachusetts—in a race to fill the seat once held by Ted Kennedy.

If a liberal senatorial candidate can be defeated in Massachusetts, eleven months after the Obama hope-and-change blitzkrieg, it is hard to believe that any liberal seat is necessarily safe anywhere.

So the real story is not a populist backlash, but a growing populist backlash, whose ultimate nature and magnitude are as yet unknown. What's going on?

BUYING JOBS?

Voters are sick and tired of a terrible year of big spending and big deficits—especially the sight of Obama and his congressional allies almost daily talking breezily about spending what we do not have.

Voters went for the hope-and-change Obama in part because he promised fiscal sobriety after the Bush $500 billion deficit. Instead, in utterly cynical fashion, Obama trumped that red ink four times over. In the process, he developed a terrible habit of promising favored constituencies a hundred billion here, a hundred billion there as if it were all paper money—rather than real borrowed currency that will have to be confiscated in the future from the beleaguered taxpayer. It only makes it worse that the more the administration borrowed, printed, and spent, the higher unemployment rose and the lower economic activity plummeted.

Most have had enough of pie-in-the-sky talk of massive new health-care entitlements, cap-and-trade taxes and regulation, more stimulus, and more takeovers of private enterprise. The country is broke and the people want to pay off, not incur more, crushing debt. What got us into the mess was too much borrowing, skyrocketing debt, and reckless spending—not too many balanced budgets and too much lean government.

PROPHETS CAN'T MISLEAD?

No politician quite gets a pass for deception and prevarication. Obama in his narcissism thought his sonorous rhetoric made him exempt from a "read my lips" or "I didn't have sex with that woman" moment. It didn't.

People heard his serial promises about airing the health-care debate on C-SPAN, his new-transparency/no-lobbyist vows, and his monotonous boasts to close down Guantanamo within a year. All that is now "inoperative." The problem was not just that Obama made promises that he broke, but that he made them so frequently and so vehemently—and so cavalierly broke them. That brazen campaign deception is problematic for a politician, but proves fatal for a self-appointed messiah.

A CESSATION OF CORRUPTION

We went from a Republican "culture of corruption" to a liberal cesspool of corruption. Sen. Chris Dodd lectures Wall Street while he gets sweetheart loans and vacation-home deals. Few could make up a story that the nation's top tax lawmaker, House Ways and Means Chairman Charles Rangel, is a tax dodger, and the nation's top tax enforcer, Secretary of the Treasury Timothy Geithner, is an even more egregious tax dodger. When the Democratic Senate leadership started buying health-care votes at $300 million a clip, our Congress became little more than the praetorian guard, auctioning off its support to any wannabe late Roman emperor. The idea of a muckraking Obama nominating Tom Daschle as his Health Secretary—the liberal populist who skips out of thousands of dollars in taxes on his free corporate limousine service—was the stuff of satire.

BUSH REALLY, REALLY, REALLY DID DO IT

No one likes a serial whiner. It has been a year now—and Obama still blames George W. Bush ad nauseam. He did it in Massachusetts again—and on the eve of the election, no less. Blaming the past for the mistakes of the present gets old quickly. And when one adds in the constant What's the Matter With Kansas? brand of condescension about naïve yokels not knowing what's good for them, it gets even worse.

Yet Obama still pontificates that angry deluded voters will "suddenly" come to appreciate how he rammed health care down their otherwise ignorant throats: "The American people will suddenly learn that this bill does things they like and doesn't do things that people have been trying to say it does. . . . The worst fears will prove groundless. And the American people's hope for a fair shake from their insurance companies—for quality, affordable health care they need—will finally be realized."

Good luck with that, O philosopher king!

WALL STREET POPULISTS

Elite liberals are not good class warriors. Factor in multi-millionaire Nancy Pelosi's government mega-jet or Barack Obama's various overseas junkets or the big Wall Street money that went into Obama's near billion-dollar campaign coffers, and it is hard to take seriously Obama's constant war against "them." The voters have figured out that their president likes the elite plutocracy and the lower middle classes, but not so much the wannabe rich who aspire to cross his hated $250,000 income threshold—at which point suddenly they become unpatriotic, unwilling to pay their fair shares, and reluctant to spread the wealth around.

It is not particularly smart to constantly demonize the entrepreneurial classes, promise to raise income, payroll, health-care, and inheritance taxes on them, and expand government regulations—and then wonder why they are not creating more jobs.

ELMER GANTRY

Devotees turn on false prophets with a special vengeance. Obama is beginning to grate. His flip-the-switch-on, evangelical cadences at rallies sound more like a Harvard nerd doing blues imitations than Martin Luther King Jr. Purple-state presidents don't appoint Van Joneses and

Anita Dunns, or turn the NEA into a quid pro quo Ministry of Approved Culture. A healer doesn't start in on the "rich," "Wall Street," the "big" oil companies, drug companies, insurance companies, or "fat-cat bankers"—especially when he has done his best to shake them all down for campaign money, hire as many of them as he can in his own administration, and arrange cut-rate loans, insider deals, bailouts, and guarantees for all of them.

Obama's populism is beginning to sound more like a bought boxer who belatedly has second thoughts about throwing the fight he previously contracted. In short, Obama's ideological presidency hinged on his post-racial, post-national mesmerizing presence that reassured reluctant Democrats to vote against their local constituencies.

If cap-and-trade or health care reform polled below 50 percent, a worried congressional supporter could always call in Him to charm bolting voters. But now? We have in a blink gone from Obama as the bankable 10 percent edge, to Obama as a non-factor, to Obama as a real liability. In short, why vote for an agenda as unpopular as its albatross author?

LIKED BY ALL, RESPECTED BY NONE

Obama thought the antidote to "smoke 'em out," "dead or alive," and "bring 'em on" braggadocio was bowing to the Saudis, promulgating new and undiscovered great moments in Islamic history, and reaching out to Ahmadinejad as he rounded up and beat down reformers in the streets of Tehran.

It's one thing to accuse Bush of shredding the Constitution, quite another to adopt his anti-terrorism protocols like tribunals, renditions, Predators, intercepts, and wiretaps. Somehow Obama offended his base by such duplicity, and then his opposition by his tokenism of trashing Bush, promising the architect of 9/11 a show trial a few blocks from the former World Trade Center, and using touchy-feely euphemisms to suggest we are not in a war against terrorism emanating from the radical Islamic world.

Ahmadinejad, Assad, Chávez, the Castro Brothers, Putin, and others for the first six months liked us as much as they had little respect for our sycophancy; now they openly show contempt. We accept that obsequiousness cannot earn respect, but it apparently cannot earn affection either.

The best thing that could happen to Barack Obama is more Democratic losses in hodgepodge elections that might yank away our young transfixed Narcissus from his mesmerizing reflecting pool.

Almost immediately after Obama showed his ideological cards last spring, I suggested in the first weeks of his presidency that the bait-and-switch president would soon face a Carter/Clinton moment in which he could either press on with his polarizing ideology, damage his party for a generation, and eventually end up churlish and sneering at the electorate, who did not appreciate his exalted morality and genius—or triangulate and follow the Dick Morris/Bill Clinton model of talking and acting sort of centrist.

Who knows after Obama's Scott Brown moment? We now may hear once again the old "no more Red State/Blue State" tropes, the stale campaign promises of presidential vetoes, claims of financial sobriety, the return of a "war on terror," and smaller government

We're either down to all that—or Obama's more principled road to perdition.

JANUARY 27, 2010

Obama Versus Obama

Will the real Barack Obama (if there is one) please stand up?

There is little need any more to offer consistent opposition to Barack Obama, since he himself is already running hard against the many previous incarnations of Barack Obama.

The first one we met was Barack the radical progressive, in his primary campaign against Hillary. Then in the general election we were introduced to the centrist Obama, who promised to invade Pakistan if need be, called for an end to partisanship, and lectured about fiscal sobriety.

Then with congressional majorities, soaring public support, and obsequious media attention came the leftist ideologue President Obama, who tried to ram through a statist health-care regime, gobbled up private enterprises, and gave us Anita Dunn and Van Jones.

Now we are back to sorta centrist Obama, who is going to fight terror, not apologize any more to the Muslim world, and freeze spending rather than give us another $2 trillion in debt.

These serial reset Obamas are quite astonishing even for a politician.

Take the examples of public advocate Obama's once idealistic promotion of C-SPAN broadcasts of the health-care debate, and Obama's current fiery lamentations over the Supreme Court decision overturning elements of the McCain-Feingold limitations on corporate campaign donations.

But Obama, the current reformer, seems to be railing at Obama, the cynical backroom organizer, who would never dare televise anything about his thousand-page health-care mess. Yet Obama II not only nixed Obama I's repeated promises of C-SPAN debates, but outsourced his health-care bill to congressional insiders, who did more backroom-dealing, vote-buying, and quid-pro-quoing than at any other time in recent memory.

So there is no consistency even in the flip-flopping. Obama III as the sudden guardian of campaign-financing curbs is antithetical to Obama I, the rejectionist of any government interference. In 2008 Obama I destroyed the idea of public campaign financing of presidential elections. Indeed, in his efforts to raise a billion dollars of private money, Obama became the first presidential candidate in the general election in over 30 years to back out of public financing, an idea which is now more or less kaput.

So what is the present-day Obama III? Nothing and everything. We have no idea whether he is against corporate campaign contributions, given Obama I/II's voracious appetite for them. Will he accept public campaign financing in the future? Only if his money machine stalls? Is C-SPAN necessary for or irrelevant to public debate?

Take also terrorism. Obama 1.0, the champion of civil liberties, based the entire foreign-policy side of his 2007—08 campaign on the notion of George W. Bush's shredding the Constitution in his unnecessary War on Terror and his venture into Iraq. Obama at one time or another attacked almost every Bush protocol—e.g., renditions ("shipping away prisoners in the dead of night"), military tribunals ("flawed military commission system"), preventive detention ("detaining thousands without charge or trial"), the surge of troops into Iraq ("not working"), the Patriot Act ("shoddy and dangerous"). We were to have all combat troops out of Iraq by August 2010, and Guantanamo ("a legal black hole," "a sad chapter in American history," "a false choice between fighting terrorism and respecting habeas corpus") closed last week. Predator strikes, according to candidate Obama, recklessly terrorized civilians.

But Obama 2.0 seemed to be ignoring Obama 1.0. Our realist president embraced renditions and tribunals, still held terrorists in preventive detention, kept troops in Iraq, championed the Patriot Act, and apparently counted on Guantanamo to stay open. Three days after he took office Obama ordered our first reported Hellfire missile attacks inside Pakistan itself.

And Obama 3.0? His team renamed the War on Terror "overseas contingency operations" and "man-caused disasters," dithered on troop escalations in Afghanistan, allowed his attorney general to go after CIA interrogators, gave the Christmas Day al-Qaeda would-be mass murderer his Miranda rights, and plans to try in a civilian court the architect of 9/11 a few blocks from where his evil genius led to the incineration of 3,000 Americans. But wait—Obama 3.0 has also belatedly expanded the war in Afghanistan, has vastly increased the controversial judge/jury/executioner Predator attacks, and is talking more about terror and less about the mythical achievements of the Muslim world. That's quite an abyss to bridge—insisting that a known mass murderer like Khalid Sheikh Mohammed gets his Miranda rights while blasting to smithereens suspected terrorists and their families in their living rooms in Pakistan.

Obama versus Obama versus Obama could be played out in almost any venue. In 2008 he was the candidate who, in response to the

McCain-Palin "Drill, baby, drill" mantra during the energy-price spike, supported more drilling, expansion of nuclear power, and using all our energy resources. Then, in the euphoria of early 2009, it was to be cap-and-trade and the solar/wind vision of Van Jones. Now there is a nothing-and-everything energy policy, apparently depending on the polls and the price of energy at any given moment.

Candidate Obama warned that the "Bush deficits" would cripple his imaginative spending agenda. Yet President Obama damned the red-ink torpedoes and went full speed ahead into far greater deficits, resulting in an addition to the national debt of nearly $2 trillion in his first year alone. Yet reset-button Obama is already calling for a national commission to freeze (some) spending and "address" the spiraling deficit.

Two observations. First, there is a hazy pattern to the Obama tri-step: soar with progressive platitudes when there is no responsibility of governance; then as president slowly learn that a center-right country is not ready to blame itself for radical Islam or destroy the private-sector entrepreneurship that made America wealthy beyond imagination; and end up with an ad hoc, poll-driven policy of everything and nothing.

The problem with Obama 1-2-3 is that progressives rightly feel betrayed and now see their once-in-a-century savior exposed as an inept triangulator, without the Machiavellian savvy of Bill Clinton or the input of Dick Morris.

Conservatives, however, who should appreciate that Obama is still fighting in Afghanistan and has kept the Bush anti-terrorism protocols, are enraged about the KSM trial, the Abdulmutallab mess, and the demagoguing about the CIA and Guantanamo.

Second, this absence of consistency, of identity even, was entirely predictable—given what the nation knew of newcomer candidate Barack Obama in the brief two-year period we were introduced to him.

He sermonized on purple-state America after compiling the most partisan record in the Senate. He talked of political and racial reconciliation, while assembling the most radically divisive cast of intimates imaginable—Bill Ayers, Rashid Khalidi, the Rev. James Meeks, Father Michael Pfleger, the Rev. Jeremiah Wright. He soared about a new transparency, but unlike rival McCain never fully released his medical records, his college transcripts, or the details of his Senate race.

If we do not know who Barack Obama is, that may be because Barack Obama does not know who Barack Obama is. Barry Dunham? Barry Soetoro? Barack Soetoro? Barry Obama? Barack Obama?

Is he the racial healer who called his own ailing grandmother a "typical white person"? The white middle-class prep-schooler, or the authentically African-American community organizer?

The hip, yuppie multicultural agnostic—or the devotee of the them/us wacky old-time religion of Trinity Church?

The working-class populist who ridiculed the culture of rural Pennsylvania?

The modern-day Cicero who needs a teleprompter?

The Harvard Law graduate and Chicago law professor who gets confused about everything from Cinco de Mayo to the number of states? The Chicago progressive who regularly voted present? The reformist Senate candidate whose rivals in both the primary and general elections mysteriously found their divorce records leaked?

By pleasing his immediate audience with his mellifluous rhetoric and clichés about his racial transcendence, Obama has always charmed his way up his cursus honorum. Why worry about the nonexistent record, broken promises, empty platitudes, and self-contradictions when his mesmerized audiences believed that he believed in them, and lapped up the inexpensive absolutions for their assorted past sins?

The only catch is that Barack Obama no longer navigates among gullible Ivy League deans, naïve philanthropists, and inept organizers and bureaucrats. No, he is running a country that still has millions of no-nonsense truckers, teachers, small-business owners, and general skeptics who don't give a damn about either Harvard or Chicago. And in their eyes, after a year, the game is about up.

Yet in a weird sort of consistency, Obama remains what he always was. Whatever we choose to see in this glass mirror, he will sorta, kinda reflect our vision.

Obama is our first everything-and-nothing president.

APRIL 14, 2010

Mr. Obama's Nowhere Discussions

President Obama could rather easily restore his credibility. But to do so, he would have to stop talking and start making hard policy decisions.

Barack Obama has a marvelous way of sounding innovative, fresh, and novel while offering stale, predictable bromides. His policies at home are an extension of LBJ's old Great Society. Abroad we've been getting a more sonorous version of Jimmy Carter's global self-righteous sermonizing.

The public wanted a racially transcendent figure and got instead a Chicago ward boss. The problem now for Mr. Obama—reflected in growing popular discontent—is that on matters of debt, taxes, energy, jobs, and race, he apparently has very little new to offer. He just serves up in new wording the them/us divides of the past.

We are at a point where each new proposed federal initiative— health care, cap-and-trade, a "jobs bill," stimulus, education—is synonymous with more debt. Mr. Obama has exhausted the time-honored Beltway gimmicks of promising to root out "fraud and abuse," of "streaming" or "reinventing" government, of "freezing" discretionary spending.

His proposed restoration of the Clinton income-tax rates does not come in a vacuum, but coincides with massive new taxes imposed by the states, health-care surcharges, and proposed raising of the caps on income subject to payroll taxes. As the deficit still grows, talk of a new federal value-added tax spreads.

In other words, when one piles up over $3 trillion in debt in less than two years of governance, all the soaring rhetoric in the world, all the borrowing from Japan and China, and all the new taxes cannot change the fact that the money is running out. There really is a finite sum that we can continue to borrow at low interest or to collect in taxes from "them." End of discussion.

Obama has never addressed our dependence on imported oil, other than by borrowing billions to subsidize wind and solar power, alternative energy sources that so far have been more inspirational than concrete in easing the immediate energy crunch. When the worldwide economy rebounds (and it will, regardless of the degree of American "stimulus"), the price of gas at the pump will soar. It is well over $3 a gallon right now in California.

Again, all the gimmicks in the world will not change our immediate need for foreign fuel. Loud but disingenuous pledges to drill offshore and tap new gas fields do not actually equate to pumping more oil and tapping more natural gas in places like Alaska and off the California and Florida coasts. Bold new statements about nuclear power matter little; that we haven't built a plant in three decades matters a lot.

So Mr. Obama can once again soar with "millions of new green jobs" and point to all sorts of innovative new energy sources; but for the next five years rising gas and power prices will crush the American public unless he is serious about developing the energy sources we have that could carry us through the crisis until private enterprise creates viable alternatively fueled transportation and electrical production. End of discussion.

Unemployment seems stuck at right under 10 percent. When it was under 6 percent during the 2004 campaign, the media tore George Bush apart with the charge of a "jobless recovery." That's not what they're saying now. Instead we hear of an ongoing recovery from the downturn. But we won't get robust job growth until Mr. Obama comes clean with the private sector and honestly lists how much additional revenue it will need to generate to pay his higher taxes.

The psychology of uncertainty really does matter. As long as those in industry and commerce hear that the government is the solution to the problems that they supposedly created, browbeaten individuals will not take risks and begin hiring. All the populist rhetoric, all the sympathetic statistical gymnastics from the liberal pundits, all the euphemisms of "jobs saved," still won't change the fact that American business believes Mr. Obama wants to take more of their money to redistribute rather than empowering them to hire and make a profit. Again, end of discussion.

Mr. Obama is also at an impasse in matters of race. His promise of a postracial era was wounded by the revelations about the Rev. Jeremiah Wright and his own racialist quips about "typical" white people, those who "cling" to guns and religion, and police who indulge in racial stereotyping and who act "stupidly." His pledge was put into a coma with Van Jones's racist remarks, Eric Holder's "cowards" smear, and Justice Sotomayor's lectures about the superiority of a "wise Latina."

Fairly or not, the president has lost all credibility as a racial uniter. The public now expects an elite to mine any trace of racial insensitivity in order to create grievances, bank sympathy, and translate that into political capital—while avoiding the promised honest discussion about race.

That taboo debate would inevitably address the degree to which the depressing per capita statistics on incarceration, illegitimacy, violent crime, gangs, entitlement dependency, and lack of education within the African-American community are due to residual racism, and to what degree they stem from a failure of the black leadership to address personal responsibility, or the disastrous entitlement policies of the federal government. Giving preference to the children of a Valerie Jarrett, an Eric Holder, or a Barack Obama to enter Harvard or Yale, or wading out into a crowd of tea-partiers in hopes of snagging a racial slur for political purposes, does nothing to alleviate the tragedy in the D.C. school system or the implosion of Detroit.

So we know what lies ahead for the next two years. Sympathetic observers in the media will detect racism in the tea parties and in non-mainstream-media coverage of Mr. Obama's disappointing performance. As never before, any African-American politician mired in ethics problems (e.g., Charles Rangel) or facing political oblivion (e.g., David Paterson) will claim he is a victim of racial intolerance.

Privately, a majority of Americans accepts that the African-American elite enjoys a particular leeway in promiscuously leveling accusations of racism—and that such exemption from criticism ultimately derives from the fact that on a percentage basis much of the African-American community is not doing as well as the rest of America, and the culprit must be either racism or a lack of government financial assistance. End of discussion.

In short, we are witnessing a public soon asked to pay higher taxes as the debt grows and jobs remain scarce, while its energy costs spike—and popular protests over any and all of that earn charges of racism.

Mr. Obama could rather easily restore his credibility by offering a plan to balance the budget that matched his tax hikes with tough budget cuts. He could offer a jobs plan centered on incentives for business and psychological support for entrepreneurs. He could offer a landmark new tax code that rewards income and savings, and taxes consumption. A multifaceted energy program might tap all the oil, coal, gas, and nuclear power we could produce as a bridge to next-generation fuels without bankrupting the Treasury or endangering our autonomy. And a fair-minded discussion of race would explore how obsession with elite racial grievances has little to do with the causes of a too-large African-American underclass.

Until then, the more mellifluously the president lectures, the more he will exhaust the voters.

JULY 14, 2010

The Psychology of Recession

Obama and his team speak the language of redistribution and entitlements—not the language of opportunity and prosperity. And Main Street is listening.

I asked a businessman two weeks ago why he said that he was neither hiring nor buying new equipment. He started in on "rising taxes."

"But wait," I interrupted. I pointed out that income-tax hikes haven't taken effect. The old FICA income caps are also still applicable. Health-care surcharges haven't hit us yet.

He countered with "regulations" and "bailouts." I said, "Come on, get specific." He offered up "cap and trade" and "the Chrysler creditors." I parried with more demands that he tell me exactly how the federal government has suddenly curbed his profit margins, or how his electric bill had gone up since January 2009, or whether he had lost money on any investment because the government had violated a contract.

Exasperated, he talked now instead of more cosmic issues—the astronomical borrowing, the staggering national debt, and the new protectionism. I pressed again, "But aren't interest rates historically low? Inflation is almost non-existent, isn't it? New products are still comparatively cheap? Rents and new business property are at bargain-basement prices?"

This give-and-take went on for ten minutes; but you get the picture. Private enterprise is wary, hesitant, even frightened, but nevertheless hard pressed to demonstrate in concrete fashion how Obama has quite ruined them in just 18 months. So why are a lot of cash-solvent financial firms, banks, and manufacturing companies not hiring, not expanding, and not buying new operating equipment as they did in past bottoming-out recessions?

In a word, fear. Remember that capitalism is in large part psychologically driven. Confidence, optimism, and a sense of calm about the future foster risk and investment, while worry, pessimism, and a sense of foreboding ensure timidity and stasis.

Barack Obama—who is mostly a creature of the university and the dependable government payroll—does not seem to grasp that fact. If one were to deconstruct any one speech, any particular piece of proposed legislation, or any single executive order, one might not necessarily conclude that Obama's agenda bodes poorly for the creation of capital. But after 18 months, put the pieces together, and the once jumbled-up jigsaw puzzle starts to form a disturbingly coherent picture.

First, there are the appointees and their various public statements—again, insignificant in isolation, but telling in their totality. Why would any executive hire the self-avowed Communist gadfly Van Jones as his adviser for "green" jobs? Regulation is one thing, but an interior secretary promising a "boot on the neck" of a company is quite another. Why does a labor secretary reassure, gratuitously, illegal aliens that they are not really subject to lawful enforcement of the laws?

What is California agribusiness to make of the energy secretary's prediction that Golden State farms will soon dry up and blow away? Is that a promise or a prediction? If the latter, is it lamented or welcomed?

Was not Mao the world's most lethal Communist? Why then would a White House communications director see him as an inspirational figure?

NASA historically marries private enterprise and government purpose to study and explore space; why then would President Obama direct its head to put "foremost" the use of our resources to make Muslims feel good about their scientific past? Why ram through on a recess appointment a new health-care czar who has repeatedly warned that good health care is synonymous with redistribution of resources and wealth?

Second, there is Obama's own history, which suggests that his subordinates are competing in parroting the world view of the man at the top. On the campaign trail, Obama touched upon the need for "redistributive change," a desire for "skyrocketing" energy prices, and the imperative of "spreading the wealth" in a fashion that sounded like a refined version of the Rev. Jeremiah Wright's crude liberationist socialism. But the reversal of the payout to Chrysler creditors, the absorption of large insolvent private companies, and the promises for intrusive cap-and-trade energy legislation only seem to confirm that the president has no understanding of the historical role of entrepreneurship and businesses in creating the sort of wealth that he takes for granted can be redistributed. Obama, past and present, seems always to talk of how someone else's money should be spent, dispersed, and redistributed, but never to worry about how it can be made in the first place.

So, fairly or not, when the president talks, business people do not gain confidence that he knows, or cares, much about them or what they do. If he thinks even surgeons are greedy profiteers, who then escapes presidential disdain?

Third, the real worry is not for 2010—after all, few revolutionaries create their utopias in a mere 18 months—but for the years to come, for which business people must right now schedule purchases, hire, and in general gamble that their investments will pay off when the boom returns. Yet at one time or another some administration official has talked of new inheritance taxes, new FICA tax schedules, new income-tax rates, new health-care surcharges, or a possible VAT or federal excise tax—all at a time when state income and sales taxes are climbing.

It does not matter whether all or some of these proposals are merely trial balloons. They still have a depressing effect in reminding the productive classes that the government is going to take a much larger percentage of their rewards and spend it for purposes that might just make things worse still. That notion kills rather than spurs investment.

And climbing taxation is not the only reason why business is now worried about fiscal policy. There is also a depressing realization that any additional revenue will hardly balance the budget, given the astronomical spending. Do not underestimate the psychology of deficits. The owner of a tire store or a pool-cleaning company may not like handing over more hard-earned money to government, but he hates the notion that it is all in vain anyway—already pledged away as interest on the rising debt before it is collected.

Out-of-control government spending depresses small businesses in other ways beyond leaving them with less cash. Growing government entitlements and redistribution are seen as undermining personal initiative. The more we provide subsidies for housing, health, education, food, and entertainment, the more the individual seems to want more compensation for less work—and the more the employer feels he has been had, as he works while others do not.

Finally, business operates best under the assumption that the law is applied equally and that there are no insider cronies who are favored by government because of their contacts, cash, or politics. The problem with socialism as we see it practiced abroad is not just that it hates private business in general, but that it hates some private businesses far less than others. Crony capitalism is the statist habit of farming out government concessions to friends and fellow travelers who spout the same revolutionary slogans, or who promise bribes or jobs to their particular government overseers. We would have more readily believed Barack Obama's Wall Street populism had he not been the largest recipient of Wall Street cash in presidential history, and Goldman Sachs's largest political beneficiary.

So when immigration law is unenforced; when an arbitrary $20-billion punitive payout is mandated from BP; when some creditors are deemed more important than others; when some states are sued for racism, but cases against racist individuals are dropped—then a general impression takes hold among business people that it is safer to lie low and avoid the gaze of government—lest a particular law be applied in punitive fashion.

Why is this recovery L-shaped? It is not just what Barack Obama has done, but far more what he most certainly would like to do in the future. When business people look at the confiscatory government in Venezuela, crony capitalism in Russia and China, democratic socialism in Greece, and sky-high taxes in most of the European Union, they do not see a connection between those policies and individual prosperity and freedom. So even the faintest hint that America is no longer exceptionally at odds with state-run systems, but may in fact wish to emulate them, simply stuns private enterprise into inaction.

That is mostly where we are now, as an unpopular president tries to convince the wary, time-out private sector that what he said so emphatically in the past is now not quite what he really meant to say.

Good luck with that.

AUGUST 27, 2010

The Sources of American Anger

Barack Obama, the great healer, is proving to be the most divisive president since Richard Nixon.

Behind the anger over the Arizona immigration mess, the Ground Zero mosque, the economy, and the new directions in foreign policy are some recurring general themes that reverberate in each particular new controversy. In sum, they explain everything from the tea parties to the wholly negative perception of Congress to the slide in presidential popularity.

1. Two sets of rules. The public senses there are two standards in

America—one for elite overseers, quite another for the supposedly not-to-be-trusted public. The anger over this hypocrisy surfaces over matters from the trivial to the profound. Sometimes the pique arises because the spread-the-wealth, we-all-have-skin-in-shared-sacrifice presidential sermons don't apply to those who do the preaching, as in the president's serial polo-shirted golf excursions or Michelle's movable feast from Marbella to Martha's Vineyard.

More profoundly, an Al Gore, a Timothy Geithner, a John Kerry, a John Edwards, a Charles Rangel—the luminaries who call for bigger government, higher taxes, and more green coercion—now appear to the public as disingenuous, living lives in abject contradiction to the utopian bromides they would apply to others.

So too with the media. The opinion makers at a failing New York Times, Newsweek, or CBS lost readers and viewers not just because of changing technologies, but because of incessant editorializing in which the educated and affluent, the winners in our system, berated the less educated and less well off, the strugglers in our system, as bigoted or selfish or both. How, for example, can Americans be asked to pay higher power bills in a recession to subsidize wind power, when the green Kennedy clan worries about windmills marring its vacation-spot view?

2. The bigot card. In reductionist terms, the public now accepts that when particular groups fail to win a 51 percent majority on a particular issue, they resort to invoking racism and prejudice—odd, when candidate Obama promised a new climate of unity and tolerance. Moreover, that disturbing trend has something to do with the president himself, who has injected racial grievance into everything from the Skip Gates controversy to the debate over the Arizona immigration law.

When the open-borders interests, or the gay-marriage advocates, or the adherents of the Ground Zero mosque cannot convince a majority of Americans that their agenda bodes well for the country, they almost instinctively fall back on the charge that America is xenophobic, homophobic, or Islamophobic. Yet the public infers that these charges reflect sour grapes rather than honest analysis: Had Arizona legislators or California voters supported the progressive agenda, then, as with the 2008 Obama victory, they would have been praised in Newsweek and on NPR for their moral sense and compassion. In short, the bigot card has played itself out and is now not much more than a political ploy to win an argument through calumny when logic and persuasion have failed.

3. The law? What law? Americans accept that they cannot pass legislation in violation of the Constitution. But they do not believe that a single judge can nullify the electoral will of millions without good cause. Thus in Arizona and California, there is a sense that judges who favor open borders or gay marriage are willing to use the pretense of constitutional issues to enact such agendas despite their current unpopularity. In a general landscape in which contractual obligations are nullified, as in the Chrysler bailout, and punitive fines are imposed quite arbitrarily, as in the BP cleanup, many believe the Obama administration applies the law in terms of perceived social utility. What is deemed best for the country by an elite few is what the law must be molded and changed to advance.

If there are, for example, not sufficient votes in the Congress to pass amnesty through legislative means, why not bypass federal law through a cabinet officer's executive fiat?

4. The futility of taxes. We talk of returning to the Clinton income-tax schedules. Yet in the late 1990s, those hikes ended up, along with the Republican cuts in mandates, balancing the budget—without new health-care surcharges, or talk of a VAT, or caps lifted off income subject to Social Security taxes. Not now. The public recognizes that the advocates of higher taxes are not willing to make the sort of across-the-board spending cuts that once succeeded in balancing the budget. In other words, those who will start paying much more of their income to the government in the form of taxes fret that, unlike the 1990s, this time the additional federal revenue won't balance the budget, and will be all for naught.

Worse still are two corollaries. First, we are in a ceaseless spiral in which each new tax increase will lead to justifications for more spending and thus to still higher taxes. Public employees, fairly or not, have morphed in the public mind from civil servants to pigs at the salary and pension trough, and from disinterested government workers to members of a liberal social movement that will perpetuate a federal agenda of race, class, and gender politics and higher taxes through payback bloc voting at the polls.

Second, there is a growing suspicion that this administration believes in a "gorge the beast" philosophy, the antithesis of Reagan's "starve the beast."

In other words, redistribution may be a desired end in and of itself. If greater spending demands higher taxes, perhaps that is socially preferable, since income is an arbitrary construct predicated on some sort of social injustice. In turn, the remedy demands that the federal government impose an equality of result to correct the inequities of the cavalier free market that so unfairly pays some too much and others too little.

In short, are our taxes not merely paying for federal expenditures, but also quite justifiably serving to confiscate income that we did not rightfully earn?

5. Disingenuousness. There is also a growing belief that the Obama administration is advancing an agenda that it cannot be fully candid about, because that agenda does not command broad support. As a result, we are habitually asked to believe that what administration appointees or supporters say is not what they really mean, or at least was taken out of context.

Justice Sotomayor did not really mean that wise Latinas make better judges than white males. Van Jones did not really mean that George W. Bush was in on 9/11, or that white youths are more likely to be mass murderers, or that whites are chronic polluters of the ghetto. Eric Holder no more meant that Americans are cowards than one of Anita Dunn's heroes really is the mass-murdering Mao. We should not believe that the top priority of the head of NASA is to advance Islamic outreach, or that the president himself thinks that police routinely act stupidly, stereotype, or arrest innocent people on their way to get their kids some ice cream. Imam Rauf did not really say that we created bin Laden, or that we kill more innocent Muslims than al-Qaeda kills innocent non-Muslims.

All this dissimulation started with the Rev. Jeremiah Wright, whose mistake was not saying the outrageous things he said—Mr. Obama and the compliant media had contextualized his corpus of hate well enough—but finally insulting the media at the National Press Club. The former was seen as a misdemeanor; the latter proved a felony.

Do Obama supporters, then, reveal their true beliefs only in gaffes and unguarded moments, while filling their official statements and communiqués with pretense?

6. A culpable America? Finally, the public has added up the apology tours, the bowing, and the constant emphasis on race, class, and gender crimes, and concluded that this administration sees America, past and present, as the story of a culpable majority denying noble minorities their rights—period.

In addition, Obama and his crew see America in isolation, without comparison to the wretchedness that exists in so much of the world outside our borders. So a logical disconnect is never quite explained. If America is so xenophobic and culpable, why would millions of Mexicans or Middle Eastern Muslims wish to immigrate here—and what exactly is America doing to attract them that their own countries are not? If Michelle Obama felt that she could not be proud of America before Barack Obama's accession, was it the free-market system that both provoked her ire and created the capital for her to jet to Marbella?

In other words, with the race/class/gender critique of the Obamians comes very little appreciation of the bounty, freedom, and affluence that they so eagerly embrace. Surely someone in the past—perhaps even white males—must have been doing something right for America to evolve into a place that our present-day critics apparently enjoy.

How will all this play out?

There are many millions of Americans who have a rising stake either in receiving reallocated federal money or in administering its distribution. For nearly half a century, the public schools have been telling millions of children that America's preeminence is ill-gotten, based largely on exploitation of less fortunate others, here and abroad. So the country is divided, and a president claiming to be the great healer of our age is proving to be the most divisive chief executive since Richard Nixon—and, in the view of an increasing majority of Americans, by his own intent.

SEPTEMBER 15, 2010

Obama's Washington Animal Farm

If you make more than $250,000 a year,
you're greedy and undeserving—unless
you're addressed as Mr. President.

S ince the moment he announced his presidential candidacy, Barack Obama hs waged a tireless, now four-year-long spread-the-wealth campaign against the more affluent.

He drew his mythical them/us line at $250,000 in annual income: If you went into the dark territory above that level, all sorts of promised punishments would kick in. At various times his administration has called for higher income taxes on this group, health-care surcharges, and removing the caps on income subject to Social Security payroll taxes—all to be added to higher state and local taxes. And, of course, higher capital-gains and inheritances taxes as well.

The president is not interested in nuances. He does not care that 40 percent of Americans pay no income taxes, or that the top 1 percent of earners pay 40 percent of aggregate collected income-tax revenue. Yet many of the people in these brackets were not always so rich and probably won't be for long. Top incomes are transient. Millions of Americans strive to reach them for a few years to provide for retirement, or college expenses, in the expectation that they will fade quickly. A quarter of a million dollars in annual compensation is great money in North Dakota, rather less so in Manhattan or the Bay Area.

Furthermore, most of these upper-income earners are the owners of small businesses, which simply calibrate proposed taxes in terms of money not available to hire employees and buy equipment. In contrast, the president assumes that a hardware-store owner or a small manufacturer already concedes that he makes too much money. The idea seems to be that, in penance, he will cut his profit margin and, for the public good, will gladly pay more of what profits remain to an Ivy League technocracy that knows far better than he how to spend his ill-gotten revenue on others more deserving.

Obama, the supposedly savvy politician, oddly has little appreciation of the psychology of business. Millions of job creators still have only a vague idea of the net effect of Obama's policies—except that they will probably mean less profits, and they are being enacted in a punitive spirit for past sins.

Obama's policies are also seen as malleable and predicated on notions of social justice rather than on absolute adherence to the law—as in the reordering of the Chrysler creditors and the recent threats against health insurers who do not toe the federal line. Employers are human. Call them greedy, undeserving of their profits, and prone to party at Vegas—and in hurt they will sit on their money and wait such castigation out.

There also seems to be little appreciation of how one creates wealth—not surprising, since Obama and his economic architects are mostly salaried elitists who have spent much of their lives on various tenured government payrolls. Almost none were entrepreneurs who had built businesses from nothing.

The result is that Obama has little insight into the mentality of a businessperson, whose values and world view are antithetical to those of the salaried and tenured employee who accepts stability and a monthly check as he does the changing of the seasons. But to the self-employed, the world is an often hostile place in which a bad back, a chance fire, an unethical employee, a wrong guess, or a national recession can destroy years of hard work in a blink.

Nor do the Obamians appreciate that the possibilities for wealth creation are infinite: The more rewards the audacious see, the more they take risks to turn ideas into new products and services. That energy enriches us all. Instead, there is now the return of the old peasant mentality of a limited good. With a finite pie, one slice to someone must mean one less to someone else. The relative wealth of a few, not absolute wealth for all, is what matters.

Implicit here is Obama's progressive notion that wealth is unfairly allotted, ill gotten, and ill spent, and therefore should not be entirely one's own. Surgeons in countries without socialized medicine, he has told us, make money by gratuitously slicing off limbs or ripping out tonsils. High earners can go to Vegas or the Super Bowl without thinking twice about it, given the superfluity of their riches. "I do think at a certain point you've made enough money," the president pontificates—a variation on his earlier lament that the Supreme Court had never demanded "redistributive change." Where that "certain point" rests, we do not know, though we suspect it is high enough to allow vacationing at the Costa del Sol and Martha's Vineyard.

In his mind, government simply cannot allow one person to make $10 an hour digging a ditch, and another $300 an hour sitting behind a desk closing a deal. The old tragic justifications of the inequality in compensation inherent in capitalism—one rises up the job chain, and recompense is not rigid and fixed; the successful entrepreneur takes more risk, may have greater skills and education, can create more wealth for others, is luckier, more motivated, or healthier, accepts more stress, does not necessarily want the more moral or enjoyable life—mean little to the therapeutic Obama. His Manichean world is fixed: suspect rich and noble poor.

As a materialist he judges equity in life by income. Thus he sees the government's proper moral obligation not as ensuring equality out of the starting gate, but as guaranteeing that we all reach the finish line at the same exact moment.

Abroad, this same notion of enforced equality explains our new foreign policy. The bowing, the apologies, the contextualization of America as neither exceptional nor especially moral, the cold shoulder to Europe and the emphasis on the Pacific and on the Arab and Muslim worlds—all that assumes an anti-imperialist and anti-capitalist world view.

Abroad, as at home, wealth is not a result of risk, luck, talent, or mastery of capitalist practices. A nation is not necessarily wealthy or poor depending on the degree to which it adopts proven successful formulas that ensure private property rights, transparency in the judicial and financial sectors, free markets, low taxes, sober accounting practices, consensual government, separation between religion and state, and meritocracy in lieu of tribal preference.

Most students of such matters know all this to be true as they com-
pare South Korea with its northern counterpart, the old East Germany
with the old West Germany, Cubans in Miami with those in Cuba,
China in the 1960s with the country of the new millennium, an oil-poor
Chile with an oil-rich Venezuela, or free-market Israel with statist
Egypt. Not Obama.

In contrast, in his view, oppression and exploitation better explain
wealth and poverty. The United States is wealthy largely because of
profits from past exploitation—slavery, racism, class prejudice, theft of
land from Native Americans, and robber-baron policies abroad that
stole the resources of other nations. We owe the world contrition, not
guidance about how to emulate our success.

Once again, in the peasant view of a limited world, wealth is finite:
If we have three-car families, people in a basket case like Zimbabwe
pay for our excess by having none. To suggest that Zimbabwe's problems are entirely its own doing, and are not connected to post-colonial
trauma or to exploitative wealth creation by the West—and that with
radical social, cultural, political and economic changes Zimbabwe
could easily be another Switzerland (which lacks Zimbabwe's natural
resources)—is to reject almost all that Obama has learned from his
teachers and friends, and as an astute navigator in the world of identity
politics.

Finally, note that crucial to this equality-of-result world view is the
notion of exemption. Where Michelle chooses to vacation, how many
holes of golf Barack plays, what sort of home they insist on buying,
how they travel abroad and the influence they enjoy as emissaries of a
wealthy capitalist United States—all this is not contradictory to what is
so easily mandated for others.

Our progressive elites are educated almost as gods. They are
prepped to bring about change for less astute and sensitive others. To
the degree they are accorded and enjoy privilege, it is simply a necessary means to an end—better homes, transportation, leisure, and material appurtenances are not matters of enjoyment, but are the needed
tools to more efficiently enact social change. A tax-avoided $7 million
Kerry yacht allows the anointed senator the necessary recharging to
repeal the pernicious Bush tax cuts that "those" over $250,000 enjoy at

the expense of others. The restorative sanctuary of a John Edwards or Al Gore mansion is integral to obtaining social justice or a greener future for the less privileged.

The new technocracy need not worry over an embarrassing Marbella vacation (why not stay at the UAW's vacation compound in Michigan?). There is no contradiction in a bloated public sector far better compensated and pensioned than its private counterpart. Persistent tax cheating by members of Congress, and by grandees like a tax-raising Treasury Secretary Geithner or would-be HHS secretary Tom Daschle, is merely a series of accounting errors.

To expect otherwise would be to ask the indoor pigs of Animal Farm not to don clothes and walk on two legs as they sacrificed to ensure that the animals outside the farmhouse window were properly equal—or else.

SEPTEMBER 22, 2010

Obama's Glass House

America's discontent may stem in part from suspecting that the administration thinks we're stupid, fearful, cowardly racists.

P reachers and professors have it hard as presidents. They sermonize too much. Finally the public gets tired of being lectured by those whom they increasingly see as no more upright than themselves. Prophets crumble from feet of clay, and stones shatter glass houses. So it was with Woodrow Wilson and Jimmy Carter, and so it is now with Barack Obama.

The Obama administration is throwing stones at a lot of people—John Boehner, Republicans, tea-partiers, Fox News, Glenn Beck, doctors, insurers, Wall Street, and business in general.

Such invective invites a response, and here the White House is becoming as fragile as glass. We saw that recently in the presidential petulance at supposedly being talked about "like a dog," and in a touchy press secretary Robert Gibbs unloading at everyone from Rush Limbaugh to Forbes magazine.

Last February, Attorney General Eric Holder, self-appointed racial philosopher as well as the nation's chief law-enforcement officer, lectured his fellow Americans: "In things racial, we have always been and continue to be, in too many ways, essentially a nation of cowards." Professor Holder went on to complain that "certain subjects are off limits and that to explore them risks at best embarrassment and at worst the questioning of one's character."

Fair enough: Most Americans would be willing to engage Holder in his desired racial seminar—if it were two-sided, and did not devolve into something like the imbroglio over Harvard professor Henry Louis Gates. Before even hearing the facts of that case, remember, the president of the United States, as arbiter of racial relations on campus as well as commander-in-chief, rushed to condemn the Cambridge police for acting "stupidly" and then accused law-enforcement officers in general of racial stereotyping.

In contrast, did Eric Holder's proposed conversation include questions of welfare dependency, anti-social cultural messages, or lack of personal responsibility—in addition to racism—to explain much higher than average rates of illegitimacy, illiteracy, failure to graduate from high school, and criminal behavior among some minority groups?

So far, Holder himself has never dared to raise such "off-limits" controversial issues. Yet in the case of the Arizona immigration statute, the attorney general was hardly so reluctant. He lambasted the legislation as "unfortunate," possibly unconstitutional, and leading to racial stereotyping—all before he had even read the law. Cowardly?

Recently, Michelle Obama advised Americans to eat better foods to combat the national epidemic of obesity. She envisions using government power to teach restaurants how to restructure their menus, and helping targeted communities with federal money to improve their collective diets.

Fair enough once more: As a nation we are probably too fat, and First Ladies often seek to better the American condition. But as in the Holder case, does the First Lady, as first professor and preacher, really wish to lecture the American people on their personal sins and to follow that up with federal programs and expenditures? If the issue is to promote better health by using the bully pulpit of the First Family in symbolic fashion, then Michelle Obama might first more quietly start at home with her errant husband.

The presidential role model is secretively a chain smoker—a habit that promotes both heart disease and cancer, and kills millions of Americans each year. At almost every photo op, President Obama is enjoying hot dogs, ice cream, and beer. The president deserves a private life, and his smoking and consumption of fatty foods are his business alone—unless his spouse is suggesting simultaneously that the rest of us must not only avoid such behavior, but seek to fund and institutionalize its antithesis. A voter might well respond to the First Lady's lectures on diet with something like, "First convince the first husband to stop smoking and to eat better, and then I'll listen to your advice about my own diet." Otherwise one might conclude that smoking can keep down weight as effectively as restricting one's diet can. Such are the wages of a White House of "Do as I say, not as I do."

We saw more of this disconnect between sermons and behavior when the president lectured us that in rough times we all had to cut back: "Everybody's going to have to give. Everybody's going to have to have some skin in the game." Apparently that did not mean giving up one's vacation at Martha's Vineyard or the Costa del Sol. Lectures have consequences.

Businesses and banks are increasingly criticized for not hiring and lending while they're sitting on trillions of dollars in cash. Both charges—made by the administration and the unions—are true. But does greed and self-interest alone explain these organizations' reluctance to spread their wealth to others?

Maybe private companies were stung by the Obama administration's reordering of the creditors in the Chrysler bankruptcy case. Or maybe their hesitancy derives from the serial anti-business references during the Gulf oil-spill disaster, such as the ones about putting a boot on BP's neck and forcing it to cough up $20 billion in clean-up costs. Or maybe it has something to do with the stereotyping of insurers and doctors as greedy. Or with the refrain about suspect earners who make over $250,000, and who thus owe the rest of us higher income taxes and health-care surcharges.

Again, our average voter might respond, "If you want a two-way conversation on recovery, why not question the unions' anti-democratic tendencies, haphazard productivity, and inflexibility, or the tax avoidance of allies like Charles Rangel, Chris Dodd, Maxine Waters, and dozens of White House staffers, or the mismanagement of Fannie Mae and Freddie Mac, the wasted stimulus, or the new bureaucratic empires that can only hamper commerce?"

Then we come to radical Islam. The president weighed in repeatedly on the so-called Ground Zero mosque. Here too he wishes to use the symbolic prestige of his office to offer a teachable moment about a local controversy. But to play sermonizer-in-chief requires at least appearing fair-minded.

At various times, the president misrepresented the disagreement as one of legality rather than of taste and common decency. Obama finally implied that his illiberal opponents were lashing out at Islam because of rough economic times—reminiscent of his earlier psychoanalyzing of rural Pennsylvanians who voted against him in the primaries supposedly out of fear of immigrants and those "not like them" rather than because of opposition to the policies he was promising to implement.

When Mr. Abdulmutallab tried to blow up a Detroit-bound airliner, we first heard that he had "allegedly" done so—the same sort of tentativeness we witnessed in the president's first interview with Al Arabiya. There he suggested that American problems with Islam were due in part to past American policies and presidents. In the Cairo speech, one would have thought Córdoba—a Western city conquered by invading Muslims—was a modern-day Amsterdam rather than a typical medieval city in which the dominant religion forced other faiths to pay obeisance.

So an enlightened president likes to lecture less-informed Americans that Muslims are not more likely than other people to promote, or be silent about, radical Islamic terror. Again, fair enough.

But is he as worried about the reality that, of the 31 major foiled terrorist attacks against the United States since 9/11, all of them involved Muslims? Again, our mythical voter might say something to the effect that "I will be careful to honor the right of Muslims to build a $100 million mosque near Ground Zero if you will at least ask the Muslim community to condemn Western Muslims who keep trying to kill those about them."

The terrorist impulse simply does not abate. We saw it most recently in Britain, when police broke up a plot by Algerian immigrants to kill Pope Benedict—who four years ago was a target of Muslim death threats for quoting a Byzantine text. Americans know that even as the president lectures them about being intolerant of Muslims, additional Islamist plots to kill them will be uncovered—and will probably not earn as much presidential moralizing as the Ground Zero mosque.

When an attorney general, a first lady, and a president offer lectures to the American people about their purported unfounded fears, bad habits, and prejudices, like any sermonizer they invite reciprocal scrutiny, both about their own conduct and about the fairness of their critiques. As a result, a stone-throwing White House is becoming a shattered Glass House.

SEPTEMBER 29, 2010

Carly Fiorina: Robber Baron, Traitor—and Outsourcer!

If we still had a well-educated workforce and reasonable taxation and regulation, outsourcing wouldn't be the wedge issue it is.

One of Sen. Barbara Boxer's sharpest charges against challenger Carly Fiorina is that, as CEO of Hewlett-Packard, she allowed thousands of jobs to be outsourced overseas—depriving U.S. workers of income while piling up profits for executive grandees like herself.

Outsourcing of both manufacturing and service jobs has become a wedge issue. It stings especially when times are tough. By Election Day, outsourcing will be portrayed as equivalent to child-molesting in its depravity. But the charge of greed and lack of economic patriotism is disingenuous for a variety of reasons.

Remember that outsourcing can be insidious—it knows no political bounds. When presidential candidate Sen. John Kerry once equated outsourcing with treason by promising to go after "any Benedict Arnold CEO or company [that moves] jobs overseas," he was forgetting that his wife's billion-dollar-plus fortune and thus his own luxury power boat were derived from the profits of the American-based H. J. Heinz Company, which made such gargantuan profits in part because it moved dozens of its American operations all over the globe. Take the most liberal icons of the business world—from Bill Gates to George Soros—and you will find ownerships of, or investments in, American companies that outsource production overseas.

Second, is there something called "insourcing" to explain why a Toyota or a Honda relocates plants to the United States, depriving Japanese workers of high-paying jobs in order to maximize profits for its corporate hierarchy? When Mercedes opens an American car-making plant, are we supposed to applaud a foreign company's hiring our workers and attempting to share some of its success with the homeland of its customers or lament the loss of German jobs? Mercedes is a hero to us but a traitor to Germany?

Do we complain that China and India seem to have outsourced most of their higher-education responsibilities—from engineering PhDs to MBAs for CEOs—to American universities? And in turn are we even angrier that a number of American universities are opening branch campuses in China and the Middle East—depriving Americans of both staff and instructional jobs—to better capitalize on this new global market in higher education? Are there Japanese Barbara Boxers demanding an end to Nissan plants in the American South or Indian populists running Boxer-like campaigns by crying to stop sending Indian talent to be educated at an outrageously expensive Yale?

So apparently the problem is not so much shipping some jobs overseas, but shipping more jobs out than are shipped in. Or does the anger arise because we draw in foreign capital for our own labor in some areas, but not enough in others to balance it out? Should we worry that we are assembling some American-designed printers overseas or be relieved that we are taking over more and more of the intricate manufacturing of the most sophisticated jumbo jets in the world?

In other words, no one knows exactly all the real costs and benefits of outsourcing, or how to turn the equation to our sole advantage, or why we seem to do well in one area, but not so well in another, or whether outsourcing helps many of the very developing countries that buy our American-designed products. When we fail to beat the competition in high-end, highly skilled manufacturing, then we turn to damn those who sometimes outsource the fabrication of products that require less skill.

Neither a Democratic nor a Republican president has been able to reverse the ongoing trade deficit. As Senator Boxer damns the outsourcing of Hewlett-Packard jobs, she offers little in the way of concrete answers as to how to stop it. Would she raise tariffs on imported goods (in expectation that other countries would not retaliate), or pressure a dollar-rich China to kindly devalue its Yuan and politely quit its mercantilist policies, as both Bill Clinton and George W. Bush tried but failed to do? Or perhaps she could reverse her stance on the cutoff of California water deliveries, increase the acreage of the state's productive farms, and thereby win back more jobs for California as America was again able to export agricultural products as it once did?

Democrats privately know that free trade and cheap manufacturing abroad result in cheap consumer goods at places like Walmart and Home Depot, which expands the purchasing power of the strapped American consumer. Republicans stress that in the open arena of trade, the more competition, the more pressure on American firms to stay lean and turn out better products at lower costs.

One reason why a Hewlett-Packard, or an Apple or a Microsoft, is so successful is that the skilled engineering, administration, and financing of such global high-profit operations draw on unique American talent and labor, while the often less-skilled fabrication of the resulting consumer goods is in part outsourced to places where labor regulations, wages, and attitudes tend to be very non-American. Would we prefer it the other way around—$100,000-a-year Chinese engineers traveling to

San Jose or Gilroy to teach our unskilled workers how to assemble their hot-selling, freshly designed electronic gadgets at the rate of $1 an hour?

Because we do not wish to lower wages to China's levels, or emulate the working conditions of Mexico—or see our companies go bankrupt with goods priced well over unforgiving global going rates—the only answer is upping the value of American labor and skill sets. That way we can continue to design the world's top appurtenances, and to figure out the practical problems of their fabrication, while allowing the less-skilled labor of developing countries to put the actual product together—and we can do that to such an overwhelming degree that we keep everyone from design engineers to accountants to manual writers employed at very high wages. They in turn can afford to pay everyone from hard-working baby-sitters to carpenters to restaurant workers wages that are likewise well over the global norm.

But such an idea requires that Americans encourage business innovation, ensure the world's most educated and flexible work force, and create a tax climate where productivity is encouraged rather than punished. All of that would require a radical change in the political class's understanding of the effects of taxation and regulation. It would also require radical changes in American education—questioning the ethics of teachers' unions, reconsidering ossified ideas like tenure, and junking an increasingly uncompetitive and therapeutic school curriculum.

Instead, at present—given a radical divergence in work ethics, wages, and business climates—there is a reason why most foreign automobile manufacturers that locate here do so in the South rather than near Detroit. European or Asian high-tech firms go to places like North Carolina's Research Triangle and California's Silicon Valley, where the local schools ensure a competent work force, and not to rural California, where school test scores are at or near the bottom of the country in math and English.

But again, all of that is too complicated for a Barbara Boxer. Instead, outsourcing is demagogued as greed versus liberality, patriotism versus treason. The subtext is the looking-glass notion that our middle-class and poor citizens must be able to buy iPods and DVDs at Walmart at rock-bottom prices, while we demand that the workers who manufacture them get paid over $20 an hour.

Like it or not, globalization has done away with such fantasies, especially the notion of a privileged U.S. populace that by birthright deserves its exalted position. From here on out, our lifestyles and our very futures hinge on our collective productivity, innovation, and imagination. If we still had the best educated and most highly skilled work force, the most productive work ethic, the most business-friendly environment, and the most responsive and fiscally sound government, then a flexible and constantly changing America would always be creating high-end jobs for its citizens, well ahead of the competition, with little worry over the fact that some lower-end tasks of assembling consumer products at times might migrate elsewhere.

Anger over outsourcing is thus a symptom of a larger malaise. Our politicians assume that Americans deserve both cheap consumer products and high-wage manufacturing jobs—and that we will get both because Americans are the best educated and most productive workers in the world, and our managers and designers operate in the most fertile business and intellectual environment on the planet.

The current financial and political climate suggests that is not quite any longer true. So anger follows when unemployment is over 12 percent in a bankrupt state like California. On cue, in comes a railing Barbara Boxer—whose policies had a lot to do with punishing taxes, layers of government red tape, and therapeutic education—charging that Hewlett-Packard built some things overseas when it could not make a profit doing so here.

If that is to be the analysis of and solution for outsourcing, then California and this country will see far worse days ahead.

OCTOBER 6, 2010

The Gift of Obama's Foreign Policy

As the antithesis of Bush is learning, foreign dictators are likely to bite the hand that strokes them.

The Obama reset foreign policy has, in an unintended way, brought clarity to America's traditional role in the world. After 2004, "blame Bush" proved an easy way for Europeans and American liberals to delude themselves into thinking the world's problems neither predated nor transcended George W. Bush: Tensions arose, America was at fault, Bush was the culprit, presto! Remove Bush, elect his antithesis, and a natural state of calm would return.

But suddenly Barack Obama's brief tenure has reminded us that, in fact, almost all the world's crises arose before the Bush presidency and continued during and after it. Examine current American foreign policy toward every region, and one of three general patterns emerges: Either things are no better since the end of 2008, or they are much worse, or the Obama administration has reverted to the Bush way of doing things—despite constant assurances to the world that Bush was at fault, American foreign policy was now reset, and global animosity arose out of past misunderstanding, insensitivity, and American hubris.

Take first our most vocal and overt enemies. Fidel Castro, after a few mixed messages, is still recycling his 1960s anti-American boilerplate. Syria's Bashar al-Assad is cementing relations with Iran and Hezbollah, and doing nothing to help matters either in Iraq or in the Mideast generally, despite being assured by Obama that he can do business with someone who is not "smoke 'em out" George Bush.

North Korea's unhinged rhetoric and occasional missile or torpedo shots escalate. Hugo Chávez is becoming more authoritarian and more anti-American the more he need no longer call Bush a devil. Iran's Mahmoud Ahmadinejad told the world at the United Nations that the United States might well have planned to kill the 3,000 of its own citizens who died on Sept. 11, 2001; apparently the tired American apologies for the removal of Mossadeq nearly sixty years ago still do not register.

Note that in each of these instances, appeasement—failing to support the Iranian freedom protestors, ignoring the abuses of the Cuban and Syrian totalitarian regimes, and keeping silent about the destruction of democracy in Venezuela—has resulted in even more animus, just as appeasement of the unhinged and dictatorial always does. One might almost conclude that dictatorships hate American freedom, the global stature and power of the United States, and our propensity to oppose aggrandizement, and that they do not much care who happens in any given year to be in the White House.

Then there are the big four. China is more confident today in confronting the Japanese and its other neighbors in the Pacific. It sees no obstacle to being the new ascendant power, flexing its growing muscles as Japan did in the 1920s, and imperial Germany at the turn of the 20th century (and we know how all that ended up). Turkey wishes to become the new Ottoman Empire, and it sees the United States as largely indifferent to its ambitions, and perhaps even quietly sympathetic. Relations with India are no better than they were under Bush, and perhaps less friendly. Russia, in contrast, seems to be quite fond of the Obama administration—to the degree it is given concessions in return for empty promises. It weighs the downside of having a nuclear Islamic Iran in its neighborhood against the upside of having such a rogue state, which, at least in the short term, is more a problem for America than for Russia. Chaos in the Middle East, Putin knows well, is always good for the oil business.

Pressuring Israel did not bring any Middle Eastern breakthrough. To the extent that there has not been another intifada, it is largely a result of a mini economic boom on the West Bank, which continues despite, rather than because of, American negotiating.

Are our other allies—like Japan, South Korea, and Europe—suddenly much more friendly owing to Obama's hope-and-change proclamations? Not really. All, for the first time in 60 years, have some suspicion that just maybe the sort of liberal American administration that they have so longed for might not be as ready as past administrations to come to their aid in the next crisis. Certainly, we have spent far more effort in winning over Putin than emphasizing our old alliances with Germany, France, and Britain. Japan and South Korea are starting to sense that their respective Communist rivals, China and North Korea, will soon become more their own problems than ours.

The situations in Iraq and Afghanistan are now simply evolutions of the policies that George Bush had established when he left office. The "bad" war in Iraq that Obama campaigned against has become a better war than the "good" one in Afghanistan that he had hoped was over by virtue of NATO and U.N. approval.

Despite Obama's interview with Al Arabiya, his Cairo speech, and his editorializing about the Ground Zero mosque, there has been no letup in radical Islamists' efforts to kill us at home, as we saw in the cases of Major Hasan, Abdulmutallab, and the would-be Times Square bomber. What good Obama has achieved by resonating more effectively with the Middle East's tired and poor is offset perhaps by the impression, fair or not, among would-be terrorists that he would not quite be as unpredictable and dangerous as past presidents, should there be another 9/11-like attack. As far as Muslim sensitivities go, serially promising to close Guantanamo Bay seems no better than quietly keeping it open.

Why, then, is the Obama reset policy a positive development?

Obama's efforts, and the global reactions to them, are reminding the world that global tensions still arise out of perceptions of self-interest, regardless of who is in the White House. When nations act contrary to American interests, they can be finessed somewhat by empathetic American officials, but they remain largely unaffected by apologies, bowing, promulgations of pseudo-history, and therapeutic mythologizing. Leaders like Putin, Assad, and Ahmadinejad act in their own perceived self-interests, calibrating to what degree a constant desire to maximize influence, stature, and wealth at someone else's expense is balanced by the risk of any confrontations that might ensue and the possibility that they might lose—all such calculations being more likely when the players are, like these three, autocratic in nature.

In the end, Obama's Carteresque sermonizing over the past two years has achieved the opposite of its intended result. The preaching, confessionals, and outreach, from the ridiculous bowing to Saudi princes to the supposedly sublime Cairo mythmaking, have reminded the world that anti-Americanism transcends alike the unfair caricatures of George Bush and the hokey apotheosis of Barack Obama. If we can avoid the wages of this naïveté—and not suffer another annus horribilis in the fashion of 1979—then Obama's inadvertent primer on unchanging human nature will have been worth it.

OCTOBER 6, 2010

How to Turn a Recession Into a Depression

Destroy business confidence, cozy up to socialists abroad, send deficits through the ceiling— that should do it.

I t is hard for a president to turn a recession into a long-term downturn in the United States, given the inherent resiliency of private enterprise and America's open and free markets. But if you were to try, you might do something like the following.

First, propose all sorts of new taxes. Float trial balloons about even more on the horizon. Subordinates should whisper about a VAT/national sales tax. Other aides should revisit campaign talk about lifting the caps on income subject to payroll taxes. A centerpiece of the effort would be to insist on bringing back the Clinton income-tax rates—but this time targeting only high earners and not putting commensurate caps on federal spending. For insurance in making things worse, raise capital-gains taxes. And why not add a new health-care tax surcharge? Let inheritance taxes kick back in. Hope that the states do their synergistic part by raising their own taxes at the same time. The trick is to dissuade businesses from taking risks, by making clear that any new profits are illegitimate and therefore will go to the government.

Second, business expansion is predicated on confidence in the future. Destroy that, and depression can become far easier to achieve. Often the decision to hire or to buy new equipment is psychological in nature—predicated on hope in the larger business climate. So to ruin that landscape, you might unleash a barrage of anti-business, anti-wealth rhetoric to remind job creators that they are already too rich from exploitative practices. The president himself might lead the attack against Wall Street, CEOs, doctors, and insurers. Now and then it would be wise to spice it up with a nice socialist quip such as "I do think at a certain point you've made enough money"—or digs about the wealthy needlessly jetting to the Super Bowl or Las Vegas. Try out lines like "keep the boot on their necks" and "know whose ass to kick." Turn Koch Industries in the public imagination into something akin to IG Farben. Make the Chamber of Commerce the equivalent of Enron. Create a pantheon of good capitalists like George Soros, Bill Gates, and Warren Buffett, who never speculate, hedge, or seek monopolies, and set them against bad ones like Charles and David Koch. Remember, the aim is to let businesses know on a very visceral level that you simply do not like them.

Third, create an artificial economic divide of them/us. Pick an arbitrary figure, say $250,000 in annual income. Families above that figure are suspect and need to pay far more of their ill-gotten gains in income taxes—their "fair share"—to "spread the wealth" and achieve "redistributive change." Once the capital of small businesses is demonized, they will either stop making any more or hide what they have. Either way, the economy fortunately slows.

Fourth, if one is really serious about undermining business confidence, then attack the very structure of law, statute, and custom. Reverse the legal order of creditors in the Chrysler bailout case to favor labor unions. Call the investors and creditors "speculators." Pick a big number—why not $20 billion?—for BP to fork over for the Gulf oil spill. Have your labor secretary go on record as saying that illegal immigration is not really illegal; e.g., "Every worker has a right to be paid fairly, whether documented or not." Sue the state of Arizona for trying to enforce immigration laws. Excuse sanctuary cities that openly flout such laws. Apologize to foreign governments, like the authoritarian Chinese, for Arizona, and then encourage other nations to join in on law suits against Americans. Again, the point is to fire a volley across the bow of businesses, letting them know that social awareness and progressive ideology trump strict enforcement of legal statute—and so they had better make the necessary adjustments.

Fifth, bring as many academics into the administration, and as few people from private enterprise, as possible. The point is to assure the private sector that those who are tenured and for most of their lives have been given guaranteed annual pay raises, who pontificate and theorize rather than create and build, will oversee their antitheses in the business community. Then just when their entire Keynesian blueprint is operative—have them all quit their jobs and return to places like Berkeley, Harvard, and the Council on Foreign Relations. If the image of hostility does not work in slowing down private enterprise, this impression of incompetence—and even cynicism—surely will.

Sixth, overregulation is a powerful tool for prompting a depression and should not be ignored. Promise to go well beyond passing cap-and-trade energy taxes ("an extraordinary first step"); convince businesses ("who can afford it") with "price signals" that if higher taxes cannot take all their profits, their new energy bills most certainly will. Again, the point is to assure the business community that all that pop socialist talk on the campaign trail was serious stuff. If the president once joshed that energy bills were going to rise dramatically, now in a recession is the time to remind employers that, in fact, they will. Dovetail new energy regulations with vast new health-care and financial regulations. Once again, the message is that the wasteful, cruel private sector must be corralled by the far better public sector.

Seventh, gorge the beast. Try to get annual federal deficits up to the $1.3—$1.5 trillion range. Reagan tried to "starve the beast"—that is, to lower federal spending by lowering taxes. Why not do the inverse and borrow so much money, pile up so much debt, that even fiscal hawks will concede that higher taxes are necessary? It is a win/win/win/win/win proposition: Bigger deficits mean more federal spending, which means more federal employees, who will find more regulations to impose, which will cost employers more money and require higher taxes.

Eighth, take over as many private businesses as possible, the bigger the better—auto manufacturers, banks, insurers. Heck, absorb the entire student-loan program while you're at it. Remind private businesses that their once-comfortable world of free-market capitalism isn't so free any more. Dream up a cash-for-clunkers program that destroys the used-car market and lets government borrow billions to buy up old automobiles. "You're next" is a valuable tool in warning businesses to keep a low profile and slow things down.

Ninth, do not forget to reset foreign policy. Let it be known that socialist systems abroad are no longer suspect. Reach out to Iran, Syria, Cuba, and Venezuela; snub free-market Israel and Colombia. Pick a fight with Germany over borrowing. Run down the value of the dollar. Talk about Keynesian deficits as a proper global model. Mimic the social policies of the European Union. Talk of protectionism and trade wars with China to come. Oppose free-trade agreements.

Tenth, assure businesses that they need more unions. Elevate the profile of the SEIU and ACORN. Get Andy Stern into the White House as much as possible. Make sure Hilda Solis over at Labor keeps up with those videos about exploited illegal aliens coming to her for help. Remind everyone how the UAW's pensions, wages, and benefits are now protected by Government Motors. Ensure that in campaign appeals you list special-interest groups—"black folks," young people, unions— to the deliberate exclusion of employers and businesses.

If this ten-step program were to be followed, we might just get unemployment up to near 10 percent, consumer confidence down to historical lows, food-stamp use to record highs, the dollar to a new low, and annual budget deficits at levels previously unimaginable. That way we will never waste a crisis, since all sorts of new possibilities open up once we turn a normal recession into a genuine old-fashioned depression.

CHAPTER NINE

WE ARE GOING TO MAKE IT

JULY 4, 2008

Reflection Day

These two truths should be self-evident.

O n this Fourth of July of our discontent—with spiraling fuel prices, a sluggish economy, a weak dollar, mounting foreign and domestic debt, continuing costs in Iraq, a falling stock market, and a mortgage crisis—we should remember two truths about America. First, the United States remains the most free and affluent country in the history of civilization. Second, almost all our problems are lapses of complacency, remain relatively easily correctable, and pale in comparison to past crises.

By almost any barometer, the United States remains the most fortunate country in the world. We continue to be the primary destination of immigrants, who risk their lives to have a chance at what we take for granted. Few in contrast are flocking to China, Russia, or India. The catalyst for immigration is primarily a phenomenon of word of mouth, of comparative talking among friends and families about the reality of modern-day living, not of scholarly perusal of social or economic statistics.

When one compares any yardstick of material wealth—the square footage of living space, the number of consumer appurtenances— Americans are the wealthiest people in the history of civilization. Why so? Others have more iron ore, as much farmland, greater populations, and far more oil reserves. But uniquely in America there remains a system of merit, under which we prosper or fail to a greater extent on the basis of talent, not tribal affiliations, petty bribes, or institutionalized insider help. More importantly still, we are impressed by those who advance rather than envious of their success. The lobster-barrel mentality is a human trait, but in the United States uniquely there is a culture of emulation rather than of resentment, which explains why neither Marxism nor aristocratic pretension ever became fully entrenched in America.

Our system of government remains the most stable and free. Consider the constitutional crises in Europe where national plebiscites continue to reject the European constitution that grows increasingly anti-democratic in order to force its vision of heaven-on-earth on its citizenry. There is no need to mention the politics of China, India, and Russia whose increasing affluence ensures a rendezvous with unionism, class concerns, suburban blues, minority rights, environmentalism—all long known and dealt with by the United States. Elsewhere the remedy for tribal and sectarian chaos in Africa or the Middle East is usually authoritarianism.

The current challenge of America is not starvation or loss of political rights—we have been far poorer and more unfree in our past, but the complacence that comes with continued success, to such a degree that we think of our bounty as a birthright rather than a rare gift that must be hourly maintained through commitment to the values that made us initially successful: high productivity, risk-taking, transparency, small government, personal freedom, concern for the public welfare, and a certain tragic rather than therapeutic view of the human experience.

In that regard, most of our present pathologies are self-created. In fits of utopianism we felt we could be perfect environmentalists, no longer develop our ample oil, coal, and nuclear resources, maintain our envied lifestyle, mouth platitudes about "alternative energies," and yet be immune from classical laws of supply and demand. In truth, with a little national will, within a decade we could both be using new sources of energy and producing our entire (and decreasing) appetite for oil without importation at all of foreign supplies. When our petroleum runs out, we will find other sources of energy; when a Saudi Arabia's or Venezuela's fail, so goes their entire national wealth as well.

Our budgetary laxity is a bipartisan stand-off in which free-spending pork-barrel Republicans mouth platitudes about reductions in spending while Democrats continue to vote for increased government programs, assured that either military cuts or tax increases will pay the tab. We still await some gifted statesman who will convince us that we

can increase revenues and cut spending without loss of essential gov-
ernmental services or oppressive taxes.

Iraq is expensive, but draws on a fraction of a $12 trillion economy;
for all the acrimony over the war, Iraq is stabilizing, al-Qaeda has been
discredited, and the notion of constitutional government in the heart of
the ancient caliphate is not longer caricatured as a neocon pipedream—
an accomplishment beyond the military of any other country.

Slumping house prices are a concern, but we forget that nearly 95
percent of homeowners meet their monthly mortgage payments, that
housing prices are merely returning to their 2002 levels—to the relief
of first-time potential buyers—that many of the problems were caused
by housing speculators who wished to flip properties for instant profits,
by overzealous lenders who warped the rules, and by misplaced liberalism that sought to put everyone in his own home, despite the historical fact that between 30 percent and 40 percent of the population either
should not, or does not wish to, own their homes.

Given the strength of our system and culture and our inherited values and wealth, as long as we don't tamper with our Constitution, a
uniquely American entrepreneurial culture, and the melting-pot notion
of shared values rather than balkanized tribes, races, and religions, we
can easily rectify our present mistakes without much reduction in our
soaring standard of living. In America alone—for all our periodic hysterical self-recrimination—there is still comparatively little danger of
coups, nationalization of foreign assets, crippling national strikes, sectarian violence, terrorism, suppression of free speech, or rampant government and judicial corruption that elsewhere lead to endemic violence and economic stagnation.

On this troubled Fourth we still should remember this is not 1776
when New York was in British hands and Americans in retreat across
the state. It is not 1814 when the British burned Washington and the
entire system of national credit collapsed—or July 4, 1864 when
Americans awoke to news that 8,000 Americans had just been killed at
Gettysburg.

We are not in 1932 when unemployment was still over 20 percent
of the work force, and industrial production was less than half of what
it had been just three years earlier, or July, 1942, when tens of thou-

sands of American were dying in convoys and B-17s, and on islands of the Pacific in an existential war against Germany, Japan, and Italy.

Thank God it is not mid-summer 1950, when Seoul was overrun and arriving American troops were overwhelmed by Communist forces as they rushed in to save a crumbling South Korea. We are not in 1968 when the country was torn apart by the Tet Offensive, the assassinations of Martin Luther King Jr. and Robert Kennedy, and the riots at the Democratic convention in Chicago. And we are not even in the waning days of 1979, a year in which the American embassy was seized in Tehran and hostages taken, the Soviets were invading Afghanistan, thousands were still being murdered in Cambodia, Communism was on the march in Central America, and our president was blaming our near 6-percent unemployment, 8-percent inflation, 15-percent interest rates, and weakening international profile on our own collective "malaise."

We live in the most prosperous and most free years of a wonderful republic, and can easily rectify our present crises that are largely of our own making and a result of the stupefying effects of our unprecedented wealth and leisure. Instead of endless recriminations and self-pity— of anger that our past was merely good rather than perfect as we now demand—we need to give thanks this Fourth of July to our ancestors who created our Constitution and Bill of Rights, and suffered miseries beyond our comprehension as they bequeathed to us most of the present wealth, leisure, and freedom we take for granted.

DECEMBER 30, 2008

A Year Like None Other

It usually takes decades to fit in all the tragicomedy of 2008.

T
he three great stories of 2008 were the financial meltdown, the turn-about in Iraq, and the Chicago Way. All of them conveyed a certain sense of the surreal—whether the vaporization of the nation's 401(k)s in a few hours, or Harvard Law School graduate Barney Frank asking Harvard Law School graduate Franklin Rains of the soon-to-be bankrupt Fannie Mae whether he felt under-regulated, or Tony Rezko making a cameo appearance in almost every Illinois scandal of the last decade.

What happened in mid-September not only destroyed the classical concept of trust and fair-dealing, but the entire Wall Street premise that those with MBAs from Ivy League business schools, or years of work with the SEC, or long tenure with brokerage houses with 19th-century pedigrees know anything. In other words, goodbye to all those titles and business cards. We are now back to hometown insurance agents and the local tow-truck driver offering just as insightful stock tips.

Greed and excess gave way to panic, as the primordial emotions broke free from their thin veneer of culture. Without a blink, we went back to 1929—the only difference being that the baby-boomer generation blames everyone but themselves, under oath and amid clicking cameras, rather than privately and quietly jumping out the window.

In the aftermath of the financial meltdown, 50 years' worth of careful thinking and hard-won wisdom were erased, as the Reagan Revolution, the work of Milton Freidman, and the classical free-market ethos were suddenly Trotskyized. In their place, the government printed more money to cover its hourly check-writing. The only entertaining element of the tragedy was the sheer shamelessness of a Barney Frank and Chris Dodd—who both once peddled their wares to banks and Freddie/Fannie at Ground Zero of the meltdown—now with flashing

eyes and sagging craws pontificating each evening about Wall Street greed and excess.

After Bernie Madoff (the "by the way, $50 billion is sorta gone" guy), Wall Street finance will have its chronology delineated by BM and AM. It calls to mind a group of five-year-olds scrambling when the song cuts out during a game of musical chairs, or those smudged mimeographed pyramid scheme chain-letters that we used to receive, or those bizarre e-mails from "Sir Reginald Oboke, esquire, a barrister representing a Nairobi Bank who wishes to deposit $1 billion in your name if you can please supply me with your necessary social security and banking routing numbers."

Well over halfway through the month of December, only two Americans have been lost in combat operations in Iraq—about the daily body count in a major American city. What is incomprehensible is not just that Gen. David Petraeus turned around an entire theater— Americans from William Tecumseh Sherman to Matthew Ridgway had done just that amid media gloom and doom—but that his efforts when begun were so roundly demonized, and when nearly ending in success so roundly ignored.

We forget that the Democratic primary once hinged on who was to apologize the loudest for authorizing the war, that the Sen. Majority Leader in mediis rebus declared the war lost, that the New York Times once ran at a discounted rate the "General Betray Us" Moveon.org ad, that Sen. Clinton once derided the general's testimony as requiring a "suspension of disbelief" (i.e. "you are lying"), and that President-Elect Obama once all but said the surge would make things worse—and when it began to work claimed that it hadn't.

Quite suitably we end the war year with an Egyptian-based Iraqi journalist trying to hit the president of the United States with his two shoes—being canonized by the Arab Street and not-sot-secretly appreciated by the American Left (far more interested in the Miranda rights of the assailant than the breach of security that allowed not one, but two projectiles to target their president). The irony was not just that, had he tried that with Saddam Hussein he would have been brush shredded in the basement, but that such a self-described crusading journalist would not even dare such theater in Mubarak's authoritarian Egypt. It was

more of the same old, same old from the blame 'em Middle East: "We hate you for doing business with our oppressive dictators; and we also hate you for losing blood and treasure to liberate us from our oppressive dictators and fostering democracy, and we also just hate you since so many of you seem to want us to hate you."'

The year 2008 also reintroduced us to Bill Ayers, Hot Rod Blagojevich, Rahm Emanuel, Father Pfleger, Tony Rezko, the Right Rev. Wright and the rest of the Chicago Pals. What was so uncanny about them all was not just that they were proverbial spokes to Barack Obama's hub, but that each revealed how the Chicago Way proved so interdisciplinary in nature.

Bill Ayers started out as a scion of the rich Chicago elite, did his "terror thing" so to speak, and then ran back home to Chicago for his sinecure, inheritance, and security blanket. He has ended up as the wrinkled, balding version of the narcissistic spoiled brat he started out as. How perfectly Chicagoan that old Mayor Daley once battled Ayers et al. in the Chicago streets (cf. that mug shot of the smug, slouching, saucy, and ambivalent-looking Ayers after his 1968 arrest), and young Mayor Daley now comes full circle to the defense of his sullied reputation.

Blago did not just sound crooked on tape. No, what astounded Americans was his apparent furor that anyone anywhere might in fact follow the law—how un-Chicagoan could that be? His only saving grace was that as Americans recoiled from his sinister musings, they suddenly cracked a laugh at least at his audacious quip, "The seat is a f—ing valuable thing, you just don't give it away for nothing."

For most of 2008 we were lectured how suave tough guy Rahm Emanuel played winning hardball. Then in November we were told by the media how tough guy Rahm Emanuel would knock heads and bring dreamy Obama down to earth. And then in December we were suddenly told yet again that it made sense that tough guy Rahm Emanuel was horse-trading for hours with Hot Rod on Prosecutor Fitzgerald's wiretaps.

Father Pfleger proved that only in Chicago could a Catholic priest sound just as creepy as the proverbial evangelical pompadoured preacher in a leisure suit.

What was strange about Tony Rezko—and unlike his counterparts in New Jersey and New York—was that he didn't take a cut to get the container ships unloaded, the cranes in place, or the garbage picked up, but that everything that the anti-Midas Rezko touched wound up a failure. Never has someone taken so much from so many for so little.

When the hate-spouting venomous Rev. Wright was compared by now President-Elect Obama to his late "white grandmother" who had devoted her latter years to raising young Barack, we suspected something was terribly wrong with our prospective commander-in-chief's judgment. That assessment was reaffirmed when Obama swore to us that the hate-mongering preacher in his various ridiculous costumes and rants-of-the-day was not the Rev. Wright he once knew—and proven thrice when Rev. Wright reiterated his racism in almost everything he has uttered in the year since.

This year turned out to be the Roaring 20s, the bleak 1930s, and the Sixties—all rolled into one.

FEBRUARY 26, 2009

A Funny Sort of Depression

It is no longer 2005, but that does not mean it is 1932 either.

Are we headed to something like the Great Depression? There is clearly much to be worried about. Most of America's private retirement 401(k) accounts have significantly decreased in value since last autumn's crash. Home equity has plunged. The unemployment rate is above seven percent and climbing.

We had negative GDP growth last quarter. Stock prices are the lowest in ten years. Almost daily some company announces layoffs. Some big banks may be nationalized. The American auto industry will not survive as we have known it for nearly a century. Abroad, the news is worse. European banks have lost trillions of euros in bad loans to

Eastern Europe and Asia. Countries like Iceland, Ireland, and Greece are teetering on insolvency. China's export industries may have to lay off millions of workers.

Given all that news, we are in a funny sort of depression. Our spiraling national deficit is being financed by China, Japan, and other overseas concerns at almost no interest—saving the United States trillions of dollars in debt service costs.

Nearly 93 percent of those Americans in the workforce are still employed. The difference between what the banks pay out in interest on depositors' savings and what they charge borrowers for loans is one of the most profitable in recent memory.

The sudden crash in energy prices may be hurting Iran, the Gulf monarchies, Russia, and Venezuela. Yet Americans, who import 60 percent of their transportation fuel, along with natural gas, have been given about a half-trillion-dollar annual reprieve. The reduced price of energy could translate into more than $1,500 in annual savings for the average driver, and hundreds of dollars off the heating and cooling bills for the homeowner.

For the vast majority of Americans with jobs, the fall in prices for almost everything from food to cars has, in real dollars, meant an actual increase in purchasing power. The loss in value of home equity is serious for those who need to relocate for work or want to downsize and move to an apartment or a retirement community. But when averaged over the last decade, real estate still shows a substantial annual increase in value.

Moreover, the vast majority of American homeowners—well over 90 percent—meet their mortgage payments. They have no plans to flip their homes for profit. For them, the fact that they have lost paper equity, or even owe more than their homes are currently appraised at, is scary—but not equivalent to a depression. Most are confident that after a few years their houses will appreciate again. As for now, working young couples have a chance to buy a house that would have been impossible just two years ago.

The same holds true for many retirement accounts whose decline is terrible for those retirees who count on drawing out each month what they put away or must cash out their depleted accounts at vastly reduced value. But the majority of working Americans are not yet pulling out their sinking retirement funds. Most are still putting away pre-tax money each month, apparently confident that within a few years their portfolios will return to their former value. Some are even consoled that they are now buying mutual funds at rock-bottom prices rather than investing in sky-high investments at the peak of a bull market.

Times are bad for those out of work or those who bought expensive homes with paltry down payments. Yet for those hurting, there is a vast array of government help. Both private companies and public agencies offer all sorts of ways to either walk away from mortgage obligations or have them renegotiated. The same is true for credit-card debt. Unemployment insurance, welfare, food stamps, and even more new social programs on the way have redefined poverty from what our grandparents told us of the Great Depression.

I live in southeastern Fresno County, one of the poorest regions of a now nearly bankrupt California. Many people are hurting. Yet to go to the local Wal-Mart is to see late-model cars in the parking lots and plenty of cell phones, iPods, and BlackBerrys among the shoppers. Carts are stuffed with consumer goods, lots of food, and Easter confections.

So are we in a depression that justifies a vast redefinition of government and a massive takeover of the private sector? Not quite. What we are a witnessing instead is a sharp downturn from the most affluent era in the history of civilization. For the last two decades, we borrowed and spent as if there were no tomorrow. Now we are living in that tomorrow of cutting back and making do.

In relative terms, it is no longer 2005, but that does not mean it is 1932 either.

MARCH 2, 2009

Triumph of Banality

Obama didn't invent dishonesty in political discourse—but he had a talent for it.

O ne of the most tired rhetorical tropes in Washington starts with, "We must . . . " In the age of Obama, this is now usually followed by "Get the cost of our health care under control," or "Invest in the education of our youth," or "Spend wisely." Such promises usually devolve into pleas for more money. They rarely explore how we ended up in the first place with such severe crises in health care and education—and with trillions in borrowing to spend trillions more that we do not have.

The cost of health care is spiraling out of control, and not just because the proverbial evil "they" (fill in the blank: pharmaceutical companies, insurance companies, medical corporations, trial lawyers, etc.) charge too much. Such profit-mongering entities may well gouge us, owing to a lack of competition, fear of lawsuits, or government mandates and interference.

Yet the larger culprit is, of course, we the people. The cost of our health care is soaring because, to be frank, that health care is usually very good, and it does things routinely that almost no one else in the world contemplates—such as providing 83-year-olds with heart-valve replacements, 78-year-olds with hip and knee replacements, and those who drink, smoke, and are chronically obese with drugs and weekly doctor visits.

When I grew up in rural California in the 1960s, an obese uncle in his early 70s had "heart trouble." That translated into some nitroglycerin tablets, and otherwise about the same regimen offered President Eisenhower after his in-office heart attack: Try to quit smoking, eat less, more bed rest—and good luck!

Forty years later, that same patient would have a bypass, and an expensive battery of medications and weekly follow-up doctor visits—

and would make it not to 73 years old (as my uncle was when he died), but to 78 or 80, or even 90.

If we wish to get health-care costs under control, then we should at least be honest with the American people and admit that we are all paying a collective fortune largely for three reasons: (1) to keep functioning into their 60s those who drank, smoked, and ate too much and in a past era would have passed on at 60; (2) to give us all an extra three to five years of mobility and functionality after we reach 75; (3) to fit us up with IVs, feeding tubes, and respirators so that in our last six months of life we can die in a rest home or among machines and specialists in a hospital rather than in our own home with a few morphine tablets for pain and a bowl of soup with a straw on the nightstand.

My dentist warned me in 1962 to brush three times a day, since he could predict a depressing train of events to come for most of the more fortunate rural patients who could pay for his care: surely fillings in your 20s and 30s, hopefully caps in your 40s, maybe root canals and crowns in your 50s, and, unfortunately, false teeth after that. And now? We confidently expect all sorts of restorative dentistry and tooth implants to such a degree that the old common sight of a normal American middle-class fellow with a couple of missing teeth or even a shiny, crass glistening gold incisor is now the exception.

Again, health care is expensive because Americans, with some good reason, have decided that the ancient tragic view—we all age and break down, and pay for the sins of our 20s and 30s in our 50s and 60s—can at last be replaced by the therapeutic promise of vigor and health into our 80s.

What could be done? President Obama could try some honesty. Thus he might say, "We are spending hundreds of billions to keep us healthy, vital, and alive in ways unimaginable a few years ago. To keep our part of the bargain, we must then encourage the aging to remain active and working—and delay retirement. If we are living to 80 rather than 65, then surely we can start receiving Social Security benefits at 67 rather than at 62. What we save in postponed payouts can go to the greater cost of keeping us alive to 80."

President Obama also promises historic new rates of high-school and college graduation. Again, he seems to think the present problem is the absence of money—as if brilliant, gifted, and motivated young people are ending up at McDonald's rather than doing quantum physics because the bogeymen "they" raised the bar and didn't give them enough college scholarship support.

More banality. The truth is quite different. First, too many of contemporary minority youth—the growing Hispanic and African-American underclass that may well soon make up 40 percent of our nation's student body—for a variety of reasons beyond the government's control (e.g., from inordinate patterns of illegitimacy; greater absence of two-parent families; above-average parental drug use, incarceration rates, and felony convictions; and a pervasive ethic of machismo that disdains "acting white" with your nose in a book), simply are not as competitive as other students in grade and high schools. In reaction, the good-hearted state, at the 11th hour of college entry, seeks to ensure an equality of result through affirmative action, set-asides, de facto quotas, and government subsidies. When poorly prepped minority students subsequently do not graduate from college at rates commensurate with other groups, the Left cries "racism"—and we are again back to asking for more money rather than a radical change of heart.

President Obama apparently cannot say, "Americans—each time you have a child out of wedlock, each time you take an illicit drug, each time you break the law or go to jail, each time you romanticize brutality rather than honor scholarship, each time you allege the racism of the others rather than look into your own soul, you do your own small part in ensuring that we might not educate your child as we should—no matter how many thousands of dollars we lavish upon him."

Second, for all American youth, too much government money, not too little, is pouring into education. From some 20 years' experience in higher public education in California, I have come to know a familiar student profile:

Age: 18–30
Units enrolled: 6–9
Residence: Still at home
Job: 20 hours a week at minimum wage to pay for car, insurance, video games, entertainment incidentals (but not rent, food, laundry, etc.)

Major: Either undeclared or changing
Goal: Return to school every other semester, work part-time, party, and put off becoming autonomous.

Such students, in today's grade-inflated university, are able to get Cs and Bs for F and D work, to cobble together state and federal loans, student work assistance, and grants—and to delay growing up while they sleepwalk through a largely therapeutic curriculum. Eric Holder may call us cowards for not discussing race more openly, but if he were to examine the current class offerings at a California public university, or read the syllabi of the courses, he would quickly discover that race, class, and gender are the common themes—an approach designed to encourage grievance and separatism, which consumes precious student hours at the expense of real learning in the liberal arts and hard sciences.

If President Obama is serious about education, then he might also remonstrate with universities to bare their books, keep their costs below the rate of inflation, mandate a cutoff of student support after four years, insist that the BA or BS degree be contingent on some sort of final exit examination, re-examine tenure—and invest in vocational and trade schools rather than continue subsidizing community-studies, sociology, education, and physical-education degrees. One brilliant plumber, gifted carpenter, or adept auto mechanic does more for the American economy (and our collective values) than a dozen 20-something sociology majors in progress.

All government officials talk of spending wisely, but they never tell us the true extent of their financial malfeasance. Imagine if last week, in his address to Congress, President Obama had said something like the following: "We must cut spending, since the borrowed money must come from somewhere. Either we print more paper dollars, and eventually ruin the value of our currency in the manner now common in Zimbabwe or Argentina; or we continue to borrow from the Chinese, Japanese, and Europeans, and therefore mortgage both our honor and our autonomy; or, in the manner of War Bonds during the Second World War, we will have to ask you all to forgo stocks, 401(k)s, and real-estate investments, and instead each month, as part of your patriotic duty, buy

U.S. government savings bonds that garner almost no interest, to subsidize our nation's lavish borrowing and spending."

Only that way could we have an honest national debate on whether the proposed high-speed rail between Vegas and LA is worth making Americans soon pay $10 for a Big Mac; or whether federally subsidized community organizing justifies more begging for help from the Communist government in Beijing; or whether we would all like to accept 0.05 interest on our government bonds to finance the mortgage bailout of those in arrears on their home debt.

In short, for each word devoted to spending, we need one word of honest exegesis about "paying for it."

For the last 20 years, all our presidents have talked much about health care, education, and spending, while saying little. Either they were not honest enough to tell us the truth—or they were convinced that, like children, we simply couldn't handle it if they did.

APRIL 9, 2010

Our American Catharsis

Will Obama-time be a transitory experience or an enduring tragedy?

For years conservatives have railed about the creeping welfare state. They have tried to tag liberals with being soft on national security, both for courting those who faulted America and for faulting others who courted it. The parameters of all these fights were well known, as talk radio, the blogs, and cable news hourly took up hammer and tongs against the creeping "liberal agenda."

But for all the furor, there were few unabashed leftist gladiators in the arena who openly fought under the banner of radically transforming the country into something that it had never been. Bill Clinton was a centrist pragmatist who put Bill Clinton's political interests well above any ideology. His brief flirtation with Hillary's hard leftism was rendered inoperative after the Republicans took Congress in 1994. Indeed, Hillary herself eventually ended up running as a blue-collar, Annie Oakley centrist alternative to Barack Obama.

One-termer Jimmy Carter remained a Democratic embarrassment. He was elected on the fumes of Watergate—and through his own efforts at convincing voters for a few crucial weeks in the autumn of 1976 that his folksy Southern Christian Democrat persona was no veneer, but the natural expression of a true conservative.

By 2000 even Democrats talked more fondly in retrospect of the Reagan years than of the era of appeasement and stagflation of 1977–80. The old progressive dream of electing a genuine leftist president was rendered quixotic by the disastrous campaigns of Northern liberals like George McGovern, Walter Mondale, Michael Dukakis, and John Kerry.

All this is not to say that statism did not make advances. By 2008, almost 40 percent of the population was either entirely, or in large part, dependent on some sort of government handout, entitlement, or redistributive check. The size of government, the annual deficit, and the aggregate debt continued—no matter who was president—to reach unprecedented highs.

Nonetheless, until now we had not in the postwar era seen a true man of the Left who was committed to changing America into a truly liberal state. Indeed, had Barack Obama run on the agenda he actually implemented during his first year in office—"Elect me and I shall appoint worthies like Craig Becker, Anita Dunn, and Van Jones; stimulate the economy through a $1.7-trillion annual deficit; take over health care, the auto industry, student loans, and insurance; push for amnesty for illegal aliens and cap-and-trade; and reach out to Iran, Russia, Syria, and Venezuela"—he would have been laughed out of Iowa.

It was not his agenda but his carefully crafted pseudo-centrism that got Obama elected—that, and a dismal McCain campaign, weariness over the Iraq War, a rare orphaned election without any incumbent candidate, the September 2008 meltdown, and the novelty of the nation's first serious African-American presidential candidacy.

Now, however, for the first time in my memory, the United States has an authentic leftist as president—one who unabashedly believes that the role of the U.S. government at home is to redistribute income in order to ensure equality of results through high taxes on a few and increased entitlements for many, while redefining America abroad as a sort of revolutionary state that sees nothing much exceptional in either its past role or its present alliances—other than something that should be "reset" to the norms embraced by the United Nations.

In sum, for years the loud Right warned Americans about what could happen should they vote for a genuine leftist. We mostly did not believe their canned horror stories. But now the country has got what it unwittingly voted for—and at last we have evolved beyond the rhetoric and entered into the real liberal world of the way things must be.

In just a year, the manner in which Americans look at things has changed radically. Something as mundane as buying a Ford or a GM car now takes on ideological connotations: The former company, in politically recalcitrant fashion, resists government takeover; the latter has been transmogrified from Michael Moore's Roger & Me bogeyman into a sanctioned, government-subsidized brand. Toyota went from the good green maker of Priuses to a foreign corporate outlaw whose handful of faulty accelerators symbolizes the non-union threat to fair-play American production.

The whole notion of capital and debt has changed—mostly on the issue of culpability. Buying too much house at too high interest is the bank's fault. Not being able to pay a debt is certainly negotiable and most certainly nothing to feel bad about. Maxing out credit cards and getting caught with high interest is proof of corporate malfeasance. Cash in the bank earns little, if any, interest. Owing lots of money costs little, and it does not necessarily have to be paid back, if one is able to stake a persuasive claim against "them."

The reaction to a hated and greedy Wall Street is now to be an omnipotent, all-wise, and all-caring state technocracy. Today there is nothing so simplistic as the actual "unemployment rate"; "jobs saved" by government borrowing is the better barometer of who is actually working and who is not. A $200-billion shortfall is a "deficit"; a trillion-dollar one is "stimulus."

Not purchasing a cheap catastrophic-health-care plan is quite understandable. The Department of Motor Vehicles, Amtrak, and the

Postal Service are models of what good government can do. Social Security and Medicare are not unsustainable or insolvent; those loaded adjectives are simply constructs of a wealthy class unwilling to pay the taxes needed to fund them.

Worrying about the deficit or national debt is a neurotic tic. Why fret, when millions in the oppressing class have enough money to eliminate these problems whenever we acquire the backbone to make them pay what they owe us? We are in a them/us, winners/losers zero-sum age, one in which a forever static pie must have its finite slices radically reapportioned.

Colin Powell and Condoleezza Rice were not paradigms of racial equality, as we once assumed. The new correct protocol of unity and togetherness is not to ignore race but to accentuate difference whenever possible. Thus we have a uniter and his flock talking of a "typical white person," of white country folk who "cling" to their fears and superstitions, of "cowards" who refuse to discuss racial matters, of a "wise Latina," of police who "stereotype" and act "stupidly," and of polluters and high-school mass-murderers identified as typically "white." In place of real civil-rights marches, we have psychodramas where congressmen wade into a crowd of protestors in search of a televised slur. To this president, the tea-partiers are sexually slurred "tea-baggers," in his Manichean worldview of opponents to whom we are "to get in their faces" and "bring a gun" to their knife fight—all as we praise "unity," "bipartisanship," and "working across the aisle."

Fourteen months ago, the number $250,000 meant little. Now the arbitrary figure is an economic them/us Mason-Dixon line seared into our collective thoughts. Those who cross it are the proven greedy who profit inordinately and must have their payroll, income, and health-care taxes commensurately increased. But those who earn below it are still kind and decent folk deserving of credits and entitlements.

I used to think that old-stand nations like Britain, Canada, the Czech Republic, France, Germany, Israel, Norway, and Poland were our natural friends by virtue of a shared Western heritage and values, commitment to constitutional government, and acknowledgment of a distinguished intellectual history. Today their leaders are to be snubbed, ignored, or lectured; we are unsure only whether their sin is post-imperialism, post-colonialism—or pro-Americanism.

In contrast, more revolutionary states that bore America ill will, and certainly despised George W. Bush, must ipsis factis have been onto something—and therefore can be courted. Iran, the Palestinians, Russia, Syria, and Venezuela are, at worst, misunderstood. At best, their strong leaders are somewhat sympathetic for their prior opposition to much of what America has done and stood for.

In 2008 I had no idea of what an "overseas contingency operation" or "man-made disaster" was. And even Michael Savage could not scare me into thinking that the U.S. government would attempt to try the beheader and architect of 9/11, the self-avowed jihadist Khalid Sheikh Mohammed, in a civilian courtroom, replete with Miranda rights, lengthy appeals, and government-appointed lawyers—all that a couple of thousand yards from the scene of his own mass murdering.

The watchdog media have become a house kitten that purrs rather than barks at such radical change. Mass assemblies—so common in protests against wars during the last decades—are now racist and subversive. Grass-roots political expression like talk radio and cable TV is in need of government-enforced fairness. Hollywood no longer produces movies like the anti-war, anti-administration Redacted and Rendition; Knopf no longer publishes novels like Checkpoint; and there are, we may be thankful, no longer docudramas about shooting presidents—the latter would be both unpatriotic and clearly defined as hate speech. Filibusters are not traditional ways of checking Senate excess; the "nuclear option" is now a slur for legitimate majority legislative rule; and recess appointments don't thwart the legislature's will but resist its tyranny.

In other words, the last 14 months have been a catharsis of sorts. At last the world of Rush Limbaugh's fears and Sean Hannity's nightmares is upon us, and we can determine whether these megaphones were always just alarmists—or whether they legitimately warned of what logically would follow should faculty-lounge utopian rhetoric ever be taken seriously. Europe screamed for a multilateral, multipolar, nonexceptional America. Now in place of the old Johnny-on-the-spot NATO colossus, they are quickly getting what they wished for—America, the new hypopower. Perhaps the European Rapid Reaction

Force will take on the Milosevices and Osamas to come.

Keynesians have sermonized for decades about a truly appropriate mega-debt. Now we're quickly on the way to achieving that vision, to testing just how much debt a country can incur and still survive. If Reagan and Co. talked about "starving the beast"—cutting needless government spending by first reducing tax revenue—this is the age of "gorging the beast": borrowing and spending as much as possible to ensure later vast increases in taxes, and with them proper redistributive change.

Politics is high-stakes poker with real losers and winners, not a mere parlor game. The country voted for the party of Pelosi, Reid, and Obama, and for once such statists are governing in the manner of their rhetoric. Time will soon tell whether this strange American experience is transitory and so becomes a needed catharsis, or whether it will be institutionalized and thus result in an enduring tragedy—this rare moment when the dreams of a zealous few are at last becoming the nightmares of a complacent many.

DECEMBER 30, 2010

The American 21st Century

America's rivals lack the culture necessary to sustain greatness.

The current debt, recession, wars, and political infighting have depressed Americans into thinking their country soon will be overtaken by more vigorous rivals abroad. Yet this is an American fear as old as it is improbable.

In the 1930s, the Great Depression supposedly marked the end of freewheeling American capitalism. The 1950s were caricatured as a period of mindless American conformity, McCarthyism, and obsequious company men.

By the late 1960s, the assassinations of John and Robert Kennedy and Martin Luther King Jr., along with the Vietnam War, had fueled a hippie counterculture that purportedly was going to replace a toxic American establishment. In the 1970s, oil shocks, gas lines, Watergate, and new rustbelts were said to be symptomatic of a post-industrial, has-been America.

At the same time, other nations, we were typically told, were doing far better.

In the late 1940s, with the rise of a postwar Soviet Union that had crushed Hitler's Wehrmacht on the eastern front during World War II, Communism promised a New Man as it swept through Eastern Europe.

Mao Zedong took power in China and inspired Communist revolutions from North Korea to Cuba. Statist central planning was going to replace the unfairness and inefficiency of Western-style capitalism. Yet just a half-century later, Communism had either imploded or been superseded in most of the world.

By the early 1980s, Japan's state capitalism along with emphasis on the group rather than the individual was being touted as the ideal balance between the public and private sectors. Japan Inc. continually outpaced the growth of the American economy. Then, in the 1990s, a real-estate bubble and a lack of fiscal transparency led to a collapse of property prices and a general recession. A shrinking and aging Japanese population, led by a secretive government, has been struggling ever since to recover the old magic.

At the beginning of the 21st century, the European Union was hailed as the proper Western paradigm of the future. The euro soared over the dollar. Europe practiced a sophisticated "soft power," while American cowboyism was derided for getting us into wars in Afghanistan and Iraq. Civilized cradle-to-grave benefits were contrasted with the frontier, every-man-for-himself American system.

Now Europe limps from crisis to crisis. Its undemocratic union, coupled with socialist entitlements, is proving unsustainable. Symptoms of the ossified European system appear in everything from a shrinking population and a growing atheism to an inability to integrate Muslim immigrants or field a credible military.

As we enter this new decade, we are being lectured that China is soon to be the global colossus. Its economy is now second only to

America's, but with a far faster rate of growth and with budget surpluses rather than debt. Few seem to mention that China's mounting social tensions, mercantilism, environmental degradation, and state bosses belong more to a 19th- than a 21st-century nation.

Amid all this doom and gloom, two factors are constant over the decades. First, America goes through periodic bouts of neurotic self-doubt, only to wake up and snap out of it. Indeed, indebted Americans are already bracing for fiscal restraint and parsimony as an antidote to past profligacy.

Second, decline is relative and does not occur in a vacuum. As Western economic and scientific values ripple out from Europe and the United States, it is understandable that developing countries like China, India, and Brazil can catapult right into the 21st century. But that said, national strength is still measured by the underlying hardiness of the patient—its demography, culture, and institutions—rather than by occasional symptoms of ill health.

In that regard, America integrates immigrants and assimilates races and ethnicities in a way Europe cannot. Russia, China, and Japan are simply not culturally equipped to deal with millions who do not look Slavic, Chinese, or Japanese. The Islamic world cannot ensure religious parity to Christians, Jews, or Hindus—or political equality to women.

The American Constitution has been tested over 223 years. In contrast, China, the European Union, India, Japan, Russia, and South Korea have constitutional pedigrees of not much more than 60 years. The last time Americans killed each other in large numbers was nearly a century and a half ago; most of our rivals have seen millions of their own destroyed in civil strife and internecine warring just this past century.

In short, a nation's health is gauged not by bouts of recession and self-doubt, but by the durability of its political, economic, military, and social foundations. A temporarily ill-seeming America is nevertheless still growing, stable, multiethnic, transparent, individualistic, self-critical, and meritocratic; almost all of its apparently healthy rivals, by contrast, are not.